ASCENSION AND ECCLESIA

ASCENSION AND ECCLESIA

*On the Significance of the Doctrine of the Ascension
for Ecclesiology and Christian Cosmology*

DOUGLAS FARROW

William B. Eerdmans Publishing Company
Grand Rapids, Michigan

First published 1999
in the UK by
T&T Clark Ltd
59 George Street
Edinburgh EH2 2LQ
Scotland
and in the United States of America by
Wm. B. Eerdmans Publishing Company
255 Jefferson Ave. SE
Grand Rapids, Michigan 49503

Printed and bound in Great Britain

Library of Congress Cataloging-in-Publication Data

Farrow, Douglas.
Ascension and ecclesia : on the significance of the doctrine of
the Ascension for ecclesiology and Christian cosmology / written by
Douglas Bryce Farrow.
p.   cm.
Includes bibliographical references (p.   ).
ISBN 0-8028-4683-1 (paper : alk. paper)
1. Jesus Christ — Ascension.   2. Church.   3. Lord's Supper.
4. Cosmology.   I. Title.
BT500.F37   1999
232.9'7—dc21   99-40388
                                                    CIP

for Anna
with much love and gratitude

Contents

Preface

Not since the time of Paul has the question of ecclesial identity been a more pressing one than it is today. Then again, not for at least a millennium and a half has the identity of the church's founder (and I do not mean Paul!) been more hotly disputed. 'Who was Jesus?' is the question that most exercises New Testament scholarship. Theologians, of course, may prefer the present tense, 'Who is Jesus Christ for us today?'; or even the future tense, 'Who is the Christ we should expect?' However it is asked, the question about Jesus underlies the question about the church.

It was reflection on the eucharist, which forces us to grapple quite directly with the link between the identity of Jesus and the identity of the church, that first aroused my interest in the doctrine of the ascension. For it quickly became clear that the 'Who?' question (as Bonhoeffer knew and dogmatic history attests) is to some extent bound up with the 'Where?' question. And since a good detective, they say, begins the search where the subject was last seen, that doctrine seemed to call for closer attention.

An esoteric adventure? Not as it turned out. For what I eventually discovered, to my own surprise, is that doctrines of the ascension are woven into the most diverse theological projects from the fathers to the reformers, and indeed into the major theologies of our own era. So much is this so that I must acknowledge that I am in some danger of having overreached both my ability as a sleuth and the practicalities of such a work as I am now presenting. A great many topics are passed over lightly or merely returned to from time to time and from various angles; others are more consistently examined but without any real attempt at resolution. What is worse, in sketching the general evolution of my subject matter – a task forced upon me by the paucity of similar works – I have omitted some important contributors and made reference to a number of others with whom (and whose times) I have not engaged to the degree that might be desirable. Certainly I cannot pretend to have done equal justice to all, or indeed full justice to any, yet I may hope that the most critical connections have been drawn out or at least have begun to appear. Others, perhaps, will supply what is wanting and make corrections in doing so.

Now it has been said that too much attention to christology is actually bad for the church, distracting it from the wider horizons of its relationship with the world, but the charge is a specious one. That relationship, as the present study will show, is one of the very things persistent inquiry into the person and work of Christ requires us to face up to. Indeed, the opposite charge might more easily be laid, namely, that christology regularly invites us to transgress the boundaries of other disciplines or fields of discourse in order to be true to its own insights. From this I have not always shied away.

My forays into cosmology, without which it is not possible to pursue the doctrine of the ascension, are a case in point. Let it be noted by way of explanation that I am using the term quite broadly to indicate any attempt to see the world as an ordered whole, or at least to articulate the conviction that it is, or was, or will be, such. Cosmology in that sense is not the special province of scientists; others also have contributions to make. Certainly the church, just because it believes that God in Christ has given himself to creation as its *Lord*, has something unique to say about the way creation is ordered. And even if it admits, as it should, that there can be no such thing as a complete understanding or interpretation of the world – lusting for which leads to great error! – the church can hardly avoid giving an account of its christocentric perspective, which even today it must regard as much *more* important than the contributions of the scientist, the humanist, the artist, etc. Fluctuations in that account are inevitable, of course. These fluctuations and their impact on the identity questions are what I will be watching for.

What follows is both an examination of the Christian tradition in its broad contours and a programmatic essay calling for substantial change. Obviously no single doctrine provides an entirely satisfactory key to the tradition, nor can it lead by itself to a balanced agenda for the present time. We must not seek to bring the whole theological enterprise into subjection to one set of interests, much less reduce the economy of the incarnation to but one of its features. Yet each aspect of Christ's life is capable of supporting a lifetime of reflection, as von Balthasar has observed, and the ascension is, I think, a subject richer and more instructive than is commonly recognized. Indeed, what I have attempted here seems to me little more than a prolegomenon, on which I hope later to build in the context of a more direct discussion of ecclesiology, and with greater regard for the (still equivocal) postmodern shift.

Lacking, for good or for ill, the continental fascination with method, and preferring a centre to *strictness* of order, I have taken as far as possible a story-like approach to my study. In the matter of style, accessibility has been my aim. There is undoubtedly a price attached to these decisions, which I hope is not too high. To compensate somewhat I have resorted in places to a rather heavy use of notes, which should be of service to the more demanding reader. Above the line or below it, I have written with a keen sense of the gravity and urgency of the questions that set me going.

To those colleagues, friends and family whose support and guidance were so selflessly given along the way, I offer my sincere thanks. Professor Colin Gunton, who supervised this work at an earlier stage, deserves special mention. David Ford, Christoph Schwöbel, Alan Torrance, Francis Watson, Tom Wright and John Zizioulas have all seen or heard drafts of various parts of the work, again at an earlier stage, as have others associated with the Research Institute in Systematic Theology at King's College, London. Their comments, whether approving or disapproving, have been instructive (in some places they will wish rather more instructive) but none bears any responsibility for the work's deficiencies or eccentricities. Above all, it needs to be said that the advice and shared stamina of my wife, Anna, have been indispensable. But to list the generous contributions of family and friends, both in Britain and in North America, is a hopeless task; so I may simply state the fact that it is they who, time after time, have given me hope. It is my prayer that what I have written will in some way serve to multiply that gift.

Douglas Farrow
McGill University

I

Thinking about the Church

Every journey needs a place to begin, and a reason for beginning. Ours begins where it will end, not with the doctrine which is to be the chief focus of our study but with talk about the church, a concern for the health of which is one reason for setting out on this particular expedition. Is it wrong in a work that is intended to serve the academy as well as the church to draw attention to such a reason? Not if it is sound method to indwell one's subject. Not if the church itself is a consequence of the ascension, as we believe, and not merely the inventor of a doctrine of the ascension. But with that primary presupposition stated, and the reader forewarned as to which side of the road we are travelling on, let us not delay our beginning; the journey will be a long and demanding one.

Eucharist and Ambiguity

There is no context in which to ground serious thought about the church but the eucharistic assembly. Here Christian theology in general takes root in its own proper soil.[1] Here ecclesiology is furnished with the object of its special consideration. We quite agree, then, with John Zizioulas, who in his book *Being as Communion* calls for a recovery of 'the lost consciousness of the primitive Church concerning the decisive importance of the *eucharist* in ecclesiology.' He goes on to argue, in fact, that it is the eucharist which constitutes the church, not the reverse,[2] a point some find difficult. But whoever is at least prepared to assert, with a well-known Faith and Order paper of the World Council of Churches, that 'it is in the eucharist that the community of God's people is fully manifested,'[3] must also admit that just there the nature of the church is laid open (in a qualified way) to genuine observation and interpretation.[4]

[1] 'A heuristic impulse can live only in the pursuit of its proper enquiry. The Christian enquiry is worship' (M. Polanyi 1962:281).
[2] 1985:20f. (see also P. McPartlan 1993); cf. Hans Frei 1975:159.
[3] *Baptism, Eucharist and Ministry*, Eucharist §19.
[4] Vatican II's *Constitution on the Sacred Liturgy* makes this very point, reminding us that 'it is through the liturgy, especially, that the faithful are enabled to express in their lives and manifest to others the mystery of Christ and the real nature of the Church' (A. Flannery 1975:1).

I

Other starting points for thinking about the church are common enough, of course. Denominational concerns override doxological ones; political arenas compete with the eucharistic assembly as the dwelling place of ecclesiology; sociologists or scientists become the doctors of the church. But the fact remains that the church itself is established only by 'the upwards call of God in Christ Jesus,' and that call is made concrete precisely in the eucharistic liturgy. *Sursum corda!* is the cry that heralds the possibility of ecclesial being, and to that possibility ecclesiology is naturally bound.[5]

Is this really an assumption the whole church can share? Even if we grant the priority of a doxological starting point over a strictly institutional or perhaps an ethical one, must we name the eucharistic assembly specifically? Let us turn the question around. Where *shall* we begin if not at the very place where the bond between head and members is proclaimed, where the church's identity is renewed in memory and hope, where its unity is plainly set forth?[6] The simple answer is that no other situation presents itself as an adequate alternative. All the various resources on which we must lean for insight into the church – scripture, creed, tradition, baptism, the experience of the faithful – live and move and have their being in a community knit together around a common table.

Immediately we are faced with certain consequences of conceding that the eucharist provides the axis along which the heuristic impulses that govern a sound ecclesiology will run. First, we cannot approve of an ecclesiology that attends primarily to the past, that is dominated by a ponderous history of traditions perspective and related concerns about formal unity. Such an approach is too abstract. Neither, then, can we afford to substitute an ecclesiology that is focused primarily on the future, very much the modern temptation.[7] By this we mean both the church's own future (its institutional viability) and that of the world. Where the latter is concerned it must be asked, not out of pessimism or hysteria but for reasons known only to itself, whether the church should not be quite dubious about its prospects.[8] In any event the church, unlike the world,

---

[5] The transcendent dimension of the church requires an internal and strictly doxological engagement for its interpretation (cf. Phil. 3:14, Rev. 1–5). Interfaith dialogue may have something to contribute; even the secular paths to understanding the church are not devoid of insight (cf. J. Moltmann 1977:4ff.). But it is not *vis-à-vis* the world's own social, religious or scientific communities that the truth about the Christian communion is ultimately to be uncovered.

[6] Or *denied*, which helps to account for our ecclesiological confusion. Cf. G. Wainwright 1978:140f.

[7] According to Jürgen Moltmann (1988:23), 'the basic question of modern times is the question of the future. Therefore Christian theology of modernity must necessarily be a theology of the future.' But cf. 1979:16.

[8] See Matt. 24, e.g., or Rev. 8:1–5 (a specifically liturgical passage). That the same need not be said of the church itself is due entirely to its eucharistic possibilities. What we mean by that will later become clear; but it will already be clear that we are no longer speaking in a way that typifies the WCC.

takes its bearings not so much from planning committees and strategic summits as from the new meaning given to its *present*, as in the Spirit it actually meets with the one it remembers and for whom it hopes. A eucharistic ecclesiology must reckon faithfully with that fact, seeking first of all to accompany and assist the church as it inhabits the present in a transformed and transforming way.[9]

Second, and more profoundly, we are brought face to face with the eschatological nature of ecclesial being as we know it. Zizioulas and Geoffrey Wainwright are among those who have drawn to our attention the fact that the eucharist is in every respect an eschatological act. No doubt there are different ways to articulate this, not all of which are compatible. But since it is only Christ who can make the church the church, perhaps the best way is to point directly to the central paradox of the *Christus praesens* and the *Christus absens*. The one around whose table we are said to gather is 'in a manner present and in a manner absent,' to borrow Calvin's way of putting it.[10] Is there anything about the church that is unaffected by this peculiar ambiguity at its very heart? The oddity of the eucharistic situation must never be overlooked, even if we are ashamed of the quarrels it has occasioned! For it is in its eucharistic ambiguity that the church is marked off from the world ontologically and not merely ideologically. It is in confessing that ambiguity that its appeal to the Holy Spirit is spared the banality, or rather the blasphemy, of reducing to self-reference. It is in knowing the provisionality of its own existence that the church is able to speak with some integrity of a reality that lies beyond itself and beyond the world in which it lives. To put the matter more positively, there is something more to the church than meets the eye, and that 'something more' belongs to the christological enigma which the eucharist introduces.

To grapple with the mystery of the *quodammodo praesens et quodammodo absens* is indeed ecclesiology's constant challenge. Where either side of that mystery is neglected the mystery of the church itself is undone. Not long ago a rather cheeky editorial in *Theology Today* encouraged us to learn to appreciate 'the presence of the absence,' something we propose to do; but to take such advice at face value, eschewing the eucharistic movement from absence to presence, would be to give up believing in the church altogether.[11] On the other hand, those who are content to build lopsidedly on the wonderful promises of presence in Matthew 18:20 or 28:20, for example, will still find it difficult to press through to a serious view of the church. In neither case are presence and absence brought into their right relation, for they are not seen *together*, as the eucharist demands.

---

[9] As Zizioulas (1985:180) points out, in the eucharistic community the Spirit 'brings the eschata into history,' confronting 'the process of history with its consummation, with its transformation and transfiguration,' thus transcending its linearity.

[10] Quoted by J. B. Torrance 1996:82 (see Chap. 5 below).

[11] Hugh T. Kerr 1986:1ff. (see Chap. 6 below).

3

Thus the intimate association between ecclesiology and eschatology is lost from view and the church is gradually assimilated to some more or less worldly agenda.[12]

Third, it becomes clear (how did it ever become unclear?) that the liturgy of the sacrament and the liturgy of the word also belong together as different dimensions of a single reality.[13] Just because Jesus Christ, even in his eucharistic parousia, is in some sense still absent or yet to come, it is plain that neither his presence as word nor his presence as sacrament is meant to stand alone. Disembodied word or mute substance would be unnaturally divided aspects of his self-giving to the church. Each needs and qualifies the other, testifying jointly to the provisional nature of his presence and the graciously contradicted fact of his absence. Where they are prised apart the consequences are always negative; only by correcting any imbalance here can the church hope to keep properly in touch with its Lord, and so to guard its worship and its theology from subjection at critical points to the restricting canons of worldly orthodoxy.[14]

* * *

In our day the liturgical net has been strained by a catch of bewildering variety, but the simple pattern laid out by Justin Martyr in the middle of the second century will suffice to set before us these two moments of Christian worship in their natural relation. Justin's description runs like this:

> And on the day called Sunday all who live in cities or in the country gather together to one place, and the memoirs of the apostles or the writings of the prophets are read, as long as time permits; then, when the reader has ceased, the president verbally instructs, and exhorts to the imitation of these good things. Then we all rise together and pray . . .[15]

In other words, scriptures, sermon, and prayers are the backbone of the liturgy of the word, in the church as in the synagogue. If we allow that the prayers may take many forms (confessions, intercessions, psalms, hymns, etc.), and if we leave room for the fact that words of instruction

---

[12] i.e., a self-generated eschatology of some sort arises to impose an ecclesiology of its own making. Ironically, this problem is common to the anti-sacramentalist traditions *and* to the sacramentalism they have learned to fear.

[13] Gregory Dix (1945:36f.) reminds us that in origin the synaxis and the eucharist were distinct, and remained detachable, though the normal custom was to combine them in regular Sunday worship. All we are claiming here is that there is indeed an organic connection between them in the life of the church (cf. Frei 158).

[14] The imbalance fosters both rationalism and a false mysticism, which is paralleled by a dangerous dichotomy between the church as visible institution and as mystical body, wreaking havoc with Roman and Protestant ecclesiology alike (cf. T. F. Torrance 1988:270ff., 1993:5ff.).

[15] First Apology §67 (*Ante-Nicene Fathers*, 1).

and exhortation may not be confined to the president, this outline still fits most churches today. Only one major element has been added and hallowed by more than a millennium of common tradition: the recitation of the creed. That distillation of the essential content of the liturgy of the word, though it arose under pressure of controversy, quickly became a vital doxological act in its own right.[16]

Much might be added about the messianic pattern of receiving and responding to the word of God, but we must go on to speak of the transformation of the contents of the liturgy of the word as they are ultimately caught up and fulfilled in the eucharist itself. Justin continues:

> and when our prayer is ended, bread and wine and water are brought, and the president in like manner offers prayers and thanksgivings, according to his ability, and the people assent, saying Amen; and there is a distribution to each, and a participation of that over which thanks has been given, and to those who are absent a portion is sent by the deacons.

In this manner words are transfigured by and into actions. The kiss of peace is put in place of mere reminders of brotherly regard; gifts are presented in place of mere acknowledgment of indebtedness to God; above all, communion together in the body and blood of Christ through the power of the Holy Spirit replaces mere confession of a common hope and need.[17]

Just here the eschatological character of the liturgy comes to the fore, together with its cosmic scope and ramifications, as Justin's conclusion indicates:

> But Sunday is the day on which we all hold our common assembly, because it is the first day on which God, having wrought a change in the darkness and matter, made the world; and Jesus Christ our Saviour on the same day rose from the dead.

This observation helps us to set the mystery of the church in a much wider context; that is, in the context of a more mundane ambiguity, the ambiguity of the whole world that is owed to the fall. The eucharistic event, as a movement from absence to presence, is as such a movement from chaos to order, darkness to light, death to life. It is an inventive, ordering event on the same plane as the act of creation, though its actual results are largely withheld from our view. It is an event aimed at nothing less than the restoration to creation of its own proper goodness, and of its lost transparency to the goodness of God.

We are quite right, then, if following the habit of the eastern church we insist on connecting that movement with the appeal to the Holy Spirit

---

[16] That it is widely ignored in churches that concentrate mainly on the liturgy of the word is odd; that it is now regarded only as 'the language of love' by many churchmen and theologians in the sacramental churches is a clear sign of the twofold malaise of rationalism and mysticism.

[17] See §65f. for details.

(i.e., with the epiclesis, to use the technical term). Was it not the Spirit, hovering over the waters of our world at its birth, who brought it into being *as* a world? Likewise, the Spirit is the one who brings the church into being as a new creation in Christ by making possible its communion with him. The ἐπίκλησις and its answer, complete with the χαρίσματα, are entirely necessary if any genuine response is to be made by us to the ἄνω κλῆσις or upwards call – that is, if any real fellowship with Jesus in the presence of the Father is to occur. For it may indeed belong to the church to make claims that embrace heaven and earth, yet of itself it has no claim on either; without the Spirit its ambiguity is not at all paradoxical but quite mundane.[18]

The movement itself, however, is christologically grounded, and it is dramatized by the handling of the bread that is presented. Gregory Dix, a twentieth-century liturgist, has highlighted the fourfold action of taking, blessing, breaking and distributing which is at the core of every eucharistic liturgy.[19] What this drama declares is the sanctification of our humanity through the life and passion and heavenly intercession of Jesus – what for economy's sake we will often refer to as Jesus-history – a sanctification that actually takes effect in us as we and our histories are made by the Spirit to overlap with him and his.[20] That overlap, it is plain, requires the deconstruction and reconstruction of the reality belonging to us, as the sacrament of baptism likewise declares. That is why the *Christus praesens* is and remains for us the *Christus absens*, why the Spirit himself is given only in pledge form. For the course marked out by Jesus, the movement that reverses the fall and leads 'upwards' to the new creation, is a radical departure from our own.

* * *

About the eschatological qualification of ecclesial being much more must be said, but there is here an epistemological rebound we do well to observe at the outset. Is it not ecclesiology's special contribution to the theological enterprise to draw attention to the fact that all its labours are in vain if

[18] Otherwise put, it is only by appealing to the Spirit – Justin is careful to include mention of the Holy Spirit alongside the Son – that we can insist on the *Christus praesens* at all, a point our study is intended to underline (cf. W. Kasper 1989:186ff., A. Heron 1983b:152ff.).

[19] 1945:48ff. Dix, though not in this context, supports the idea that the 'primitive eucharist is above all else an "eschatological" rite' (see 256ff.); cf. G. Wainwright's *Eucharist and Eschatology*.

[20] If the centre of that overlap is the holy communion – and why should we wish to deny that there *is* a centre? – its periphery is as wide as the experience of the faithful. Yves Congar (3/228ff.) rightly describes the life of the church as 'one long epiclesis.' But that means that we must be careful not to divorce the consecration of the gifts from that of the people who present and receive them; for the work of the Spirit is to bring about a change in the onto-relations not only of the bread and wine but of the eucharistic assembly itself and its participants.

they are not grounded beyond themselves in the mystery of the kingdom of God? That the moment they propose to be self-sufficient, to deal only with what is publicly accessible, they cease to be churchly and hence to be Christian?[21] Ecclesiology is, or ought to be, the conscience of biblical studies, by which we seek to clarify our reading of scripture; of dogmatics, by which we strive to comprehend the faith embodied in the creed; of practical theology, through which we hope to translate the prayers of God's people into a thoughtful course of action consistent with the upwards call. It ought to remind those disciplines (and itself) of their liturgical footing and *raison d'être*, of their epicletic dependency.

Unfortunately, ecclesiology itself is prone to move in just the opposite direction, displaying a keen interest in the church's self-justifying and self-serving agendas. By subtly transferring the church's ambiguity to Christ himself, a process we shall witness many times over in the course of our journey, it stands the eschatological relation on its head.[22] Small wonder, then, if biblical studies often gives the impression that the identity of *Jesus* is a great, perhaps an insoluble, problem; if systematics has detached itself from the creed; if practical theology has for some time looked to the sociologists and scientists for direction. Small wonder if ecclesiology is a discipline that divides rather than unites; if the table of the Lord has become the table of this or that ecclesiastical authority. But to dig further into these matters we must look into the ground of the eucharist itself.

Two Histories

On the road to Emmaus, where only two or three traveled together, they found Jesus in their midst. His path fell alongside theirs and the liturgy of the word began, burning deep into their hearts and minds though their eyes remained veiled. At the house of Cleopas eyes, too, were opened at the breaking of bread. The one who was present was finally recognized, and that decisively, but in the recognition was suddenly found to be absent again. The new creation had apparently begun, but not without its ambiguity.[23]

This remarkable vignette, a prophetic scene situated at the church's foremost border, introduces in narrative form the problem we have already

---

[21] If the *ordo cognoscendi* must follow and obey the *ordo essendi*, as Karl Barth attempted to impress upon us, then there is in the eucharist this most fundamental implication for theology and theologians: Our thinking about the church, and all our thinking for the church, must be done in a *churchly* way.

[22] In this light consider again Zizioulas' really quite vital point that the church does not constitute the eucharist but the eucharist the church.

[23] E. Ellis (1991:276) points out that Luke has structured his account to present this meal as Jesus' eighth meal with his disciples, the first of the new creation. Note the parallels with Adam and Eve walking and talking in Eden with the Lord, and eating the fruit in his absence, with the result that their eyes are 'opened;' here the situation is reversed. We may also observe with J. Nolland (1993:1208) that 'a nice irony emerges' at the outset of this encounter, with the disciples remarking on what they suppose to be the ignorance of *Jesus*.

identified as the central challenge of ecclesiology, the problem of the presence and the absence. Jesus is seen here as one who still moves in parallel with his people, if with considerably greater freedom of movement than theirs. He is resurrected to walk the old roads, but without being subject to all their usual conditions. In some sense he is already in a manner present, in a manner absent; perhaps even in a manner here, in a manner there. The privilege and the need of his people is to find him at least momentarily visible or tangible in their midst, instructing them and nurturing them for the journey together – for without him it is not at all clear that they *are* a people. The eucharistic assembly is to be the place where this will happen. It is the place where Jesus will reveal and interpret himself; where the church, therefore, will also interpret itself in his presence and renew its gospel mandate.[24]

But how and when and in what way precisely will these paths touch in the necessary manner? With the cross and resurrection the history of Jesus has taken a startling turn, and so also the history of God's people; that is the beginning of the good news. How, though, are the two to be held together? Has not the sudden turn in Jesus' own history to some extent thrown his people off his track, at least temporarily, so that it is difficult to speak of parallel paths? We cannot avoid the fact that the Easter events introduced a discontinuity into the life of Jesus which renders the kind of links we are used to impossible and irrelevant. The path of Jesus cannot be traced as if by some kind of extrapolation.[25] How then are we to speak sanely about his presence, and thus to speak also and secondarily of our own ecclesial existence?

Many answers to this critical question, which has been posed under a great variety of guises, have been attempted down through the centuries. The problem of the presence and the absence, of the Lord who is seen but not seen, who is at table but not at table, who is both with us and away from us, who is walked with yet awaited, has dogged ecclesiology from the beginning. According to Dietrich Ritschl, the question 'What does it mean that Jesus Christ makes himself present?' lies at the center of christology itself, and of all theology.[26] He attempts to show that the notion of a timeless God, accompanied by a negative view of ordinary world history and an insistence that God's decisive actions lie in the past, has led the west as a whole into a theological impasse precisely through an inability to come to grips with this question. Only a new focus on the *Christus praesens*, he contends, a new starting point for theology in the ongoing 'history of God' as the present subject of our own lives, can move

[24] Cf. Frei 135ff., 149. See also Dix's comments (56ff.) on the last supper as a *chabûrah* meal, a concept which helps to link the Emmaus story to the church's eucharist. It is not a eucharist, of course, but a pre-Pentecost encounter with the risen Jesus.
[25] Mapping Jesus-history by extrapolation (e.g., L. van den Brom 1994) is for those who do not reckon with that history as Jesus' *own*.
[26] 1967:20f.

us ahead.[27] We may ask, however, whether Ritschl's thought-provoking analysis really penetrates to the heart of the problem. We may even ask whether a new focus on the *Christus praesens* is possible without at once attending more seriously to the *Christus absens*. For the history of God with which scripture and the creeds have to do is the history of the man Jesus, and Jesus, as we have said, has a course all his own.[28]

A course all his own? We have not yet mentioned the ascension directly, but then it is remarkable (as J. G. Davies observed in his Bampton lectures on the subject) how little mention the ascension gets these days.[29] Once it was seen as the climax of the mystery of Christ:

> He was made known in the flesh,
> vindicated in the Spirit,
> beheld by angels,
> preached among the nations,
> believed on in the world,
> taken up in glory.[30]

Once too it was celebrated as the crown of Christian feasts and the ground of the sacraments.[31] Today it is something of an embarrassment. Both exegetically and theologically the ascension is quickly assimilated to the resurrection.[32] Its festival is commonly passed over as a redundant marker on the road to Pentecost, allowing it little or no impact on the shape of Christian life and thought. It is said to smack of the triumphalism we intend to put behind us or of the remoteness of God we want to overcome. For many the very idea conjures up an outmoded cosmology; for a few, something more sinister.[33] But perhaps its greatest offence is that just here the eucharistic dilemma of the two histories, and with it the troubling ambiguity of the church, stubbornly asserts itself. For with the ascension

---

[27] Ibid. xii, 6f.; cf. 1986:171ff.

[28] If christology is not to collapse eventually into a vague pneumatology, if it is not to be employed simply as a means of saving the appearances in an evolving church, the discontinuity between his history and ours must not be glossed over. Ritschl is not as clear about this as he might be.

[29] 'Of all the articles in the Creed there is none that has been so neglected in the present century as that which affirms our Lord's Ascension into heaven' (1958:9).

[30] 1 Tim. 3:16; note the complex parallelism set up by the combined use of couplets and an abc/abc pattern.

[31] Davies (1969:16) quotes Augustine in support: 'This is that festival which confirms the grace of all the festivals together, without which the profitableness of every festival would have perished . . .'

[32] 'According to the dominant line in the New Testament witness, resurrection and ascension may be considered as different aspects of the one reality of the risen and exalted Lord.' That is all that *Confessing One Faith* (Faith and Order Paper No. 140, §158) has to say about the ascension.

[33] G. Jantzen, in a recent editorial in *Theology*, has even managed to link it with sexism and to read it 'as yet another of the many biblical "texts of terror."'

the track of Jesus-history, still genuinely visible in some sense on the Emmaus road, passes beyond all ken. 'Where I am going you cannot come.'[34]

* * *

It is the divergence of Jesus-history from our own that gives to the ecclesia its character and its name. It is the divergence of Jesus-history from our own that calls for a specifically *eucharistic* link: for the breaking and remoulding, the substantial transformation of worldly reality to bring it into conjunction with the lordly reality of Jesus Christ. The kind of ecclesiology we wish to do is quite impossible, then, without careful attention to the ascension, however difficult and unpromising that doctrine may appear today. Certainly it is true that the divergence in question began at the beginning, that is, with the conception of Jesus. His devotion to the Father, his sinless life, was a profound deviation from our history. His death too was unique, a fact to which its jarring, tomb-opening effects bore witness. With the resurrection and brand new beginnings for Jesus all doubt about his uniqueness disappeared, at least for the disciples, and the ecclesiological problem also came into view.[35] But it was not with the resurrection or on the road to Emmaus that the church began. Its footings were laid on higher and firmer ground. It was not with the resurrection that Jesus' link with his people became inscrutable and enigmatic.[36] Only with his establishment at the right hand of God – 'separated from sinners, exalted above the heavens'[37] – did ecclesial being become possible. Only then did its eucharistic form become necessary, somehow anticipating a second and more profound 'change in the darkness and matter' that is yet to come.

When we want to think about the church we are therefore obliged to think about the ascension, and that is what we propose to do in the present work. We are not unaware of the skeptical response we are inviting even from within the church; beyond it the project can commend itself only as an exercise in the history of Christian dogmatics, on which we hope to shed some further light. The embarrassment of our subject does not much concern us, however. We will come in due course to a consideration of the cosmological difficulties which today beset the notion of Jesus' ascension, only remarking here that there never has been a cosmology into which that part of his story could be fitted without impossible strain. On the other hand, the same must be said of Jesus-history as a whole and

---

[34] John 7:33ff.; cf. 20:17, also Luke 24:36ff.

[35] Where Jesus' identity was concerned, says Frei (149), the ambiguity was over. But plainly a new kind of ambiguity came into being, an ambiguity in the identity of his followers which also requires our attention.

[36] Not for nothing does the fourth Gospel bracket its magisterial treatment of the ecclesial situation (14–16) with references to Jesus' absence and exhortations to guard against anxiety, a concern which also informs Jesus' high-priestly prayer in chap. 17.

[37] Heb. 7:26, RSV.

of the eucharistic community as such, which brings us back to what we have called the troubling ambiguity of the church.

What exactly do we mean by that? In Jesus covenant history was reduced to the history of one single man, on whom, Christians claim, the covenant community has become entirely dependent for its true identity.[38] But the outcome of Jesus-history was something so radical, in the proper sense of that word, as to leave that community stripped of every earthly distinction from the rest of humanity. Jesus, broken on the cross and restored in the resurrection, was 'taken up in glory' as the representative and judge of all people. Since the ascension the only thing standing in the way of the community's complete dissolution into the world (hence into what is commonly called universal history) is its eucharistic reincorporation into the society of one whose course is known to God alone.[39] The church, then, is marked off from the world, insofar as it is marked off, not by race or culture or even by religion (marks which are definite enough by worldly standards and more or less acceptable) but by its mysterious union with one whose life, though lived *for* the world, involves a genuine break with it.[40]

Now the church is only really itself when it accepts and embraces this situation of radical continuity, and equally radical discontinuity, with the world. But that can hardly be taken for granted! Most of the really thorny issues in ecclesiology, as in Christian spirituality, arise where this uncomfortable tension is rejected and a more stable (or at least condign) identity is sought. So too do the great betrayals of ecclesial integrity to which history bears witness, among which the greatest is surely the church's attempt to hand over its own proper scandal to the Jews, deflecting the animosity of the world onto their shoulders by encouraging the exaggeration of their racial and cultural and religious differences. For insofar as the church seeks to alleviate the eucharistic pressure – usually by denying or falsifying its own much more profound discontinuity with the world – it is bound to spend much of its time and energy trying to cover up for that discontinuity. A surprising amount of ecclesiastical history can be accounted for in just that way.[41]

---

[38] Cf. Frei 137.

[39] It is a weakness of Frei's work that the ascension is taken too little into account, and the eucharist too, so that the tension of the presence and the absence is eased by talk of 'indirect presence.' That leads (155ff.) to a different construction of the ecclesiological problem as a tension between Christ in the church and Christ in the world. Frei does not overlook our concern altogether, however.

[40] That break is represented by the ascension no less than by the cross; where this point is overlooked the cross itself becomes a mere religious symbol.

[41] It does not follow that Christians should cease to proclaim the gospel to the Jews, or that our theology must be reduced to theodicy, a defense of 'the God and Father of our Lord Jesus Christ' against crimes committed in his name. Only a theology constructed on its own proper ground, its course set not by our agendas (not even that of a wounded conscience) but by God's own agenda in the life, death, resurrection and ascension of Jesus, will suffice.

What is not surprising is that the doctrine of the ascension (if it is not rejected outright) is often pressed into service here, precisely by refusing to allow it to teach a doctrine of absence and hence of discontinuity. The following excerpt from a theological dictionary illustrates how readily the ascension is converted into a prop for the notion of universal presence:

> Thus, even if Jesus appears to be absent from his church, in one sense, he is, in fact, more profoundly and intimately present to the church, in another sense. For he is now in 'heaven' with God – in the heaven which, according to the biblical tradition, is a symbol not only of God's transcendence and inaccessibility but also of God's omnipresence. Paradoxically, being in heaven with God, Jesus is also present in the world in the way that God is present.[42]

No doubt there is an element of truth in this, not to mention a quite different intention behind it. But in what way *is* God present, and how can Jesus be present in that way? How does his presence in the church differ from his presence in the world, or does it? (If not, what is the church?) How is he to return from such a heaven, and what can heaven possibly mean for the rest of us?[43] Above all, what does the ascension, so interpreted, do to his humanity? Is there not a marked tendency towards the de-humanization of Jesus, and thus towards that confusion between him and the Spirit that is so prevalent today?[44]

The notion of Christ's universal presence is an exceedingly common one, as we shall see. Whatever its other merits it nicely sidesteps the question of the two histories and the difficult ecclesial situation that goes with it. The burden of the cosmological and the ecclesiological challenge of the ascension is lightened, but at the cost of trifling with Jesus' identity too.[45] What is sacrificed for the sake of this *Christus praesens*, as Calvin noticed long ago, is his specificity as a particular man. Christ everywhere really means Jesus of Nazareth nowhere. In the

---

[42] L. Swain, *A New Dictionary of Theology* (Komonchak 63). On the whole the entry is a good one, but we cannot resist noting this Sunday School parallel culled from the *Church Times* ('Growing in Faith,' 12 May 1995): 'once Jesus stopped being present in one place at a time, he could start being present everywhere at once. Does that seem strange? . . . Drop the tablet [representing Jesus] into the water. You cannot see the tablet now, but it is still present in the water. Jesus was going to heaven; but he would still be in the world.'

[43] J. Ratzinger (1975:46) suggests that 'it would be a misunderstanding of the Ascension if some sort of temporary absence of Christ from the world were to be inferred from it.' But surely that assertion leads more or less directly to another, *viz.*, that a visible return should 'not be taught as a certainty' (thus the Congregation of the Sacred Office in 1944; quoted with some amazement by Karl Barth, *CD* 3/2:510).

[44] Gordon Fee's massive study, *God's Empowering Presence*, essays for the sake of pneumatology to reclaim the distinction between Jesus and the Spirit in the letters of Paul. Our own first concern is with the integrity of christology, but the health of each depends on the other, and the health of ecclesiology on both.

[45] See Heb. 13:8.

ascension he becomes ἄτοπος in the most literal sense: he is unnatural, absurd, for he has no place of his own.[46] (Vague talk among modern theologians about 'a change of state, not of place' hardly alleviates that difficulty, however effective it may be in turning aside impolite inquiries as to Jesus' actual whereabouts.) For that reason, and others we will encounter later, we begin to hear of the 'post-existent' Christ or about the period *after* the incarnation. In other words, just when the gospel has taught us to think of salvation in the most concrete terms, as an act of God in the flesh and for the flesh, the story of Jesus is turned against itself. His humanity is betrayed and marginalized after all. The ascension means, not the consummation, but simply the *end* of Jesus-history.[47]

When that happens, of course, the problem of the church's own identity is badly compounded; for it is no longer clear who it is that it confesses as Lord. The next step is almost always to fix even more strongly on one or another aspect of its own structure or mission as a guarantee of its fidelity and continued relevance – 'seeking to grasp identity from the fear of nonidentity,' in Hans Frei's phrase.[48] That in turn throws up barriers to eucharistic unity by creating competing notions of the church which must be jealously guarded.[49] In fact, the more the church struggles to establish an identity that can be clearly delineated in worldly (i.e., non-eschatological) terms, the more it suffers fragmentation along its political and cultural fault-lines. And in *that* brokenness it shares less and less with its Lord; at the same time the glass through which it sees grows darker and darker.

* * *

We have, then, a second reason for taking up the doctrine of the ascension, since it is chiefly by way of that doctrine that the church's eucharistic ambiguity is passed on (all in vain) to Jesus. We shall find ourselves arguing what is perhaps an unusual line. It is frequently said that the humanity of Christ used to be the great problem for theology but that today it is his divinity which is distracting and difficult. Our study suggests that the case is otherwise. It is still the humanity of Christ over which we are prone to stumble, and what is required today more than ever is a doctrine of the ascension that does not set his humanity aside.

Such a doctrine will actually require a new and more coherent relationship between the disciplines of christology, ecclesiology and

---

[46] Frei's main reference to the ascension (see p. 49) is an attempt to counter this notion, but he offers no hints as to how we might do that.

[47] 'Christ is not confined to Jesus of Nazareth . . . I dare not cling too closely to Christ as past event, lest I miss the incarnation present now' (J. Nelson, *Body Theology*, 193).

[48] p. 154 (the context is not ecclesiological).

[49] Cf. 1 Cor. 3:1ff., 11:18f.

cosmology.[50] How that relationship is commonly understood, and what we believe to be a more right-minded approach, we will leave to unfold with the work itself. For we do not intend to launch directly into a systematic consideration of the ascension but to examine at some length its treatment in scripture, tradition and the modern context, making our systematic observations along the way. We will of course keep a constant watch on the manner in which the doctrine of the ascension is brought to bear on the doctrine of the church, and return in our concluding chapter to the concerns of the present one. Our main sub-thesis in ecclesiology may be stated in advance, and it is this: To the extent that the doctrine of the ascension *is* used to dissolve Jesus' humanity, ecclesiology also deteriorates into the impersonal and, indeed, the irrelevant. But we shall have to fill this out from the tradition in order to make much sense of it.

To open up a fruitful discussion of the ascension today (if we may offer this broad hint about the realignment of disciplines) we must be prepared to take Jesus-history far more seriously than our own. Christians have never believed that the cross was the end of that history, nor even the resurrection. To adopt such a view would put us in the strange position of having to fall silent midway through the creed. Yet to continue in full voice is not possible without renewed commitment to the absolute priority of Jesus-history. And here we may recall another occasion, recounted by Luke no less than three times, when after the ascension a small band of travelers again met up with Christ upon their road. This time it was not Jesus whose path was temporarily arrested at a mortal's bidding, but just the reverse. Only one of the travelers saw anything specific at all, but what he saw and heard completely overwhelmed the confident categories of his own existence. The collision knocked him from his seat, provided *him* with a new identity, and thoroughly rearranged his theology in the process. That is what may be called a new starting point!

---

[50] It will also require new efforts on the part of biblical scholars. Once it was decided that Jesus' identity had been determined by the church, rather than the reverse, the history of tradition – not Jesus' own history – became the proper object of scholarly investigation, and New Testament studies became a branch, albeit a highly independent one, of the self-absorbed ecclesiology we criticized above. But things have already changed somewhat; a new interest in Jesus himself is emerging. We mean to urge that interest on towards the climax of his story.

2

The Ascension as Story and Metaphor

What St Paul encountered on the road to Damascus, namely, the disrupting and transforming power of the ascended Jesus, Daniel perceived from afar in prophetic visions which 'passed through his mind as he was lying on his bed':

> In my vision at night I looked, and there before me was one like a son of man, coming with the clouds of heaven. He approached the Ancient of Days and was led into his presence. He was given authority, glory and sovereign power; all peoples, nations and men of every language worshiped him. His dominion is an everlasting dominion that will not pass away, and his kingdom is one that will never be destroyed.[1]

Like Paul, Daniel was disturbed by the unexpected revelation, and inquired about 'the true meaning of all this.' We must do likewise, for it is a most helpful (if often neglected) passage in getting to grips with the significance of the ascension within the biblical framework. First, however, it is necessary to speak directly of the New Testament witness.

We begin with Luke, who is the only one to offer an actual account of Jesus' departure, and with the difficult question of the genre of that account. Is Luke attempting to describe the ascension more or less as it happened, leaning on apostolic testimony, or was the story conceived, like Daniel's dreams, in the comfort of a bedroom or study? Certainly there are reasons for questioning the historicity of Luke's story. That it appears only in his writings (if we discount the longer ending of Mark) has frequently been pointed out, ever since Reimarus remarked that Matthew and John write 'just as if they knew nothing about it or as if it were a mere trifle.'[2] That the story is told twice, in a not entirely consistent way, has been taken to suggest either some confusion or the liberty of invention, precedent for which is discovered in other assumption stories of that period. It is not surprising, then – given its native ability to provoke

---

[1] Dan. 7:13–14, NIV.
[2] §32 (1971:197); cf. e.g. W. Pannenberg 1972:116, 2/354f.

incredulity – to find that the story of the ascension is often regarded as a pious fiction.[3]

There are some, however, who consider that judgment a hasty one. A number of lines of evidence converge to suggest even to the skeptical a second look. That the story of Jesus' ascension is, in its context, quite unlike its supposed parallels is evident. That Luke's two versions of it are not mutually contradictory more sympathetic commentators have shown.[4] That the story itself is of great importance to Luke is becoming increasingly clear.[5] This last point in particular invites our closer attention, for it will lead us eventually to a consideration of the ascension elsewhere in scripture. By 'consideration' we do not mean anything like a proper scholarly investigation, of course; that is a task for others to perform. All we mean to do is to draw attention to the fact that our subject is a worthy one, and to show up something of the seriousness with which it is treated. If what we have to say is sufficiently suggestive (or provocative, for we shall have to take many risks) to encourage further investigation, so much the better.

A Lukan Artifice?

The ascension episode, twice-portrayed, is the hinge on which Luke's two-volume work turns, a fact that can be acknowledged without immediate prejudice to the question of genre. Whether as history or as a bit of New Testament apocalyptic, this remarkable scene first provides a dramatic closure to the story of Jesus and then a hermeneutical key to the new history of the people of God. It serves to inform us that it is from the standpoint of the vindication and exaltation of Jesus that Luke intends to recount that history, and to account *for* it.[6] So much Peter's Pentecost sermons already make clear, but more can be said.

---

[3] Harnack (1909:157ff.), e.g., regarded the ascension myth as one of the 'semi-doctrinal legends' developed by second-generation believers in the interchange between Jewish and Hellenic ideas. Luke had access to more primitive traditions, which included nothing of the sort, but gradually embraced the invented version – not his only slip of credulousness. Though Lukan studies have come a long way since Harnack, his view is still a common one.

[4] The main point of conflict is the insertion in Acts of a forty-day period between the resurrection and the ascension, which is explained in a variety of ways. C. F. D. Moule (1957:207) suggests that Luke received new information, but can we not allow him the licence to condense before unfolding? Mikeal Parsons (1987) is very helpful on this and related matters; cf. R. Tannehill (1990:10f.) whose discussion is less satisfactory.

[5] Even Leslie Houlden, whose skepticism would appear to be quite settled, acknowledges that the ascension provides 'the climax or watershed of Luke-Acts, and makes sense of the conceptuality of that novel work as a whole' ('Beyond Belief' 178). His response is to isolate Luke from Paul and the rest of the New Testament.

[6] Cf. Parsons (17f., 185), who notes the claim of R. Maddox (1982:10) that 'the ascension is for Luke the point of intersection of Christology, eschatology and ecclesiology.' Whether as a so-called 'pre-narrative' or as actual history, the story's theological significance is not in doubt; how precisely to interpret it belongs to the wider question of Luke's theological agenda. See R. O'Toole (1979:106ff.) for a summary of the debate.

Among those who have argued strongly for the centrality of the ascension narratives in Luke's overall design is Eric Franklin. Franklin develops the somewhat controversial thesis that the ascension is used by Luke not to *abandon* eschatology for history, as the 'delay of the parousia' scholars would have it, but to bring history into the *service* of eschatology, in view of growing uncertainty about the timing of the parousia. For Luke, he maintains, it is no longer the end of history which is to guarantee 'the claims made on behalf of Jesus;' the ascension and heavenly session provide that guarantee already. The ascension (not the resurrection or the parousia) thus becomes the climax of Jesus-history and *the* eschatological event, fulfilling all the prophetic hopes of Israel. And this eschatologizes what is left of history by setting it within the tension of his departure and still-impending return.[7]

Franklin, we think, is on the right track, though his work requires some rethinking in view of the much more radical criticism now being aimed at the eschatological assumptions of those with whom he is taking issue. Today it begins to appear (as some suspected from the start) that the delay of the parousia crisis was strictly a modern one,[8] which leaves us to confront the fact that the return of Jesus to establish his kingdom was, and remained, a very central element in the kerygma. What we need to notice here, however, is that Franklin does not commit himself on the question of genre, in spite of making such strong claims respecting the ascension in Luke. Luke's scheme, he suggests, appears to be 'an artificial one and is most likely of his own making.'[9] Historical considerations are in any case secondary to theological ones.

More recently, Mikeal Parsons has pointed to the centrality of the ascension narratives by means of an extensive literary analysis. In *The Departure of Jesus in Luke-Acts* he attempts to show how the ascension resolves a number of key tensions in Luke's Gospel, while setting in motion the entire plot of the book of Acts. Regarding genre, Parsons also takes a mediating position. An underlying tradition, historical or otherwise, was moulded by Luke's considerable literary prowess (which is 'at its best in the ascension narratives') to the requirements of the project in which he was engaged.[10] In short, 'Luke shaped an ascension story inherited from

---

[7] 1975:6ff., 41ff.; cf. 1970:194ff.: Luke's efforts to come to terms with ongoing history led him 'to see the Ascension as the climax of God's action in the history of the Jewish people, and to view history since the Ascension as witnessing to it as the moment of the enthronement of Jesus at the right hand of God.' But history 'does not take the place of eschatology;' the absence of Jesus must be respected.

[8] See N. T. Wright 1992:285f., 462f. (also Neill and Wright 20ff., 376ff., 398ff.), who is not alone in rejecting the line of Baur, Strauss, Harnack, Bultmann, Käsemann, Conzelmann, Köster *et. al.*

[9] 1975:33. J. Maile (1986:46ff.) notices the inconsistency in this retreat.

[10] Cf. P. Benoit 1/244ff., and the popular view of van Stempvoort (1958). Parsons does not pass judgment on the historicity of the tradition, but is persuasive that an ascension story belonged to it.

primitive tradition into a final departure scene in Luke 24:50–53 and a heavenly-assumption story, complete with apocalyptic stage-props, in Acts 1.' Fittingly enough, the former was given the form of a priestly benediction, the latter that of an invocation, as it were.[11]

Naturally such monographs invite and receive their own share of criticism, but perusal of their contents makes it difficult to dispute the presence of the ascension as a major motif in Luke. On the other hand, even those who so regard it are frequently inclined to speak of Luke's narrative as an artificial device, one that works well structurally and symbolically but not as history *per se*.[12] The historical kernel within it, if such there be, is not very accessible and seemingly of little importance. But this should not go unchallenged, if only because it turns upside-down the relationship between history and theology.[13] For a theology that wishes to take its own departure from Jesus-history, it is far from irrelevant whether the ascension should have its own place as a distinct event in the life of Jesus, and if so whether it should be understood as having taken place in this way or that. Indeed, the greater the place accorded to the ascension in Luke or elsewhere, the more urgent this question becomes. We must continue to ask, then, whether the ascension is Luke's story only – an artful metaphor by which he means to unpack something of the meaning of the resurrection – or whether it belongs in the first place to Jesus himself as part of *his* story. A metaphor it may be either way, but whose metaphor is it?[14]

Suppose in answering our question we simply set aside Reimarus' charge of fraud against Luke, a charge the faithful have always rejected and which few biblical scholars today are prepared to repeat. Suppose, too, that we reject Rudolf Bultmann's completely unfounded suggestion that what is now *in*credible was credible enough in the first century.[15] What reason

---

[11] pp. 63, 150; see 111ff., 189ff. See also now A. Zwiep 1997, a work we may hope to engage elsewhere.

[12] Even J. G. Davies (1958:56ff., 63f., 168f.) finds Luke's version historically 'unreliable.'

[13] Nor has it, of course. For Moule (1957:209) the ascension is a distinct moment in the Christ-event which 'carries its own special significance as the closing moment of one chapter and the opening of the next . . . As such, it seems to demand a position "in history" as truly as the others.'

[14] The value of such a metaphor or 'enacted parable' (W. Temple 1962:154) is not in question here. But just as it would be a mistake to miss the metaphor by seeing nothing but physical movement, so (for reasons we will come to) it would be a mistake to miss the actual movement.

[15] 'What meaning can we attach to . . . "ascended into heaven"?' asks Bultmann (Bartsch 1953:4f.). 'No one who is old enough to think for himself supposes that God lives in a local heaven.' The scientific outlook no longer permits us to 'accept the story of Christ's descent into hell or his Ascension into heaven as literally true. We can no longer look for the return of the Son of Man on the clouds of heaven or hope that the faithful will meet him in the air.' Between Reimarus and Bultmann lies D. F. Strauss, of course, who regarded everything miraculous in the biographies of Jesus as a smothering 'mass of mythical parasites.' Without stopping to refute in detail his handling of the ascension (see 1879 §98), we may object to two things in particular which he shares with Bultmann: the mistaken notion that Luke's

will we then put forward for deciding that Luke's story is an artifice? Today Luke is recognized as a theologian in his own right, but it will be granted that he is indeed a historian, that it was not his intention to write fiction or apocalyptic or some kind of picture-theology.[16] It will be granted, too, that the fullest version of the ascension story (Acts 1:6–11) falls in the middle of what is in other respects a very traditional historical prologue. Are there, then, clear signals that Luke wishes – suddenly and briefly – to effect a change in genres? Does this plain and concise passage, highly remarkable for its restraint,[17] display some quite different form or style than what precedes or follows it? If we *are* dealing with a bit of apocalyptic, say, or creative myth-making, against which the charge of fraud ought not to be made, where are the usual semantic markers? Certainly there is no visionary framework, no tell-tale symbolism (in canonical literature clouds and angels are thin proof), no feel of the primitive, no hint of the universal.[18] Is there not instead a sense of stubborn realism, even to the almost humorous rebuke of the disciples for having their own feet stuck *too* firmly to the ground as they gape incredulously into the skies? What is there to contradict the feeling that Luke, at least, believed what he was writing, as Bultmann also supposed? But if that is so, then we must not only admit that he was representing a more primitive tradition, but also that it is unlikely that that tradition existed in a merely fanciful or obviously apocryphal form. For we can hardly turn around and accuse a writer of such sensitivity and 'literary prowess' of being less astute than his peers.[19]

---

presentation has something to do with the 'delay of the parousia,' and the obvious circularity of the wider argument. If one has already rejected 'the thick and murky cloud of Jewish error and superstition' (§99), determining to decide matters theological in isolation from the biblical witness to God's acts, then certainly one must accuse the Evangelists of employing invented stories to show that Jesus fulfilled Old Testament expectations. But what if these Jewish expectations are *not* mere superstitions, and what if Jesus actually did so?

[16] Should we contend that Luke has in some way or other stylized his story (his shorter and longer versions are proof of that) no further conclusion follows. 'An author is not to be suspected of having invented what he narrates because he arranges his narrative for the benefit of his theological teaching' (Benoit 1/250).

[17] No comparison with imperial apotheosis stories (satirized in Claudius' case by Seneca's *Apocolocyntosis*) commends itself, except perhaps, as Tom Wright has suggested to me, on a theo-political level. Nor does Luke attempt to match the much more dramatic story of Elijah's departure, e.g., even though that famous prophet is closely linked to Jesus by the transfiguration episode and the forty-days motif.

[18] If we follow G. B. Caird's lucid definition of myth (1966:66, 1980:219ff.) the ascension story will not fit that category; nor does it fit the aims of apocalyptic (cf. K. Koch 1972:24ff.). Hans Frei rejects a mythological reading of these narratives as *diametrically opposed* to their actual character, which is designed to bring out the irreducible particularity of Jesus (1975:139ff.; cf. 1974, and see also J. Alsup 1975:272).

[19] Cf. Parsons 137ff. Even Harnack (1909:161) noted among fellow critics of Acts that some appeared to lack sufficient acquaintance with the 'unwieldy collection of fabulous stories' available in Luke's day. 'If they knew them,' he remarked, 'they would not make so much ado about the stories of miracles in Acts.'

Of course, there is still the point about Luke being the only one actually to tell the story, but the argument from literary and theological design is a double-edged sword. If we wish to maintain that one Gospel writer incorporated an ascension story (invented or otherwise) only because it suited his peculiar purposes, we can scarcely deny that others may have left it out simply because it did not suit theirs. The real issue, then, is whether its omission elsewhere implies that only Luke saw in this particular element of the tradition something especially noteworthy. Even that is by no means a foregone conclusion, for the omission of an account of the event and its absence from the work itself are not the same thing.[20] Whatever we make of the longer ending to Mark, it must be said that there are several vital passages within that terse Gospel – including no less than three direct allusions to Daniel 7:13f. – which justify its reference to the ascension.[21] Matthew's conclusion, surely, is highly redolent of the ascension. Since he is presenting Jesus as the 'prophet like Moses,' his book reaches its natural climax with Jesus on a mountaintop, at the fringe of the gentile world, commissioning the disciples like so many Joshuas. But in that commissioning it is made clear that Jesus, unlike Moses, will not have to let go of the reins of authority as he departs to *his* hidden place of Rest. This suggestive scenario, with its allusion to Daniel 7 in verse 18 and its sidelong glance at Jewish tradition, does not rule out Luke's story but points towards it, in substance if not necessarily in detail.[22] As for John, at once the simplest and the most sophisticated Gospel, we find that it is powerfully charged with the ascension motif *throughout*, a matter we will touch on later. But of course it is only Luke who took up the challenge of carrying on the gospel story into a history of the early church. Is that not explanation enough why he alone among the Evangelists concerned himself with an account of Jesus' departure? His work required it, theirs did not.

The historical flavour of Luke's account has been argued by C. F. D. Moule and others; we see no reason for rejecting their findings.[23] We may

---

[20] Cf. W. Milligan 1892:8ff. Strictly speaking, even the resurrection is not narrated – what happens in the tomb being as inscrutable as what happens in the cloud which receives Jesus out of his followers' sight (Acts 1:9).

[21] Mark 8:38, 13:26ff., 14:62; Dan. 7 imagery is strong throughout. See Davies 1958:35ff. for discussion of these passages, and of ascension imagery and typology in the account of Jesus' baptism.

[22] On Matt 28 see Davies 1958:43f., 64, who elsewhere (62f. n.13, following H. Schrade 1930:89f.) observes that early iconography suggests a parallel with Moses (cf. N. T. Wright 1992:384ff.). But Matthew may also intend a contrast – rumours of Moses' permanent ascent into glory (Josephus, *Ant.* 4.8.48) being contradicted by Deuteronomy.

[23] 1957:205ff. M. Hengel (1979:68f.) comments: 'We only do justice to the significance of Luke as the first theological "historian" of Christianity if we take his work seriously as a source . . . The radical "redaction-critical" approach so popular today, which sees Luke above all as a freely inventive theologian, mistakes his real purpose, namely, that as a Christian "historian" he sets out to report the events of the past that provided the foundation of

add that the case for an historical genre is considerably strengthened when we face the fact that removal of the ascension episode would render unintelligible other significant material in Acts. The thrice-repeated Damascus Road episode is a case in point. It is sometimes conveniently overlooked that Paul's pivotal confrontation with the risen Jesus was remarkably unlike the pre-ascension encounters of the disciples. On the way to Damascus Paul did not sit down to eat and drink with the risen Christ. He met up with the Lord of Glory, whom mortal eyes cannot behold without dramatic consequence. As an apostolic witness he was, by his own early testimony, 'one abnormally born.'[24] The differences we have in view have nothing to do with any alleged spiritualizing tendency in Paul, but everything to do with the fact that the situation of *Jesus* had changed.[25] And just here we find ourselves in opposition to another highly popular idea.

It is common today to insist on equating the resurrection with Christ's full glorification. For many this is a primary reason for sitting lightly to Luke's account. Even those who are prepared to allow that the latter is by and large historical are therefore obliged to treat it as only a lesson designed to put an end to the disciples' expectation of further 'visitations' from heaven.[26] Were the disciples then capable of being taught the mysteries of the kingdom but quite incapable of grasping in any other way that their visits with Jesus were only a temporary arrangement? And why *should* the arrangement have been temporary if Jesus had already entered upon his heavenly glory? Why should he not have continued to come and go in their midst at his own pleasure, taking up his kenotic disguise from time to time? As a matter of fact, the only solid New Testament evidence for a visitation from heaven concerns Paul. If certain

---

the faith and its extension. He does not set out primarily to present his own "theology."' We agree, without imagining that this settles the credibility question, which *cannot* be settled on historical criteria alone.

[24] It is false to suppose with J. Dunn (1975:115) or J. Fitzmyer (1984:422) that the inclusion of Paul's experience in a list of other resurrection encounters in 1 Cor. 15 means that these were all of a piece, or to conclude that at this early stage no distinction was being made between resurrection and ascension. When in v. 8 Paul admits to being born abnormally – ἔσχατον δὲ πάντων ὡσπερεὶ τῷ ἐκτρώματι ὤφθη κἀμόι – is he not pointing to the fact that he did not walk and talk with the resurrected one in the manner of the other apostles, and to the fact 'that Christ had in some way to do violence to the ordered scheme of salvation to bring about Paul's vocation' (*Catholic Dictionary of Theology* 1/165)? Moule (208) rightly argues that he holds to the pattern of resurrection first, then ascension and glorification, a pattern he also translates into the expectation of believers (cf. 1 Thess. 4:16f., Phil. 3:14).

[25] Benoit (1/221ff.) rejects the 'frankly anachronistic' idea that the resurrection was first interpreted in spiritual terms, then gradually materialized; F. Watson (1996:127f.) is also suspicious. Cf. Dunn 108, 120ff.

[26] It is 'nothing more than *the* appearance from glory in which Christ took his final leave from the community . . . .' Though Luke has not invented it 'he has *historicized* it in a way no other NT writer has' (Fitzmeyer 424).

other texts could be read that way, none need be.[27] And when they are, it ought to be admitted that the resulting construction – which is indeed a new and strange form of kenoticism – is a highly problematic one. It leaves Jesus looking rather like one who has moved away somewhat reluctantly, and who for a time keeps finding excuses to pay his friends a visit.[28]

Some, of course, try to evade the problems by speaking of the resurrection appearances rather as visions, and of the ascension as a departure vision, but that is expressly ruled out by all four Evangelists. To hold such a view is to make the resurrection itself as doubtful as this so-called departure. It is not for nothing that the concreteness of Jesus is always underlined in his resurrection appearances, the last being no exception, since Luke describes it as taking place 'before their very eyes.'[29] Visions of Jesus did not cease with the ascension but rather commenced. What Jesus 'began to do and to teach' in his earthly ministry, says Luke, he did and taught 'until the day he was taken up into heaven.' It was then that his ministry took on a brand new form, a pentecostal form in which visions of various sorts were and are commonplace.[30]

To move away from Luke's story is of necessity to write a different one, an exercise that inevitably creates more problems than it solves. For our part, we will proceed on the assumption that what Luke has to say about the ascension ought not to be dismissed, or even admired, as an artifice, but pursued as the indication of an essential component of salvation history. That can be done by looking at the wider framework in which it is set. Along the way it may be that we will find further and even better reasons for affirming the traditional view of the ascension as (in some sense) a space-time event with its own proper claim on our theological reflection.

The Larger Story

It has been observed that the journey motif is the most prominent organizational element in Luke-Acts. In the Gospel the large, seemingly disorderly central section admits of no obvious superstructure other than the slow, tortuous, but deliberate advance of Jesus from the desert of

[27] The heavenly authority with which Jesus bestows the Spirit in John, or commissions the disciples in Matthew, supplies no decisive objection; these acts require and look towards Pentecost for their fulfillment. On the other hand, if John's experience in Rev. 1 is regarded as something more than a vision, its very different character only reinforces our point. But we do not so regard it, except perhaps in its eucharistic dimension (see Chap. 6 below).

[28] See e.g. M. Harris 1985:50ff. When Harris says that the ascension 'does not lead to the exaltation but looks back to that event which it visually dramatises as an acted parable of the raising up of Jesus to cosmic dominion' (84), we quarrel not over its dramatic form but over its detachment from the actual history of Jesus.

[29] As the NIV aptly translates it: καὶ ταῦτα εἰπὼν βλεπόντων αὐτῶν ἐπήρθη καὶ νεφέλη ὑπέλαβεν αὐτὸν ἀπὸ τῶν ὀφθαλμῶν αὐτῶν. Cf. 2 Kings 2:9f.

[30] See e.g. Acts 2:17, 7:55f. Cf. Strauss 1879 §98, according to whom 'the billows of excited mental life became calmer and calmer.'

temptation beyond the Jordan to his final hour of trial in Jerusalem.[31] N. T. Wright points out how Luke thus sets the life of Jesus carefully alongside that of David, presenting him as Israel's true king and heir of the covenant promises. In Acts the travels and trials of Paul, especially, imitate and so bear witness to those of Jesus.[32]

Acts begins, however, where the Gospel leaves off, by furnishing a fuller version of Jesus' departure on his own ultimate journey – the journey that leads from Jerusalem to God's heavenly sanctuary and throne, completing the exodus of which he spoke at the transfiguration when the glory cloud enveloped him briefly in an anticipatory way.[33] From there, the angels avow, he will someday return.[34] For his ascent to heaven, like his ascent to the cross, is a journey undertaken on behalf of God's people and with a view to the realization of their kingdom hopes. That is the context in which the disciples are commissioned for *their* journeys; the outwards spiral of the apostolic mission is the ripple in the sea that marks the upwards passage of Jesus to receive what was promised.[35]

In this light, Franklin's notion that Luke's entire story comes to rest on the ascension must be confirmed. And when we stop to consider (as Wright and others bid us do) that the story Luke is telling plainly belongs to a very much longer one, we are finally in a position to allow the full force of that episode to make itself felt. Carried along by the central currents which generate the Bible's seemingly impossible unity, we are brought to a place where we can see this particular journey as marking the very climax of salvation history.[36] For without the ascension not only would Luke's story begin to disintegrate,[37] but the biblical story as a whole would lack the outcome it demands. Within the parameters of the present study, unfortunately, we can do little more than suggest a vantage point from which the reasons for making such a claim can be glimpsed. And that brings us back to Daniel 7.

---

[31] See 9:31, 51ff., 18:31, 23:5, which drive home the point; that is not to say, of course, that there are no other structural or thematic considerations in play. Cf. Parsons 90.

[32] 1992:379f.

[33] Cf. Franklin 1975:54. The cloud motif is a highly prominent one in scripture and has a number of different overtones, all connected with the divine Presence. See e.g. Gen. 1:2, Exod. 40:34ff., 1 Kings 8:10f., Isa. 6:4, Ezek. 1 and 10, Dan. 7:13, Luke 1:35, 9:34, 1 Thess. 4:17, Rev. 11:12. M. Kline (1980) is particularly helpful in this matter.

[34] Jerusalem is still to be the polestar of the new creation. The cloud which now receives Jesus outside and above the city recalls, however, the temple vision of Ezekiel in which the Glory of Israel departs and stands at a distance, judgment on the present Jerusalem having been pronounced (cf. Ezek. 8–10, Luke 21:5ff.).

[35] Pentecost, of course, being the link between the two. See below (Chap. 4) on Augustine's abuse of this insight; cf. Wright 373ff. for a suggestion as to Luke's own agenda in bringing it to light.

[36] Renewed sensitivity to the wholeness of scripture has begun to pay off in a number of useful works of different shapes and sizes; see e.g. N. Frye (1982), W. Gage (1984), W. Dumbrell (1985). In particular, Wright's *The New Testament and the People of God* will be teaching us how to read 'the larger story' for some time to come.

[37] Cf. Frei 1975:123.

In this purely visionary ascension scene, which belongs to a popular apocalyptic dream sequence, we are invited to observe the action not from below, with anchored feet and craned necks, but from above. It is neither a departure nor an assumption story we are offered, but an *arrival* story – arrival at the end of a long and painful pilgrimage, disclosed in advance to a footsore people. Here we do not see what those bound to the paths of this present world must be satisfied to see; we see instead from the other side of the mysterious theophanic cloud, and from the other end of history. To be sure, what we see 'from above' is something which at the end of the age will take place in human history, namely, the people of God being exalted over the destructive chaos of the nations. (That is what we are told in the *pesher* rendered to Daniel by 'one of those standing there.') And that means that we are glimpsing something of the world's own destination, when the human *imago dei* has been reformed as the priest-king within creation through the perfecting and vindicating of the saints.

This much any diligent student standing within the Hebrew theological milieu could have made out without a great deal of difficulty.[38] Since the true dominion of man over the earth was lost in his expulsion from Eden, man (and creation with him, as Romans 8 tells us) has been on a long journey of rediscovery. This journey, hopeless but somehow full of promise, by divine election has been compressed into the journey of Abraham and his descendants. These, unfortunately, even at their faithful best, have suffered the enmity of the Babel-building beast-nations engaged in a lawless drive to generate a dominion of their own making.[39] But Daniel is assured that at the end of the journey the court will sit to settle the matter of just dominion once and for all; and thus God's people will arrive at their appointed place. Towards that everything moves, if in hidden ways and by secret channels.

What has all this to do with Luke? Daniel and Luke-Acts are clearly engaged in telling one and the same story, about the same great journey of God's elect, with an eye deliberately fixed on that journey's end.[40] Peter's sermon in Acts 2, leaning on three or four royal and liturgical Psalms, rings out the triumphant note sounded already by Christ during his trial: 'from now on, the Son of Man will be seated at the right hand of the mighty God.'[41] That is Daniel's note, of course. The difference here is that the story has moved along in a most surprising way. In the specific

---

[38] Obviously we are taking a good deal for granted in a very controversial passage. See Wright 291ff., whose general line we find convincing; cf. Dumbrell 1985:187.

[39] The cursing of Cain in Gen. 4:12 already establishes the paradigm both of the wandering journey of man and his pursuit of an artificial sanctuary and dominion – 'Cain was then building a city' – which becomes a violent parody of Eden. Cf. H. Blocher 1984:196ff., Gage 49ff., Kikawada and Quinn 55ff.

[40] Thus Lactantius, *Epitome* 47 (see Davies 93f.). Cf. Wright 374, 382, 400f., 462.

[41] Acts 2:33; cf. Luke 22:69. Peter quotes from Pss. 16 and 110, but M. M. B. Turner (Rowdon 1982:176ff.) and others have argued persuasively that Psa. 68 is also of fundamental importance to his claim (note esp. v. 18, 'When you ascended on high . . .'). There appear to be allusions to Psa. 18 as well.

person of the once despised and crucified Jesus of Nazareth, Adam-Israel has indeed been led into the presence of the Ancient of Days to receive dominion over all things.[42]

What Daniel envisioned from above, therefore, Luke is now able to chronicle from below; this he does, conscious of his task. Jesus' ascension has actually been witnessed by the disciples, with their craning necks. News of his coronation in heaven (still hidden from view) has reached earth in the pandemonium of Pentecost. His universal authority is already becoming manifest through the power of the gospel in every place and people. His glorious return, leading to the promised restoration of all things, is expected. Moreover, in this whole turn of events – fulfillment for the many in the person of the one – a nagging anomaly in Daniel 7 begins to clear up, namely, the statement that 'all peoples, nations and men of every language worshiped him.' For it is evident that the one in question is not just any one, but himself the Holy One of Israel.[43]

Luke thus sets out to share with us the realization in history of the ancient dreams and promises. The unifying climax of the whole story is contained in the ascension, which carries forward the journey motif to its natural conclusion. His accounts of this (coming from below) are simple and brief but strategically employed, powerfully illuminated by their context.[44] Acts 2 openly expounds the vital importance of the ascension episode within the flow of biblical history. In spite of the circumstances giving rise to Peter's address, it is not a sermon on the Holy Spirit we hear; nor is the focus on the resurrection. What we are offered is a sermon on the ascension of the risen Jesus to the throne, that is, to Israel's throne *and* the throne of the Presence from which the Spirit goes forth.[45] It is the

---

[42] Cf. Luke 21:27. Note also the extended genealogy in Luke 3 – Jesus is ultimately 'the son of Adam, the son of God' – and the prayer in Acts 4:23ff., which begins with a reference to God's dominion over creation, then draws on Psa. 2 in order to attach this to Jesus.

[43] The verb in Dan. 7:14 (*plḥ*) is consistently used with God as its object; though subsequent Jewish literature knew other putative co-occupants of this Throne, only of Jesus are claims made that would fully justify the statement quoted. (Cf. e.g. Luke 1:26ff., Psa. 99, etc.) Though we are not following him here, we note that Wright in his most recent work (1996:612ff.; see esp. 642f.) sketches out a full-scale interpretation of Jesus-history in terms of the promised return of Yahweh to Zion. He proceeds only as far as the crucifixion, however, and his own treatment of the vindication of Jesus is focused on the events of AD 70 (360ff.). We await with interest his treatment of the resurrection, and fuller treatment of the ascension/parousia complex, in a subsequent volume.

[44] The continuity of reference is necessarily matched by a *discontinuity* of genre. If Luke really is telling the story of Jesus as 'a story which he intends to be the *true climax* of the story of Israel' (Wright 1992:382), he can hardly be restricted to the tools of figurative language.

[45] J. Nolland (1993:1228f.) denies that Luke has any interest in a priestly christology, while pointing out that Luke 24 casts the ascension in a form that parallels Sir. 50:20ff. Surely that alone is weighty evidence for such an interest. Are we not invited throughout (another uniquely Lukan story, about the boy Jesus in his Father's house, deserves mention here) to see in Jesus something of Samuel as well as David, and of the priestly as well as the kingly? But this question belongs to a discussion of Luke's temple theology, which we do not have room to consider.

unifying of these thrones on a Melchizedekian model which occasions the unleashing of the Spirit, thereby signaling both the beginning of the last days and the imperative of Jesus-worship.[46] Pentecost is thus interpreted as witnessing to the actual arrival of Jesus at journey's end. It is the audible earthly echo of what is at once a great liturgical procession and a victory parade, in the fashion of Psalm 68.[47]

Such is the logic of Pentecost as Peter exposes it. The manner in which the central notions of kingship and priesthood are here gathered up testifies to its rightness and invites our attention. For it was chiefly through these two institutions that Israel guarded within its own corporate life the great quest for the rediscovery of human destiny, and kept its bearings for the journey. Or rather, that is how it was supposed to be. In the Gospel we are shown how persistent unfaithfulness (the prophets' constant preoccupation) terminated in a mortal conflict between Jesus and the keepers of the temple, and with the wicked King Herod as well.[48] All the same, it belonged to the nature of cult and monarchy, especially in their central rituals, to point the people of God towards their goal: not simply ascension *over* the nations but ascension from the chaos and contamination of the nations into the presence and blessings of God, and thus into the promised image-bearing dominion over creation. Peter's Pentecost sermon, the theological frontispiece of Acts, is nothing more nor less than an argument that this goal has finally been reached in the person of Jesus – anointed, ascended and crowned. The point is clinched with the quotation from Psalm 110.[49]

Luke thus completes the Daniel 7 picture by adding an arrival story, also witnessed from below (i.e., in a historical rather than a visionary way), to the departure story he has already twice told. Though the emphasis varies, each scene supports the other in a consistent witness to a single movement which by its very nature reunites earth to heaven in fulfillment of the great biblical promises. On that fulfillment, with the ascension as the consummating element and the promised return as the *dénouement*, rests the integrity of the new Christian gospel; on it all that follows in Acts depends.[50]

* * *

We must stress the point that it is indeed the ascension towards which the biblical story constantly strives, especially in its messianic dimensions,

[46] It is the thrust of Turner's article to show that Jesus' right to 'administer the operation of the Spirit' – this being 'the *means* of his heavenly reign' – was understood to have christological implications of the highest magnitude.

[47] Cf. Eph. 4:7ff.

[48] See esp. Luke 13:31ff.

[49] L. Houlden (177) admits 'a degree of consensus' in the New Testament around Psa. 110:1, 'early Christianity's sheet-anchor text.'

[50] R. Maddox (185ff.) points to the significance for Luke-Acts of two words from its preface: πεπληροφορημένα and ἀσφάλεια.

not the resurrection in and of itself. In the Bible the doctrine of the resurrection slowly emerges as a central feature of the Judeo-Christian hope. But if, synecdochically, it can stand for that hope, the hope itself is obviously something more. Resurrection may be a necessary ingredient, since death cuts short our individual journeys, but it is not too bold to say that the greater corporate journey documented by the scriptures continually presses, from its very outset and at every turn, towards the impossible feat of the ascension.

There is no shortage of evidence with which to back this claim, the full weight of which systematics must eventually shoulder. The cosmic mountain motif offers another avenue of approach. The biblical story begins with Eden, of course, the mountain-garden of God from which Adam was forced to descend, at the foot of which was the flaming sword of the guardian cherubim, which would frustrate any attempt to return.[51] The pattern of descent and ascent is furthered (and proleptically fulfilled) in the story of the great flood, during which it is granted to one man, his family and representatives of the animal creation with him, to rise far above even the highest places of our fallen, chaotic world, until he comes to rest on Ararat.[52] Next is the man-made mountain of Babel, provocatively pushed upwards in the very face of the cherubim, a mountain which Yahweh himself stooped to level. Its positive counterpart is Sinai, which God graciously invited Moses to ascend on behalf of his people, on which the seventy elders also 'saw God' in table fellowship. There on Sinai the pattern was laid out for the holy tabernacle, in which the high priest was to ascend by stages into the divine Presence once each year, and from thence descend to bless the people.[53] When this tabernacle (containing the ark of the covenant as the earthly version of the heavenly throne) itself comes to rest on Mount Zion, kingship in Israel is co-opted with it, so that ascent to the Davidic throne likewise comes to hold promise of access to the lost blessings of the mountain-garden of God.[54]

[51] See Gage 49ff. for a brief summary of the cosmic mountain motif. The enigmatic oracle of Ezek. 28 and various references to the cherubim or 'living creatures' in that book and in the Apocalypse suggest that these represent creation itself, in its mandate to render obedient worship to God through the mediation of man. In that case the distortion of creation, i.e., its dislocation connected with the fall of its anointed mediators, is itself the barrier to recovery of the Edenic heights.

[52] See Gen. 7:17ff., where we are told that the waters, carrying the ark with them, 'rose . . . rose greatly . . . rose and covered the mountains' (on the consummate literary design of this chiastically structured passage, see Kikawada and Quinn 97ff.). This episode is tied by analogy to the resurrection and ascension of Christ in 1 Pet. 3:18ff.

[53] The Cloud of the Presence, in which Moses communed with God on Sinai, descended into the camp – after Moses, like the creator, 'finished the work' – and dwelt in the inner sanctuary (Exod. 40). It was into this cloud that the high priest was to ascend yearly. The tabernacle itself represented cosmic order, just as the whole redemptive history and liturgy of Israel is presented in the Pentateuch as a microcosm of the original creation. (See Gage 66ff., Kline 42ff.; cf. Kikawada and Quinn 108ff. on the Babel-like overtones of the Solomonic temple.)

[54] Dumbrell 1984:150ff. For an outline of the above, see Appendix A.

So it goes throughout the entire body of Old Testament literature. The prophets work endlessly with modifications of these themes, testifying at one and the same time to the centrality and to the provisional nature of the institutions enshrining them, until the coming of the one through whom every hope will be fulfilled. Along the way, every would-be high priest is thrust out again from the holy of holies, barred for another year. Every would-be king is carried down from his throne in exile or in death. Certainly every charlatan and imposter, whether he ascends in the midst of Israel or rises among the nations, is warned, rebuked, ridiculed. The failures of the best and the worst of the messianic forerunners are documented together by scribes and prophets, as the Spirit of prophecy drives their dissatisfied thoughts ever forward to the coming of the anointed one. When he finally does come, he comes himself as a prophet, but it is plainly towards this sacred ascension as high priest and king that he moves on his way to the destiny of man. He has come for nothing less.

Of course the messiah must resist every possible shortcut on his journey. He cannot ascend the heights of the temple directly, as the devil suggests,[55] for the temple itself requires reconstruction, a reconstruction he will accomplish in connection with his own person through bitter conflict with the world, the flesh, and the devil – and especially with those who take it as their task to guard the temple.[56] Thus in the end Babel proves only a foil for the much more sinister Calvary, where Zion becomes the ironic mountain of death with its man-made trees. Then again, Ararat, Sinai and Zion in turn show themselves foils, not merely for a lost Eden, but for a new cosmic glory-temple on the heights of which man is to dwell as the true image of God, fully permeated and empowered by the overshadowing Spirit.[57] Jesus, enabled by the Spirit, is the builder of this temple and the first embodiment of this image. Through his resurrection and ascension he will realize in the presence of God the fruit of the work he accomplished here with us, when we in our own crude parody of the ascension lifted him up on the cross.

To cut short the journey of Jesus by conflating resurrection and ascension, however, is to alter the goal of salvation history. How? First of all, it puts in jeopardy the continuity between our present world and the higher places of the new order established by God in Christ. For in that conflation the ascension, insofar as it can still be distinguished from the resurrection, is regarded as an event with no *historical* component, separating it from Old Testament expectations.[58] This eventually rebounds

---

[55] Luke so orders the temptations as to make this the climax.

[56] See John 2:12ff.

[57] This theme is important to Luke in building up to the ascension; see 1:35, 9:26–36, 21:25ff., and cf. Acts 7:55f.

[58] We cannot agree with Bultmann (1/45) or with John Macquarrie (1990:409f.), e.g., that the ascension has no historical dimension. Ratzinger (1975:46) is wise to insist that the ascension 'is not wholly confined to the realm of the "other-worldly" and the suprahistorical,' though he too errs by way of this conflation with the resurrection.

on the doctrine of the resurrection itself – if indeed it is not already the sign of a docetic version of that doctrine – and binds it closely to an other-worldly eschatology that has little in common with that of scripture. Resurrection comes to mean 'going to heaven,' which in some theologies makes it rather hard to distinguish from dying! The doctrine of the parousia either falls away or signifies simply the end of the world. Thus the very point the angels of Acts 1 were concerned to safeguard, the return of 'this same Jesus,' is overlooked and the verdict which Daniel heard in his dream is set aside. That in turn puts in jeopardy the proper *discontinuity* between Jesus-history and common history, leading to the substitution of our own story (the story of man's self-elevation) as the real kernel of salvation history in the present age.[59] That is a process we will have adequate opportunity to expound in later chapters; suffice it for now to say that it tends to the very obverse of Daniel's vision.

In the last analysis, then, to go back on Luke is to risk going back on the larger story itself. But if we are to stick with Luke, we are obliged to direct our attention to certain awkward questions. For if we allow that Jesus was raised in such a way that he was still a participant in our history – albeit in some profoundly new and liberated engagement – then the ascension plainly entails *a parting of the ways*. On the far side of his suffering and death the resurrected one had, and at the proper moment took, a different direction.[60] What are the implications of this parting and how, if at all, shall we attempt to conceive it? Does the ascension of Jesus fit nicely into the biblical worldview or does it do something *to* that worldview?

To answer such questions we need not confine ourselves to Luke. Indeed, if we are on track with what we have said so far, we should expect to find a bold theology of the ascension growing throughout the New Testament. We are not disappointed.

Breaking Boundaries

It is sometimes suggested that there is little of the ascension as an event with its own distinct significance to be found in the New Testament outside of Luke 24 and Acts 1.[61] That is an entirely specious claim, as others have been quick to observe. In his Bampton lectures J. G. Davies

---

[59] This substitution is openly advocated in modern times by Strauss (1879 §100), e.g., but its roots are in early Christian gnosticism on the one hand, and in Constantinianism on the other. (Wright, 1992:382, having explained how Luke subverts other contemporary readings of the story of Israel by retelling it as the story of Jesus, astutely accuses Eusebius of subverting Luke's story in turn by combining it with the story of Constantine. Note that Eusebius, *Dem. Ev.* 6.9, was among those who followed Origen in spiritualizing the ascension.)

[60] 'Do not hold on to me, for I have not yet returned to the Father' (John 20:17).

[61] P. E. Hughes (1989:372ff.) notes Emil Brunner's rejection of the ascension on this basis, a rejection that goes hand in hand with 'a spiritualization or dematerialization of the doctrine of Christ's resurrection.'

shows the contrary in a convincing manner. 'The witness of the New Testament writings to the ascension of Christ is remarkable in its universality,' writes Davies. He cites evidence from all four Gospels together with Acts, and several important examples from the Pauline corpus, including both the disputed and undisputed letters, along with 1 Peter and the Revelation. We have outlined some of the most obvious of these references and allusions in an appendix, but the evidence is even greater than Davies supposes and more revolutionary in character than he perceives.[62] Serious reflection on the ascension appears to have contributed to important breakthroughs in biblical thought about God, man, and the universe, and to have shaped ecclesiology in a quite fundamental way. In support of this claim we will look briefly (much too briefly to qualify as a full demonstration) at three other New Testament theologians, each of whom we believe to have developed a penetrating insight into the significance of the ascension for a Christian worldview.[63]

* * *

Paul, as ferocious in his pursuit of theological integrity as of frightened Christians on the road to Damascus, was naturally the first to grapple with the problem. The *Christus victor* theme which runs through all his letters was no mere theory to him but an unshakeable conviction born of his confrontation with the ascended Jesus. Pauline scholars have with good reason traced back to this experience his devoted reworking of basic Jewish doctrines about God and salvation into the foundations of the Christian faith. Some have also discussed his forays into cosmology, especially in terms of Christ's triumph over the δαίμονια, subjugation of the στοιχεῖα, relation to the πλήρωμα, etc. Hemmed in by faulty assumptions about Hellenization, however, this latter debate has produced more confusion than clarity. In interpreting the lordship of Jesus, Paul's building blocks were the materials provided by the Jewish scriptures. God's design for human dominion and stewardship, creation's fall into slavery and its coming liberation, the elect 'shining like stars' in the darkness of the pagan firmament, the resurrection of the dead and the eventual advent of the

---

[62] Whether this is a result of backing away from Luke's account others may judge. He suggests (1958:27) that to follow the ancient habit of approaching the ascension through Luke is very possibly to miss other references which do not conform. That may be so, but we would reverse the charge: *not* to take St Luke's approach with full seriousness is to risk seeing in those other references less than they actually contain. See Appendix A.

[63] No one, cautions Bultmann (Bartsch 3), 'can adopt a view of the world by his own volition – it is already determined by his place in history. Of course such a view is not absolutely unalterable, and the individual can even contribute to its change. But he can do so only when he is faced by a new set of facts so compelling as to make his previous view of the world untenable. He has then no alternative but to modify [it] . . . or produce a new one.'

30

messianic kingdom – such ideas continued to form the horizon of his theology. Paul was no dualist or Hellenizer.

It is clear enough, however, that all of these interests took on new dimensions as he wrestled with the significance of the exaltation of Jesus. Jesus' own U-shaped course (in Philippians the descent–ascent pattern of the Old Testament is adopted as a framework for christology) completed in the midst of history was a thoroughly unexpected affair that called for a new estimation both of the God who works in history and of history itself. We are not thinking only of the question of Jesus' divinity, for this cannot be thought at all except in terms of this one man in his actual relation to God and the world. And if in the case of this one man all the promises had already been fulfilled, if the ἄνω κλῆσις τοῦ θεοῦ had already been heard and answered, a radically revised worldview was unavoidable. Salvation history was no longer comprehensible in strictly linear terms; cosmic structures and powers were no longer fixed or immovable determinants of human existence. Heaven itself, as Andrew Lincoln has pointed out, had to be reinterpreted.[64] In his advent and enthronement the long-awaited messianic Son had reorganized, not just the nations, but the whole of creation around himself.[65]

In short, the alteration of the world order anticipated in Daniel and the prophets had now to be expressed in terms that went well beyond those of political, social, or religious possibilities. The vessel of Jewish apocalyptic expectations had to be enlarged and reshaped; the cosmic imagery of the prophets had to be given more weight; the (hitherto largely unspeculative) doctrine of the resurrection had to take on new connotations.[66] 'The form of this present world is passing away':[67] this was now to be proclaimed with a profound sense of the ontic link between creation and the cross, or rather between creation and the Christ through whose death, resurrection, and ascension a quite new reality had been forged out of the old. For the one who confronted Paul on his journey to Damascus was regarded by him as nothing less than the Lord of creation. To him all things had been made subject; in him all things were seen to cohere; by him all things would reach their goal. Even the highly paradoxical conclusion that through him all things derive their being forced itself upon Paul. 'For us,' he confessed, 'there is one God, the Father,

---

[64] 1981:170ff. For Paul 'what God has done in Christ has given a special content to the concept of heaven, for it has become involved in a new way in that act of the drama of redemption inaugurated by Christ's resurrection and ascension' (184). 'It is not as though Christ is fitted into a system that Paul already firmly holds. His adherence now is clearly to Christ in a way that requires the reshaping of old patterns of thought' (173).

[65] Cf. Phil. 3:20f. We note Markus Bockmuehl's (1997:19ff.) similar yet very different conclusions regarding Phil. 2:6ff. and 3:21. To place Paul in the mystical tradition as Bockmuehl does is to place him in the docetic tradition as well, where eschatology is concerned (see Chap. 4 below).

[66] 1 Cor. 15:35ff.; cf. Wright 1996:217f.

[67] 1 Cor. 7:31

from whom are all things and for whom we exist, and one Lord, Jesus Christ, through whom are all things and through whom we exist.'[68] History itself, then, belonged to the one who had ascended ἵνα πληρώσῃ τὰ πάντα.[69] A new ontology and a new christocentric cosmology were being conceived, at least in broad outline.

All of this was implicit in Pauline ecclesiology and indeed necessary to it. The baptized derive their new existence from their union with Jesus (a claim the boldness of which left nothing to the mystery religions). The church is a community of Jew and gentile, slave and free, because it is one man in Christ. It stands poised at the consummation of the ages because it exists with Christ on high and not only in a world whose σχῆμα has been condemned. These ideas and others like them demand something more than a purely 'spiritual' interpretation. E. P. Sanders points to a certain maddening, elusive element in Paul, bound up with his so-called Christ mysticism:

> We seem to lack a category of 'reality' – real participation in Christ, real possession of the Spirit – which lies between naive cosmological speculation and belief in magical transference on the one hand and a revised self-understanding on the other. I must confess that I do not have a new category of perception to propose here. This does not mean, however, that Paul did not have one.[70]

Paul was, as Sanders claims, a coherent thinker, even if his writings were more pastoral than systematic; it is therefore reasonable to suppose that he did in fact develop such a category, or at least a framework for it.

May we not look to his insight into the implications of the ascension for understanding here? Ephesians, for example, makes it quite plain that the church is founded in and with the ascension of Christ, who by virtue of his heavenly session is given to it as 'head over everything.' The ecclesial communion as such is the prophetic sign to the world that God has organized all things around the one whom he has enthroned at his right hand. The church has cosmic significance, precisely in its anticipation of

---

[68] 1 Cor. 8:6, RSV. Karl-Josef Kuschel (1992:285ff.) wants to keep this passage firmly in the sphere of history and of eschatology. It is quite definitely to the exalted *Jesus* that it refers, not to some pre-existent heavenly being. Thus far we concur. But he also wants to limit it to soteriology, i.e., to the new creation not the old. To follow him here means trading the θεός/κύριος parallel for a 'polarity' that is difficult to justify, while also accepting an untenable distinction between τὰ πάντα and τὰ πάντα. On Kuschel's wider argument see Appendix B, where Col. 1:15ff. is also discussed.

[69] Eph. 4:10; on the ἵνα clause, cf. Jer. 23:23ff.

[70] Sanders (1977:522f.) is interacting here with Bultmann, whose interpretation of Paul does not do justice to Paul's ontological claims. For Paul, 'Christians really are one body and one Spirit with Christ, the form of the present world really is passing away. . . .' Jesus' lordship meant 'that a real change was at work in the world and that Christians were participating in it.' (Sanders, of course, supposes that Paul's beliefs have failed to prove themselves; but such *were* his beliefs.)

the appearance of that order. It is the community of the *recapitulation*.[71] To pursue this point we would need of course to explore at some length Paul's sense of the eschatological tension introduced into the basic structures of reality by the events of Jesus-history, and in that light his doctrine of the Spirit, the eucharist, and of suffering. Unfortunately we cannot attempt that here. But we will make so bold as to say that these matters are not better understood in part because the boundaries and horizons of our *own* cosmologies are generally very stubborn, and resistant to the lessons of the incident on the road to Damascus.

* * *

That Paul began forging new categories of existence with which to work out his theology is not to be doubted; the exact role of the doctrine of the ascension may be a matter for dispute. For the author of Hebrews, on the other hand, the ascension is that which determines both the shape and the content of his great epistle. Many commentators miss the marvelous symmetry and rhetorical power he derives from this motif, which we have tried to outline in an appendix.[72] We can be thankful, however, for those whose work has laid to rest the unhappy notion that Hebrews is a work of Christian Platonism, opening the way for more fruitful attempts at interpreting the book and for reckoning with its eschatology in particular.[73] Hebrews is the classic Christian restatement (in the context of, and over against, an educated *diaspora* Judaism) of the Old Testament journey motif. The journey in question is the exodus, viewed here as a pilgrimage into 'the world to come.'[74] The book thus serves as a treatise on the destiny of the faithful, who will accompany Christ into the glory tasted by Moses and the elders at Sinai. A familiar frame of reference is marked out by Psalms 8 and 110, which parallel Daniel 7. Of course, Hebrews is also a treatise occasioned by the needs of a suffering church, and that is where the ascension motif really asserts itself. All the encouragement it has to offer flows from a single contention about Jesus, namely, that 'he sat down' in the presence of God as the Melchizedekian priest-king. This bit of ascension theology, repeated at key intervals, is the focal point which holds Hebrews together.[75]

---

[71] See Eph. 1:9f., 1:18ff., 3:8ff.; cf. e.g. 1 Cor. 6:2f. Later on we will observe the faulty elaboration of this high standing of the church into a de-eschatologized 'κόσμος of the cosmos' doctrine.

[72] Appendix A.

[73] e.g., C. K. Barrett (1954), L. D. Hurst (1990), B. Lindars (1991).

[74] 'Τὴν οἰκουμένην τὴν μέλλουσαν, about which we are speaking' (2:5). See below, 261f.

[75] 1:3, 8:2, 10:12, 12:3. Hebrews works on the premise that Jesus fulfills entirely the goals of both cult and monarchy (cf. P. Church 1982), such that the Christian way has a surety and solidity about it which renders the old Jewish way no alternative at all.

The suggestion of Aileen Guilding that the book is in fact a sermon built up around the synagogue lections for Pentecost has much to commend it, we think.[76] Hebrews is nothing if not a celebration of the grace associated with the accession of Christ to the heavenly throne and to ministry in the heavenly sanctuary. Its very structure (as our Appendix shows) embodies the invitation to 'share in the heavenly calling' of Jesus by following in his train, and that *is* the Pentecost message from a Christian point of view. But what we are especially interested in is the power of the ascension motif to shape, not only a sermon, but a worldview and a vision of the church.[77]

Like Paul, the author of Hebrews finds that what happened with and to Jesus compels us to think of his life as the actual consummation of the age – he has appeared, before us and before God, ἅπαξ ἐπὶ συντελείᾳ τῶν αἰώνων. This consummation includes and indeed rearranges worldly existence from the foundations up. It creates a new and higher order that stands in judgment on that with which we are familiar.[78] The permanent reception of Jesus into the heavenly sanctuary as the λειτουργὸς τῶν ἁγίων signifies that in him our humanity has been rendered truly presentable to God ('perfect' in the cultic sense) through the Spirit.

Here again the logic is not linear, as we admit when we speak of a higher order. Jesus' ascension, considered as a priestly act, begins already on the cross; or rather his whole life is seen as an act of self-offering that culminates in the cross. In the ascension this offering is received on high. It is Jesus in the totality of what he was and did who 'passed through the heavens' to the divine sanctuary that is 'not a part of this creation,' to minister there.[79] But he does minister there, in a new way; the cross is the sacrifice that makes possible the ascension, not the ascension itself.[80] The reference therefore is not to an ideal or supra-sensual realm but to the

---

[76] Guilding points out that the readings in the three-year lectionary included Psa. 110, Gen. 14–15 (the Melchizedek story), Exod. 19 (the arrival at Sinai), and Num. 18 (Aaron's budding rod), all touched on in Hebrews and woven into the enthronement motif established by the doxology with which it begins. From its opening lines the epistle's rhetoric shows a sermonic character and structure, and it closes with the advice ἀνέχεσθε τοῦ λόγου τῆς παρακλήσεως, a common way of referring to a synagogue sermon (see F. F. Bruce 1964:xlviii).

[77] It is remarkable, writes Paul Ellingworth (1986:340), 'how often the author's view of who Jesus was and what he did does involve presuppositions about the universe . . . . The author thinks synthetically, not analytically: for him, what Jesus did, who he was, and how the universe is framed, belong together, though the last is least important for him.'

[78] See esp. 9:24ff.; cf. 1:10ff., 9:10 (μέχρι καιροῦ διορθώσεως ἐπικείμενα), 8:13 ('what is obsolete and aging will soon disappear,' NIV).

[79] H. U. von Balthasar (1967:287) speaks in another context of the 'refounding' of history from the new beginning contained in the resurrection and ascension, in which Christ integrates 'in himself everything he was on earth, in order to take it away into the sphere of this miracle, to translate it, to heighten it . . . .'

[80] 'The point of what we are saying is this: We do have such a high priest, who sat down at the right hand of the throne of the Majesty in heaven, and who serves in the sanctuary . . .' (8:1f., NIV).

divine Rest from which the present creation has been barred, but which Jesus has entered. Once more highly paradoxical conclusions are drawn as to the significance of Jesus for all of God's works from the very beginning.[81] Once more a profound eschatological tension comes into view.

The author of Hebrews does not shy away from pressing the liturgical pattern through to its conclusion. He who appears before God on man's behalf will also reappear before man on God's behalf, to bestow the fullness of his high-priestly blessing. But that reappearance will mean a thorough shaking of the αἰῶνες, so that whatever cannot be made presentable with and through him will be removed. Only thus will the rest of creation, strengthened and confirmed by his blessing, enter into the place of Rest.[82] For the reality Jesus knows and inhabits is both continuous and discontinuous with that which we know and inhabit. Fulfillment has an ontological depth that failure and futility lack. His life in its consummation is rendered substantial to such a degree that it not only surpasses but calls into question, subjects to judgment, the history it leaves behind – that is, the obsolete ages and structures of this fallen world. But the eucharistic community, sustained by the manna of 'the heavenly gift,' does not belong to that obsolescence, for it shares even now in the reconstituted reality that belongs to Christ. It is drawn upwards in an invisible way; or to use temporal language, 'the powers of the age to come' are already at work in it, rendered operative in the Spirit through Jesus' priestly ministry.[83]

Such is the language and logic of Hebrews, crudely condensed from the persuasive form in which it is applied to the insecurities of its recipients, who were under pressure to join in the self-deception of fading worldly forces – for that is how its author was forced to regard even the religion based on Moses in its position *post Christum*. The resulting world picture, in spite of certain deliberate similarities, is neither Platonic nor strictly Jewish, but represents the filling up of the Hebrew vision of history with something so substantial that the mould itself is made to fall away. Two religious cosmologies, not one, are thus subverted and replaced. Such was the heuristic power of the doctrine of the ascension.

* * *

[81] His priesthood, based as it is on 'the power of an indestructible life,' is without beginning or end (chap. 7); he is 'the same yesterday and today and forever' (13:8). He has appeared to the world 'once for all at the consummation of the ages,' and has in turn 'entered heaven itself, now to appear *for* us in God's presence' (9:24ff.). In keeping with this we have argued elsewhere that the opening eulogy does not reflect a three stage pre-incarnate, incarnate and post-incarnate christology but refers throughout to Jesus himself as the one mediator (1986:129f.; cf. Kuschel 354ff.).

[82] 'Like a garment they will be changed,' 1:12 (Psa. 102); cf. 9:28, 12:26ff., 13:14.

[83] 6:4–5

John's Gospel, as we observed earlier, contains an abundance of references and allusions to the ascension in spite of the fact that an account of it is lacking. The absence of such an account is no more to be held against the historical facticity or significance of that event than in the parallel case of the last supper, an account of which is also lacking in this most eucharistic of Gospels. Both these interests are set forth in provocative dialogues but held back, in a tantalizing way, from the narrative itself. The veil that is drawn in front of them only heightens the reader's interest.[84]

We are not so brave as to offer an interpretation of John, but we ought at least to notice what is openly stated about the ascension. *Where* Jesus goes, we are told, is to the Father, whence he also came.[85] *Why* he goes is to prepare 'in his Father's house' a place to which others will eventually come. 'You cannot follow now, but you will follow later.' *That* he goes makes him the way.[86] *How* he goes is along the path of the cross and the resurrection.[87] And the *consequence* of his going is a mission of the Spirit aimed at the proclamation of the Father's open house, a mission that hails the advent of ecclesial man, whose being is in communion.[88] Already there is too much here for us to digest properly, but it will suffice for our purposes simply to indicate that John forces to the forefront of our reflection the following matters.

First is the pneumatological dimension of life in the Father's house, towards the exposition of which any theology of the ascension ought to move. What is accomplished in the ascension is a decisive opening up not only of the Father's house but of human being, which through the Spirit now realizes its true nature in a 'perichoretic' and communal form of existence – that is, in the *co*-existence of the faithful with Jesus and his Father. This is the main subject of the great discourse, beginning in chapter 14, that culminates in chapter 17 with the so-called high-priestly prayer.[89]

---

[84] Even Jesus' baptism is present by absence, i.e., by dialogue rather than description. Given this pattern (cf. C. K. Barrett 1978:67ff.) we may certainly reject the idea that an actual ascension was unknown to John; but we may also need to question C. Pickstock's interpretation (1998:264ff.) of his intention in omitting it.

[85] 16:5ff.

[86] See 13:31–14:31. 'I am ascending to my Father and your Father, to my God and your God' (20:17; cf. 8:21ff.).

[87] Jesus' departure is a twofold one, for it *begins* with death; but 20:17 makes clear that neither the cross nor the resurrection are his return home. (Francis Watson rightly points out against Brown and Schnackenburg that ἀναβαίνω has a future reference – cf. ὑπάγω in 8:21, 13:33, etc. – as οὔπω γὰρ ἀναβέβηκα suggests.)

[88] Cf. 20:21ff., of which Barrett (570) observes: 'That John intended to depict an event of significance parallel to the first creation cannot be doubted.' The man born of water and the Spirit stands as the answer to the man of dust because of this inbreathing of trinitarian Life.

[89] Since in his ascension Jesus becomes the spring whence the river of the Spirit flows, he is not only the high priest, of course, but the temple itself (cf. 2:12ff., 7:37ff., Ezek. 47, Rev. 21f.; see also Dumbrell 1985:66ff.).

Second, and closely related, is the cosmic status accorded to Jesus in view of the fact that his personal history is defined in terms of a coming and going from the Father's side.[90] Paul's ground-breaking insights are very much alive in John, whose whole work (not the prologue only) displays a cosmological awareness. The unreserved identification of Jesus of Nazareth with God's own Word requires new ways of thinking and speaking about him. He is the true *beth-el*, the oasis where heaven and earth are joined.[91] The times of other men and women are relativized to the real temporal priority of his history. Indeed, in the book that has rightly been described as the alpha and omega of the New Testament, Jesus is portrayed as one who stands equally at the beginning of time and at its end, and just so at its creative centre: 'Truly I say unto you, before Abraham was, I am!'[92]

Third is what we can only refer to as the retroactive effects of the ascension. In John the one who will ascend speaks and acts as if he has already done so; his descending and ascending somehow interpenetrate, so that the latter recapitulates and lends power to the former.[93] Later we will have to reckon with the different ways in which dogmatics has dealt with this interpenetration, but for the moment we will say only that Jesus-history as we find it in John's Gospel also defies any interpretation that moves strictly within a linear framework.[94]

Fourth is the way in which John heightens the tension between the presence and the absence by frequent talk about Jesus *leaving* the world in order to go to the Father, and through his close association of the cross and the ascension. The comfort of the *Christus praesens* is clearly grounded in the stubborn and troubling fact of the *Christus absens*. Among other things, this prevents any confusion between christology and

---

[90] 1:18, 3:13, 6:46, 7:33, 8:14, 13:3, etc. A question arises here as to the relation between descending-and-ascending and coming-and-going. Should we simply equate these (cf. e.g. G. Nicholson 1983:21ff.)? We think not, for reasons which will later become clear, though they plainly overlap.

[91] 1:51

[92] 8:56. 'He who comes after me has surpassed me because he was before me' (1:15; cf. Rev. 22:13). Such statements ought not to be referred away from Jesus. J. A. T. Robinson (1985:366, 383ff.) rightly takes issue with the view that John represents a late christology interested in the coming and going of a divine being – a view, he says, that makes Christ 'a cuckoo in the human nest.' It is the 'pre-existence' and the 'ultimacy' of a *man* with which John is concerned. But Robinson (like Kuschel, 363ff., who argues similarly though he accepts a late date) rejects the language of ontology with respect both to the incarnation and to the cosmic status of Jesus. This is an unjustified retreat; see further Appendix B.

[93] Cf. e.g. 1:18, 3:13, 13:3. Benoit (1/233) remarks that John 'narrates the life of Jesus in terms of the glorified state.' Kuschel (384ff.) speaks of a 'fusion' of times. The whole debate over pre-existence in John is bedeviled by a failure to come to grips with this matter, which is something more than a mere literary device.

[94] Departing and returning also interpenetrate, of course, so that C. H. Dodd is quite correct in settling on the statement, 'The time is coming and now is,' as a summary of John's eschatological outlook (Caird 1980:253).

pneumatology.[95] It also allows John to press upon us, in subtle and not so subtle ways, a question we will eventually have to deal with at some length: Where, from our point of view, *is* Jesus?[96]

Last, but by no means least, is the link between the ascension and the eucharist to which we have already pointed. That link, which is quite deliberate, is made explicit by John precisely at the point where the common capacity of these doctrines to offer offence – or to break down barriers – is underscored. Addressing the dispute that broke out among his followers over the seemingly coarse and foolish notion of eating his flesh and drinking his blood, Jesus asks: 'Does *this* offend you? What if you see the Son of Man ascend to where he was before!'[97] May we not find here a vindication of our claim that the ascension is the greater mystery on which the lesser mystery of the eucharist rests, such that we must interpret each in the light of the other? That properly understood they imply an unsettling worldview not derivable from any other source than the remarkable outcome of Jesus-history? At all events, we will take from it courage for a journey into dogmatic history that in exploring some of these matters is likely, though not intended, to cause some small offence of its own. But first let us turn back for a moment to Luke's story in order that we may bring the present chapter to a conclusion.

The Master's Metaphor

Leslie Houlden (whose line is not at all like ours) is quite right to speak of Luke's story as 'an obstinate presence.'[98] That Luke's rendering of the ascension as a distinct event in the life of Jesus has a claim on our attention is made more certain by the creative thinking the ascension apparently evoked in the other New Testament theologians. But what of the event itself? One thing about which there can be no doubt at all is that the journey thus undertaken was one that cannot be comprehended by those left behind! 'A cloud hid him from their sight.' Nevertheless, since we have insisted on a historical component, and see no reason to abandon Luke's proffered description, let us try to say something sensible about it.

---

[95] See 14:1ff. It is the task of the Spirit to keep Jesus squarely in the centre of the picture in spite of his absence; *pace* Kuschel and others this is precisely *not* a 'Spirit-christology.'

[96] 'Now I am going to him who sent me, yet none of you asks me, "Where are you going?"'(16:5) Houlden maintains that the Where? question, asked in 'literal' terms, is a *non*-question. But how can we eschew literal terms altogether without falling into gnosticism, i.e., without actually running together the cross and the ascension by ignoring the resurrection appearances? (Cf. Nicholson, 165 n. 5, for whom the latter 'fit awkwardly' into the scheme of the Gospel.)

[97] 6:61f. (see 25ff.). Can there be any doubt in the present climate, were it not for our long familiarity with the eucharist, that our reaction to it would be the same as theirs? And how long will we maintain this doctrine if our intellectual and cultural revulsion gets the best of the doctrine of the ascension?

[98] p. 174

We spoke earlier of the ascension episode as a metaphor. All that we have said since has been in support of the claim that the metaphor in question was not so much Luke's, or even the tradition's, as Christ's own. Nor was it merely a metaphor. It was a real departure, the exchanging of a shared – though no longer a fully common – history for an altogether distinct and unique one. That this departure and exchange took place in the form of a dramatic gesture is plain enough; space travel was never in view. But it did take place. Let us call it, then, with an eye on the priestly cast the scriptures give to it, a *liturgical* metaphor; for it was an act which both imitated and also effected its aim.[99] And what was the aim? To leave the world and go to the Father? Then let us say further, with the Venerable Bede, that it was that particular liturgical act on which every other such act depends.[100] For it was the act in which the link between our fallen world and the new creation was fully forged. Moreover, it was the act in which the problem of the presence and the absence came into being, the problem that defines the eschatological situation and necessitates the peculiar sacramental form of the people of God.

It is important to understand exactly what is at stake here. If there is no genuine this-worldly component – if the act of ascension is one of pure transcendence capable of any number of really quite arbitrary historical manifestations but incapable of being carried out in a historical way[101] – then Christ is indeed atopic and atemporal, and it is above all his personal human identity that is beclouded in his ascension. Again, if in the ascension the movement *within* our corrupted space and time is not as real as the movement *beyond* it, then the church's sacramental acts are devoid of meaning; for that is where and how they also take place. Then the church's distinction from the world does indeed reduce to something that is purely ideological or ethical or social. Or, put the other way round, if we wish to take the eucharist and the church seriously we must also take the ascension seriously in both its dimensions.

Could that not be done, it may be asked, by holding to an ascension on the same day (Luke 24) rather than forty days later (Acts 1)? We reject this proposal for two reasons: first, because it pits Luke against himself; second, because it still refuses to take the leaving as seriously as the going.

---

[99] Torrance (1976:108f.) reminds us of the cultic significance of the verb ἀναβαίνω used in Acts 2:34.

[100] Bede, in a remark not without insight, compared the gift of the sacraments to the cloak that Elijah left Elisha at his assumption (*Hom.* 2.9; see Davies 1958:158f.). Bede died on the Eve of Ascension in AD 735.

[101] See Balthasar's discussion (1990:246ff.) of the views of G. Koch. Cf. O'Donovan 1986:36f.: 'The incarnation is not simply a mythic portrayal of the fellowship between men and God, nor the ascension of the triumph of the cross. Insofar as these transitions have one foot in our space and time, they are seen there as *events* – events which, however, have another end to them beyond the historical sequence of which, at this end, they form a part.' The new Roman *Catechism* (§660) speaks similarly of 'the historical and transcendent event of the Ascension.'

In biblical terms the ascension involves a real departure of Jesus of Nazareth. That is the basis on which we find ourselves compelled to speak of two histories rather than one. Covenant history and world history have divided in this departure, for in and with Jesus the former has already reached its goal. In the resulting gap a place has opened up for the eucharistic community as a genuinely new entity within world history, albeit a peculiar one with its own peculiar view of the way things are.

3

Cosmologies and Ecclesiologies, I

Cosmologies and ecclesiologies are inseparably linked, we are convinced, though the relationship is one that generally receives little attention. But we must not get ahead of ourselves. On this score our last chapter indicated only that reflection on the ascension, and on the notion of ecclesial communion as a real participation in Christ, was accompanied by the opening up of new horizons in cosmology as well. With the appearance of a discrepancy between the two histories, and the revision or deepening of Jewish eschatology, that was inevitable. The task before us now is to trace these connections, and in particular the role of the doctrine of the ascension, into the later reflections of the church. If we have read rightly the movement of thought in the biblical witness, and if it has (for all its diversity of expression) the inner coherence we suspect, then it will surely prove instructive to approach subsequent developments with the same interests in view. In that way we will be able to add historical sinews to the theoretical bones of the conviction just stated, and demonstrate something of the significance of our subject for the evolution of the church.

Before proceeding, however, it will be helpful to set the stage a little further by reminding ourselves of the general context in which the ecclesiological interests of the early church took shape. We may appeal for assistance here to the summary of a well-known New Testament scholar.

A Precarious Position

In his Didsbury lectures Professor C. K. Barrett argued the paradox that 'in the New Testament the church is at the same time central and peripheral.' This strange feature reflects something of the church's own nature, he suggests, as 'the community of the interim' between the resurrection of Jesus and his parousia. The consequence of its present provisional character, however, is that the church as it faces the world 'had and has an impossible task, for it can affirm itself only at the cost of denying its own proper being.' The paradox upon which Barrett reflects translates on the practical side into the problems of church order, and on the theoretical side into the question of the way in which the being of the church is conditioned by grace, in a manner suited to the present fashion of things. That is to say – if we may be permitted this recasting of the paradox in terms of our own systematic interests – it thrusts upon us the whole complex of issues connected with the enigma of the presence and the absence which we introduced already in Chapter 1.[1]

Now according to Barrett the church in the first century had not yet hardened into rigid forms of self-expression. Ministry and sacraments provided 'some of the necessary apparatus of permanence,' but the tension between its historical needs and its eschatological orientation was for the most part successfully maintained. If here and there we discern signs that the balance was being tipped towards the former, signs of retreat into a dangerous sort of institutionalized self-security, it was not until later on that these elements coalesced into anything like the *Frühkatholizismus* of which we hear so much, usually in pejorative terms. We might say, in other words, that the Pauline emphasis on κοινωνία with Christ in the Spirit prevailed as the guiding light of ecclesiology throughout the critical early phases of the church.

But of course far-reaching changes did take place, however gradually. Some of the key developments (as they would later prove to be) can be seen quite clearly even in the writings of Clement and Ignatius, at the turn of the century.[2] In facing the challenges thrown up by the unexpectedly long historical course of things, the form and self-understanding of the worshiping church underwent a great many adjustments. Barrett rightly rebukes those who cannot look upon this evolution with empathy; change was always and necessarily part of the picture. But he does take care to point out what he sees as a growing 'deficiency in theological criticism,' such criticism as keeps Jesus central and the church itself peripheral.[3] On the reasons for that deficiency he does not speculate, though the paradox itself may appear as explanation enough.

Whatever the causes, and they are surely several, in retrospect it is difficult to deny that the characteristic emphasis on a Christ-centred κοινωνία, which feeds primarily on eschatological realities, slowly faded into the background.[4] It was above all a creeping institutionalism that took its place, in which (many are prepared to admit) the whole framework of ecclesiology became badly distorted. Even now, four centuries

---

[1] See *Church, Ministry, and Sacraments in the New Testament* (quotations from pp. 9, 77f.). Barrett himself does not attempt to identify or deal with the theoretical side of the problem directly.

[2] Cf. Barrett 88ff.

[3] i.e., both the person and *example* of Jesus (ibid. 100f.; cf. Mark 10:41ff.).

[4] Where the eucharist itself is concerned, Zizioulas (1985:20f.) contends that this fading did not reach the critical point in east or west until about the twelfth century; like W. Kasper (1989:157), however, he is overly generous.

after the heated battles of the Reformation, the church is still struggling to set things right. For our part, we think it reasonable to suggest that the deficiency of theological criticism which permitted this evolution was aggravated, not only by the insecurity generated by the prolonged absence of Jesus, but by a loss of grip on the provocative cosmological dimensions of the eschatological framework developed in embryonic form by the leading New Testament thinkers. That loss could only result in a certain confusion about the fact that the church exists – and *can* exist at present – only in the most painful and precarious of positions, namely, as a community with a foot in each of two radically diverging histories.

Yet such an existence is by nature incapable of submitting altogether to institutionalizing tendencies, even if the church is constantly tempted to seek relief in that direction.[5] In any event, even in theological criticism there were both advances and retreats, which we hope now to underline in our own way. Of course there are far too many threads here to trace out anything like a complete depiction of this story within the greater tapestry of concerns to which we have just made so brief a reference. Thus we will have to settle for looking at only a few representative theologians, chosen both for their overall significance and for their attention to our primary subject, the ascension. Again, if the special complex of ideas we have selected for consideration is but one of a number of relevant lines of inquiry into the evolution of ecclesiology, we are at least bold enough to think that it is more important than is usually perceived. For the ascension forces us to grapple with the inner logic of the church in a way that highlights its paradoxical situation, a thorough understanding of which is essential to its welfare and its mission.

Preserving the Tension

Christian dogmatics makes its first appearance in the second-century struggle with gnosticism. Like most philosophical movements of a religious variety, gnosticism was heavily occupied by the problems of evil and of finitude, and the possible connection between them.[6] Squatting upon ground hallowed by the ancient Hebrew tradition and newly cultivated by the Christian church, it was attempting in its own largely Hellenic way to cope with the basic antinomies of human existence which our world is always thrusting upon us, as those who have eternity in our

---

[5] By 'institutionalizing tendencies' we mean all efforts to carve out a secure identity for the church at the expense of its eschatological character. These tendencies assume different forms at different times, of course, and pass through revolutionary stages which may appear rather *anti*-institutional. Such is the situation today in some places, but we do not want to be understood in that way. Creeds and canons are not inherently uneschatological; indeed, adherence to such may be an eschatological act.

[6] Cf. *The Ante-Nicene Fathers* 1/3 10.

hearts but are bounded by suffering and death.[7] The challenge it posed to the church grew ever more intense as the latter moved further away from its Jewish roots, and it boiled down to this: a dispute over the relation between creation and redemption.[8] How were the antinomies of human existence to be overcome, by the rejection of that existence as innately flawed (the common pagan view) or by its full and happy repair (the Judeo-Christian view)? In other words, was redemption the antithesis of creation or its fulfillment? That was the question, and the increasingly energetic activities of the various gnostic schools forced it onto the dogmatic agenda at a very early stage. Indeed this question, already a cosmological one, virtually created the discipline of dogmatics.[9]

The first theologian of genuinely catholic stature in these times, and the great Christian champion against the gnostics, was Irenaeus, bishop of Lyons. A man firmly convinced that the true faith is 'ever one and the same,' he was nonetheless a creative thinker, no simple steward of tradition(s) as some have supposed.[10] In turning the gospel to face the rising tide of intellectual and moral deviations with which the second-century church had to cope, Irenaeus was not afraid to follow the fresh lines of thought which beckoned him from within the apostolic witness. By reason of this constructive interest his work retains an even greater relevance than many imagine, and there is a richness to his thought that is only the brighter for being set in the dark background of the often tedious speculations he sought patiently to destroy. In any event, his thoroughgoing repudiation of gnostic and docetic revisions to the Christian message still rewards his readers nearly two millennia on,

---

[7] Cf. Eccl. 3.

[8] 'For whatever all the heretics may have advanced with the utmost solemnity,' writes Irenaeus, 'they come to this at last, that they blaspheme the Creator, and disallow the salvation of God's workmanship . . .' (*AH* 4. pref. 4). English quotations of this work are taken from the *ANF*, with occasional deviations in punctuation or capitalization (pronouns being rendered in the lower case); quotations of *The Demonstration of the Apostolic Preaching* are from J. A. Robinson.

[9] Here we agree with Harnack (1/129ff., 252ff., 326ff.), but only in part. For Harnack the very possibility of dogmatics is bound up with the prior inclination to ask and answer such questions with a Hellenist slant, a slant introduced by St Paul (i.e., by his alleged spirit–flesh dualism and the 'secularizing' cosmological speculation to which it contributed). For us dogmatics took its start from a highly perceptive rebuttal of Hellenist misreadings of Paul and John, misreadings which have nonetheless proved attractive to many, including Harnack.

[10] Irenaeus has been charged both with a lack of originality *and* with a rather unsuccessful experimentation with his sources, but neither of these charges can be made to stick. G. Wingren (1959:xvff.) supports Emil Brunner's highly positive evaluation of Irenaeus 'as the most fertile and creative of the early theologians . . . No other thinker was able to weld ideas together which others allowed to slip as he was able to do, not even Augustine or Athanasius' (1934:249, 262). In what follows we shall not concern ourselves directly with his sources but with his theological vision.

especially those who have an eye for the refined and subtle forms of those heresies which have gained so much ground again today.

In *Adversus omnes haereses* Irenaeus takes for his compass the baptismal confession by which Christians identify themselves.[11] He evidently believed that in this trinitarian formula, which wraps itself around the history of Jesus, there was an arsenal of insights adequate for any theological task. Thus he set out not only to expose the great 'tissue of falsehoods' woven by the gnostics in support of their private rites of initiation, but also to lead his readers through to a deeper grasp of their own 'celestial' faith.[12] But what is immediately interesting to us is that Irenaeus frames this first-ever theological textbook with passages containing pointed references to the ascension. Coming to the third article of the confession, he reminds us that the Spirit

> proclaimed through the prophets the dispensations of God, and the advents, and the birth from a virgin, and the passion, and the resurrection from the dead, and the ascension into heaven in the flesh [*et in carne in caelos ascensionem*] of the beloved Christ Jesus, our Lord, and His manifestation from heaven in the glory of the Father 'to gather all things in one' [*ad recapitulanda universa*], and to raise up anew all flesh of the whole human race, in order that to Christ Jesus, our Lord, and God, and Saviour, and King, according to the will of the invisible Father, 'every knee should bow . . .'[13]

Then in the closing lines of the work, when his exposition of this christological foundation is complete, he sums up the larger vision to which it leads as follows:

> For there is one Son, who accomplished His Father's will; and one human race also in which the mysteries of God are wrought, 'which the angels desire to look into;' and they are not able to search out the wisdom of God, by means of which His handiwork, confirmed and incorporated with His Son, is brought to perfection [*conformatum et concorporatum Filio perficitur*]; that His offspring, the First-begotten Word, should descend to the creature, that is, to what had been moulded, and that it should be contained by Him; and, on the other hand, the creature should contain the Word, and ascend to Him [*et factura iterum capiat Verbum et ascendat ad eum*], passing beyond the angels, and be made after the image and likeness of God.[14]

And between these two prominent references to our subject there are, as we shall see, a good many others. Irenaeus was, in a remarkably insightful and well-rounded way, a theologian of the ascension.

---

[11] The church has but one voice, heard in all the members of its household: 'I believe in one God, the Father Almighty . . . in one Christ Jesus, the Son of God . . . and in the Holy Spirit . . .' (1.10.1; cf. *Demo.* 99f.).

[12] 1.9.4; cf. the preface to Book 5.

[13] 1.10.1. Notice the deliberate use of the words 'in the flesh,' which Justin also uses but not regularly (cf. *Res.* 9 and 1st *Ap.* 21, 42, 45f., 50f., 54).

[14] 5.36.3.

Perhaps we should not be surprised, since it is precisely the doctrine of the ascension which both affirms the importance of the gnostic question and forces us to deny the rightness of their answer to it. On the one hand, the ascension (or rather what we might call the ascension/parousia differential) highlights the discontinuity between the present world and the world to come. On the other hand, ascension in the flesh, as the bishop puts it, demands that we understand the former as something incorporated and perfected by the latter. Continuity and discontinuity are held in tension, and that tension – the very same that belongs to the eucharist – is what Irenaeus sought to preserve in defense of the Judeo-Christian hope.[15] In doing so, and in particular by rejecting the gnostics' mytho-logizing treatment of the ascension for one with an historical dimension, he opened up vast tracts of fruitful theological discourse for us to explore, tracts regularly passed over by expositors whose eyes are elsewhere. So significant is his contribution that we will devote the remainder of the present chapter to his ideas, which will then stand as a measuring rod for the subsequent handling of the doctrine as outlined in the next two chapters.[16]

***

Within the framework of gnostic dualism ascension was a strictly vertical affair. It meant dissociation from the corrupt realm of material existence, a movement of the inner man that entailed a repudiation of the temporal

---

[15] His emphasis naturally falls on the positive pole (i.e., on continuity rather than discontinuity) since it was at that end that the attack had come. We will eventually discover, however, that it makes little difference which end is attacked or which defended; the important thing is the tension itself.

[16] Alastair Logan, introducing his study of gnosticism as an early form of Christian Platonism, remarks that the classic gnostic myth 'could not but develop differently from the "orthodox" version by its downgrading of the Old Testament, its Creator God and his prophets, its preference of the heavenly Son/Christ of Paul, John and Hebrews to the earthly Jesus of the Synoptics, and its focus on baptism and chrismation rather than on the eucharist as the climax of illumination and salvation, but its claim to be a valid interpretation of the Gnostic's ecstatic experience of and identification with the heavenly Revealer/Redeemer, i.e. Christ, should not be doubted' (1996:xx). Though it is not our purpose to expound gnosticism but to expound Irenaeus, we will have to touch, directly or indirectly, on each of these differences. Dr Logan will forgive us, however, if we object to his way of putting the matter. The conflict between classical gnosticism and early ecclesial orthodoxy does not arise from a 'downgrading' of the Old Testament or from a 'preference' for one strand of the New Testament over another, much less for one sacrament over another – as if we might find the roots of that conflict in the scriptures or the sacraments themselves, and see that they needed only the warmth of an alternative religious experience to cause them to flower. Irenaeus claims, and we agree, that (with or without such experiences) the choice of myth over history, and the contents and implications of the myths themselves, represent a falsification of the scriptures in whole and in part, and of the sacraments in whole and in part, and of the Christ himself – who cannot be taken apart!

creation with its inherently unstable mixture of flesh and spirit.[17] It was not so much a fact of Jesus-history as a kind of antidote to *all* history.[18] Against this Irenaeus set the apostolic teaching. In the ascension of Jesus the temporal and material dimensions of his being were affirmed and maintained, and by no means repudiated.[19] But that conviction, allied as it was to belief in redemption *of* the world rather than from it, obviously required a radically different way of thinking about spirit and matter, heaven and earth, eternity and time – indeed about God, man and the universe. Irenaeus did not shy from the task, though it meant challenging not just the self-styled gnostic gurus ('these perverse mythologists,' as he called them) but also the great philosophers and 'all that are ignorant of God, poets and historians alike.'[20] It was time for the Christian faith to discover within itself a proper alternative even to that more ancient and reputable tradition of dualism which belonged to Plato and the rest, since it too was incapable of acknowledging the incarnation, or of answering to the climactic events of the life of Jesus and the promise they contained for the whole creation.[21]

How did Irenaeus proceed with his attack on dualism? Guided by the rule of faith, he opened an assault on several fronts, each one requiring a shift away from the sub-personal categories of the gnostics to the relational categories of the creed. First, he threw out together both the anthropomorphic *theology* he discerned in his opponents and the rationalist *epistemology* from whence it sprang.[22] The true nature of God cannot be got at, he said, by projecting into the divine being distinctions which may to some extent hold true in the analysis of human being, as the philosophers supposed and the gnostic (Valentinian) theory of aeons implied. God is 'simple, uncompounded being' in whom thought, will, word, and action cannot be separated or marked off in gradations. He is

---

[17] See e.g. 1.21.5. Irenaeus, we note, is widely regarded as essentially accurate in his representation of gnostic doctrines, and as justified in responding to them (as he frequently did) according to their family resemblance.

[18] Otherwise put, it belonged to a primal or universal history that was effectively self-cancelling. Ascension represented a 'return of like to like,' to be consummated when 'all that is spiritual has been formed and perfected by gnosis' (1.6.1; cf. 1:21.5, 1.25.1f., 2.29). The temporal and material creation would then come to an end.

[19] 3.16.8; cf. *Demo.* 84.

[20] 2.14.4; cf. 1.10.3, 1.25.6, 4.1.1. Irenaeus recognized that the gnostic faith was based on the same foundation as that of the Greek tradition generally, and accused their teachers of a low sort of plagiarism. Their systems, he said, were 'sewed together out of ancient dogmas redolent of ignorance and irreligion.' In Plato, however, he does find things to commend over against gnosticism (3.25.5). Would he have been a little kinder also to Basilides, e.g., had he access to the latter's own teachings (cf. G. May 1994:62ff.)? Or did he?

[21] The charge of inadequacy applied also to Stoic monism, since it was no more possible for the materialists than for the idealists to comprehend how God could 'impart immortality to what is mortal, or bestow incorruption on what is corruptible.' All maintained rigid cosmological clamps on soteriological possibilities.

[22] Cf. Justin *Dial.* 3.

totus spiritus operans, existing in such a way as to transcend entirely the divisions and polarities which we find in ourselves or in the cosmos. If we have specific and definite knowledge of him – and we do – it is a gift. God addresses himself to us through his Word, and his Word is himself.[23]

Of course there was general agreement on the simplicity of God's being, and hence on the danger of anthropomorphism and of an overly rationalized theology. It was the glaring inconsistency here that Irenaeus challenged with persistence and wit.[24] But not only the inconsistency! For there was a pronounced contrast between his concept of divine simplicity and that of the gnostics or of other more classical theologians (including Origen and Plotinus, e.g., who resisted gnosticism less effectively). Unlike them, Irenaeus did not build his theology around a philosophical opposition between the one and the many. Nor did he build on a preconceived principle of divine apathy. In a departure demanded by the scriptures, he built instead on the freedom of God to involve himself with his creatures. For 'the Father of all' is already in his transcendent simplicity the triune God, who with his two hands – Word and Wisdom, the Son and the Spirit – is well able to embrace the world, and has in fact done so. That is *how* we know him, and *who* we know him to be.[25]

This cuts completely across the grain of any Greek construction. The God of Irenaeus is not trapped by the failed transcendence of Hellenic deities. He is capable of dealing directly with our world.[26] He is wholly other and genuinely accessible at the same time. For the glory of God must be considered under a twofold aspect: not only from the standpoint of the greatness which renders him incomprehensible, but also from the standpoint of the love and kindness by which he comes to meet creation,

---

[23] D. Minns (1994:38ff.) and other commentators do not put sufficient emphasis on Irenaeus' rejection of natural theology, a rejection that goes hand in hand with the one feature that distinguishes him from all Hellenist theologians – his Johannine rejection of any breach whatsoever between God and his Word. Cf. *Demo.* 7, *AH* 1.9, 2.13, 2.25ff. (esp. 2.28) and 3.12.6: 'But the advent of the Lord will appear superfluous and useless, if He did indeed come intending to tolerate and to preserve each man's idea of God rooted in him from of old.'

[24] See e.g. 2.6.3, 4.33.7; cf. Minns 32f.

[25] 'Thus, therefore, was God revealed; for God the Father is shown forth through all these [operations], the Spirit indeed working, and the Son ministering, while the Father was approving, and man's salvation being accomplished' (4.20.6; cf. 2.13.8, 2.30.9). Irenaeus borrows the image of God's 'two hands' from Theophilus, of course, but his closer co-ordination of these hands with the trinitarian history at the heart of the *regula fidei* (including his equation of wisdom with the Spirit) sets him apart from the apologists before him and the Alexandrians after him. Among other things, it prevents him from paying homage to the notion of absolute oneness (Ἑνάς), hence from requiring, like Origen, a distinction between θεός and αὐτοθεός in order to speak of God's 'hands.' But does his description of God as 'simple, uncompounded Being, without diverse members' (2.13.3; cf. *Demo.* 47) suggest that his trinitarianism is merely economic? No. To postulate that God *becomes* a compound being in order to deal with the world would destroy his whole argument.

[26] 'The majestic handling of the idea of God's free, historical activity is an essential theological achievement of Irenaeus' (G. May 174).

lending to man the capacity to know him. Those who *would* know him must engage with him, not by some vain effort to ascend to him in their minds, but by obedience to one who in the incarnation has already adapted himself to them.[27] That is the context in which the bishop issues his famous warning against 'knowledge falsely so-called,' which is built up, layer upon layer, by the speculative imagination or the autonomous intellect. For in the last analysis we can speak of God 'only according to the love we bear him.' Γνῶσις is relational, not simply rational. Knowledge of the triune God is by nature personal and communal, which is to say, ecclesial.[28]

Second, Irenaeus began to attack pagan *cosmology*, not merely in its various gnostic forms but at its roots. Having broken the chain of being with his doctrine of transcendence, this move followed naturally enough. The biblical notion of *creatio ex nihilo* now emerged in full bloom, with the bishop stressing time and again that creaturely being is the immediate object of God's free action and affection. It is not by nature degenerate being, disintegrating being, mediated by declining stages of the Pleroma or generated by some evil demiurge. On the contrary, it is a positive being-in-relation-to-God that is willed *by* God.[29] Irenaeus was not content to rest with that, however. Nor yet was he satisfied when he had reaffirmed that humanity and the material world are made for each other (scripture's own anthropic principle, if you please, in which human activity also assumes genuine ontological significance).[30] Taking his cue from the ascension of Jesus and its pentecostal consequences, and building conceptually on the fruitfulness motif from Genesis – that 'faculty of increase' given to creation – Irenaeus pushed things a step further. In doing so, he developed a worldview which completely reversed the gnostic scheme of things.

According to Irenaeus the creaturely may indeed be said to be disintegrating, falling into non-being, but not by nature (i.e., simply by reason of its finitude or its material aspect). By nature it may be frail, but

---

[27] See 4.20 in its entirety, one of the most impressive passages to be found anywhere in the fathers. Its opening lines indicate the proper 'method of discovery' (2.27.2) in theology: 'As regards His greatness, therefore, it is not possible to know God, for it is impossible that the Father can be measured; but as regards His love (for this it is which leads us to God by his Word), when we *obey* Him, we do always learn that there is so great a God . . .'.

[28] See 2.13.4, 2.27f., 5.20 (cf. P. Hefner 1964:294ff.).

[29] See 2.7ff. (e.g. 2.10.4, 2.30.9). Here Basilides affords a useful comparison. Though he pushes 'negative theology' to its extreme, he nonetheless illustrates the failure of transcendence mentioned above. As May points out, he himself approximates a doctrine of *creatio ex nihilo* – but only in a determinist, deistic form. It is to Theophilus and Irenaeus that we must look for the proper founders of that doctrine, then, and to the latter in particular. (See 67ff., 80f., 164ff. May however stops short of a full appreciation of Irenaeus' contribution, since he does not reckon directly with the christological and trinitarian features which govern his thinking.)

[30] Cf. 5.29.1. In Irenaeus there is no conflict between anthropocentrism and cosmocentrism; humanity is 'the centre of the divine art' (von Balthasar 2/74) and the mediator of cosmic perfection.

by vocation it should nevertheless be on the way to that *fullness* of being with a view to which God bestowed the faculty of increase.[31] In other words, the falling away into corruption which presently mars our world is not the consequence of a defect in the creator, as the heretics suggested, and hence something inherent in the creation itself. Rather, as Genesis tells us, it is related to man's deliberate moral dysfunction, which by virtue of his leading role in creation cannot be contained or isolated but has cosmic consequences. Creation is therefore found to be working against itself. Only through the faithfulness of God embodied in his incarnate Word (a faithfulness to himself, as to us) is its course rectified. For 'God is he who gives rise to immortality,' overcoming corruptibility and bestowing on created things the capacity to transcend both frailty and fallenness, leading them on triumphantly 'to their own proper result.'[32]

Irenaeus thus adopted both an epistemology and a cosmology into which the dynamic of personal relations was fully factored. Obviously we shall have to say more about this; for the moment, what we need to notice is that creation is not only *ex nihilo* but in progress. This notion (which should not be too quickly identified with similar sounding proposals popular today) is easier to assimilate when we remind ourselves that, for the bishop and his opponents alike, true being is certainly eternal being. But if for his opponents the temporal world, the world of creaturely becoming, was thus excluded by definition, it was not so for Irenaeus, who gave 'temporal' and 'eternal' new meanings. In the light of the ascension of Jesus, the eternal is something to which the temporal may aspire without abandoning its temporality. There is in fact a creaturely form of eternity, consisting in an existence that is fully engaged with God, open to the inexhaustible possibilities generated by communion with God.[33] If the temporal world is not yet so engaged, its very temporality is the consequence of God's invitation to such engagement; it has, therefore,

---

[31] This idea refers to much more than mere physical reproduction; it is tied together with the notion of bodily ascension: God 'fashioned man, and bestowed the faculty of increase on his own creation, *and called him upwards from lesser things to those greater ones which are in His own presence* . . .' (2.28.1, italics ours; cf. 4.11.1f.).

[32] The God whose will 'is the substance of all things' is certainly no slave to necessity – i.e., the necessity of creaturely dissolution – but lends to his creatures possibilities springing from his own freedom. He has however permitted our fall that we may learn that we are not naturally *like* God but naturally *dependent* on God for his likeness; in short, that our proper being is indeed a being-in-relation to God (see 2.14.4, 2.29.2, 2.30.9, 3.20.2, 3.23.3, 4.38f., 5.5, 5.13.3, frag. 6, etc.; cf. Zizioulas 1989/90 for a different treatment of this point).

[33] It is said that Plato's contrast between being and becoming is fundamental to Irenaeus, and so it is (cf. Minns 68ff.). But he takes up that contrast in an unplatonic way: First, the primary contrast is between God and his creatures, not between things grasped by the intellect and things grasped by the senses. Second, becoming is good, since it leads (through communion with God) to the realization of creaturely being even where sensual things are concerned. Third, God himself is capable of this becoming and freely invests his own being in it. Fourth, the creature can therefore become something that 'becomes' eternally, since God's investment is inexhaustible.

a proleptic reality lent to it by God himself along the way of that invitation.[34] By the same token, however, its reality is also pending, its time reversible. What is that decaying time which is our common experience but a function of our *rejection* of communion with God, marking a collapse of 'those things among which transgression has occurred, since man has grown old in them'?[35] Fortunately, this corrupt time of ours is destined to give way to the saving time of Jesus Christ, who hears and answers the upwards call. In his time, 'the fullness of the time of liberty,' man enters upon such entire intimacy with the creator that he is 'always holding fresh converse with God,' a revitalizing converse that precludes growing old. In the kingdom, says Irenaeus – that *vera plantatio* – we will forget to die. Our temporality will be invested with eternity through friendship with God.[36]

Thirdly, then, Irenaeus worked out a new approach to *anthropology*. Man himself is still in the making. It is not his unmaking which is wanted, but his finishing; not the liberation of the spirit from the body sought by the gnostics and by pagans generally, but the life of communion vouchsafed to us in Christ. Adam himself, he argues, was a provisional sort of creature with a provisional sort of existence: an infant, an animal with a spiritual umbilical cord and not yet truly a man. For by no means was he all that God intended him to be when he attempted to push away the two hands by which he was being formed. Having received but the beginning of his creation, he was merely a tentative thing, 'a creature of today.'[37] This situation the fall made over into something it was not, namely, the law of his existence. He was unnaturally confined to today, trapped by the στοιχεῖα τοῦ κόσμου; which is to say, the fall put the becoming of man into reverse, and creation with him. Thus it came about that a true man – one who is more than a creature of today, one who by virtue of his unreserved reciprocity with God has become the master not the slave of his creaturely condition – did not appear in our history until much later. That occurred only when the Word of God penetrated our fallen estate and the Spirit rested upon him, raising him up again into the presence of the Father.[38] Here at last was a fruitful man, who unlike Adam

---

[34] God 'made the things of time for man, so that coming to maturity in them, he may produce the fruit of immortality,' thus receiving from God eternal things as well (4.5.1; cf. 2.29).

[35] 5.36.1 (cf. Shakespeare, Sonnet 62). All of this is in sharp contrast to the Eleatic tendency to spatialize time, which was intended 'virtually to eliminate it' (M. Čapek, P. Wiener 4/389).

[36] Cf. 3.20.2, 4.22.1, 5.12.6, 5.36.1, frag. 39.

[37] Cf. 2.25.3, 4.38f.

[38] By descending and ascending he 'established fallen man' (2.20.3), rendering him 'receptive of the perfect Father'. 'For never at any time did Adam escape the hands of God, to whom the Father speaking, said, "Let us make man in our image, after our likeness." And for this reason in the last times . . . his hands formed a living man, in order that Adam might be created after the image and likeness of God' (5.1.3). In connection with Christ, then, we are those 'whose creation is still being carried out' (4.39.2).

yielded a proper increase. For 'the wages of Christ are human beings,' men and women who in the Spirit are themselves spirit, heirs of a fecund creation without corruption and 'without restraint.'[39]

We shall have to say more about Irenaean anthropology as well. But we have already found ourselves on the fourth and really decisive front of the bishop's battle with dualism, which was of course *christology*. It was the unmaking of Jesus in particular which (as the crowning act of their blasphemy against the creator) was the gnostics' most grievous offence, an offence which drove Irenaeus to the harsh but justified conclusion that their teachings were nothing short of homicidal![40] For these self-taught men had spared not even the saviour from the implications of their pessimistic worldview. In order to confront their scheme of things properly Irenaeus had therefore to consolidate all his advances by articulating a christology that safeguarded the integrity of Jesus himself against the impact of the gnostic myths. His shorthand for that christology, or at least for the scheme of descent and ascent with which it is associated, is the term ἀνακεφαλαίωσις or *recapitulatio*, and it is to this rather difficult but crucial topic that we now turn. In due course it will bring us round also to Irenaean pneumatology and eschatology, and thus to his ecclesiology.[41]

* * *

In a fascinating section of *Against Heresies* that forms the climax to Book 3, Irenaeus takes up the dispute about the ascension in earnest. Among the gnostics it was not uncommon to hear that Jesus of Nazareth was merely the receptacle of some secret agent from above, who, having descended to declare through him 'the unnameable Father' (i.e., he who is *not* the creator), eventually returned to the Pleroma 'in an incomprehensible and invisible manner.' Irenaeus promises to call on 'the entire mind of the apostles regarding our Lord Jesus Christ' in order to show that it was not so. In carrying out that promise, he charges the heretics with the two fatal errors by which they now wander completely from the rule of faith: Turning from that Father who is the maker of all, they also refuse to acknowledge Jesus as his Son and to find in him the true centre of all God's works; what is more, they effectively 'set the Spirit aside

---

[39] 4.21.3, 5.32.1; cf. 3.17f. Note that the invisible Spirit given through Christ for the completion of man does not negate the visible *plasma*, but reforms and perfects it (5.9.3). This of course constituted a direct attack on the tripartite anthropology of the gnostics, who were dismissive of man's 'animal' and material aspects.

[40] 3.16.8. Book 4, preface, singles out here the Valentinian doctrine 'as a recapitulation of all the heretics.'

[41] We move then, with Irenaeus, from the first article of the creed to the second, and thence to the third, but it will already be obvious that their contents cannot be taken separately.

altogether.'[42] These errors (the christological and the pneumatological) occur when they extract the agent of our salvation first from God, then from the man of Nazareth – who for them is not the Word in person but only a dispensable instrument of the Word, an instrument discarded at the cross. By thus subdividing our Lord along the lines of their hierarchical worldview these men serve up to their unfortunate disciples no saving γνῶσις, says the bishop, but a poisonous concoction which disagrees with their God-given constitution.[43]

Leaning on the scriptures and refusing to let go of the story they tell, Irenaeus offers the antidote: It is Jesus himself who, having suffered the cross, rose and ascended into heaven, and is seated at the right hand of God. It is Jesus himself who is the Word of God and 'truly God' (i.e., God with us).[44] Rather than allow him to be torn asunder by a fragmented cosmology, we must reckon with him as the one in whom all things hold together. Is he born of a woman, in his own place and time? He is also the King Eternal. Does he stoop low, even unto death? He is also the ruler over the living and dead. Things visible and invisible, things temporal and things eternal, belong to him. He, the incarnate one, gives substance, shape and (through the Spirit) direction to the whole creation. 'Being indeed one and the same, but rich and great,' the Son of God who is also the Son of Man 'fulfills the bountiful and comprehensive will of his Father.' He arranges all things 'in perfect order and sequence' and draws them to himself in the fullness of time. In his own undivided person he becomes the guarantee of the unity and goodness of all God's works, and of the continuity between creation and redemption.[45]

Here already are the rudiments of recapitulation, that Pauline doctrine which assumed great prominence in Irenaeus just because he too refused to allow cosmology to control christology. To begin to understand it – and it is not generally well understood, for it defies all ordinary interpretations of the world, whether religious or secular – we must keep in mind three closely related points.[46] First, as far as Irenaeus is concerned

---

[42] 3.16.1, 3.17.4. This turning away from the Father is *already* a turning away from the Son and the Spirit; cf. *Demo.* 7, 99f.

[43] See 3.16.5ff.; cf. 1.30.12ff.

[44] Irenaeus has already sketched out his position in the opening pages of his work by rebutting the heretics' use of John 1: 'Learn, then, ye foolish men, that Jesus who suffered for us, and who dwelt among us, is himself the Word of God' (1.9.3). How could it be otherwise, if indeed he 'who descended is the same also that ascended' (Eph. 4:10; cf. 3.6.2, 3.16.6, 3.18.2f., 3.21.6)?

[45] His name is twofold because his works are twofold, says Irenaeus. He is named 'Christ' because through him 'the Father anointed and adorned all things,' and 'Jesus' because 'he became the cause of salvation' (*Demo.* 53; cf. *Demo.* 5f., 53ff., AH 3.16ff., 4.20.7). We will touch later on the fact that Jesus is also the guarantee of the unity of the covenants and of the scriptures, which the heretics likewise divide and distort (see 4.5ff., esp. 4.9.1).

[46] Wingren (xv) suggests that 'the best confirmation that a particular interpretation of Irenaeus is a correct one will be whether or not we have given the terms *recapitulatio* or ἀνακεφαλαίωσις a definite and objective meaning.' We concur, without necessarily being

the divine speech-act by which God addresses himself to creation cannot be divided up into discrete phrases. That is, there are not several independent dispensations of the Logos as the gnostics imagined, only one of which is connected with Jesus, but a universal disposition of creation itself in connection with the Logos who *is* Jesus:[47] 'There is therefore, as we have shown, one God the Father, and one Christ Jesus our Lord, *veniens per universam dispositionem, et omnia in semetipsum recapitulans.*'[48] That makes Jesus, as Irenaeus is quick to recognize, the ground of creation as such. Creaturely things are called into existence for his sake, not he for theirs. Indeed, he pre-exists them, not they him.[49] The doctrine of recapitulation, in other words, does something more than reserve for Jesus a pride of place at the apex of salvation history, as the one who sets right what has gone wrong. Its first task is to signify that no realm whatever lies beyond the pale of his domain, that there are no autonomous times or spheres over which he is not the Lord – and because the Lord, also the redeemer.

The position Irenaeus takes up here stretches the limits of language and pushes him, as Robert Jenson observes, into some 'violently paradoxical' formulations which can easily be misread.[50] But we must not seek to detour around the difficulties it poses by appealing to a λόγος ἄσαρκος who takes on a human mode of existence only in an *ad hoc* way. Such a move would bring us dangerously near to the gnostic conviction that Jesus himself is somehow incidental to the Word. Flirtation with that idea was and is common enough, of course, preserving even among orthodox theologians traces of the gnostic bias against the redemption of the material world, but Irenaeus will have none of it. As Harnack rightly

---

satisfied that Wingren – who manages, like most interpreters, to ignore the ascension – takes us as far as we need to go. It is worth noticing, perhaps, that in the concluding chapters of Book 3 one finds about a dozen references to our subject alongside the half dozen to recapitulation.

[47] Likewise, then, there are not several Sons or Christs but one only, albeit one who through the Spirit graciously dispenses 'paternal glories adapted to the times' (4.20.6; cf. 4.5ff., esp. 4.9.1, and 4.25.3, 4.28.2, 4.33.7).

[48] 3.16.6. Two of his favourite texts, 1 Cor. 8:6 and Eph. 1:10, supply the language and the frame of reference; cf. also Col. 1:15ff.

[49] 3.22.3; cf. 5.1.1. We must not attempt to weaken the force of this claim by diverting it into familiar channels. The pre-existence Irenaeus has in mind is not isolated to a divine element in Jesus, nor could it refer to anything remotely like the gnostic *Urmensch*. Even a more Hebraic interpretation – that Jesus is 'known' by God before all others and so exists more truly than they – is not entirely adequate. Signs 'in the depth below and in the height above' (i.e., the virgin birth and the ascension, 3.21.6) point to something more than that: 'existing before all and going before all,' he is 'a perfect Master for all' (2.22.4).

[50] Jenson (1982:69f.) illustrates from 3.9.3: 'neither was Christ one and Jesus another: but the Word of God – who is the saviour of all, and the ruler of heaven and earth, who is Jesus, as I have already pointed out, who did also take upon him flesh, and was anointed by the Spirit from the Father – was made Jesus Christ . . .'

points out, he does not append the name Jesus to the Greek λόγος in the manner of the apologists. Rather, this and every other christological title is appended to the name Jesus.[51] The bishop knows no Word *sine carne* in the Greek sense, for in the final analysis he believes us to be confronted with just one 'short' Word through whom God says everything he has to say and accomplishes everything he wishes to accomplish.[52]

Now in teaching the coherence of all things around the incarnate Word Irenaeus was safeguarding not only the integrity of Jesus but the integrity of every particular; that is, he was postulating a creaturely unity which does not exclude the plurality of our human personhood or of our bodily existence. That is the second thing we must keep in mind in order to understand the doctrine of recapitulation. Whereas the gnostics saw in the redemptive work of the Logos 'the separation of what was unnaturally united,' Irenaeus saw in Jesus the reunion 'of things unnaturally separated;'[53] where they looked for the dissolution of the material world, he looked for its eternal flourishing. This disagreement, of course, had as its corollary their dispute over the proper locus of the doctrine of evil, which for the gnostics belonged in ktisiology and for the bishop in hamartiology. When the existence of evil is put down to the fact of creation rather than to the actions of sinning creatures, creaturely existence is that which must be overcome, not sin and its consequences.[54] The search for salvation thus becomes a search for a lost *divine* unity that does not include but repels the finite particularity which belongs to our creaturehood – making it impossible to accept that Jesus really is the unifying Logos. But the second task of the doctrine of recapitulation is to show that the gnostic search is a false one, that the unity constituted by God in and for creation through Christ embraces genuine otherness and plurality.

The doctrine of recapitulation remains largely inaccessible, then, not only to those who want to retain a λόγος ἄσαρκος but also to those who do not recognize that it is carefully interwoven with Irenaean notions of growth, freedom, and creaturely fecundity. These are themes to which we shall return in connection with his teaching on the Spirit. Meanwhile it is necessary to observe parenthetically that Loofs, Harnack and Bousset have argued that Irenaeus badly undermines himself here by way of his own speculative interest in union with God. Though he seeks to ground this union quite differently – that is, in the incarnation – his crudely constructed 'physical redemption' theory, and the doctrine of recapitulation with it, ultimately tails off into a gnostic-like mysticism in pursuit of that

---

[51] See 1.9.2 (cf. Harnack 2/262f.). Not until Karl Barth has anyone pressed this point with the same rigour.

[52] Cf. 1.9.3, 2.2.4f., 3.11.3, 3.16.6, 3.21.4, 5.18f. , *Demo.* 86f.

[53] Harnack 2/238, 272ff.

[54] See Farrow 1995:335f. While Irenaeus (2.28.7) rejects any speculation about the origin or cause of evil, he is clear about its systematic context.

Greek holy grail, deification. A new foothold for Hellenism is found by focusing on the incarnation as a bare fact, which is drawn into the service of a foreign soteriological scheme interested not in *our* world but in some other.[55] On this way of reading him, *Cur deus homo?* is made out to be the critical question in Irenaeus, and its well-known answer – that man might become God – his chief interest. Just how mistaken this line of thought is, however, will become clear as we continue.

The third and most important thing to keep in mind is that the doctrine of *recapitulatio* or ἀνακεφαλαίωσις has a reduplicative force – the logic of transformation as well as of headship – which belongs to it precisely because the tension between creation and redemption has been contained *within* christology rather than being allowed to co-opt and disintegrate christology. This is where the dispute about descending and ascending comes into its sharpest focus, and where the bishop's incarnational theology bites the deepest. For Irenaeus, descending and ascending are certainly not the actions of some novel entity such as Valentinus and other gnostic teachers dreamt of. Their putative saviour came without warning to announce a deity previously unknown and uninvolved with our world. The saviour himself was not quite God and not quite man, but a *tertium quid* whose task it was to set men on the way to God by leaving their humanity behind them.[56] *Tertium quid* christologies, we might say, are by design christologies of cancellation; but an incarnational christology, if it is not compromised by some hidden docetism, moves in a completely different direction. Here descending and ascending are acts of God himself (the covenant God) *as* a man. They do not cancel, but restore and consummate, human existence.[57] And in so doing they answer not to a defect in the creator or in his handiwork as such; they answer to man's fall.

---

[55] It does so, says Harnack, only after shifting the attention of Christian thought away from its proper object, that is, from the life and teachings of Jesus and from the ethics of actual Christian existence. Harnack (2/230ff., 3/103ff.) and Bousset (1970:420ff.) offer treatments which are often stimulating but deeply flawed. To portray Irenaeus as one who sought to juggle a simple biblical faith with Hellenist speculations and religious piety – who in the final analysis is best interpreted 'from the mystical side' – will not do at all.

[56] Obviously we are using the word 'humanity' in a loaded sense. For the gnostics true humanity was the divine spark in them (identifiable with the πνεῦμα or νοῦς) which required to be liberated from its compromising entanglement with the merely animal and carnal features of their present existence. That liberation is what the divine Man or Son of Man was sent from heaven to accomplish, taking a 'body' appropriate to the task, which naturally was not a carnal one. Just as obviously, we are speaking critically when we refer to a *tertium quid*: Whatever divisions and separations the heavenly man must undergo to complete his mission, he remains in some sense 'consubstantial' with God; so indeed do the γνώστικοι themselves. But that is just the point. What we have here is not a mediation between God and human beings, but between the original purity of heavenly divinities and a subsequent earthly impurity.

[57] The one who came *per universam dispositionem* did not come invisibly and incomprehensibly but in the flesh, in which he also suffered; and in the flesh the gates of heaven were opened to him, that he might indeed 'possess the supremacy' over all things. Cf. 3.16.8f., 3.19.3.

Note well, then, that it is not with incarnation in the abstract but concretely with Jesus-history that Irenaeus occupies himself.[58] Which is to say, he is concerned in the doctrine of recapitulation not with one descent only, but with two. He does of course acknowledge a descent of *God* in connection with the incarnation as such – a descent which is both invisible and an inappropriate subject for investigation.[59] Since man can neither reach up to God on his own, nor yet live without God, the Son of God becomes the Son of Man that he might join man to God.[60] That indeed is quite fundamental. Moreover, it is a thesis lent considerable urgency by the fact that Irenaeus wants to argue against the Hellenists, on the one hand, that man is not by nature divine, not even in his inner being; and against the Ebionites, on the other hand, that man is in truth made a partaker of the divine nature by adoption.[61] But what is equally fundamental is that the Son of God becomes the Son of Man in a way that adequately addresses our fallen condition. This soteriological thesis must be carefully distinguished from the ontological one just stated, or both will be falsified (as indeed they commonly are). Man has created for himself an unnatural plight; by joining in the devil's apostasy he has become alienated from God and hence from himself.[62] The descent of the Son must be so arranged, then, as to meet that need as well. If he descends as God to man so that man may ascend to God, he also descends *as* man so that alienated man may not fail to ascend with him:

> For as it was not possible that the man who had once for all been conquered, and who had been destroyed through disobedience, could re-form himself and obtain the prize of victory, or again, as it was impossible that he could

---

[58] Redemption is dependent on what Jesus *does* as well as what he is. Brunner (1934:249ff.,) was quick to spot the false dichotomies (between work and person, existence and essence, etc.) and the open contradictions which those who take Harnack's line are forced to find in Irenaeus. Cf. also J. Lawson 1948, G. Wingren 1959, G. Aulén 1969:16ff., and especially T. Hart 1989:152ff.

[59] *Demo.* 70, 84 (cf. 3.19.2). Cf. Thomas Aquinas *ST* 3/57.1.

[60] Two of the bishop's best known *dicta* point out the ontological necessity (from our side) of the incarnation: If 'God cannot be known without God,' and if 'the life of man consists in beholding God,' then God must come among humans for there to *be* humans (see 4.6.3ff., 4.20.4ff.). Zizioulas (1975:434 n.1) notes that Maximus is the first to state explicitly that the *fact* of the incarnation is not contingent upon the fall, even if the shape of Jesus-history is; but the position itself clearly derives from Irenaeus.

[61] See 4.33f., 5.1. He who is not novel in the gnostic sense – who does not therefore reveal a new and previously unknown God – does however bring about 'all novelty' (4.34.1), quickening humankind by his long-awaited advent and bestowing on it those divine mysteries into which even the angels long to look. Both gnostics and Ebionites turn aside from this. The latter do not recognize the true dignity of their high calling in Christ; the former make themselves out to be gods *before their time* (4.38f.; cf. 2.26.1). Irenaeus is especially hard on the gnostics, of course, since by refusing to await 'the time of increase' they ascribe to the creator the weakness of their own nature, demonstrating in their confusion between God and man (a confusion articulated in their invisible Christ) that they really know nothing of either.

[62] Forsaking his divine *vocatio*, man has been 'alienated contrary to nature' (5.1.1).

attain to salvation who had fallen under the power of sin, the Son effected *both* these things – the Word of God springing forth, descending from the Father, and being incarnate, and descending even to death, and consummating the arranged plan of our salvation . . .[63]

Now it is only when we reckon with this other descent – that is, with descent and ascent as a twofold movement in the flesh, as a complex form of creaturely temporality – that the full impact of the bishop's blow against gnosticism can be measured. For the third task of the doctrine of recapitulation is to show that Jesus of Nazareth resolves the real problem of evil (*viz.*, the alienation and fragmentation introduced by human sin) in his own personal history, in order that we and our world might flourish after all by attaining to genuine 'union and communion' with God. The third task, if we may put it this way, is to show that creation time and fallen time – though quite distinct – are brought together in Christ, and that the conflict between them is overcome at his own expense.[64] This is the very obverse of the gnostic position, which begins to appear in its true colours as the consequence of something more than a mere cosmological problem.

What do we mean? Let us think back to where we began. By divinizing spirit and demonizing matter – that is, by dislocating the doctrine of evil in the usual pagan way – the gnostics also separated Jesus from the Christ. In this they not only denied Jesus' bodily resurrection and ascension, but effectively bypassed his cross. Or rather they approved and affirmed it by tearing him apart all over again with their false doctrines! Wanting no part themselves in the way of the cross, they were prepared to dissolve and redefine the saviour rather than to allow that the saviour had redefined and dissolved our alienation from God. It was against such perverse ingratitude (diametrically opposed to the church's eucharistic mindset) that Irenaeus developed the doctrine of recapitulation, proclaiming one Jesus Christ who descends and ascends, in the flesh to redeem the flesh.[65]

* * *

---

[63] 3.18.2 (translation modified). We observe that this double 'descending' should not be understood as sequential but as coincidental, since 'descending' in the first sense qualifies Jesus-history simply as such.

[64] In an image borrowed from Justin (*1st Ap.* 60) Irenaeus speaks of the crucified Christ as 'inscribed crosswise' on the entire universe (*Demo.* 34; cf. 5.18.3).

[65] See 1.9.3, 3.6.2, 3.16.5ff., 3.18.2f., 3.21.6, etc.; cf. Rom. 10:6f., Eph. 4:10, Phil. 2:6ff. For Irenaeus there is an invisible descent (that of God in giving himself as a man) and a visible descending and ascending (that of the God-man who suffers for us and leads us to glory). For the gnostics, there is an invisible descending and ascending (that of the 'Christ' who suffers nothing) and a visible descent *without* a corresponding ascent (that of the crucified Jesus, who also required to be redeemed from the flesh).

With so bold an alternative, then, does Irenaeus scorn the disconnected planes of the gnostic picture of reality, and protest against their 'lowering and dividing' of God's Son. From every angle he encourages us to confess that there is no saviour but Jesus, in whom the goodness of creation and the goodness of redemption are seamlessly combined. But what of the Spirit, whom the heretics (he submits) more or less paint out altogether? We have not firmly grasped the doctrine of recapitulation as an antidote to homicidal innovations until we have spoken also about *pneumatology*, gnosticism's missing ingredient.[66]

It has already been intimated that Irenaeus allowed Jesus-history to serve as a commentary on Genesis 1 and to govern his view of the creation of man. Thinking together Jesus' baptism, his ascension to the Father, and the appearance of the ecclesial community, he developed the thesis that it is of the very essence of man to advance, to grow and become fruitful, through communion with God.[67] Freedom in and for that communion became for him the *conditio sine qua non* of genuine human existence. Only the man continually fortified by 'the increase of God' is the man of God's making, the man in God's image. Now the freedom and fortification in question are the peculiar work of the Holy Spirit, who is poured out from heaven to 'absorb the weakness' of man, whose capacity to commune with his creator does not lie in himself. 'Where the Spirit of the Father is, *there* is a living man,' says Irenaeus;[68] nothing else qualifies.

Here is a noteworthy treatment of the *imago dei* which eschews the rationalism of the Greek tradition for a relational ontology based on the gift of the Spirit. That which makes man man is not to be found in the soul or intellect, but in a uniquely communal *modus vivendi*; nor is human unity to be located somewhere behind human beings in a Universal Man, but in the actual lives *of* human beings insofar as they live out the possibilities for communion granted to them by the Spirit.[69] Would that

---

[66] Irenaeus was well aware, of course, that the gnostics had much to say about a Holy Spirit. But to separate Jesus from the Christ is in fact to 'set aside' the Spirit, *viz.*, as the creator Spirit, as the Spirit who spoke through the prophets to announce Jesus, and as the Spirit given to the church through Jesus. Nor was the bishop afraid to point out that the gnostic sects did not enjoy the gifts and powers of the Spirit (cf. 2.31f., 5.6.1).

[67] See especially 3.17. Cf. 4.11.1f.: 'For he formed him for growth and increase, as the Scripture says: "Increase and multiply." And . . . truly, he who makes is always the same; but that which is made must receive both beginning, and middle, and addition, and increase . . . For the receptacle of [God's] goodness, and the instrument of his glorification, is the man who is grateful to him that made him . . . '

[68] Even if the man in question is being martyred (5.9.3)! See 5.6–10, a crucial passage which addresses the false anthropology and eschatology of the gnostics by insisting that the so-called 'spiritual' or 'perfect' man exists only insofar as the human animal – body and soul – receives the Holy Spirit and lives accordingly (cf. 1.5ff., 2.29ff.).

[69] God's love 'is the life of man' (2.26.1); 'the soul herself is not life, but partakes in that life which is bestowed on her by God' (2.34.4; cf. Justin *Dial.* 4f.). This is a life which can only be understood christologically and pneumatologically, hence also ecclesiologically. It is as a *church* that man is 'fashioned after the image' (4.37.7; cf. 4.33.7ff.).

later theologians had been more careful to follow up this move! But our point in noting it here is to underline the fact that Irenaeus saw the creation of man as a job for both of God's hands, not one only. The gift of the Holy Spirit is as fundamental to the emergence of the *imago dei* as is the incarnation of the Son.[70]

We are not surprised, then, to find that Irenaeus also provided a pneumatological exposition of recapitulation. If Jesus is head of the human race from Adam to the last generation, if indeed he is lord of all creation, it is as and because the Spirit lends to that creation a perichoretic form of existence which is centred on him.[71] Conversely, if creation becomes fruitful and fecund, flourishing in all its particulars as God intended it too, it is because through Christ the waters of the Spirit flow upon it. And if Christ descends and ascends, incorporating the song of redemption into the melody of creation, he does so precisely in order to introduce the life-giving Spirit into the desert of human intransigence. Descending, he accustoms the Spirit to dwell in an unreceptive environment, making room for him in the fallen creature; ascending, he reconstitutes that environment by means of the same Spirit, and in so doing makes room for the creature in the Father's presence. Overcoming all obstacles, he makes the *Spirit* to be the head of man, his 'ladder of ascent to God.'[72] For he came

> commending to the Holy Spirit his own man, who had fallen among thieves, whom he himself compassionated, and bound up his wounds, giving two royal *denaria*; so that we, receiving by the Spirit the image and superscription of the Father and the Son, might cause the *denarium* entrusted to us to be fruitful, counting out the increase to the Lord.[73]

Christ's ultimate mission, in other words, was to draw the Spirit into man and man into the Spirit, that man might truly become a living being. Once again this analysis of descending and ascending contrasts sharply

---

[70] 'For by the hands of the Father, that is, by the Son and the Holy Spirit, man, and not [merely] a part of man, was made in the likeness of God' (5.6.1).

[71] In this light consider the 'reciprocal rejoicing' of 4.7.1 (cf. 4.22.2, 4.36.7f.). Zizioulas (1985:109 n.109) warns against bringing in the Spirit as a *deus ex machina*; a serious ontology is called for, in which 'being and relationship must be mutually identified' (ibid. n. 108). Irenaeus is certainly working towards such an ontology.

[72] See 3.24.1, 5.20.2; cf. 3.17.1f., 3.20.2, 4.14.2, 4.20.4. For the musical analogy (though Irenaeus himself is fond of such) we are indebted to the opening pages of J. R. R. Tolkien's *The Silmarillion*.

[73] 3.17.3. This passage is one of many, by the way, which suggest that Irenaeus did *not* draw any careful distinction between *imago* and *similitudo*, the oft-quoted but notoriously difficult 5.6.1 notwithstanding (cf. e.g. 3.18.1, 4.33.4, 5.8.1, 5.10.1, 5.16.1f.). In 5.6.1 *similitudo* does serve to bring out the dynamic dimension which is definitive for true image-bearing as a function of the gift of the Holy Spirit, through whom 'we see and hear and speak' in unity with Christ. What is particularly noteworthy there, as here, is first of all that Irenaeus refuses to accept any notion of a human being which marginalizes *either* the body or the soul (with its intellectual, volitional and aesthetic powers) and, second, that he understands humans to have 'spirit' only by *being* spiritual, i.e., by virtue of a dynamic relation to God established and sustained by the two hands of God.

with that of the gnostics, who by dispensing with the human Jesus conflated christology and pneumatology, rendering the latter more or less redundant. Theirs was a one-handed theology, built around a synthetic spirit-Christ.[74] A mere parody of Christian teaching, it was at once backward-looking and highly presumptuous. It talked of entering into the life of God, not by receiving our creation, but by shedding it. Gnosticism, according to Irenaeus, could lead only to a wretched abortion of God's anthropological project. It was an attempt to defraud us of our proper *ascensus* or ἄνοδος, that is, of our 'promotion' beyond the angels into the image and likeness of God, of our adoption in Christ into the Father's own house.[75] That is because it recognized neither the incarnate one nor the Spirit of adoption vouchsafed to us in him.[76]

This observation brings us, penultimately, to a closer consideration of Irenaean *eschatology*. But we may pause to remark, anticipating a later chapter, that the one-handed theology of the gnostics (and the very different eschatology that goes with it) has today reappeared in the west. The weaker trinitarianism of the western tradition is often blamed for this, but there is also a connection to certain dubious concepts of deification arising from that much-quoted eastern maxim, 'God became man that man might become God.' Common opinion notwithstanding, this bit of theological shorthand neither comes from Irenaeus nor could satisfy him.[77] Its pneumatological content, if it has any, is obscured by its abstract form, so that it does not adequately confront gnosticism's homicidal streak. So far from conjuring up images of creaturely freedom and fecundity such as we find in the concluding chapters of *Against Heresies*, it even permits a reading of which the gnostics themselves would approve, namely, that it is the condition of being human – rather than the human condition – which the mission of Christ must overcome.

We can be quite sure that Irenaeus had nothing like that in view when he summed up the doctrine of recapitulation by insisting that 'the Word of God, our Lord Jesus Christ . . . did through his transcendent love become what we are, that he might bring us to be even what he is

---

[74] For Irenaeus, on the other hand, 'in the name of Christ is implied he that anoints, he that is anointed, and the unction itself with which he is anointed' – i.e., the threefold God, Father, Son, and Holy Spirit (3.18.3).

[75] 3.19.1; cf. 3.25.6, 5.1.1, 5.36.3.

[76] Cf. 5.11.1: 'the things which save are the name of our Lord Jesus Christ and the Spirit of our God.'

[77] V. Lossky (1978:137), e.g., puts this in the mouth of both Irenaeus and Athanasius, as something 'repeated by the holy fathers and theologians of every age.' Athanasius did of course say that the Word 'was made man that we might be made God' – if we may render θεοποιηθῶμεν so literally – adding that 'he manifested himself by a body that we might receive the idea of the unseen Father' (*Inc.* 54). But he is not so close here to Irenaeus as to Clement (*Prot.* 1.84): 'the Logos of God became man so that you might learn from a man how a man may become God.'

himself.'[78] Here, while we are still talking about recapitulation in terms of the gift of the Spirit, is the place to treat this famous equation, which is a formula for 'deification' only as authentic humanization. By now it should be clear that the love of which Irenaeus speaks is twofold. It is first of all the love by which the divine Son becomes human, so that humanity might be given a filial character and definition.[79] But that filial character can only be stamped upon us by the Holy Spirit, and we are those who live as if the Spirit were not.[80] Hence the love of which the bishop speaks is also and especially the love by which the Son pursues us into the place of our fallenness, engaging himself with us as we actually are, in our decline rather than our advance.[81] He who by nature *is* the man of the Spirit posits himself for our sake as a man in need of the Spirit. Invading 'the land of sepulture,' he passes through every phase of human life and through every stage of our own backwards career, placing all within the redemptive remit of the Spirit.[82] In that way he brings into being the man of the Spirit even out of *homo indecorus et passibilis*, that the Spirit in turn might create a living and fruitful man out of *homo mortis reus*. That is how he brings us to be even what he is himself: not God, for in being God he is unique; yet certainly those who are able in their very flesh 'to receive and to bear God,' that is, to become partakers of the Spirit.[83]

---

[78] *qui propter immensam suam dilectionem factus est quod sumus nos, uti nos perficeret esse quod et ipse* (5. pref.). Lossky, who misquotes, does not miss the pneumatological point (cf. 1974:97, 103).

[79] How can the ἄνοδος at which the incarnation aims be a letting-go of our humanity, if it is grounded in God's taking up our humanity? The Son of God becomes the Son of Man 'for this purpose, that man might also become the son of God' (3.10.2). Cf. Wingren 206ff., Zizioulas 1975:438ff.

[80] Indeed we live where in some sense – but for Jesus – the Spirit *is* not, though he works from the beginning 'in all the dispensations of God' (4.33.1; cf. John 7:37ff.).

[81] 'For it behoved him who was to destroy sin, and redeem man under the power of death, that he should himself be made that very same thing which he was, that is, man *qui a peccato quidem in servitium tractus fuerat, a morte vero tenebatur . . .*' (3.18.7; cf. 3.20.2, 5.14.2).

[82] Many commentators suggest that Christ's was a separate Edenic humanity, but that does not do justice to the relational terms in which Irenaeus thinks. In his solidarity with us the Word recapitulates the *entire* sixth day of creation, including our time of bondage (5.23.2). From the standpoint of God's creative love, the incarnation already entails the humbling of Christ, that he might begin with beginners, and not with the immortal glory which belongs to him in the Spirit (4.38.1f.). Soteriologically, however, from the standpoint of God's grace, it means 'not despising or evading *any* condition of man,' including decline and death (2.22.4; cf. Wingren 85ff., 116ff.). We note that the bishop's earnestness here even drives him to the unnecessary conclusion that Jesus lived to some 50 years of age, the 'old man for old men' after whom Padre Blazon yearned in Robertson Davies' novel, *Fifth Business*.

[83] Through the overflow of his unction the righteous in every age are gradually accustomed *capere et portare Deum* (5.8.1; cf. 3.9.3, 3.18f., 4.31, 4.38), and 'not indeed *sine carne*'! The full argument.is summed up in 5.1.1: 'Since the Lord thus has redeemed us through his own blood, giving his soul for our souls, and his flesh for our flesh, and has also poured out

Now humanization with Christ in the Spirit is just what Irenaean eschatology is all about, as the doctrine of ascension in the flesh suggests that it should be. When Christ ascended 'to the height above, offering and commending to his Father that man which had been found,' he made 'in his own person the firstfruits of the resurrection of man,' opening up the time of increase which will answer to the present time of decrease and condemnation.[84] This time of increase – the time of our promotion – is described, in that wonderful vision of the *consummatio mundi* in Book 5, as a renewal of 'the inheritance of the earth' and a reorganization of 'the mystery of the glory of sons.'[85] With Christ's appearance before the Father, what he has commended to the Spirit in his own person is commended *in toto*. The Spirit takes possession of creation.[86] And in this act of possession he brings everything into subjection to Christ, enabling him to grant fruit to what is barren, wholeness to what is broken, vitality to what has become lifeless. Creation is liberated from every form of alienation and from everything contrary to the life of communion. Humanity is restored to the open horizons of paradise, and brought by stages into readiness for the new heavens and earth, in which gifts will be bestowed which have never yet been seen or heard or conceived by man.[87] For we ascend by the Spirit to the Son, and with the Son to the Father, who in due course will bless us 'after a paternal manner,' confirming and establishing the work of his two hands.[88]

Since we really have been dealing with this subject all along (Irenaeus' quarrel with gnosticism is nothing if not a quarrel about eschatology)

---

the Spirit of the Father for the union and communion of God and man, imparting indeed God to men by means of the Spirit, and, on the other hand, attaching man to God by his own incarnation, and bestowing upon us at his coming immortality durably and truly, by means of communion with God, all the doctrines of the heretics fall to ruin.'

[84] 3.19.3.

[85] *Utique haereditatem terrae ipse novabit, et reintegrabit mysterium gloriae filiorum* (5.33.1). The whole passage is eucharistic; see below.

[86] In *Demo*. 9 Irenaeus speaks in the common way of a world 'encompassed by seven heavens,' but as J. A. Robinson notes (1920:77f.) he 'strangely connects the Seven Heavens with the Seven Gifts of the Spirit.' Actually this is not so strange, since on his view heavenly things *are* the things of the Spirit (cf. 2.30.8) which are made accessible to us in Christ.

[87] In our present condition we dwell only 'on the way to paradise' (*Demo*. 16), having through disobedience lost 'that robe of sanctity' which we had from the Spirit and been 'cast out thence into this world' (3.23.5, 5.5.1). Restoration to paradise will be the 'prelude to immortality' because paradise is that condition of man in which he is free to advance towards God.

[88] 5.36; see 5.30ff. The people of God thus 'advance through steps of this nature' (5.36.2, cf. *Demo*. 7), 'the Spirit truly preparing man in the Son of God, and the Son leading him to the Father, while the Father, too, confers incorruption for eternal life' (4.20.5). The link between the doctrine of the ascension and the doctrine of the Trinity will appear again in our study. We should point out here, however, something which at first glance may not be obvious: namely, that only a trinitarianism which is neither Sabellian nor subordinationist can sustain an eschatology like that of Irenaeus, in which creation is not made to collapse in on itself as it advances toward God.

and will return to it in discussing the church, there are just a few matters which require our attention here. The first concerns the bishop's insistence against the gnostics, and indeed against some who are 'numbered among the orthodox' but have 'entertained heretical opinions,' that the Spirit takes possession of the *whole* man not just a part of man.[89] Is Irenaeus forgetting that flesh and blood cannot inherit the kingdom? On the contrary, he has made it quite clear that neither the visible nor the invisible aspects of human being have in themselves the capacity to receive the divine blessing. That capacity comes with the blessing itself, that is, with 'the vivifying Spirit.' Flesh and blood, then, 'can be taken *for* an inheritance into the kingdom of God,' along with our whole dissipated and decaying world, in order that the righteous may rule over it and re-order it as they will. For what has been redeemed by Christ, what he has committed to the Spirit, what therefore belongs to the saints in eternity, is just this world of ours.[90]

The second concerns the relation between the time of increase and the time of decrease. How shall we interpret that relation, given what has just been said? Irenaeus was moving towards an open, relational understanding of temporality that would do justice to the Christian gospel, and we must learn to think in terms of that gospel. Just as the descending and ascending of the Son are both sequential and non-sequential – that is, both historical and a redemptive 'inversion' or reworking of history – so then with our time and kingdom time: The latter follows the former, but in the sense that the former is 'thrown open' by Christ as an inheritance for his brethren. That is, it follows only in and with the parousia, which does not happen to the last generation only but 'comes alike to all.'[91] This complex relation between the time of decrease and the time of increase, which is not strictly linear, is everywhere implicit in the doctrine of recapitulation, even if it is inconsistently developed or applied by Irenaeus (whose chiliasm, though ontologically interesting, is certainly open to criticism). We will revert to it later on, when we think more specifically about the implications for ecclesial time.[92]

---

[89] 5.31. Irenaean ideas about the resurrection and ascent of man – beyond the angels! – stand quite apart from the increasingly angelomorphic interests of such 'orthodox' thinkers, who, by neglecting to give up the Greek habit of identifying the image with the νοῦς, further compounded the difficulty of making room in their heavenly vision for the physical creation. According to the bishop, the destiny of the righteous is foreshadowed already by Enoch and Elijah, who exhibited prophetically 'the assumption of those who are spiritual, and that nothing stood in the way of their body being translated and caught up; for by means of the very same hands through which they were moulded at the beginning, did they receive this translation and assumption' (5.5.1). After all, what *is* the 'heavenly' but the *Spirit* (5.9.3), who through Christ is invested in the earthly?

[90] Cf. 1.30.13, 2.29.1f., 5.9.1ff. Ταῦτα δὲ κληρονομεῖται ὑπὸ τοῦ πνεύματος, μεταφερόμενα εἰς τὴν βασιλείαν τοῦ οὐρανόν.

[91] Cf. 3.22.4, 5.27.1, 5.33.1.

[92] P. Forster (1985:140) also points to this difficult feature of *Against Heresies*: 'Irenaeus would appear to be attempting to see time on two levels, a linear, progressive level being

The third and last matter concerns the nature of the time of increase, and its goal. What is inherited for the kingdom must be fitted for glory through a process of 'fulfilling, extending and widening.'[93] The time of increase is not a time for laying aside the things of creation, as those who entertain heretical opinions imagine, but a time for the emergence of 'real men' who will eventually dwell with Christ in a 'real establishment,' as fit receptacles for the ever-increasing blessings of the Father. This process is one in which the inner workings of creation itself are adapted to the purposes of God's communion with man, and to the purposes of a humanity that is being personalized by God through and for that communion.[94] The *consummatio mundi* will occur not 'when all that is spiritual has been perfected by γνῶσις,' as the Valentinians taught, but when man, as the centrepiece of creation, has been readied by obedience and love. And what will that consummation look like? The bold simplicity of Irenaeus' ultimate vision – which represents a rare triumph for the personal and the particular – may come as a surprise, but in fact he has been preparing us for it all along: The new heavens and earth, he says, are an establishment in which the saviour shall be seen *everywhere,* 'according as they who see him shall be worthy.'[95]

---

overlaid by what we may term a recapitulating level, in which time and eternity definitely meet. Alternatively we might describe Irenaeus' understanding of time as comprising two aspects: fallen, linear time, which is being redeemed, and the redeemed time of the incarnate Christ, by which it is being redeemed. These two aspects correlate with the twin Irenaean themes of growth and *anakephalaiosis* . . .' We may improve on these helpful remarks by observing that Forster's alternatives are in fact complementary, since in the doctrine of recapitulation we must reckon *both* with 'comprehension in unity' *and* with redemption or 'going over the ground again' (to borrow Lawson's terminology, p. 143). Now regarding comprehension in unity, we are not to think in terms of a christological *nunc stans* as a counterpoint to linear progress, but of a pneumatological intersection of times, where time itself is understood as a function of personal existence, and personal existence as a function of communion with God through co-humanity with Christ. (Cf. 4.38.3, with its 'sequence' *and* 'harmonies.') As for redemption or 'going over the ground again,' here we are to think of the transformative effect on the whole nexus of human existence achieved by Christ's descending and ascending, which alters the direction of temporal 'progress.' That alteration is what prevents us from understanding the future of creation as a linear projection from its past.

[93] Note the qualification in 4.13.3: 'the more extensive operation of liberty implies that a more complete subjection and affection towards our liberator had been implanted within us.' Cf. Ezek. 40ff. (esp. 41:7).

[94] See 5.35f. Millennial time is ontologically interesting in Irenaeus because it is ascension time, the time in our personal and corporate histories which corresponds to Jesus' return to the Father. And let it be said in just this context (where Irenaeus is much criticized) that one of his greatest achievements is to make process an essential feature of the creator–creature relationship, while refusing to allow that process to *undermine* our creatureliness.

[95] 5.36.1. Having developed in various ways the point that obedience, love and communion are among the most fundamental of ontological categories, Irenaeus here posits a direct link between human development and spatio-temporal structures. He also neatly trumps the gnostic claim that Christ only seemed to carnal men to have come in the flesh,

Now if this final stroke should seem over-bold, we may at least recognize that it is just what the doctrine of recapitulation calls for. It constitutes both a decisive rejection of the marginalization of Jesus (that, not the Spirit, is what unites the heretics!) and an attempt to press through to a coherent Christian worldview. That worldview is one in which belief in the mediation of Christ as the ground of our existence is backed by a relational ontology based in the perichoretic power of the Spirit, so that in his ascension he does indeed fill and fulfill all things, as Ephesians teaches. In short, it is a doxological worldview that traces out the trinitarian lines of Christian worship to form an image of the finished creation in which there is no higher category than communion. 'For the glory of God is a living man, and the life of man consists in beholding God,' in the Spirit and through the Son, who is 'the visible of the Father.'[96]

Let us try, in a final stroke of our own, to give that worldview a name. Is it not essentially a *eucharistic* model of reality for which Irenaeus is contending in his quarrel with gnosticism? On the alternative he offers – guided if not inspired by reflection on the ascension – Jesus of Nazareth stands at the centre of God's handiwork. His descending and ascending is revealed as a priestly movement which impinges sovereignly and graciously, in an epicletic way, on every aspect and corner of creation. Through him there is an inverting of the inverted (a *conversio*, if you please) from which emerges a new kind of creaturely existence, built around a fruitful humanity that is defined at its roots by 'union and communion' with God.[97] But if we are thinking along the right lines here that will surely declare itself as we come at last to Irenaeus' doctrine of the church.

Eucharistic Ecclesiology

The subject of ecclesiology is not always treated as something integral to the bishop's project. Some are content merely to search his work for surviving metaphors of primitive ecclesial life. Others watch for this or that aspect of the creeping institutionalism to which we referred at the outset, focusing on apostolic succession and primacy, perhaps, or on the canon of truth, or on liturgical questions. Little effort is made to relate what he has to say about such things to larger issues.[98]

---

i.e., that what people saw or might have seen at the time 'would have differed according to their spiritual capacity' (H. Chadwick 1967:38). We should add that the Latin variant in this passage – *Deus* for σωτήρ – is wrong and misleading; see Harvey's explanatory note (2/428 n.2), and cf. 4.20.9.

[96] 4.20.7.

[97] Again, we can do no better than to point the reader to 4.20 in its entirety, with which cf. Eph. 3:14–4:16.

[98] But cf. Zizioulas 1985: 78ff. Perhaps this is the place to indicate to the reader that the title of this section, while inspired in part by friendly contact with John Zizioulas, is otherwise unconnected with the same terminology as used by one of his interpreters, Paul McPartlan (1995).

One of the reasons for this unfortunate state of affairs is the influence of Harnack. Harnack claimed that Irenaeus inherited a simple, non-theological notion of the church as an aggregate of spiritual individuals who shared common convictions and a common hope, but was forced in doing battle with the gnostics to betray that original simplicity in favour of ideas which led to the entrenchment of a more formal conception. More or less unwittingly, he became a transitional figure in ecclesiology. The emerging 'Catholic' view, that the church is rather 'the visible communion of those holding the correct apostolic doctrine,' did not yet hold sway; but Irenaeus certainly aided its ascendance, especially by making episcopal transmission of the apostolic *magisterium* a front-line defense against the heretics.[99]

Harnack's picture is badly distorted, however. In the first place, the more primitive conception that Irenaeus inherited – the Pauline notion of the church as a Christ-centred κοινωνία – was nothing so naïve as he suggests. If the bishop was fond of speaking, for example, about 'the communion of the brethren,' that was no substitute for serious ecclesiology but an expression of his most systematic themes, and already an answer to schismatics.[100] Nor, in the second place, did his appeals to the church as the locus of truth, or to its overseers as guardians of the truth, comprise a dangerously independent line of argument, as Harnack imagines. On the contrary, even the institutional strands of his ecclesiology are thoroughly embedded in his relational ontology. What fascinates Irenaeus about the church is that 'we, being many, [should] be made one in Christ Jesus.'[101] The continuity of its bishops is but one manifestation

---

[99] Harnack (2/77ff.) allows that Irenaeus himself retained a strong emphasis on the Spirit and did not employ an openly hierarchical construction; the primitive notions and the new ideas existed side by side, and more or less independently, but it was the latter which prevailed in future generations.

[100] See e.g. 3.11.8f.

[101] 3.17.2. Harnack's notion of communion is too thin to support the synthesis between being and truth with which Irenaeus is working. Where the former sees only a collection of individuals in a 'common relation to a common ideal and a common hope' – a typical enlightenment vision projected back into the second century – the latter sees a community with a highly distinct ontology. As for the supposedly primitive concept of 'the personal Christianity of the individual Christian' (2/73) which he is alleged to have put at risk, Irenaeus would not even have heard of it; arguably it was not invented until after the radical Reformation. It may be, as Harnack claims, that Christian truth gradually came to be conceived by some as 'a law and aggregate of doctrines' of doubtful practical aim, and that 'catholicity' came more and more to be understood in terms of submission to that law. But the process was a very slow one, and Irenaeus cannot be understood as a contributor. He was quite clear that even the formal aspect of catholicity, the *ordinatio ecclesiae* to which all adhere, springs from participation in the divine life, which embraces the people of God in every time and place and constitutes them as such. (See e.g. 3.4.2, 3.24.1 and 5.20.1f., which argues *from* the fact that around the world 'all receive one and the same God the Father, and believe in the same dispensation regarding the incarnation of the Son of God, and are cognizant of the same gift of the Spirit,' etc., *to* the notion of catholicity.) Zizioulas' remark here is one which Irenaeus *would* have recognized: 'We cannot understand catholicity as an ecclesiological notation unless we understand it as a Christological reality' (1985:158).

of that; likewise with the consistency of their teaching. For the pillars of the church are not its offices or doctrinal traditions as such, but 'the gospel and the Spirit of life,' which join it to Christ and cause it to 'breathe out immortality on every side.'[102] If the heretics lack consistency, if their behaviour is infamous and 'the footsteps of their doctrine are scattered here and there without agreement or connection,' it is not for want of an episcopal pedigree but for want of the Spirit, through whom 'we see, and hear, and speak' in the unity of Christ.[103]

Irenaeus' ecclesiological response to the gnostic threat goes much deeper, then, than his contention that the church is distinguished from heretical movements by adherence to its bishops, its scriptures, and its rule of faith (though he rightly saw that the gospel demands doctrinal measurements in the church, and that deviations from the faith are in fact deviations from the Lord himself).[104] It is through his ecclesiology that he occupies, as it were, the whole of his anti-gnostic edifice: The church is the place where knowledge of God is really possible, because it is the place where people commune together with the Lord and learn to walk in obedience to him. The church is the place where the goodness of the creator and the creation are faithfully celebrated. The church is the place where authentic humanity, in the image and likeness of the triune God, is already emerging. For it is only ecclesial man, corporate man – 'strengthened through means of joints and bands by the increase of God' – who is actually able *capere et portare deum*. None of this is blind loyalty, we hasten to add. Irenaeus is quite aware that the serpent of hypocrisy exists in the church as well as among the heretics.[105] Nevertheless, 'communion with Christ

---

[102] 4.20.5. If the church preserves the faith from generation to generation with the help of its presbyters, it is even more true that this faith itself preserves the church, for it is entrusted to her 'as breath was to the first created man' (3.24.1). Ever renewing its own youth by the Spirit, it renews the church's youth also.

[103] 5.20; cf. 1.10.2. 'True knowledge' consists not only in the episcopal traditions, etc., but also in 'the pre-eminent gift of love.' Note well that Irenaeus (4.33.8f.) rebukes the *heretics* for relying exclusively on a set of doctrines as a sufficient basis for union, and for denying that more complete forms of witness-bearing (martyrdom in particular) are 'at all necessary.'

[104] To reject the κανὼν τῆς ἀληθέιας, or to pull apart the *membra veritatis*, or to 'disregard the order and connection of the Scriptures' by 'dressing them up anew,' or to hold oneself 'aloof from the communion of the brethren,' is to turn away from the beauty and majesty of the one in whom they cohere (1.8.1, 3.11.8f., *passim*; cf. Torrance 1988:31ff., 260ff.). *Contra* Marcion it was this same beauty and majesty which already governed the ancient prophets and made them, in Justin's phrase, 'friends of Christ' (*Dial.* 8), indeed *members* of Christ (4.33.10). For 'one and the same householder produced both covenants, the Word of God, our Lord Jesus Christ, who spake with both Abraham and Moses, and who has restored us anew to liberty, and has multiplied that grace which is from himself' (4.9.1).

[105] See e.g. 4.26.2, 4.33.7. In the former passage he warns especially against those 'who are believed to be presbyters by many, but serve their own lusts . . . and are puffed up with the pride of holding the chief seat,' etc. As for the heretics, however, 'everything connected with these men is unreal' (4.33.5)!

has been distributed throughout it, that is, the Holy Spirit, the earnest of incorruption . . .'[106]

Now of the many things we might say about his ecclesiology there are only two which really matter here. The first is his unusual stress on the Spirit as the source of Christian κοινωνία. Who among the fathers sounds this exuberant note with more clarity or consistency? If Ignatius could say, 'Where Jesus Christ is, there is the catholic church,' Irenaeus would rather say: 'Where the church is, there is the Spirit of God; and where the Spirit of God is, there is the church, and every kind of grace.'[107] That is because for the latter the church is significant precisely as proof that the man of the Spirit has come into being with the ascension of Jesus. This already puts paid to any charge of formalism. Irenaeus' most characteristic thought about the church is not (as J. N. D. Kelly suggests) that it is 'the sole repository of the truth,' but rather that it is the wine press of the Spirit dug by God in the midst of creation, *paradisus in hoc mundo*.[108]

The second is his orientation to the eucharist, evident in a host of allusions and in more than one extended discussion. Theologically speaking, the bishop has indeed drunk deeply from the holy cup, as we suggested above: '*Our* opinion is in accordance with the eucharist,' he insists, 'and the eucharist in turn establishes our opinion.' Let those who deny the creator, the incarnate one, and the future of creation cease from offering to God creatures of bread and wine! Let those who do not believe in the resurrection of the body, or in 'the fellowship and union of the flesh and the Spirit,' refrain from receiving them! For the eucharist witnesses unmistakably to all of these things, and so to the continuity of creation and redemption. What is more, it imparts to us a share in the priestly humanity of our Lord, and interprets to us our ecclesial vocation.[109]

---

[106] et in eo est disposita communio ipsius Christi, id est Spiritus sanctus, arrha incorruptelae, et confirmatio fidei nostrae, et scala ascensionis ad Deum (3.24.1; cf. 4.18.5).

[107] Ignatius, *Smyrn.* 8; *Adv. Haer.* 3.24.1. It is extraordinary how modern commentators have failed to appreciate the impressive pneumatological component in his theology. J. Pelikan (1/156), e.g., shifts the emphasis of this Irenaean *dictum* from the Spirit himself to the ecclesiastical means he employs, but this is not justified. The Spirit – not the sacraments – is 'that most limpid fountain which issues from the body of Christ.' Indeed, people are 'saved altogether by the communion of the Spirit' (5.11.1; cf. 4.38.1). Even the Montanists are rebuked, not for claiming too much respecting the Spirit, but for claiming too little (3.11.9).

[108] See 4.36.2, 5.20 (which pursues the thought of 3.24.1). If we can give any credence at all to the conclusion articulated by Kelly (1977:192), it is only because by 'truth' we *mean* communion, or rather, the Holy Spirit who effects it. *Spiritus autem veritas.*

[109] See 4.18; cf. 4.33.2, 5.2.2f., 5.33.1. The centrality of the eucharist is evident in his claim that 'the new oblation of the new covenant' is the very 'means of subsistence' (*alimenta*) which the Lord offers his church as 'the firstfruits of his own gifts' (4.17.5). It is worth noticing, however, that Irenaeus never treats the form of the eucharist for its own sake, but always for illustrating an ontological or soteriological point. Thus he avoids the opaque sacramentalism of later times.

Let us see if we can expound these two observations together, focusing especially on the question of vocation. Irenaeus understands the church as an ontologically unique community, not as a collection of spiritual individuals (a gnostic-like concept). The special calling of that community is not to escape the world but to participate in its transformation. Together with the ascended one, in the doxological ferment of the Spirit, its members are granted a depth of being out of which they are able to offer a genuine oblation of thanksgiving on behalf of creation.[110] This oblation not only distinguishes them outwardly from the gnostic blasphemers, it is an activity with profound ontic effects, transcending the boundaries and limitations of that time and place which is otherwise under God's judgment, 'increasing and supporting' that nature which is otherwise unable 'to receive and to bear God.' In other words, through a living anthem of praise the church overcomes the world's dissipating mode of existence, and its bondage to the powers of darkness, such that creation (in the form of the church) begins to take on the lively, open-textured quality which belongs to it in Christ.

Irenaeus is not at all shy about staking the claim that it is only eucharistically that creation can hope to enjoy the liberty for which it was made. His line of thought runs something like this: It is the fundamental task of man to 'sanctify what has been created' by recognizing its quality as a gift and rendering thanks for it. Only in this personal interchange between God and man is the cosmos set on a sound footing.[111] But in his Cain-like duplicity, he cannot fulfill this role. Be he Jew or gentile, he can at best make only a 'servile' oblation, which is of no existential value in that it makes no real connection with the creator, who himself gives *freely* and stands in need of nothing. Man as we know him lacks a share in the liberty (and liberality) of the Word, 'through whom the wood fructifies, and the fountains gush forth, and the earth gives "first the blade, then the ear, then the full corn in the ear."'[112] Because his heart is 'divided with envy and malice,' because he is isolated in his resolute individuality, he cannot make either of himself or of his world a proper offering. In a frustrated mockery of ecclesial transcendence he becomes intent merely on the *abolition* of boundaries, like a perverse child who is not growing up but only growing old.[113] More and more his world

---

[110] Torrance (1993:39 n.2) points out that there is one Hebrew word for oblation and ascension, '*olah*. It is by virtue of the fact that the being of the church is bound up with the ascension that it *is* eucharistic, having precisely the character of a thank-offering.

[111] Thus he encourages us to offer our gifts 'frequently and without intermission' at the heavenly altar (4.18.6), for God takes these to himself for *our* good in order to return them to us in kingdom-form.

[112] See 4.18.

[113] See 4.9, where in a warning highly germane to our own day Irenaeus speaks ironically of the 'progress' of the self-willed, who are 'turned backwards' from the Father into 'an abyss without limits.'

comes to reflect and perpetuate his own corruption, as his offering runs to dust in his hands.[114]

What is needed, therefore, if man is to regain his place in the dynamic of God's design for creation, is a change of 'species' through the implantation of the Word.[115] For that change he also requires – we must not miss the epicletic component – the 'voluntary rain' from above,[116] that is, the Spirit of liberty who turns the slave into a freeman and his corruptible offering into an incorruptible one. The evidence that such freedom really does exist, proleptically at least, is the eucharistic vitality of the church. By the unique quality of its joyful and uncompelled offerings an *indicium libertatis* is set out around the world. In its common consciousness of the Spirit, in its communion of goods and spiritual gifts, in the mutual priesthood and service of its members,[117] in its supernatural growth and rejection of heretical discord, the church provides a window on the consummation of all things. In other words, Irenaeus sees in the eucharistic prising open of man to the possibilities of ecclesial life the very stuff of the kingdom. As room is made in us for the Word, room is also found in him for us to grow and advance towards the Father, and so (at the appointed time) 'to rise with manifold increase by the Spirit of God,' like the sacred bread on which we are fed.[118]

All of this explains well enough why Irenaeus shows no inclination to try on the oversized armour of institutionalism which others were beginning to forge at the expense of the *indicium libertatis*; why he does not turn to clericalism to guarantee the integrity of the church in the way

---

[114] Here cf. 5.33.3, where it is said that in the kingdom the very clusters of grapes will cry out to the saints, 'Take me; bless the Lord through me!' It should not be overlooked, by the way, that it is the man who sanctifies the offering, not the reverse; or that the man himself is sanctified once and for all by the Word, *per quod offertur Deo*, that God might receive it 'as from a friend' (4.18.3f.; cf. 5.12.6).

[115] The change of species refers to the Christian oblation as such, since it is an offering made 'not by slaves, but by freemen' (4.18.2). Irenaeus does understand also a change in the elements, from being merely earthly to being at the same time heavenly; this correlates with the change in the worshipers (4.18.5). But later preoccupation with the elements *alone* served to obscure the whole concept – i.e., the relational dimension of the eucharist and the emphasis on freedom – marking a significant reversal in the basic framework of ecclesiology. (Cf. Dix 244ff.; also T. Guzie 1995:125, where we find ourselves in fleeting agreement with the work of a modern gnostic.)

[116] *superna voluntaria pluvia* (3.17.2; cf. 5.10.1).

[117] Irenaeus' commitment to the New Testament concept of the priesthood of all believers – 'for all the righteous possess the sacerdotal rank,' 4.8.3 (cf. 5.34.3) – is backed by his pneumatology. We may note with the editors (*ANF* 1/471 n. 6) the later politically correct rendering of this passage by, e.g., John of Damascus.

[118] As the corn of wheat decomposes and then springs up to a fruitful harvest, and having been made into bread receives the Word of God and so becomes the eucharist, we too, 'being nourished by it, and deposited in the earth,' shall rise to immortality: a process which teaches us, *inter alia*, that we have this immortality as a free gift of God and 'not from our own nature' (5.2.3; cf. 4.18.5).

that Ignatius does, for example;[119] why the legalism of Tertullian is as foreign to him as the elitism of the Montanists. It explains too why he does not look to a distinct 'heavenly' church such as 2 Clement propounds.[120] He could not possibly affirm that fateful gnosticizing move, as did some later churchmen, not even in an attenuated Platonist form. For he wished to contend that it really is this world and this humanity of ours, in all its messiness, which is offered to God in Christ for the sake of his kingdom. The church on earth is not related to a heavenly counterpart as image to reality (a construct that would eventually help to create formidable institutional symbols as mediating and perfecting hierarchies). Rather the relation is an eschatological one; the eucharistic outcome is discoverable only in the grace of the parousia and of the resurrection.[121]

More importantly, the above considerations prepare us for the last vital feature of Irenaeus' dispute with the heretics. The eucharistic frame of reference in which he contemplates the ecclesial vocation affords a bold Christian ethic which sharply contradicts the deviant *praxis* of his opponents. How so? The true gnostic, whether committed to an ascetic or to a libertine form of life, denies all obligation to the world, a stance consistent with his or her systematic pessimism and narrow soteriological expectations. The spiritual person rises above the affairs of a world destined for destruction.[122] But the church, believing in the renewal of creation, offers an oblation which commits it to a life of responsible engagement with the world for the sake of its transformation. Not that the church itself can or will accomplish that transformation from below, so to speak, or assist the world to do so. The renewal which it seeks is hid with Christ in God – there is no nascent liberation theology here, nor hint of triumphalism. Indeed, the new possibilities implanted in its oblation by the Word and the Spirit, just because they *are* eschatological, consistently thrust the church back to the cross as the ground and pattern

---

[119] Irenaeus does not take up the constant rallying cry of Ignatius (*Magn.* 6, 13; *Trall.* 3; *Phil.* 2ff.; *Smyr.* 8f.), for whom the clerical orders, and the bishops especially, were the visible surety of an invisible unity. He seems to prefer the more primitive view of bishops as teachers and examples (cf. Minns 3f.). At the same time he reverts from Ignatius' overwhelming emphasis on union and unity (see Pelikan 1/159f.) to the richer idea of κοινωνία, offering the harmonious communion of voices in hymn-singing as a true picture of the church.

[120] 2 *Clem.* 14 postulates a pre-existent spiritual church, of which the temporal earthly one is an imperfect copy.

[121] The Lord, he says, 'confers gifts upon men, that is, his own presence, and the resurrection of the dead' (4.9.2). The linking of these two is not insignificant; in the last analysis union with Christ means just this radical eschatologial transformation (hence the notion that the church *sends forward* 'a multitude of martyrs to the Father,' 4.33.9). Here surely is a point of view which militates against any self-assertive turn in ecclesiology, since its interest is not in securing Christ's presence *pro nobis* – a mistake which has often tempted the church into a false immanentism, as we shall see – but in the gift of the Spirit who secures our presence with Christ *pro Patre* by way of the resurrection.

[122] The same applied for those whose eschatology was chiefly *psychology*.

of its engagement. But in the cruciform life of the church, in the witness above all of its martyrs, is the evidence of an unrelenting devotion.[123]

We should not hesitate to admit that this introduces a more sombre note, which will be heard in any theology holding creation and redemption in their proper relation. The bishop's comments respecting the joyful nature of the church's worship show a marked contrast to later treatments of the mass, imbuing his ecclesiology with a buoyant spirit; yet he plainly recognized that the pneumatic place, the epicletic place, is the place not only of eager expectation but of groaning. It is the courageous place in which Christians reject *both* of the gnostic options, often (as Irenaeus knew only too well) at great personal cost. That is, they refuse either to become irrelevant to the world or to be in conformity with it. Withdrawal and worldliness are alike repugnant to a eucharistic worldview – forsaken not for the virtue of moderation, but for the sake of a radical love. Insofar as that love, which may at any time be sealed in martyrdom, is something the gnostic is careful to avoid, he proves his antipathy to the gospel and to the church's priestly calling.[124]

Just here, with the mention of martyrdom, the subtler and more powerful tension between creation and redemption that arises when their continuity is affirmed begins to declare itself: in the form of an unsettling dialectic between church and world. Occupying the place of eucharistic stress carved out for it by Jesus, the church is distinguished *from* the world in order to present itself *to* the world as a vehicle of salvation. Which is to say, it is placed in its precarious situation as a community straddling two divergent histories. Delineating this thesis in Irenaeus, while defending it against recent misconstruals of his thought, will allow us to bring our discussion to a conclusion. It will also enable us to clarify further the connection between his doctrine of the ascension, the cosmological commitments it implies, and the ecclesial outlook we are describing.

⁂

It is of course the apocalyptic final chapters of *Against Heresies*, suppressed for many centuries, which make plain the pressurized situation of the church in the present age. Harnack regarded those chapters, complete with their chiliastic hope, as a relic of fading primitive expectations, inconsistent with the secularizing tendencies of Irenaeus. Bousset, on the other hand, found that the bishop had there creatively introduced his favourite motif – gradual development and advance – into

---

[123] Cf. 4.31.3 and 4.33.9, where the church is compared to Lot's wife (*sic*).

[124] Irenaeus' teaching stands in sharp contrast to that of Basilides, e.g., who taught that the martyr suffers because of his or her own hidden sins (H. Blair 1986:38). But the point we are making is a larger one; cf. 2.32.4.

Christian eschatology. What he offers us is 'the idea of chiliasm evolutionistically interpreted and transfigured!'[125] It has since become common to emphasize that Irenaeus saw salvation history and the history of the human race more or less as *one*; that is, as a progressive education, a movement from childhood towards maturity, in which (to use Henry Chadwick's words) 'God has gradually brought man forward step by step in a long process culminating in the incarnation of the divine Word with a universal gospel diffused throughout the world by the church.'[126] But this, to say the least, puts a rather different slant on the relation of the church to the world. In fact, it places the church on an entirely different footing than that suggested above.

John Hick has popularized the single history view while promoting his 'Irenaean' model of theodicy. Briefly put, this model interprets creation as a process of soul-making extending over many aeons and through many worlds, the end result of which will justify the means, *viz.*, the suffering and evil encountered along the way. Though the model itself is far from complete in Irenaeus, Hick believes that many of its basic elements can be found there: the idea that humanity and the world were not created perfect; that the fall was a more or less natural, even necessary business; that the human story, individually and collectively, is one of painful but purposeful advance, of slow deification 'throughout a long course of ages.'[127] Now were we to follow such a view we might well continue to say that the church has in the present phase of things a vital role to play, a constructively critical role which will not always be appreciated.[128] But as the spirit of Jesus permeates the race that role becomes obsolete. Such discontinuity as currently exists between the church and the world must yield to an ever greater continuity. It is to something like this that the name of Irenaeus has become attached.

As it happens, however, Irenaeus himself – unlike the gnostics – does not have a theodicy worth speaking of; none, that is, but the gospel itself, which sets the good news of recapitulation in Christ over against the brute

---

[125] For Harnack (2/294ff.) Irenaeus' systematic Christ is distinct from his eschatological one, 'who will shortly come to overcome the Antichrist, overthrow the Roman empire, establish Jerusalem in a kingdom of glory and feed believers with the fat of a miraculously fruitful earth.' Since the bishop and his contemporaries still lived in this primitive hope they were 'but half-hearted in their theology,' which was a temporary defensive measure. But for Bousset (443, 451) they were men of the future, engaged in bringing radical theology down to earth in an 'ecclesiastically usable' way.

[126] 8of. Cf. Minns 58f., for whom *Augustine* is the source of the idea that human history bifurcates with Christ, whereas in Irenaeus 'the history of humankind and the history of salvation are one and the same.' But Minns' brief section on recapitulation – less than three pages – suggests that he has not fully wrestled with this question.

[127] Hick (1985:211ff., 253ff.; cf. 1993:53ff.) leans heavily on 4.38f., and on the *imago/similitudo* distinction in 5.6.1. He then moves on to Schleiermacher for further help.

[128] In Irenaeus' own words (4.34.2), and the like may be found in Schleiermacher, Christ by his advent 'fulfilled all things, and does still fulfill in the church the new covenant foretold by the law, onwards to the consummation.'

fact of evil.[129] Nor, as should by now be clear, did he regard the fall as natural. (Nothing less than the entire weight of his relational ontology forbids such a view!) That is, he did not exchange the heretics' opposition between creation and redemption, as Hick does, for a simple conflation of the two.[130] Neither then did he understand the dialectic of church and world as something to be resolved gradually through the universal suffusion of the gospel. Common opinion notwithstanding, Irenaeus taught no *general* ascent of man.

We should observe that Hick might well point at this juncture to certain contrarieties in Irenaeus, as Harnack suggests. To be precise, a Pauline fall/restoration paradigm is thought to vie with his belief in deification and hence in progress, as anti-gnostic and gnostic elements in his theology collide. In other words, the bishop is said to be oriented now to the past and now to the future, so that his eschatology sounds an uncertain note. Read in this way, his famous doctrine of recapitulation becomes, as even Bousset reluctantly concludes, a doctrine divided against itself.[131] Might

---

[129] There are three matters about which Irenaeus, for theological reasons, refuses to speculate (2:28.6f.): the production of matter, the Son's eternal generation, *and* the origin of evil. He does have something to say about why God tolerates evil, and how good can come of it (cf. 3.20, 4.38f., 5.2.3). But is this theodicy? K. Surin (1986:15ff.) argues that the line taken by Hick, which owes much to Leibniz, represents 'a conflation of two radically different, even incommensurable intellectual contexts.' He asserts that the problem of evil with which Irenaeus is concerned 'has absolutely nothing to do with this kind of "soul-making" or with anything resembling a theodicy,' but has to do rather with the evil of gnosticism as a theological method (see 2.26.1). This claim may be somewhat exaggerated, yet we are quite right to detach Irenaeus from Hick. Let us venture our own opinion that theodicy *per se* is incipiently a gnostic enterprise, for it begins in the wrong place, with God in the dock not man. In Hick's case (1976) it ends in the wrong place too, with something other than a human being in the bosom of something other than 'the God and Father of our Lord Jesus Christ.'

[130] To say that the fall happened 'easily' given human immaturity (5.16.2, *Demo.* 12) is not at all to say that the fall was natural (cf. 5.1.1). Nor indeed – since according to Hick we can no longer believe in such an event – is it to invite by way of modification the view that humans were *created* fallen, i.e., that our creation could only be undertaken as redemption. Hick is right in thinking that humanity begins at a distance from God which must gradually be overcome. That distance, however, is not so much an 'epistemic' distance as one related to man's inexperience at loving God. To fall, then, is to refuse to advance in love and so to *reject* our creation. It is true nevertheless that for Irenaeus the fall can and does serve our creation. How? The forbidden tree exhibited to us God's *otherness*, knowledge of which is essential to our love for God, both now and eternally. The fall teaches us by experience, and so even more profoundly and unforgettably, that otherness. The problem with the gnostics is that this lesson is one they stubbornly refuse to learn (4.38f.). Now if we are to regard the fall and damnnation 'as mythological expressions of aspects of our own self-awareness' (Hick 1993:62), are we not siding with the gnostics? And must we not then also (with Kant) regard our coming perfection in the same way, and our redeemer too? Hick indeed takes this path, but he is not walking with Irenaeus.

[131] Bousset, to whom Irenaeus was no less than 'the Schleiermacher of the second century,' wrestles with these cross-currents, as Hick calls them, in *Kyrios Christos*; but the dilemma goes back to Duncker and Wendt, who insisted that here was a 'real contradiction' in Irenaeus (Harnack, 2/274 n.1). Cf. Wingren 26ff., Farrow 1995.

this perhaps explain our disagreement? And would it not be better for us as modern theologians to abandon the older Pauline strand altogether, allowing the evolutionary insight to develop freely? That is what Hick would have us do. But the proffered reading of Irenaeus is actually a misreading, which obscures and falsifies his position. It is one that must be corrected if we hope to elucidate the dialectic in question.

To begin with, we note that the charge of inconsistency may be turned back on those who have made it. On the one hand, Irenaeus' supposed Hellenizing of the gospel is said to distract him from the earthiness and informality of the early tradition. On the other hand, that same Hellenizing apparently draws him out of an old static paradigm (restorationism) into a new dynamic one (what some call 'elevationism'),[132] better suited to our own understanding of the world. Can these claims really be harmonized? In any case, we have already shown that neither is accurate. Irenaean soteriology remains largely biblical in spirit, as John Lawson and Gustaf Wingren correctly maintain. And his notion of advance or progress was derived principally from the concreteness of salvation history, especially from ascension in the flesh, not from Hellenic interests; gnostic and Greek soteriologies were, after all, more rigidly restorationist than any biblical scheme.[133]

More tellingly, and this is a point which must not be overlooked, the reading we are rejecting dramatically dislocates the incarnation as an historical event. That is a danger which faces us, to be sure, even when we find in Ireneus a consistently biblical thinker. His defense against the docetism of Marcion and Valentinus called for a heavy emphasis on the Christ-event as the climactic moment in a long history of God's approach to man. Only after a protracted period of preparation does the Word appear among us – not as a retort to the old covenant or to its deity, but as that very deity in person. On page after page the bishop secures this front by expounding the relationship between Jesus and the prophets who were sent before him. It is under their tutelage that we are slowly readied to receive him, for he does not come to us unannounced. When he finally does come, of course, a great threshold is crossed and a new age begun; under the personal tutelage of the incarnate one, in the communion of the Spirit, we ourselves may now advance towards God.[134] It is quite true that if we do not follow Irenaeus here we do not follow him at all. But we have missed an important turning if we proceed to operate on the premise that the incarnation takes place at the point where mankind as

---

[132] Cf. Robert Brown 1975.

[133] Here we may record our hearty agreement with Oscar Cullmann's judgment (1964:56f.) that Irenaeus was *the* theologian of antiquity 'who understood the Greek world in its innermost nature' without succumbing, like Clement and Origen e.g., to its blandishments; but we must also record our equally strong objection to the notion that Irenaeus had 'a completely linear view of time,' or neglected 'the idea of restoration' (1963:190).

[134] See 4.5ff. (esp. 9–11).

such is truly ready for God, where sacred history can therefore broaden out at last into universal history. That is the very dislocation of which we are speaking.

Here we may shed further light on our earlier remark about the *Cur deus homo?* question. It was noted that this question is widely regarded as the most fundamental of all for Irenaeus, but in fact it is only when we give equal attention to the where and when of the incarnation (a matter he promises at the outset to deal with) that we begin to see things as he does. The incarnate one, he says, is 'a stone from the earth,' a man in history and with a history. Nevertheless he is a stone cut without hands, 'the corner one,' as the virgin birth and the ascension testify. Why then does he appear only *in novissimis temporibus, et non in initio*?[135] Why does he take up his unique place in creation (his central place!) not in Eden but in Gethsemane? Why do we meet him only at the end of a long road to nowhere, in a 'waterless' land, not merely incarnate but quite literally fastened to his own handiwork with pins?[136] When we wrestle with this question we recognize that talk of evolution is an anachronism that throws the entire discussion off the track. It is not as if God's self-insertion into history were a kind of lever applied at its midpoint, or at some crucial juncture, to move humanity onwards and upwards to a higher plane of existence. As Irenaeus sees it, through the fall our evolution has actually become our devolution. The Son does not appear at the middle of history, then, but at the end; not somewhere towards the top, but at the bottom. He comes to offer his summing up just where it is necessary for history to begin all over again. Is that not the whole point of the doctrine of recapitulation?[137]

Where then is the inconsistency, or the confusion about forwards and backwards? Because we are those who are faced away from God and moving in the wrong direction, reversal has become the precondition for progress, restoration the prerequisite for elevation. There are no warring paradigms here between which we must choose. But there *is* a choice of historics. For it would certainly be a great mistake to think that this new beginning which is made by Jesus Christ can be identified directly with our history in the so-called Christian era. If his ascension, as ascension in

---

[135] Here is a question which Irenaeus promises from the outset to answer; he will explain 'why the advent of the Son of God took place in these last times, that is, in the end, rather than in the beginning' (1.10.3). In this light cf. 3.16–23, 4.20.4, 5.14ff.

[136] See the 'plough' analogy in 4.34.4: '. . . the Word, having been firmly united to flesh, and in its mechanism fixed with pins, has reclaimed the savage earth' (following Harvey 2/272).

[137] *Quid enim huc veniebat?* asks the bishop (4.6.4), and we ought not to miss the stress that falls on the *huc*, i.e., on the 'hither' of our time and place in which sin and death prevail: 'But God the Father was merciful. He sent his creative Word, who in coming to deliver us came to the very place and spot in which we had lost life, and brake the bonds of our fetters' (*Demo.* 38; cf. 5.15.4). Of course, in just this way the bottom *becomes* the top, the end the beginning; that is what is achieved in the ascension.

the flesh, is not a vertical or atemporal affair, neither is it a horizontal one. It is not an extension of this time of ours. It is indeed a *new* beginning from an old place.[138] Christ's identification with our time, which runs into the abyss, is the time of his descent not his ascent. Ascension time (which cannot be grasped by us) is the renewal or re-opening of time through genuine converse with God. It is the basis and foundation of millennial time, which Irenaeus refused to identify with our own present or future – apart, that is, from their eucharistic transformation, which has as its *terminus ad quem* the resurrection.

Now when we reckon with this distinction of history from history we have already abandoned the idea of a general ascent of man. Irenaean theology cannot be recast in the mould of an orthogenetic evolutionary cosmology, because his doctrine of ascension in the flesh forbids it. Creation may indeed be a process, and the kingdom of God on the way, so to speak; but it is not on the way along *our* way. And if in the church 'we do now receive a certain portion of his Spirit, tending towards perfection, and preparing us for incorruption, being little by little accustomed to receive and bear God,' that is a gradualism which only serves to drive deeper the wedge between ecclesial man and the man of the world. It heightens, rather than diminishes, the eucharistic tension and the choice it thrusts upon us.[139] For the church, as the bishop argues, finds itself caught up in a decisive clash between Jesus-history and apostate history. The ascension is followed not only by Pentecost but by a 'movement of the whole earth against the church,' an escalating conflict which will lead finally to an antichristic recapitulation, that is, to a hollow summing up of iniquity in a centre which cannot hold, issuing not upwards into the presence of God but downwards into darkness.[140]

After the ascension history is thus revealed as a reverse image of what it ought to be. Drawing on the dream of Nebuchadnezzar to which allusion has already been made, Irenaeus looks ahead and sees a world

---

[138] We must question Surin here along with Hick and the rest. In repudiating gnosticism, he says, 'Irenaeus affirmed that there are not two separate and antagonistic creations, but a single creation in which human beings advance towards God . . . The principle of a slow and progressive perfecting of the human race by God in Christ is the lynchpin of Irenaeus's *apologia* against gnostic dualism.' But if we are going to talk about the event of the incarnation as 'the key to this theology of history,' and hence about recapitulation (17f.), must we not be clear that this one creation has *two* histories – an old and a new? And must we not be equally clear that to 'commence afresh' does not mean merely to regroup and carry on?

[139] 5.8.1ff. (cf. 4.39, 5.2.3).

[140] Cf. 4.33.13, 5.24ff. Ontically, the world and the church – like Cain and Abel – are moving in opposite directions, so to speak, from a common place. The nations who did not 'raise up their eyes to heaven nor returned thanks to their Maker' (a eucharistic allusion, 5.29.1) will be reckoned 'as the turning-weight of a balance, in fact, as nothing.' But the church, in 'the last contest of the righteous,' will be caught up with Christ into 'the times of the kingdom . . . the hallowed seventh day,' wherein the whole creation 'will obtain a vast increase.'

that will struggle desperately for unity but fail to achieve it. In the last days, he predicts, 'there shall be minglings among the human race, but no cohesion': just a demonic parody of ecclesial fellowship through a union of nations and peoples *without* communion. This artificial kingdom will come to nothing since it is secretly divided against itself.[141] The church too, though inwardly united, must suffer a painful dissolution; its refusal to be assimilated by the world will provoke the world, attracting its enmity as well as its admiration. For in our place and time even Jesus brings division as well as communion, ruin as well as resurrection.[142]

We would be equally mistaken, however, to conclude that if Irenaeus would reject the false optimism of modern doctrines of progress he must therefore be put down as one who embraces apocalyptic pessimism, or as one for whom history as we know it has no value. It is not Irenaeus but the gnostics who take such a view. According to the Valentinians, for example – for whom the present age belongs to the psychic Christ, who sits at the right hand of the demiurge until the pneumatic seed is perfected and received back into the Pleroma with the spiritual Christ – we are on the way to the termination of history. It is the dissolution of creation for which we should look, as like returns to like and unnatural alliances (of which the church is one) are finally undone.[143] Gnostic spiritualism and determinism leave to temporal reality nothing of substance at all. Irenaeus, on the other hand, insists that it is not the substance of the world but only its false σχῆμα, the σχῆμα we ourselves have given it, which will pass away under the judgment of God.[144] The heavenly session of the man, Jesus Christ, warrants and demands this confidence. What is more, it imparts real significance to the present age, redeeming its futility, as the age *par excellence* of human choice.

The position of Irenaeus thus transcends the facile alternative, optimism or pessimism. That is because he regards our time as one which derives its unique character from the opening up of a diastasis between the man of gratitude and the man of ingratitude, the man of obedience and the man of lawlessness. We must take decisions along these lines, and choose destinies for ourselves. These will eventually be confirmed by Jesus, at whose parousia (a subject towards which the whole Irenaean project strains, as Gustaf Wingren has observed) the gnostic expectation of a

---

[141] 5.26.1 (cf. Dan. 2:43). He warns that those who ignore these things become dupes and agents of Satan, whose representatives only *pretend* to liberate the oppressed (5.30.3).

[142] See 5.27.1.

[143] 2.29 (cf. May 116, Logan 301ff.). In utilitarian fashion, the church serves in the meantime to hold together the psychic and the spiritual in an artificial unity.

[144] 'For since there are real men, so must there also be a real establishment [*plantationem*], that they vanish not away among non-existent things, but progress among those which have an actual existence. For neither is the substance nor the essence [ὑπόστασις . . . οὐσία / substantia neque materia conditionis] of the creation annihilated (for faithful is he who established it), but "the fashion [σχῆμα/figura] of the world passeth away;" that is, those things among which transgression has occurred, since man has grown old in them' (5.36.1).

sundering of unnatural alliances will not be altogether disappointed![145] For 'the advent of the Son comes indeed alike to all, but is for the purpose of judging, and separating the believing from the unbelieving . . .'[146] Eucharistic time will then bear the inexhaustible fruit that comes from the increase of God, since righteousness and faith are powerful enough to save what has participated in them. Non-eucharistic time will lead to that deprivation to which no definition can be given but that provided by pointing to its opposite.[147]

But what does all of this signify in terms of the dialectic between church and world? That is our real concern. Where exactly is the continuity and where the discontinuity? The latter is obviously in the church's very different choice (to render thankful obedience to God through Jesus Christ) and hence in its very different destiny (to enter into the 'times of refreshing' which the parousia will bring). The former is in the fact that, by choosing to follow Jesus, the church is still choosing *for* the world not against it. It is choosing to travel with the world, for the sake of the world, without joining the world. Here then is a continuity that grows precisely by keeping pace with an ever sharper discontinuity. The church, since it belongs to him who ascended in the flesh, can neither agree with the world nor let go of it. It can only take up the cross and the offence of the cross, wrestling with the world to the bitter end in hope – a well-grounded hope! – of redeeming the time.

The point we have been labouring to make is reinforced when we notice with Irenaeus that at the parousia Jesus will not need to exercise any *new* judgment. Why not? Because by descending and ascending he judged good and evil once for all, so as to effect in himself a costly separation between them.[148] So also with the church. Situated eucharistically at the place of

---

[145] Irenaeus regards the *present* time, the time between the advents, as the time for breaking up, just as the eucharistic bread is broken – but a breaking up that takes place in just this way, as the decision of men and women about their own destinies. For the righteous that decision means, *inter alia*, 'looking forward with constancy' to Jesus' future coming in the flesh (*hominem eius firmiter excipiens*, 5.14.4; cf. Wingren 193). In all of this Irenaeus is following the eucharistic vision of the Apocalypse, though we may wish to question his reading, e.g., of chap. 20.

[146] 5.27 (cf. 1.10.1, 4.4.3). For 'the Word comes preparing a fit habitation for both' according to their option for life in communion or for death through alienation and self-isolation (5.28.1; cf. 3.25.1f., 4.28.3, 4.41.2). Epitomizing the latter is the antichrist, who is called '"the other," because he is alienated from the Lord' (5.25.4).

[147] Cf. 2.29, 5.9.4, 5.27.2. We should be reminded again that for Irenaeus man *is* what he does (Hart 166), and that what he does has eschatological consequences. 'If there were really no such thing as good and evil, but certain things were deemed righteous, and certain others unrighteous, in human opinion only, He never would have taught thus: "the righteous shall shine forth as the sun in the kingdom of their Father"' (2.32.1; cf. Wingren xivf.).

[148] If the gnostics wish to divide man into flesh, soul and spirit, and so to conquer him – i.e., do away with him as man – Irenaeus sees that Jesus has come to divide and conquer *evil* in man, that he might be *re*integrated for the sake of the kingdom (5.6.1). That this work must be carried out internally, by way of recapitulation, is one of those basic insights which set Irenaeus well above his contemporaries (cf. Torrance 1988:156).

overlap between the time of decrease and the time of increase – at the place, that is, where the one is transformed into the other by the power of the cross – it allows itself to become the sacrament of that judgment by bearing witness to it in life and death. Knowing that in Christ it does not rest in the hurtful hands of the world but in the gracious hands of the Father, knowing too that its own readiness to bear the weight of glory will come in just this way, the church willingly gives itself up with him to a painful fraction. For salvation comes to the people of God only as they too are 'after a manner broken up, and rendered fine, and sprinkled over by the patience of the Word of God, and set on fire, that they may be fitted for the royal banquet.'[149]

If the anticipated time of increase followed the time of decrease in the normal sequential manner, if there were indeed but one history, it would of course be otherwise with the church. The church could then be content merely to survive until the kingdom comes; alternatively, it could seek to bring in the kingdom in worldly ways, by an indefinite widening of its interests and extending of its sphere of influence. Neither of these options, though familiar enough to us, occurs to Irenaeus, who would not recognize them as genuinely eucharistic. Are they not in fact the product of a worldview largely unaffected by the doctrine of ascension in the flesh and the notion of recapitulation? Of such things we will speak again; but it is time now for us to redeem for weary readers the labours of the present chapter by recapitulating in the purely rhetorical sense.

One Step Forward

Harnack charged Irenaeus with producing only theological fragments. If he did, the fragments in question are surely those left in the crater where the tower of gnosticism had been going up. Admittedly, we have allowed to Irenaeus a highly sympathetic hearing (too sympathetic at points) in order to explore with him the kind of theological construct that emerges when one thoughtfully embraces the doctrine of the ascension in something like its scriptural form. In any number of places it would not be difficult to show, at the very least, that his penetration of the issues is uneven, his advance halting. It may be that his 'eucharistic' worldview is not carried through as far it requires to be.[150] But we are still confident in saying that what we have before us, taking into account the enormity of the task, is impressive both for its overall coherence and for its sheer boldness.

[149] 5.28.4. Thus even the evil that is done to the church is eucharistically transfigured and redeemed, like that done to Jesus himself. Meanwhile, 'as she has received freely from God, freely also does she minister' (2.32.4), exerting daily 'for the benefit of the gentiles' the many gifts bestowed on her by God in the name of the Crucified.

[150] The doctrine of the millennium, e.g., is really quite crucial here and in our judgment unsatisfactory. Questions about the ascension and spatio-temporal structures, about the adequacy of an ontology that is still to some extent mired in the being/becoming dichotomy,

The gnostic opposition of redemption to creation which Irenaeus had to confront involved a series of theological moves with a circular and self-supporting structure. By virtue of their radical dualism (divinizing spirit and demonizing matter) his adversaries were forced to postulate an invisible saviour or saviours behind Jesus of Nazareth, and a God behind the God of the old covenant.[151] That being done, a scheme of redemption *from* creation could be worked out, a scheme which Irenaeus denounced as a fraudulent attempt to procure an abortion of God's anthropological project. Nothing was more crucial to breaking up this scheme, or at least to overturning its Christian pretensions, than reclaiming the biblical theology of descent and ascent which its architects had misappropriated. Gnosticism, by refusing to identify Jesus as the saviour, deals ultimately in a mythology of dying and rising, for the sake of an ascension of the mind or spirit. The rule of faith deals with an historical death, that of the cross, and with a resurrection and ascension *in carne*; hence with a eucharistic mode of existence. These two schemes could not be more different, yet setting the one over against the other to good effect was no mean task. It forced Irenaeus to look more deeply than any other pre-Nicene theologian into the trinitarian resources of the faith, and into the construction of the ecclesial community itself.

He did not proceed, as others have tried to, by ignoring the many difficulties raised by the *in carne*.[152] After all, a theology not engaged with fundamental questions about the world, or about human nature and destiny, was of no use to him whatsoever. Instead he operated on the principle that christology (guided by the rule of faith) must be free to control cosmology and anthropology.[153] What happened with Jesus, according to the apostolic testimony, required one to dispense with a great many common presuppositions of ancient Hellenism and to think along quite different lines. It confirmed the Hebrew view that there is no natural connection between matter and evil, finitude and sin, temporality and death.[154] It made necessary a search for new conceptualities free of bias against the particular, and capable of taking into account personal relations as the most fundamental and constitutive dimension of creaturely

---

and about a host of difficult subjects relating to the Trinity, the incarnation, the atonement, etc. – questions whose time was not yet – might well be raised. But we are dealing, after all, with a pioneer, not with someone standing at the climax of a long tradition.

[151] See again 3.24. This God, says Irenaeus, is really 'the god of Epicurus, who does nothing either for himself or for others'!

[152] Cf. e.g. *Epistula Apostolorum*, another second-century anti-gnostic document; but we are thinking of later and more sophisticated works.

[153] Gnosticism, as Irenaeus recognized, is nothing if not an attempt to reclaim the biblical story for a Hellenist cosmological framework, with its anthropomorphic structure.

[154] Insofar as finitude and temporality are in fact wardens of decline rather than increase, that is only what we ourselves have made of them; any philosophy which obscures this point, in effect normalizing or rationalizing that decline, is itself evil, for it assaults the goodness of the creator.

reality. It suggested that old philosophical polarities (the one and the many, mind and matter, eternity and time, etc.), which threatened to shackle soteriology to sub-Christian expectations, must be reformulated. However resistant to a purely rational explanation, it demonstrated *in concreto* that redemption does not mean the prising apart of creation to liberate what is divine in it, but rather the prising open of creation to the Spirit of God that it might be filled with divine glory. Simply put, it assured us that salvation does not make us something other than human, but makes us rather to *be* human in another and truer way.[155]

By committing himself to the *in carne*, and to that whole complex of convictions represented by the doctrine of recapitulation, Irenaeus produced two results of special interest to us. The first is a thoroughgoing christocentrism, which stands in stark contrast to the christomonism that is characteristic of gnostic thought. His is a worldview which (even in its tutorial aspect) eschews all utilitarianism, and all sterile homogenization, in a powerful affirmation of the particular, beginning with Jesus of Nazareth.[156]

To be sure, the question may be asked whether the bishop has pushed this point too far. Can this man, even as the God-man, really be the Word by which each of us is both called into existence and recalled from the brink of non-existence? Can he really stand, even as the ascended one, at the beginning and end of all things? Can his hand, the very hand that was nailed to the cross under the watchful eye of the centurion, rule over the vast reaches of space and time? Irenaeus appears to think so:

> For he it is who sailed along with Noah, and who guided Abraham; who was bound along with Isaac, and was a wanderer with Jacob; the shepherd of those who are saved, and the bridegroom of the church; the chief also of the cherubim, the prince of the angelic powers; God of God; Son of the Father; Jesus Christ; King for ever and ever.[157]

Though we ourselves are of the opinion that this view is already to be found in Paul and John and Hebrews, we must still ask whether so much has been claimed for Jesus that his humanity must be crushed after all under the weight of these claims.[158]

---

[155] 'Do not err: Jesus Christ, the Son of God, is one and the same, who did by suffering reconcile us to God, and rose from the dead; who is at the right hand of the Father, and perfect in all things . . .' (3.16.9).

[156] The attempt to make the historical Jesus give way to some kind of cosmic principle is what we mean by christomonism. The gnostics sometimes styled the saviour 'All Things,' to which Irenaeus countered that Jesus was given *power* over 'all things' (cf. 1.3.4 with 1.10.1, e.g., or 4.20.2).

[157] Frag. 53. Cf. 3.16.4, e.g., or 3.19.2: *Quoniam autem est ipse proprie praeter omnes qui fuerunt tunc homines, Deus, et Dominus, et Rex aeternus, et Unigenitus, et Verbum incarnatem . . . adest videre omnibus qui vel modicum de veritate attigerint.*

[158] A. T. Hanson (1982:56f.), for one, would say so. And of course the question can be asked in the other direction as well, as it frequently is in the case of Karl Barth's sweeping christological claims: Is not *our* reality somehow threatened if we take such statements about Jesus too seriously?

Recapitulation being in fact a two-handed business, everything depends on whether Irenaeus' appeal to pneumatology will hold up. This may not be easy to decide – indeed it may be impossible – but we can at least acknowledge that the bishop's resolute faith in Jesus' universal lordship is backed by such an appeal.[159] That is to say, it is backed by an adventurous ontology of communion, the absurdity of which is simply that of the church itself. For Irenaeus believed that κοινωνία in the Spirit transcends time and place without negating time and place, and that this κοινωνία has in Jesus its definite and particular centre. Like Paul in Colossians or Ephesians, for example, he had no difficulty extrapolating from ecclesiology to the organization of creation as a whole; indeed, ascension in the flesh required him to do so even if creation can only be known in that way eschatologically.[160]

The second result, no less significant than his christocentrism or the pneumatology that supports it, is the firm link which Irenaeus forges between the doctrine of the ascension and the doctrine of the cross. The former does not negate the latter, as in gnosticism, but is all of a piece with it. Descent and ascent, as we have seen, constitute a twofold movement in the flesh and for the flesh. This movement involves a profound break with our world, but a break derived at every point from an even more profound affirmation of it. Repudiating not the fact of the world but its fashion, it reconstitutes the world in the pneumatic and eucharistic mode of being for which it has always been intended. Here then is an opposition of redemption to that which undermines or destroys creation. As an opposition of affirmation, however, it is a *costly* opposition, as the church through its participation in Christ is learning, and must continue to learn until the end of the age.

This brings us back around to C. K. Barrett's concern. With Irenaeus the kind of theological criticism Barrett is seeking takes a major step forward. For this second-century bishop not only places Jesus firmly at the centre, but in doing so works out a dialectic which keeps the church at once both central *and* peripheral in the New Testament sense. The church he describes is not self-affirming but world-affirming; yet it is world-affirming only by choosing to be quite strictly itself, that is, by choosing the cross. Eucharistically (which means, freely and gratefully) the church takes up its stance in the tension between fraction and

---

[159] To have seen that the homicidal streak in gnosticism has as much to do with a weak pneumatology as with a faulty christology is one of his best insights; another is to have seen the connection between the two. Christocentrism does *not* lapse into christomonism if christology and pneumatology are not played off one against the other. And we may add that the doctrine of ascension in the flesh may be the best guarantee of that.

[160] There are again dangers here, however, to which Irenaeus certainly appears to succumb when, thinking backwards from Christ's exaltation, he asserts that other creatures are brought into existence *in order to prevent the saviour from saving in vain* (3.22.3, 5.1.1). Is this not to risk a new form of determinism, and the collapse of the open ontology with which he is working in his theory of recapitulation? See Appendix B.

flourishing bequeathed to it by Christ. Indeed it embodies that tension within itself, permitting his infinitely gracious affirmation of the world still to be seen and heard in the place where it is so desperately required, even at the cost to the faithful of being also 'after a manner broken up, and rendered fine.'[161]

Now if (by Barrett's standard) Irenaeus sets us off in the right direction, it is not by accident. It is the result of letting Jesus-history and its ecclesial consequences govern his thinking to a most unusual degree, generating an understanding of the world which highlights rather than obscures the actual situation of the church. That understanding, encouraged no doubt by the persecutions and martyrdoms in Lyons, militated strongly against any false secularization. It also enabled him to look ahead, following the pointing finger of Jesus and the prophets, in order to warn us against the deceptive character of our age, which today more than ever gives the impression of 'minglings' without cohesion. What Irenaeus did not foresee, however, and would have been mortified to learn, was the extent to which the church itself would take on the look of iron mixed with clay, or the extent to which it would covet the sham catholicity at which worldly institutions and empires aim. In that self-controverting development the doctrine of the ascension, or rather *another* doctrine of the ascension, also had a role to play.

---

[161] 5.28.4. The ascension speaks first of God's affirmation of Jesus-history as his very own, and then also of the lordly appropriation of *our* history in and through Jesus by the Holy Spirit. The church is the witness to this latter appropriation – its visible edge, so to speak. But it exists as this witness only on the brink of annihilation. Hence the Spirit is also the 'dew' from heaven which Christ sends throughout the world to cool its members against the consuming fire, while rendering them fruitful (3.17.3; cf. Rom. 8:15-27).

4

Cosmologies and Ecclesiologies, II

The question of the relation between creation and redemption raised by the gnostics (definitely a cosmological one) has continued to occupy dogmatics to the present day. But if ideally the whole matter should have been worked through with sustained attention to the nature of ecclesial being, that did not prove possible. With good reason the focus of the debate was soon narrowed to more pressing concerns respecting its christological underpinnings; and this proved troublesome enough that the best that could be managed in the sphere of ecclesiology, on a conciliar level at least, was a protracted controversy over the use of icons, a quite telling affair of which we will speak later.

Now if it is largely to the credit of Irenaeus that a deliberately docetic approach to christology – *viz.*, one which openly severed the link between creation and redemption at the expense of the human Jesus – could never again be taken seriously, it is nonetheless true that dualist tendencies were far from being fully vanquished in the church.[1] The next really important battle makes that clear. The Arian question was more than a prolonged argument over the kind of simplicity that ought to be predicated of God for piety's sake; it was laden with cosmological freight, since the church was faced once more with a dedicated attempt to establish a notion of transcendence based on opposition to, or distance from, things temporal. That the main dispute hinged on the ontological unity of the Father and the Son, rather than on the identity of Jesus *as* his Son, should not obscure the fact that the same basic issues were again at stake.[2]

---

[1] 'Despite his initial victory over his opponents, he was unable to arrest the growing influence of Platonism upon Christianity, and many of the essential aspirations of the gnostics were soon to find welcome, and a permanent home, within the spiritual and mystical traditions of the catholic, orthodox Church' (Minns 137f.).

[2] Pelikan observes that the 'ultimate outcome of the Arian system was a Christ suspended between man and God, identical with neither but related to both: God was interpreted deistically, man moralistically, and Christ mythologically' (1/198; cf. T. F. Torrance 1988:47ff.). Leaving aside the moralism, is this not the old problem in a new guise?

We have seen how Irenaeus achieved his earlier success against the gnostics by working within the trinitarian vision of the baptismal creed, and also by exploring the full scope of its witness to Jesus-history, showing special attention to the ascension. These commitments generated a strong emphasis on the continuity between creation and redemption, without jeopardizing a proper sense of discontinuity; that is to say, a robust soteriology preserved the possibility of a truly eucharistic worldview, and with it the potential for a profound interpretation of ecclesial being and *praxis*. In principle, of course, this was shared by the Nicene theologians, to whom it was left to attend more carefully, under the pressure of Arianism, to the trinitarian logic the Christian view of God and the world required. Unfortunately, however, these fathers gave somewhat less attention to Jesus-history *per se*, and to its implications for either cosmology or ecclesiology.[3] No doubt they were distracted by the task of defending Jesus' divinity and of addressing difficult questions about what novel kind of deity Christians believed in. But the shift in focus was a dangerous one, for the risk of misleading abstractions in theological analysis (as Athanasius certainly knew) is directly proportionate to neglect of the concrete form of God's self-explanation in Christ. Nicene Christianity was thus open to acquiring an Hellenic bent in spite of itself.[4]

The danger, particularly as it touched on the church's self-understanding, was heightened by the sweeping political changes which brought Christianity into mainstream society, but also by the fact that the Irenaean solution to the gnostic problem had not been properly digested. It is well known that the most influential Christian thinker of the intervening period charted a course (with or without a good firsthand knowledge of *Against Heresies*) somewhere between Irenaeus and his opponents, in places steering more closely to the latter. From Origen onwards, in fact, much of what Irenaeus had fought for, though upheld in official doctrine, was increasingly undermined. Logos christologies of a strictly speculative kind, together with a tendency towards what may be called eschatological docetism, were prevalent even in orthodox circles. And this situation was further aggravated by the failure of the greatest post-Nicene theologian, St Augustine, to free himself from the limitations of neoplatonism and from certain features of the Origenist heritage passed on to him by Ambrose.[5]

Our readers will not be surprised when we observe that these two men, Origen and Augustine, who 'tower above all other figures in the history

---

[3] Though the middle section of the creed retained its basic task of witnessing to the actual shape of Jesus-history, even while being fortified with more technical language securing its trinitarian basis, the significance of that history for Christian anthropology, etc., was not explored with any thoroughness.

[4] The fathers' much-criticized 'ontologizing' treatment of the incarnation was entirely necessary to a robust soteriology and was required by Jesus-history itself; but it can and did prove to be a distraction from the economy.

[5] Cf. B. McGinn 1/202ff.

of early Christian thought,'⁶ accorded the doctrine of the ascension a very significant place in their overall scheme of things. For neither of them, however, did the ascension of *Jesus* play a foundational role in the development of a theological worldview. For the most part the latter was already decided along dualist lines before the former was brought into play, dictating (as it had for the gnostics) the terms in which the ascension itself would be conceived. The method of Irenaeus was thus reversed, with the greatest of consequences for ecclesiology. Indeed, such was the combined influence of these later luminaries that, in spite of certain exceptions which we will attempt to note, we find that on the whole we must regard subsequent developments as a retreat from the gains and insights outlined in our last two chapters. But all of this requires some elaboration.

Two Steps Back

Origen

Jacques Ellul's fortieth book, *The Subversion of Christianity*, opens with a provocative question. 'How has it come about that the development of Christianity and the church has given birth to a society, a civilization, a culture that are completely opposite to what we read in the Bible . . .?' His embarrassingly frank conclusions about the church's metamorphosis into something quite alien to its own beginnings we cannot go into here,⁷ let alone the larger question of the church's impact on society, which must surely be set in a more favourable light. But Ellul points in convincing fashion to the church's self-betrayal with the seductive apparatus of worldly security. He does not do so by looking directly to the most obvious source, namely, to the fateful alliance with imperial power that took place in the fourth century. Like Harnack, he notices that there is an older and distinctly theological component to be taken into account: 'It seems to me that everything goes back to a phenomenal change in the understanding of revelation, namely, the transition from history to philosophy.'⁸

---

⁶ M. Wiles, in the preface to J. W. Trigg 1983.

⁷ Ellul (154ff.) argues a less nuanced view of the paradox and precariousness of ecclesial being, pressing home with characteristic boldness the same point made by Barrett in a way that is content to ignore many serious questions. His approach owes rather a lot to Kierkegaard, and in our opinion requires a certain tempering by way of careful eucharistic thinking. He has not read Irenaeus with due attention; cf. 1989:214ff.

⁸ What he has in view (p. 23) is the kind of theology that thrives on ontological questions rather than on God's actual dealings with man in the concreteness of salvation history, forgetting 'the essential point, that God does not reveal by means of a philosophical system or a moral code or a metaphysical construction.' For Ellul this forgetfulness falsifies the whole project. The vital self-criticism of which we spoke in Chap. 3 is indeed threatened by such forgetfulness, though that does not mean that we are forced into the choice: history *or* ontology.

One does not have to endorse his analysis entirely in order to agree that an epochal adjustment in the orientation of theology, and in theological method, did in fact occur at an early stage. And however it might be described there can be little doubt, though Ellul does not say so, that it was the controversial Origen who effectively inaugurated the change. Origen was born in Egypt while Irenaeus, 'resident among the *Keltae*,' was putting pen to paper in Gaul; and just as Origen outshone Clement, his predecessor in the catechetical school of Alexandria, so too his work largely supplanted that of Irenaeus as the main sounding board of Christian dogmatics. The differences between the two are as stark as the north African landscape, even if some rather basic questions about Origen's theological vision are still in dispute today.[9]

Harnack suggests that Origen freed theology from its polemical aim,[10] but it would be more accurate to say that he brought it back into the service of theodicy. Rejecting the Marcionite and gnostic brands, which had sacrificed God the creator in order to save God the redeemer, he set out to reconcile Christian faith in the *one* God both to the cultured classes of Alexandria and to the hard facts of life.[11] He borrowed his building blocks from a variety of sources (Christian, Platonist, Stoic, Basilidean, etc.) and dressed them to his own requirements. One of the most important was the notion of free will, which he set over against the fatalism and elitism which were so pronounced among the gnostics.[12] Origen was not content merely to reassert man's moral responsibility, however, or a salvation accessible to all. He laboured also to address the problem of evil and, in doing so, to propound a universal redemption.

This effort in theodicy was closely interwoven, of course, with Origen's grand attempt to articulate a Christian spirituality capable of incorporating and superseding the best of the Platonist tradition. The combined result, it must be allowed, entailed no small modification of the faith he had received, whatever one makes of the wisdom of the project itself. To be sure, his most systematic work, *de Principiis* – which Jerome crustily

---

[9] See U. Berner (1981) for a survey of modern approaches to Origen. Whatever conclusions one might reach regarding Origen's sources, aims, and value to the church, Trigg's verdict (1983:9) is sound: 'We have Origen, more than any other single person, to thank that Athens and Jerusalem belong equally to our western heritage.' And in that sense Gregory Nazianzen's acknowledgement that Origen is 'the whetstone of us all' still holds true.

[10] Harnack (2/332) thus has Origen, for better or for worse, as the true father of ecclesiastical science.

[11] 'But what purpose is there in my unfolding and enumerating the tragic tale of human miseries, from which some are free while others are involved in them . . .' (*Princ.* 2.9.3).

[12] See e.g. *Princ.* 2.9.5f., 3.3.5. Trigg provides a helpful account of Origen's sources. In the doctrine of free will he notes the influence of Antiochus of Ascalon and Plutarch of Chaeronea, and of the Platonic tradition generally as mediated by Ammonius Saccas. He speaks of the conviction acquired through Ammonius 'that Platonism was the best antidote to Gnosticism' (71).

referred to as his 'poisoned dish'[13] – begins with the 'plain' doctrines taught by the apostles and confessed by all at their baptism. But there follows immediately the first of a series of concessions to Greek cosmology, in the form of a tacit recognition of the hierarchical structures of being and knowing.[14] To these plain doctrines those capable of receiving wisdom from on high might add and expound certain other doctrines only hinted at by the apostles. Elsewhere, in fact, Origen develops a distinction between the gospel that is for the simple and the gospel that is for the wise. This was, he maintained, the same gospel in two forms: one with a temporal focus, the other with an eternal; one resting on the λόγος ἔνσαρκος, the other on the λόγος ἄσαρκος.[15] The distinction of doctrine from doctrine, and of gospel from gospel, prepares us for other important concessions and alterations.

We must offer a quick sketch of a few of these in order to pursue our christological interests. Drawing sin and suffering into a direct causal relation (hardly his most original idea though by no means an apostolic one) Origen suggested that the inequalities and seeming injustices of our world could be accounted for by reference to individual choices in a prior state. Blame belongs with us, not with the God who made us. That the world is the way it is, that we ourselves are the way we are – material beings subject to passion and pain – is the consequence of the misuse of our wills in turning away from a primordial union with God. Committing himself to such extra-biblical beliefs as the pre-existence of the soul,[16] and putting aside any Irenaean scruples about speculative constructions, Origen went on to posit a whole progression of descending and ascending aeons as the best way to explain the problematic conditions which appertain in our own. In doing so, of course, he placed salvation history within the context of a broader controlling framework. Indeed he opposed gnosticism with a gnostic device, since he too relocated the doctrine of the fall, which he alleged to have preceded the creation of the world.[17]

There can be no doubt that he was greatly influenced here by the Hellenic prejudices Irenaeus sought to combat. For Origen diversity and pluriformity *per se* were already signs of a defection from the divine unity which creation ought more perfectly to reflect. Nor would we be wrong to link such a view to deficiencies in his concept of God. The trinitarian

---

[13] *Apol. Ruf.* 3.25. H. Crouzel (1989:163ff.) emphasizes that this much-attacked work is of an experimental rather than a strictly dogmatic nature, but in doing so only underlines the speculative tendency which it reveals.

[14] 1.pref. (cf. *contra Celsus* 6.21). We may recall that Irenaeus concluded *Adversus Haereses* with such a hierarchy, but only after it had been completely modified by his doctrine of recapitulation.

[15] Cf. *Princ.* 3.6.8, 4.3.13 (and the editorial notes); Jerome, *Ep. ad Avitum* 12.

[16] Cf. *Princ.* 1.4f., Plato's *Phaedrus* 245ff.

[17] See *Princ.* 1.pref.7, 1.6–2.3, 2.8–3.6. Basilides had already linked sin and suffering even more firmly than had Plato, as of course had Oriental religion; theories of multiple aeons and multiple lives were also common.

thinking we found in Irenaeus recedes rather than advances, unable to compete with a powerful stress on sheer oneness as the proper basis of divine transcendence.[18] Origen's God-talk is more Philonic than Christian, and more triadic than trinitarian, as is often pointed out. That is precisely because its deepest roots are not in salvation history but in that ancient (social and metaphysical) opposition between the one and the many, which is commonly rationalized in favour of the one.[19] And so long as an absolutely undifferentiated Monad remained his fixed point of reference for God-talk, his worldview was bound to be constructed along dualist lines, displaying a bias against the untidy diversity of human existence and a tendency to associate only the rational with the truly real.[20] Hence this further concession of a fall *into* fleshly existence, that is, of a connection between evil and the very fact of the spatio-temporal world.

The consequence of this concession was something of a compromise between gnostic pessimism and the optimism of the Judeo-Christian tradition. On the one hand, the world of space and time is admittedly not the world of God's original design, nor would it exist but for sin. The sin in question, on the other hand, does not consist in the generation of that world as such, a notion which conveniently shifts attention away from human failure by positing more than one god or a breakdown in the primordial deity itself. Origen, like Irenaeus, would have no truck with such impiety. He upheld the doctrine of *creatio ex nihilo*, arguing for the goodness even of matter as the gracious provision of God. But he did so by appropriating in a quite different way the widespread tutorial concept of the physical universe: Our present world is a school for souls, belonging (according to Origen) to a process of cosmic reform which includes many such worlds. Though consequent upon a defection from

---

[18] *De Principiis* begins by acknowledging the trinitarian framework of the tradition, but the *Oxford Dictionary of the Christian Church* correctly observes that 'the point of departure of Origen's doctrinal teaching was faith in the unity of God, who is altogether transcendent.' This transcendent unity is not the relational unity of Father, Son and Spirit, though there is such, but is finally the ineffable oneness of the Father alone.

[19] Here a breach certainly does open up between God and his Logos, who is not αὐτοθέος but in some sense 'a second god' (Philo). Crouzel (182f.) acknowledges the connection with middle Platonism, while contending that the latter is partially corrected by Christian insights. But this is already a major step backwards. To Origen more than anyone else we owe the hegemony of a far too narrow notion of the Father as ἀρχή or αἰτία; of the Son as λόγος or divine reason; of the Spirit as the source of an inner light which liberates one from the pitfalls of material existence. Though the Nicenes rejected his peculiar mixture of subordinationism and emanationism (J. Lyons 1982:124; cf. *Princ.* 1.3.5ff.) they did not break its spell altogether

[20] Indeed with the divine: Origen complains (*Princ.* 1.1.6f.) that some 'are unwilling to have it understood that there is a certain affinity between the mind and God, of whom the mind is an intellectual image, and that by reason of this fact the mind, especially if it is purified and separated from bodily matter, is able to have some perception of the divine nature.' This is quite in keeping with his assertion that God is 'a simple intellectual existence [*intellectualis natura simplex*] ... Unity [Μόνας], or if I may say so, Oneness [Ἕνας] throughout, and the mind and fount from which originates all intellectual existence or mind.'

the good, it has purgatorial purposes. It is intended to facilitate the restoration of rational creatures who have strayed from their ontic foundations, to instruct them by hard labour to recover their single-minded contemplation of God. If not exactly good in and of itself, it is at least good for us.[21]

Now in its utilitarianism this *via media* winds up well short of the biblical affirmation of creation, just as Origen's reform school imagery, if we may call it that, lacks the richness and warmth of the adoption imagery of Irenaeus.[22] Once again the spatio-temporal realm is considered to be the result, if no longer simply the product, of a failure or mistake. When its remedial purposes are fully achieved, it will have disappeared. For the end of the cosmic process – so goes his famous principle – will be like the beginning, when all spirits have returned safely to the realm of pure rational being from their sojourns in a strange land.[23] J. W. Trigg observes correctly that in Origen's hands even the revolutionary doctrine of *creatio ex nihilo* is made to serve an eschatology more Greek than biblical, indeed, more Greek than the Greeks' own. What has a beginning (i.e., matter) must have an end; eternity belongs to the mind and the mind to eternity. In other words, the Alexandrian employed a reversible and self-cancelling cosmology. The things of this world are to be 'left behind and superseded.'[24]

Perhaps such hybrid ideas are by nature doomed to be gnostic in the last analysis. At all events, we are able to understand the admission of Butterworth, in his introduction to the theology of de Principiis, that the descent/ascent theme 'runs through it all' in a manner reminiscent of the

[21] See *Princ.* 1.6, 2.9, 2.11.6, etc.; *Gen.* 1.10f. For background Trigg (41ff., 68ff.) looks again to Plato (see esp. *Timaeus* 41ff.) and Plutarch, and to Basilides (cf. May 79ff.) and Heracleon.

[22] To say nothing about its Pelagian tendency! See e.g. *Princ.* 2.9.8: 'All these, down to the very least, God supervises by the power of his wisdom and distinguishes by the controlling hand of his judgment; and thus he has arranged the universe on the principle of a most impartial retribution, according as each one deserves for his merit to be assisted and cared for.'

[23] *Princ.* 1.6.2; cf. 1.6.4, 3.5.4, 3.6.3ff., etc. Origen, says R. Norris (1966:126), understands the world 'as the product of two 'movements': a descending movement in which being is diffused and diversified, and an ascending movement by which it is integrated again with its source.' But must we not see in this baptism of symmetry and circularity a serious error, and a major root of subsequent distortion and neglect of the doctrine of creation? Origen's anti-fatalist egalitarianism may be commendable enough in itself, but its unhappy corollary is that *sin* is the occasion of cosmic diversity (2.9.2), and divine grace an homogenizing influence.

[24] Origen is careful to say, against the Greeks, that our eternal establishment is not 'an incorporeal world that exists solely in the mind's fancy or the unsubstantial region of thought;' but he does not mean to be mistaken for an Irenaean! (See *Princ.* 2.3.6f.; cf. Trigg 110, Crouzel 107.) Since he too wants to rescue rational spirits from the doubtful ontological status of everything that has a beginning by appealing *behind* temporal reality to a prior connection with eternity (*Gen.* 1.1f.), 'consummation' is still restitution to an immaterial mode of being.

systems of the heretics.[25] In Origen too descent can be measured by degrees of materiality. Ascent, as a soteriological movement, again means a stripping away of what belongs to our present existence, not a planting but a plucking up of the infelicitous seeds of diversity falsely pressed into the eternal field of rational being.[26] The fruitfulness motif so prominent in Irenaeus is absent, being much too earthy, too sexual; that of overcoming nature is given virtually its opposite sense. Growth and advance, to be sure, are concepts as dear to Origen as to the bishop of Lyons. Unfortunately they operate here in such a way that the realization of the inner man is inversely related to the realization of the outer. There will be no hairdressers in heaven, he remarks wryly.[27]

Shall we say, then, that Origen fails to overturn the dualist option of redemption from, not of, the creaturely realm as we know it? On the contrary, he does not even try to do so. What he does attempt is to link that redemption – the purification, illumination and perfection of the inner man, the ascent of the soul – to faith in Jesus Christ, and to furnish it with a cosmological framework at once more daring and more satisfying than those of the Platonists, Stoics or gnostics. But his is only a relative and not a radical reconfiguration. Henri Crouzel asserts that Origen 'excludes all dualism,' and that may be the case if by dualism we mean a perpetual warring of mind and matter, good and evil, etc., which will admit no resolution.[28] But it is clearly otherwise when the word is understood in the sense in which we have been using it, since the resolution for which he hopes does entail the weaning of the soul from bodily existence. *Pace* Irenaeus, the image of God is situated in man's rational nature alone, and is given with the first creation not the present one. The achievement of a true likeness based on the image is *hindered* by body, especially by a variety of gross material bodies such as we now have.[29] On the way to that likeness we should expect 'gradually and by degrees, during the lapse of infinite and immeasurable ages,' to arrive at a single

---

[25] G. W. Butterworth (Origen, *On First Principles*, liv) is following Eugène de Faye.

[26] Cf. *Princ.* 2.9.2. The tutorial of time is brought to a conclusion when all diversity and confusion has been eliminated, under precepts 'to which nothing can ever be added' (3.6.9).

[27] Trigg 114 (from Jerome, *ad Ioh. Ier.* 25f.); cf. *Princ.* 2.11.7. Origen's articulation of the themes of progress and advance (e.g. 3.6.8f.) often appear to owe something to Irenaeus, but there is simply no room in the Alexandrian's eschatological vision for what is recognizably human in any well-rounded sense – unless speculation about spherical resurrection bodies qualifies! This also has implications for the present, of course; according to Origen saints do not even celebrate their birthdays, for they are not happy to be living in 'this body of death.'

[28] Dualism in the strong sense appears to be excluded by his doctrine of God's freedom as creator, yet even here hard questions might be asked, since the original creation is said in spite of its contingency to be both eternal and necessary. Cf. *Princ.* 1.2.10, Crouzel 216.

[29] See *Princ.* 3.6.1ff. (cf. 4.4.9f.), *Gen.* 1.13, *Cels.* 4.30. In working with an *imago/similitudo* distinction Origen indicates that the end is in some sense an advance on the beginning. But in what sense – that of having overcome, by bitter experience, all temptation to subject ourselves to bodily existence?

cosmic body of 'extreme fineness.' And beyond that, when God actually becomes all in all, 'the whole of bodily nature [shall] be resolved into that substance which is superior to all others, namely, into the divine nature, than which nothing can be better.'[30]

Since it is not entirely clear whether the cosmic process of diversification and reunion is one that can be assumed not to repeat itself indefinitely, we may want to disagree with Crouzel about dualism even in the stricter sense.[31] But more germane to the doctrine of the ascension is M. J. Edwards' effort to exonerate Origen of dualism in the looser sense as well, by arguing that he ties body and soul more tightly together than do predecessors such as Irenaeus. For Origen, it is true, the very substance of the body varies according to the movements of the soul that rules over it. As the latter ascends towards God the former undergoes the requisite alteration; it is not simply abandoned.[32] His more orthodox predecessors, however, would surely have joined their heirs in asking what this means, if not that the body is purged by the soul of everything that pertains to *our* bodies.[33] They might even have suggested that binding the body quite so tightly to the soul – thus individualizing the resurrection, as Edwards points out – is not so very different from breaking the bond altogether. Origen, not yet faced with an ecumenical anathema, would only have shrugged. What can one say to folk who insist that flesh and blood are capable of incorruption?[34]

---

[30] Thus Jerome, *Avit.* 10; see *Princ.* 3.6.9, where Rufinus, as so often, has something more guarded. In 2.3 Origen has already presented (in parallel with the disciple's advance to mystical knowledge?) three possible interpretations of what happens to our bodies: the progression to a purely ethereal body; to no body at all; to 'that other world' in which a truly divine existence is possible.

[31] See *Princ.* 4.4.8 (cf. Jerome, *Avit.* 14). Is there 'a safe and most sure abode' from which no further falling can ever occur? Only, it would seem, if even the potential for bodily existence is removed in the consummation of all things, which would mean also the end of free will. (Cf. Norris 123ff.) But it may not be possible to resolve the question of the one and the many at this level. The logic of emanation and return, which Origen has tried to combine with the doctrine of *creatio ex nihilo*, will not permit it, for it is the logic of an infinite series.

[32] *Princ.* 3.6.6f.

[33] Edwards (1995:517f.) compares the resurrection body to 'the chariot of the *Phaedrus*, the astral body of Neoplatonism.' We find his argument as to its permanence unconvincing, but two other matters must also be mentioned. First, the irony in attempting to defend Origen from the charge of dualism with a statement such as the following: 'No doubt the elevation of the body entails a purging of its gross materiality, but this does not make it any less a body, just as the soul is none the less a soul when it sheds its sins' (506). Second, the error in saying that only Origen proposes 'that the body may be affected by the soul.' For Irenaeus too the soul is granted 'the reason of an artist' in order to rule over the body (cf. *AH* 2.29.1f., 2.33.4); that will not mean the purging of materiality, however, since materiality is *not* coordinated with sin.

[34] Cf. *AH* 5.3.3, 5.5.2, 5.9f.; *Princ.* 2.3.6, 2.10.3, *Cels.* 5.19. The privatizing of resurrection only reinforces our point: Origen, his 'relational' ontology notwithstanding, places the inner and outer dimensions of human being in competition. (*Pace* Edwards, J. R. Lyman 1993:47ff., *et.al.*, see again *Princ.* 1.1.5ff., 1.6ff., 3.6, 4.4.6ff.)

Naturally there are a number of questions we ourselves might like to put to Origen before turning more specifically to christology and the ascension of Jesus, questions about the coherence of his scheme and its wider implications: about the revival of determinism, for example, in his equation of protology and eschatology; or about the privative character of his own 'relational' view of time; or about the justice of charging the disadvantaged with having received neither more nor less than they deserve.[35] All that really needs remarking here, however, is that his alternative subverts both the continuity and the discontinuity crucial to Irenaeus. By standing Genesis 1–3 on its head, Origen (like Hick, who ought rather to have taken the Alexandrian for his model) conflates creation and redemption. The making of this world is already a redemptive act.[36] On the one hand, then, the sharp distinction between corruption and incorruption – the shearing effect of the cross – gives way to gradualism, absorbed in that 'immeasurable' loop of descending and ascending aeons which joins the end to the beginning. On the other hand, in this same gradualism the daring proximity between temporal and eternal life is also destroyed. A eucharistic worldview is no longer possible.[37]

* * *

Bernard McGinn observes of Origen that 'his *theologia ascendens* (to use von Balthasar's phrase) departs from Platonism both in its christocentrism and in its biblical foundation.'[38] But that departure neither undoes the

---

[35] Indeed, this may present itself to many as one of the most objectionable features; nor should it be overlooked that a causal connection between suffering and sin, in justifying God, will serve also to justify systemic social oppression as well, as it sometimes has in Oriental thought (cf. *Princ.* 1.6.2).

[36] Origen thus appears a very modern theologian – or are those of Hick's persuasion rather less modern than may be supposed? Trigg, by the way, reminds us that περὶ Ἀρχῶν was written partly as a defense of the Genesis commentary.

[37] 'The weakness of Origen's system, considered as a whole, lies in its assumption that the entire cosmic process is a mistake, due to the misuse of freewill,' writes Butterworth (lviii). Crouzel (217) too is forced to admit that this is 'certainly the most vulnerable' aspect of his thought. But let us not sidestep the implications! Eucharistic hope vanishes along with the eucharistic tension, for it is *the salvation of this world of ours* which Origen cannot conceive. Nor does his preference (*Princ.* 2.3.6) for the intra-mundane rather than the supra-mundane as a location for the 'other world' reintroduce the proximity in question. See Farrow 1998.

[38] 1/115f. The debt to Philo should be further acknowledged here. Several of Philo's moves – his allegorical reading of the Pentateuch, e.g., together with his logocentrism and his transformation of 'Platonic contemplation into a more personalistic mode' (ibid. 36) – were vital to Origen's construct. Likewise the debt to Clement, who shared with contemporary Platonists the notion of 'ascent' as a process of purification, illumination and vision, but taught Origen how to begin adapting it to the Christian message.

family resemblance nor takes him very far from the gnostics, of whom similar things might be said. In both cases the ascension theme is firmly attached to a principle, at once cosmological and psychological, which predetermines its character. In neither is it derived, as it is in Irenaeus, directly from the biblical witness to Jesus-history.

We must quickly acknowledge, of course, that the undoing of the fall is said by Origen to depend upon Jesus' revelatory and redemptive work. Indeed the descending and ascending of the whole creation finds in him, and particularly in his cross as a sign of the complete subjugation of the flesh, its turning point or hinge.[39] His own restoration to glory, however, is manifestly not a restoration in the flesh, which would be a contradiction in terms. Given his prior commitments, Origen is bound to interpret Jesus' pioneering ascension much more conservatively as a movement of the mind. In his influential work *On Prayer* we receive the following guidance:

> And let us seek to understand in a mystical sense the words at the end of the Gospel according to John, 'Touch me not; for I am not yet ascended to my Father,' thinking of the ascension of the Son to the Father in a manner more befitting his divinity, with sanctified perspicuity, as an ascension of the mind rather than of the body.[40]

Origen thus takes his leave rather of the apostolic tradition – as preached among the simple – by way of an appeal to spiritual exegesis. This is not merely a concession to his own desire, with scripture's help, 'to gallop through the vast spaces of mystic and spiritual understanding.'[41] It is completely in keeping with his belief that 'the Word of God has arranged certain stumbling blocks, as it were, and hindrances and impossibilities to be inserted in the midst of the law and the history,' lest 'by never moving away from the letter [we should] fail to learn anything of the more divine element . . .'[42] Now in disputing with Celsus he makes plain that he does not regard the resurrection stories themselves as hindrances or impossibilities. He believes with the church 'that Jesus actually rose again': historically, not mythically or in anyone's hallucinatory fever. But naturally he wants to understand this history in a

---

[39] Cf. Lyman 69ff. Origen thus agrees with Irenaeus that Christ came at the nadir of history, 'when the end of the world was near at hand and the whole human race was hastening towards its final destruction' (*Princ.* 3.5.6). But since his construct is not a eucharistic one, we are not surprised to discover that from that time 'events have begun to hasten towards the ideal of all being one as the Father is one with the Son' (3.6.4; cf. 2.3.5).

[40] τῆς ἀναβάσεως πρὸς τὸν πατέρα τοῦ υἱοῦ θεοπρεπέστερον μετὰ ἁγίας τρανότητος ἡμῖν νοουμένης, ἥντινα ἀνάβασιν νοῦς μᾶλλον ἀναβαίνει σώματος (23.2).

[41] *Rom.* 7.11 (quoted McGinn 112, in another connection); cf. *Gen.* 1.7 and *Luke* frag. 257, noting in the latter the relation between ascension as a movement of the mind and the doctrines of creation and cross.

[42] *Princ.* 4.2.9. Part of the interpreter's task is to recognize, in the New Testament as in the Old, that which is true *only* in a spiritual sense, the bodily sense in itself being misleading (as presumably in the Lukan account, e.g.).

manner consistent with his cosmology. What Thomas and the others saw was 'the body of the soul,' says Origen, 'in a form in every respect like its former shape;' for at the time Jesus was 'in a sort of intermediate state between the solidity of the body as it was before his passion and the condition of the soul uncovered by any body.' The work of the incarnation being finished, his divinity was already becoming 'more brilliant' and, conversely, his presence in the world more difficult to discern with carnal eyes.[43] The ascension, we may surmise, would complete this process of thinning and glorifying.

Like the gnostics, then, if a little more gently, he drives a wedge between the human Jesus and the exalted Christ. Certainly his sanctified perspicuity does not see in the ascension the receiving up of a Jewish rabbi into the bosom of the Father, such that the man himself is established as the ground and measure and lord of all God's works. That notion *is* a hindrance and an impossibility. It sees instead the detachment of his soul from this grosser realm, and the marking out of a path for other righteous souls to follow in escaping the tentacles of the sensual world into which they have sunk.[44] To do so they must look through and *beyond* the Jesus of history to the pre-incarnate, and now post-incarnate, Logos. For the ascension itself teaches us that it is not really his human nature which ought to interest us, but his 'superior' nature.[45]

The contrast with Irenaeus is here at its sharpest. Origen's universal or cosmic Christ, 'the truth and life of all things that exist,' is definitely not God's embodied λόγος, as spoken in the world of man. He is rather the λόγος ἄσαρκος, whom (in a curious redrafting of Colossians 1:15) the Alexandrian identifies as 'the invisible image of the invisible God.' This invisible image is the real mediator between God and creation, from all eternity. He has both divine and cosmic attributes, but in him there is nothing 'perceptible to the senses' and not 'the least reason to understand

---

[43] See *Cels.* 2.56ff. Origen here takes up the gnostic claim that different people would have seen Jesus in different ways – though Jesus is one, he is careful to say – according to their spiritual capacity. His handling of this idea is neither gnostic nor Irenaean, but again something of a compromise.

[44] We too may hope, on the basis of our forerunner, 'that after the "troubles and strivings" here we shall come to the topmost heavens,' where 'we shall always be engaged in the contemplation of the invisible things of God' (*Cels.* 6.20; cf. John 14:3, Heb. 4:14, *Phaedrus* 247b,c).

[45] On the προηγούμενη οὐσία (*Joh.* 6.154ff.) see Lyons 135f. Though Lyman (72ff.) insists that Origen remains interested in the soul of Jesus, one of the difficulties inherent in his dualist anthropology is the problem of the identity of souls. According to *Timaeus* 41 – on which he is heavily dependent – souls, so to speak, are all of a piece (see K. Wesche 1996:30ff.). Hence in that end that is like the beginning there is to be not only an abandonment of bodies but of *names* (thus Anathema 14, and this makes good sense if 'the mind will no longer be conscious of anything besides or other than God,' *Princ.* 3.6.3). Would it not then appear that the soul nearest to the Logos, indeed united to him by an indissoluble bond, is in its ascension already well on the way to divine anonymity?

anything corporeal.'[46] His union with the flesh, mediated in its turn by the pre-existent soul of Jesus, is temporary not permanent. Which is to say, the Irenaean notion of recapitulation, with its triumph of the particular, is firmly set aside. In a return to christomonism Origen exchanges it for one based on the 'totallizing' function of the λόγος, in which the full-blooded figure of Jesus plays but a brief part: at that crucial point where the history of diversification begins to reverse itself, hastening once more 'towards the ideal of all being one.'[47]

It may be allowed that Origen, in contradiction of the gnostics, confesses an actual incarnation as well as an historical resurrection; docetism is disavowed.[48] But by limiting Christ's bodily humanity to a brief soteriological phase – and certainly we are no longer to think of him 'as being confined within those narrow limits in which he once lived for our sakes,' when in fact he 'is everywhere and runs throughout all things' – Origen reintroduces the docetic heresy in an eschatological form.[49] Indeed he has to do so, given the constraints imposed by his protology. By positing a mediating λόγος more fundamental than Jesus, or at all events by positing a prior union of that λόγος with Jesus' pre-existent soul, he shifts the link between the divine and the creaturely to a sphere in which the flesh is not yet taken into account.[50] In that way he endorses the gnostic view respecting the *object* of redemption, even while differing as to the method: It is not man as we know him but the immortal soul of man (as of angels, demons, etc.) which requires and receives salvation through the condescension of the saviour. The suspicion that this is moving in a docetic direction after all is confirmed by the outcome. After completing his work in the flesh the saviour himself no longer participates in the vagaries of human existence, and neither shall we. The wine of Christ, as Crouzel observes, 'takes one out of the human.'[51]

Now this neo-docetism, which knows a descent into the flesh but no ascent *of* the flesh, does not deny to the economy an abiding significance. It does however reinterpret that significance iconically, so to speak.

---

[46] See *Princ.* 1.2.4ff. and 2.6 (cf. Lyons 117). The opening lines of the first homily on Genesis read much like Irenaeus, but by 'the saviour of all, Jesus Christ' Origen means not the incarnate Word but the invisible Word.

[47] 'The First-born is a world (κόσμος) containing the principles (λόγοι) according to which all things made by God have been created (γεγένεται),' as Lyons puts it (114). Recapitulation, then, means a 'totalling up' or 'totalling together' (συγκεφαλαίωσις) of all things as they converge under his direction into a single cosmos or a single perfect result (ἀποτέλεσμα). See *Frag. in Eph.* 6, 11.2–11 (quoted Lyons 144); cf. *Princ.* 3.6.4.

[48] See *Princ.* 1.pref.4 and 2.6.2, a moving and justifiably famous passage; cf. e.g. *Cels.* 3.28.

[49] *Princ.* 2.11.6. See Anathemas 7–10 (*Nicene and Post-Nicene Fathers*, 2nd series, 14/316ff.).

[50] *Princ.* 2.6.3. Crouzel's observation (220) that 'it is the God-man who is directly the subject of the kenosis' suggests a point of agreement not so much with Irenaeus as with his opponents.

[51] p. 129. Irenaeus, of course, believed that one discovers one's humanity in Christ.

What the Gnostics merely represented as a more or less valuable appearance
– namely, the historical work of Christ – was to Origen no appearance but
truth. But he did not view it as *the* truth, and in this he agrees with the
Gnostics, but as *a* truth, beyond which lies a higher.[52]

Our own ascent requires us to recognize this, for we cannot follow Christ
by clinging, as it were, to the bottom rung of the ladder. The one who
from all eternity 'interprets and presents to the rational creation the secrets
of wisdom and the mysteries of knowledge,' if he is to reach us in our
fallen estate, must do so in historical form, making himself the λόγος
even of our earthly knowledge of God. But his ascension invites us to
penetrate more deeply, to transcend what belongs to the earth. It points
us heavenward, towards things that cannot be grasped κατὰ σάρκα.[53]
Christ may now be adored not so much as the Word made flesh but as
'the angel of great counsel,' as Origen liked to call him, as the master
tutor who mediates to the wise those divine mysteries through which their
own souls are instructed in the art of ascension.[54]

Origen's tutorial cosmology thus produces its corollary in christology,
which also gravitates towards the pedagogical. And in this way, let it be
noted, *the problem of the presence and the absence is rationalized and
internalized along with the ascension itself.* It becomes a question of the
cultivation of a spiritual mind, of the fine-tuning of the inner person to
an invisible reality, and is no longer bound up with the matter of a man's
departure and return. In other words, it too is de-historicized. Not surprisingly, one discovers in Origen very little of the biblical tension
between two opposing histories preserved by Irenaeus, or of the equally
biblical optimism about our world which eagerly awaits its vindication
at the parousia. That eschatological dialectic is supplanted by something much more formal and sterile: the tracing of a purgatorial circle
focused on the soul's departure from and return to God;[55] that is, on

---

[52] Harnack 2/368f. Crouzel (99ff.) offers a helpful discussion of education through images,
and of the various levels, corresponding to Plato's five elements of knowledge, on which
one might learn to recognize Christ. (According to *Cels.* 6.9: ὄνομα = the prophetic revelation
which climaxes in John the Baptist; λόγος = the historical Jesus; ἐίδωλον = the Christ in
each of us; ἐπιστήμη = the wisdom found in the perfect; to which can be added, presumably,
ἰδέα = the Logos or cosmic Christ contemplated in the beatific vision. See ibid. 112f., 221ff.)

[53] J. Meyendorff (1975:176f.) draws our attention to a letter of Eusebius of Caesarea to
Constantine's sister: 'It contains a very clear exposition of Origen's doctrine of salvation.
The "form of a servant" assumed by the Logos was no longer in the realm of realities. He
undoubtedly assumed it, but in order to transform it into a divine reality; it is important,
therefore, that the Christians, if they desire to anticipate the glory that is his . . . should
contemplate God in the purity of their hearts and not in artificial images of a historical past
that is now over.' Indeed, according to *Joh.* 1.51f., the economy of the incarnation should
be left behind *as quickly as possible.*

[54] See Trigg 1983:101, 1991:35ff. (cf. Irenaeus *AH* 3.16.3; see also Blair 32ff.). That this
art includes virtue, and is not merely an intellectual art (Lyman 80f.), may be granted.

[55] Of which Jerome remarks in *Con. Joh. Hier.* 19 (quoted Butterworth 41 n. 1), though
perhaps not altogether ingenuously: 'What you admire so much we long ago despised when
we found it in Plato.'

the restoration of a rational cosmos through rational means, a distant but certain ἀποκατάστασις.

Christology, as we have said, is not allowed to correct this scheme but must support it. Only thus can we explain the really quite astounding fact that at the outset of de Principiis Origen quietly passes over the parousia altogether in setting out the apostolic faith, while transferring the themes of conflict and judgment, revelation and salvation, from the public arena of human history to the private arena of the soul.[56] The marginalization of the concrete humanity of Jesus and the privatization of eschatology – which means also its collectivization – go hand in hand. Might it not be said that the fatal transition from history to philosophy is accomplished just here, in the decapitation of Jesus-history which naturally follows any such reinterpretation of the ascension as Origen attempts? That is our own judgment; but some of the questions it raises we must set aside in order to attend specifically to the ecclesiological consequences of his project, which are enormous.

***

The fact that Origen himself has almost nothing to say on the subject in his most schematized work allows for a very simple explanation. His ecclesiology, as J. A. Lyons remarks,[57] is 'clearly a facet of his cosmology' and is largely assimilated to it, requiring no separate treatment. Indeed in Origen's case cosmology is ecclesiology, and ecclesiology cosmology. For the history of the world is the history of the fall and restoration of the church, and the history of the church the history of all rational beings.[58]

Aided by his christology, Origen employs the treacherous distinction between a heavenly and an earthly church in the service of this universalism. Just as the saviour pre-exists the temporal realms, so his church also pre-exists with him as the sum total of rational spirits, the *corpus verum*.[59] Its empirical counterpart today is the *corpus permixtum*, that community of faith (differing widely in degree of spiritual

---

[56] See 1.pref.4ff., which begins in a quite promising way but (from the standpoint of the baptismal confession) veers off course before completing the task; a fleeting reference to the parousia is made in 4.3.13, but only in connection with the distinction between the temporal and eternal gospels. Harnack (2/369 n. 1) rightly speaks of Origen's native 'aversion to the early Christian eschatology.'

[57] p. 142.

[58] Origen's *via media* thus turns out to be both less and *more* optimistic than the Christian tradition generally: less, because he is interested only in the spiritual aspect of the universe; more, because faith in the ultimate unity and stability of rational being points him in a universalist direction. The fallen bride is 'every race of men, perhaps indeed the totality of all creation,' claims Origen (*Pss.* 36.2.1; cf. *Princ.* 4.3.7), departicularizing the people of God in a completely different way than that suggested in our first chapter.

[59] See Crouzel 219f., Lyons 136f.; cf. *Princ.* 1.2.4, *Cant.* 2.8, *Matt.* 14.17.

advancement) which serves the rest of humanity much as Jesus did, namely, as model, tutor and intercessor. As an extension of his redemptive activity, it interprets to the world its destiny to ascend with the ascending saviour, while age after purgatorial age strips away the impurities that separate us from our origin and goal.

We can indicate some of the most salient features of this ecclesiology by marking briefly two characteristics that are virtually the reverse of those we found in Irenaeus. Perhaps the more obvious one is a deeply rooted individualism. Allegiance to the Greek notion of ascension as a movement of the mind makes inevitable, however paradoxically, an atomistic view of the church. The search for unity with the hidden Logos, in turning us inwards and away from the distraction of earthly particularities, turns us also from our fellow humans. An Irenaean interest in κοινωνία finds little encouragement here. Instead there is a focus on the disciplined advance of the inner man, on one's own private spiritual journey, and on the Christ who is formed in each of us.[60] This generates a tendency towards the privatization of the sacraments, and towards sacramental nominalism.[61] Moreover, where the local church fails to serve the individual's journey satisfactorily, it may be replaced by a form of community more adept at doing so; witness the rapid growth of the monastic houses, for example, which in many places were intensely Origenist.

It should be noted in passing that the intellectual mysticism which sustains this individualism is nourished in turn by a much leaner pneumatology. In Origen's worldview the Spirit is not so much the creator Spirit as simply the Spirit of wisdom and holiness. *Contemplatio* and *imitatio* are the activities that come to the fore as authentically Christian modes of being, then, while the social and material aspects of life in the eucharistic community are correspondingly downgraded.[62] No doubt this

---

[60] 'And every soul, virgin and uncorrupted, which conceives by the Holy Spirit, so as to give birth to the Will of the Father, is the Mother of Jesus' (*Matt.* frag. 281). See McGinn 125ff., who in quoting this passage notes that Origen here initiates 'a potent theme in the history of Christian mysticism.' McGinn denies that the mystical life is 'a Plotinian "flight of the alone to the Alone,"' since it is mediated to the fallen soul through 'the "great sacrament" of the church.' This agrees with Crouzel, but of course the question is – mediated *how*, and to what end?

[61] His association of infant baptism with the cleansing of the soul from the carnal act by which it enters the world already signals a privatizing tendency. And *pace* Crouzel, we think Origen's 'sacramentalism' more Platonist than Christian, since it is tied to the antithesis between perceptible and intelligible. It is not in fact a sacramental point of view if it is the 'ethical and contemplative virtue' conferred by the word (225f.) which really matters to Origen. (See e.g. *Matt.* 11.14; cf. A. Heron 1983b:68f., Pelikan 1/170, H. Wybrew 1989:24f.)

[62] Working on the ancient epistemological principle that 'only the like knows the like,' Origen naturally stresses the idea of imitating or 'following' God (Crouzel 96ff.; cf. Trigg 60). The Spirit's work (*Princ.* 1.3.5ff.) is to bring all to a 'unity of contemplation,' not to enable them to be 'real humans' in the Irenaean sense; no wonder, then, if some of the fizz disappears from the ecclesial winepress.

has something to do with the fact that the links between Spirit and eucharist – and indeed between church and eucharist[63] – are very thin in Origen, though for an explanation of that we may also appeal directly to his rejection of ascension in the flesh. A doctrine of the church 'seen mainly in its spiritual aspect' (as Crouzel puts it)[64] follows naturally enough on the heels of the disappearance of the human Jesus into a cosmic Christ.

The second characteristic evolves out of the first, which appears to require a compensatory development in the direction of the collective. It is in Origen, not Irenaeus, that we find the beginnings of an institutionalism seriously out of step with the New Testament. Let us explain. The earthly church, which (following Clement) he calls the city of God, is at once an imitation of the eternal or heavenly church and a reflection of the stratified cosmos.[65] It is, as we have said, a mixed society, embracing many who remain heavily entangled in the web of idolatry associated with perceptible reality. But at its core are the τέλειοι, who have already attained a high degree of unity with Christ in the secret places of the soul. These are the true – though not necessarily the official – priests and deacons, who function as the spiritual eyes of the church below insofar as they participate already in the church above, that κυρίως ἐκκλησία which exists timelessly in the bosom of God as its exemplar.[66] Now if this blending of formalism and spiritual elitism (sic) seems at first glance to enshrine an anti-institutional bias, it has in fact the opposite effect. The transference of spiritual leadership from the official presbyterate to the enlightened, contrary to Origen's intention, leaves room for an increasingly pragmatic and politicized view of the former.[67] More importantly, perhaps, the exemplarist framework concedes to visible ecclesiastical symbols a kind of revelatory necessity for the simpliciores, in a way that readily attracts a host of subsidiary devices to point them towards the heavenly mysteries.

It is in this last connection that Harnack charges Origen with having, ironically, 'a principal share in introducing the apparatus of polytheism into the church.'[68] And certainly the Alexandrian did lend a disturbing

---

[63] Crouzel 229.

[64] p. 221.

[65] Much of this comes from Clement; see Kelly 201ff. for references and comment.

[66] Note that the priest symbolizes the inspired exegete, and that the whole visible hierarchy 'is in fact the image of the hierarchy of holiness' (Crouzel 222). Note too that, though Christ 'runs through all things' and is the saviour of all, he remains 'the mediator of a privileged knowledge of God to a select few' (Trigg 1991:35), just because the problem of the presence and the absence has become a matter of degree.

[67] It is true that his view of church leadership 'contrasts markedly' with a merely formal approach (Trigg 1983:145; cf. 1991:50). But may we not see in this graded spirituality, i.e., in the notion of ascension by degrees, the basis of a corpus permixtum concept which later helped to justify inclusion of the lightly sprinkled masses, thus spawning the political bishop?

[68] 2/368; cf. 3/2f., where Harnack suggests a more general connection between Logos speculation, development of the notion of the mysteries, and a growing dependence of the people on the ecclesiastical institution.

new significance to the formalities of ecclesial life; esoteric and exoteric forms of Christianity were equally well served.[69] But we cannot perceive the full extent of his contribution to the institutionalism that over the centuries has so extensively transfigured the church, without reckoning also with the way in which his universalist perspective situates the people of God historically and in the public sphere. Which brings us back to our discussion about continuity and discontinuity.

By now it will be obvious that Origen is the real source of the idea of the general ascent of man, and of the doctrine of progress in a collective sense. Many elements come together in *de Principiis* to produce it: the biblical belief in salvation history, already incorporated by Irenaeus into a process-oriented anthropology; the cyclical cosmology of the Stoics, altered and opened up by the Platonist notion of free will; Christian faith in a universal gospel, transformed into actual universalism in the interests of theodicy and of philosophical theology. Unfortunately we cannot delve further into its origins, though we shall come in due course to the manner in which the idea took hold in the modern period.[70] What is important here is that Origen sees the church as *the mediator of progress*, laying down the necessary principles through its doctrine and gathering up human response through its liturgies. Indeed the church is identified as the 'internal regulative principle of the cosmos,' as Christ is of the church.[71]

We intimated earlier that Origen's purgatorial view of history – for that is what his doctrine of ascension comes to in the end – subverts Irenaeus' eucharistic cosmology. Similarly, the notion of the church as κόσμος of the cosmos deconstructs his understanding of the continuity and discontinuity between church and world. Discontinuity may be stark enough by outward appearances, as it was in Origen's own experience. But it no longer means that each is on a different course. What after all is the world but an extension of the church, the church in a more fragmented form?[72] Hence the fateful notion arises, as circumstances permit, that the

---

[69] Cf. ibid. 2/343.

[70] We may prepare for that discussion by noting, firstly, that his doctrine of progess is rooted paradoxically in an essentially *negative* view of history, which begins as an undesirable eruption of particularities that the Logos undertakes by patient persuasion to quell. Secondly, that it is bound up with a move to *universalize* the incarnation (at the expense of all *caro*). For 'with Jesus human and divine nature began to be woven together, so that by fellowship with divinity human nature might become divine' (*Cels.* 3.28), and that interweaving is slowly extending itself to all rational creatures (cf. Anathemas 12–14).

[71] Lyons 142f. The Logos 'is the initiator of order in the world and the Church its mediator,' such that the latter 'affords the precondition for the final state of the cosmos' (ibid.; see *Joh.* 6.301ff., *Gen.* 1.5). It is 'an imitation of that future kingdom' in which 'the human race will one day be constituted in the world in unity' (*Princ.* 1.6.2).

[72] Origen, influenced by the Stoic *anima mundi* doctrine, makes the Logos the 'soul' both of the church and of the universe, which is 'as it were an immense, monstrous animal' sovereignly held together by that soul (*Princ.* 2.1.3; cf. *Eph.* 9.113ff., *Cels.* 6.48). Here, in this confusion between Christ, church and world, are the beginnings of a triumphalist ecclesiology.

church ought to provide for the world a spiritual foundation for social order, supervising its advance; the mediator must have her residence hard by City Hall. Hence too the notion that the church may take its own bearings in consultation with the world. Such is the practical import of Origen's well-worn dictum, which as much as any other single factor accounts for the evolution denounced by Ellul.

Of course it may be said in reply that it is quite unfair to lumber Origen with a long history (real or alleged) of ecclesial compromise. What better proof of his own keen sense of discontinuity do we need than his strong advocacy of martyrdom, for instance, or indeed his personal zeal for that privilege? The further mention of martyrdom, however, serves only to make our point, for its meaning has undergone a significant change. In Irenaeus martyrdom is above all an expression of continuity with the world, through what we called an opposition of affirmation. In Origen it is an expression of one's rejection of the world, and hence an affirmation of opposition – the opposition of spirit to flesh.[73] With this rejection the compromise in question is not incompatible, even if Origen himself provides reasons to be wary of it. It is rather the logical outcome of the internalization of the problem of the presence and the absence.

In sum, then, it seems to us that in the ecclesiology of Origen we catch a glimpse of what will later manifest itself as the Janus-like character of the Christian church: the alienation from the world which it often encourages in the saints, and the *rapprochement* which it seeks as an institution. Given the conviction that the cross of Jesus had brought the world of becoming to its nadir, and that the course of the aeons had now been turned towards the reintegration of all things, Origen could no doubt afford to concentrate on the individual soul as the true arena of cosmic conflict. But in consequence the principle of the precariousness of *ecclesial* being was undermined. The eucharistic tension so vital to Irenaeus was exchanged for the old metaphysical ones, leaving room for the possibility that the church as an institution might sooner or later fit quite comfortably in the midst of human society, serving as its spiritual eye and conscience, just as the τέλειοι do in the church itself. Otherwise put, the soil in which the Constantinian temptation might flourish was prepared well in advance.

Now it is not at all necessary to decide whether Origen intended that his speculative enterprise, his theology γυμναστικῶς, should impose itself

---

[73] McGinn (1/127), though not making our point about Irenaeus' view, makes clear Origen's revision: 'While he still views martyrdom as an *imitatio Christi* in ways not unlike those found in earlier literature (e.g., *Exhortation* 12, 28, 36–37, 42), the martyr is now seen not so much oppositionally, as the one who confronts pagan demonism through his speaking out for Jesus, as "gradationally" (to use Alison Elliot's term), that is, as the one who brings to perfection the soul's desire to separate itself from the earthly body and material things (e.g., *Exhortation* 3, 12).' To this we have another sort of testimony – possibly malicious – in the rumour about his self-castration.

on a biblical or orthodox faith, for impose itself it did. His works contain 'the germ of innumerable developments,' as Richard Norris has said,[74] many of which are still unfolding today. Indeed, one testimony to his greatness can be found in the fact that even the anathema of the fifth council was unable to prevent that, or to suppress for long the admiration he generally commands from fellow theologians. Yet we cannot disagree either with the council or with Porphyry's famous verdict that here was a Christian who 'thought like the Greeks, inasmuch as he introduced their ideas into the myths of other peoples.'[75] We may however correct the latter by insisting that in his truce with gnosticism Origen corrupted history (Jesus-history not least) with myth. That said, it is time to turn to the chief western influence on Christian theology, tracing our second backwards step.

Augustine

We hesitate to describe the teachings of St Augustine, whether on the ascension or the church, as a backwards step. On what grounds would we do so? If we allow that Irenaeus and Origen bequeathed to subsequent theologians two opposing models – one working from a centre in Jesus-history, the other in cosmic history and the journey of the soul; one defending the faith, the other defending God; one teaching ascension in the flesh, the other ascension of the mind – Augustine might possibly be said to waver between the two. But in the end he is happy enough to take the part of Irenaeus. In his last great work (though itself a work of apologetics with a title harking back to the Alexandrians) does he not openly rebuke Origen for his pagan philosophical assumptions, and especially for his ideas about pre-existence?[76] Does he not there insist on the ascension of Jesus in the flesh, deriding that 'little coterie of skeptics' who, remaining true to the premises of Greek cosmology, were still holding out against this doctrine?

> Even if we should grant that the resurrection of the earthly body was once beyond belief, the fact is that the whole world now believes that the earthly body of Christ has been taken up to heaven. Learned and unlearned alike no

---

[74] p. 107.

[75] 'Simply the metaphysics of the age,' is Harnack's judgment (2/341), in keeping with that of Porphyry (see Eusebius, *EH* 6.19). Of course from Rufinus to Henri de Lubac and Crouzel it has been protested that Origen was at heart a biblical theologian who struggled deeply with the conclusions to which he found himself driven in his defense of God's justice and mercy, and of hope for all rational creatures. We do not need to reject either opinion entirely to conclude that his theodicy project was in fact a disaster for the church, since it meant qualifying the goodness of creation, rejecting our embodied humanity, and undermining the eucharistic identity of the church.

[76] See *de Civitate Dei* 11.4ff., 22f. (cf. 21.17). Cf. Basil, who in the *Hexaemeron* (1.5) lends some credence to them.

longer doubt the resurrection of his flesh and his ascension into heaven, while there is but a handful of those who continue to be puzzled.[77]

Who, for that matter, speaks more often of the ascension than Augustine? And was it not he who argued that the foundation of the church does not lie here with us but with Christ who ascended, thus making explicit the systematic connection we are exploring?[78] How then are we to see in his work a backwards step?

To answer this question properly we must take stock of prior developments. Apart from the contributions of Irenaeus and Origen, discussion of the ascension in the period leading up to the great councils was not extensive. Origen's influence notwithstanding, the church followed the scriptures and the baptismal creed in a doctrine which embraced rather than repudiated the bodily dimensions of man. Tertullian, Hippolytus, Cyprian, Novatian and Methodius, likewise, all spoke of 'flesh ascending' and sitting at the right hand of God.[79] Such bold thoughts (bold because they ran counter to the accepted cosmology and were indeed counter-intuitive, having nothing to do with mysticism or any other familiar mode of discourse that might make sense of them[80]) were not matched by a concerted effort to follow the matter through, however. Often as not they stood side by side with their own contraries. Certainly the problem of the presence and the absence was not faced directly, whether in sacramental theology or elsewhere, and rather dubious notions about the heavenly session naturally began to take root – as if Christ were sitting above the heavenly spheres in resplendent isolation, marking time until his return to collect the faithful.[81]

---

[77] CD 22.5 (trans. G. Walsh *et.al.*; capitalization altered, as elsewhere in our use of translations of the fathers). 'It is incredible that Christ should have risen in his flesh and, with this flesh, have ascended into heaven; it is incredible that the world should have believed a thing so incredible; it is incredible that men so rude and lowly, so few and unaccomplished, should have convinced the world, including men of learning, of something so incredible and have convinced men so conclusively.' Is the first of these, he asks, more difficult to accept than the latter two?

[78] *En. Ps.* 30 (29) ii.9f.; cf. CD 15.19, which also makes clear the eschatological dimension of the church insofar as it has this heavenly foundation. See W. H. Marrevee 1967:146f.

[79] 'Flesh and blood, yet purer than ours,' says Tertullian (*Res.* 51) – who in his defense of martyrdom remarks, with an interesting turn of phrase, that the way of ascent to heaven 'was leveled with the ground by the footsteps of the Lord' (*Scor.* 10). There were exceptions to the rule, of course, on the fringes of the church. The docetic Naasseni, e.g., with whom Hippolytus contended, taught 'a spiritualizing of Christ prior to His return to the heights' (Davies 88; see 81ff.).

[80] Cf. e.g. M. Himmelfarb 1993.

[81] And soothing God's fury with man through his heavenly intercessions (Davies 121; cf. O'Donovan 1986:37), an idea easily linked to that sacrificial view of the eucharist promoted by Cyprian and Cyril of Jerusalem which so obscured its joyful, celebratory character. Cyril (*Cat.* 14.30), by the way, insists that if the ascended Christ is absent in the flesh he is nonetheless present by the Spirit, but like Tertullian he makes no effort to explore this. In Chrysostom (or is it?) we find the same simplistic *dictum*: 'Above his body, below his Spirit for us' (Davies 119).

That was the situation when, in the heat of the Arian debate, all energies began to be directed towards one paramount goal, the confession of the divinity of Christ. Here the descent of the Logos as a movement from God to man was of more urgent interest than the descending or ascending of the God-man. And as the challenge of ascension theology was pushed into the background, the doctrine also suffered a pull in the direction of eschatological docetism. To describe that pull we must touch again on the Alexandrian formula, God became man that man might become God, which Athanasius took up in *de Incarnatione*.[82] For Athanasius this formula neatly enclosed the manhood within the godhood in a way that stressed both the divinity of Christ and the soteriological importance of acknowledging it. That the formula also threatened the manhood and distorted the soteriology went unremarked. Athanasius did not interpret either the ascension or deification as Origen did: The Son's return to the Father was not a rejection of material existence, nor does our own participation in immortality imply such a thing. In his mature theology, at least, deification meant the gift of the Spirit to the whole person, body and soul, as it had for Irenaeus.[83] Nevertheless there was an ambiguity that we do not find in Irenaeus.

The source of the ambiguity is not entirely obvious, but it certainly appears to be connected with lingering doubts about the status of material existence. These doubts begin to manifest themselves when we ask, for example, about the relation between sin and death. Is death native to us as bodily creatures, as is commonly believed, or is it, as scripture says, a consequence of sin? The Greek fathers were not quite sure, though their answer was a resourceful one. Death is native to creaturehood considered in and of itself, for to be a creature is to be given existence *ex nihilo* and therefore to be under threat of dissolution; the creature does not have life or being in and for itself, as God does. But death is *not* native to creaturehood where the creative Word is taken into account, for that Word is constant and faithful and potent. Dynamic ontological categories are thus employed in a more or less Irenaean way. Human death as an actual occurrence is indeed the result of sin,[84] and redemption from sin means

---

[82] *Inc.* 54. See *Ari.* 1.37ff., where he rejects an adoptionist view of the ascension by stressing rather the descent of the divine Word: 'Therefore he was not man, and then became God, but he was God, and then became man, and that to deify us' (39). Cf. Novatian (*Trin.* 11ff.; Davies 88), who insists that 'as he ascended as man into heaven, so as God he had first descended thence.'

[83] The ascension and parousia of 'the humanity of the Lord' (ὁ κυριακὸς ἄνθρωπος) are mentioned in *Exposito Fidei*; cf. *Adel.* 5, *Ari.* 1.41. We may recall from *de Incarnatione* 22 that 'the Lord was especially concerned for the resurrection of the body,' which he proposed to offer 'as a monument to victory over death.' Likewise, by receiving the Spirit who deifies us we do not 'lose our own proper substance' (*Decr.* 3.14).

[84] According to Athanasius (*Gent.* 41, *Inc.* 3ff.) the image in man, i.e., his participation in the rationality of the Word, is what distinguishes him from the animals and keeps him from that 'natural state' which tends towards dissolution. Rejection of the Word, through the transgression of its articulated form as divine command, turns him back to his natural

also redemption from death – redemption of the whole person. Material existence can be affirmed in eschatology as in biblical protology.

The trouble, of course, is that too often it is not so affirmed. There is a telling silence about human life in the eschaton, a slightly embarrassed withdrawal from the territory explored in *Against Heresies*, Book 5. There is also the contrary evidence of moral and pastoral theology. It is rightly asked of Athanasius on what grounds he exalts virginity to the highest rank of ethical virtues, or hallows the path of the ascetic above all other paths, or claims that 'our increase is no other than the renouncing of things sensible;'[85] or how it is that he can speak of the ascension only quite vaguely as human nature 'being deified.'[86] It is rightly asked of Gregory Nazianzen, to take another example, what conclusions we should draw from Christ's 'ascension, or restoration, or whatever we ought to call it, to heaven.'[87] Or whether in the light of that doctrine he is justified when he speaks (at his father's funeral!) of getting closer to God by shaking off the 'bodily fetters' and holding intercourse 'naked with the nakedness of the prime and purest Mind.'[88] Indeed we might ask about the implications of his advice that we ascend with Christ's *godhead*, that we may not 'remain permanently among the things of sight but . . . rise up with him into the world of thought,' discerning his true nature.[89] This is not Origenism, much less gnosticism. It is a defense of Nicene orthodoxy which alludes to our subject in a rather unusual fashion, since most

---

state, and hence to death. For though God does not 'barely' create man, as he does other earthly creatures, man nevertheless has an unstable will with which he can and does despise 'the contemplation of God' that is his unique privilege as image-bearer, and the basis of his abiding in life.

[85] *Ari.* 3.52; cf. 2.76. Wingren (211) observes that for Athanasius 'virginity or celibacy is the highest expression of the Christian life,' whereas in Irenaeus there is 'absolutely no trace of any such ascetic ethic.'

[86] Though the Word cannot be exalted as Word, he can be exalted *for us* in his manhood, 'which exaltation was its being deified' (*Ari.* 1.41ff.; cf. Gregory Nyssen, *Eun.* 6.4, 12.1). Colin Gunton (1996:181f.) criticizes Athanasius here for having nothing to say about this deified humanity *qua* humanity; his main concern being to safeguard Christ's eternal sonship it is only somewhat grudgingly that he turns to the subject at all. Nevertheless we may say in his favour that Athanasius does not give the 'for us' a strictly subjectivist interpretation, as do many moderns.

[87] *Pent.* 11

[88] *Orat.* 18, in which he speaks also in traditional Greek fashion of 'two worlds, the one present and transitory, the other spiritually perceived and abiding.' But cf. *Pent.* 5: 'The dispensations of the body of Christ are ended; or rather, what belongs to his bodily advent (for I hesitate to say the dispensation of his body, as long as no discourse persuades me that it is better to have put off the body), and that of the Spirit is beginning.'

[89] For in the incarnation 'his inferior nature, the humanity, became God,' the higher nature prevailing, that we too 'might be made God insofar as he is made man' (*3rd Theo. Or.* 18f.). Again it is not at all clear what this means. What *is* clear is that Nazianzen's advice does not so much turn us to the God-man, and through him to the Father, as to the God *in* the man and only thence to the Father – an approach followed by Augustine, as we shall see.

treatments of the ascension deny that that event *was* an event for Christ's godhead. Unfortunately the distinct lack of interest here displayed in his humanity (ascended or otherwise) may not be explained merely by appeal to the Arian circumstances, for the dualist assumptions on which the advice rests are all too evident.[90]

We might probe a little further into this ambiguity by querying the above treatment of the *ex nihilo*. Is it perhaps a mistake to attempt even hypothetically to regard the creature with reference only to itself? Is it possible that behind the obvious vestiges of dualism an inadequate concept of divine transcendence is still in play, implying some sort of opposition between creator and creature simply as such? Is the creature perceived already to be under sentence of death simply because he or she *is* a creature, and not God? In other words, are God and creation brought together in the first instance not christologically but in a correlativity of mutual negation, even though that negation is now aimed very definitely at honouring rather than dishonouring the creator?[91] If so, the only possible resolution is to go beyond redemption from sin and corruption to another kind of redemption, one that collapses the ontological space between God and man, which inevitably means a thinning out of our humanity in something like the way suggested by Origen.[92] Hence the elliptical equation, God became man that man might become God.

---

[90] Here and there something better appears. At his brother's funeral Gregory speaks of the soul receiving in due course 'its kindred flesh,' and adds: 'I await the voice of the Archangel, the last trumpet, the transformation of the heavens, the transfiguration of the earth, the liberation of the elements, the renovation of the universe' (*Orat.* 7.21). But as A. Meredith remarks in the *Dictionary of Christian Spirituality* (SCM 1983:70), 'The body, the resurrection and the sacraments do not play a large part in the spirituality of any of the Cappadocians.'

[91] This is really a question about natural theology. Though we do not accept important aspects of her analysis, we agree with Lyman (133ff.) that Athanasius has a notion of transcendence derived in part from Platonism and not fully consistent with scripture. Immutability and mutability, eternality and temporality, passibility and impassibility, etc., are categories he sometimes uses in an *a priori* way, disrupting his christologic (cf. A. Torrance 1996:191ff.). The doctrine of creation is not properly controlled by the incarnation, allowing the *ex nihilo* to be misunderstood in privative terms and image-bearing to be seen as already a form of salvation (*Inc.* 3).

[92] Is this not the only possible conclusion if, as Nicholas Cabasilas later puts it (*Vita* 3; Balthasar 1990:22), man is 'triply sundered' from God – i.e., by his *human nature* as well as by sin and by death? Why should we admit that man is sundered from God in his human nature? Or indeed, as Hilary (*Trin.* 9.38) would have it, that God is somehow sundered from God in the Son's assumption of humanity, which creates 'an obstacle to the unity', an obstacle the ascension must overcome? According to Genesis 3 there was nothing standing in the way of God's communion with man until man sinned. And it was *in* his sin that Adam falsely suggested that his distance from God was an ontological problem – 'I knew that I was naked' – when in fact it was an hamartiological one: 'Who told you that you were naked? Have you eaten from the tree which I commanded you not to eat from?' To obscure the hamartiological problem by pointing to an allegedly more fundamental ontological one is to commit ourselves to seeking a solution to the latter, which solution will always have something in it of the gnostic hatred of the flesh.

The doctrines of ascension and deification plainly do not have to go in that direction, as Irenaeus demonstrated. But he prevented them from doing so precisely by rejecting a speculative Logos christology, which the Nicenes did not. For Irenaeus the one Word of creation and redemption is Jesus Christ. He stands at the centre of the economy of creation as the incarnate one, and at the centre of the economy of redemption as the crucified and risen one, the descending and ascending one. For the conciliar fathers, on the other hand, creation is ordered by and to the Word in his divinity, the λόγος ἄσαρκος; only as fallen is it ordered to the λόγος ἔνσαρκος.[93] This construction, like the tower of Pisa, is compromised by the ground on which it is built, for it leaves open the possibility that the economy of creation will be interpreted in some other way than in the harmony between God and man that is Jesus Christ. In spite of all rectifying attempts it inclines towards the old association of flesh with sin, since the advent of the Word *as* flesh is viewed only from a lapsarian perspective.[94] Perhaps then we should not be surprised that, though Athanasius and his colleagues did indeed affirm that the incarnation of the Word was aimed at the salvation of the whole person, they found it difficult to make a clean break with the common notion of ascent as a movement away from our earthly humanity towards an incorporeal existence which more closely images the divine Logos.[95]

Now as the Nestorian and Eutychian controversies sprang up in the wake of the Nicene success with the more fundamental question of the ὁμοούσιον, the doctrine of the ascension temporarily took on greater significance. Attempts to combat those twin heresies generated more attention to Christ's post-resurrection humanity and heavenly priesthood. Thus Chrysostom, for example, who was contemporary with Augustine, offers us (as J. G. Davies notes) a sermon on the ascension rich with insight. It moves from the subject of martyrdom to that of man's reconciliation with God through the mediation of Jesus, who in his own flesh offered the firstfruits of humanity before the heavenly throne. Contrasts are made

---

[93] See e.g. *Gent.* 40ff. Cf. *Ari.* 2:73ff., which adds that 'the materials for a repair' were provided *before* the house was built; i.e., that the incarnation of the Word was foreordained as 'the economy of our salvation.'

[94] Though Athanasius rejects any correlation of flesh and sin as Manichaean (*Nicene and Post-Nicene Fathers* 4/331 n. 2) the logic of his position is against him. If the incarnate one is provided not as the *basis* for the house (so Irenaeus) but only as the means of its repair, we may conclude that, ideally, no mediation of God by the flesh of Christ is called for; this devalues all flesh. Alternatively, we may conclude that the house as originally designed is inferior to the house as repaired, and that the latter is the real goal of God's creative activity. That conclusion appears to be the correct one, but it implies that sin is inevitable and felicitous. And why inevitable? Not because as rational creatures we already partake of a 'portion' of the power of the Word (*Inc.* 3), but because as creatures of flesh we do *not*. In our judgment there is no way to avoid the correlation of flesh and sin if there is a natural affinity between God and the mind, while the Word takes flesh only because of sin.

[95] After all, even Origen (*Dial.* 7; T. F. Torrance 1988:163 n. 61) speaks of the redemption of the whole man. But cf. A. Petterson 1990:30.

between his ascension and those of Enoch and Elijah, emphasizing the new thing that is accomplished in the former and the gift of the Holy Spirit that follows from it. Ethical implications are drawn and the sermon concludes by pointing to the parousia.[96] Some genuine progress against dualism might have been made at this time, were it not for the scandalous politicization of so many theological issues, such that even Chrysostom, a severe ascetic but no proponent of Origenism, could be falsely accused of that and other vices at the Synod of the Oak. Such intrigues could only prevent real movement. Nevertheless we may illustrate further from Proclus, one of John's successors in the see of Constantinople, who expostulates in one of his own Ascension Day sermons:

> Blessed be God! The nature of creation is divided into heaven and earth; yet today the grace which unites that which is divided does not permit me to see the division.

In another he confidently announces that with Jesus 'the creator has raised creation on high together with his divinity, and has settled it in the Father's bosom.'[97]

Part of the strategy against Eutychianism especially was to resist firmly the pull of eschatological docetism. Diadochus, bishop of Photice, actually conscripts the cloud on which Jesus ascends (much more subtly treated by Chrysostom) to make the point that, thus carried and supported, he did not 'deny the laws of the nature which he had taken.'[98] Here perhaps we have ambiguity of another kind, but in order to *be* kind we may drop the matter there, and jump forward two or three centuries to the close of the conciliar age. In John of Damascus we find the same resistance at work:

> He did not put aside any of the elements of his nature, neither body nor soul, but kept possession of the body and the rational, intellectual, willing and acting soul. And thus he sits at the right hand of the Father and wills our salvation both as God and as man . . . And both the ascent from earth into

---

[96] Davies' collation of material on the ascension, which is generally invaluable, is particularly helpful here. See chaps. 6–7, and 115ff. on Chrysostom and the Chrysostom *spuria*, which appear to preserve or recover a number of primitive features.

[97] Davies 130f. (capitalization and punctuation altered). Cf. Theophanius Ceramei, who later describes the ascension for that reason as 'the crown of the mysteries of Christ' (Davies 150f.).

[98] 'Wherefore,' continues Diadochus (*P.G.* 65.1141ff.; Davies 134f.), 'the saints shall be caught up into the cloud . . . when the expected Lord comes upon a cloud. For that which is fitting to God when he became incarnate on account of the body is also fitting to those who are being deified on account of the riches of his grace, when God wishes to make men gods. Let no one suppose therefore that the denseness of human nature, which we saw the holy Word of God unite to himself, that this will be changed into the resplendent and glorious substance of God, since indeed the truth of both natures subsisted in him unconfused. But it was not in order to make his form visible that the glorious Lord was incarnate, but in order that by his participation he might destroy for ever the evil disposition sown in us by the serpent . . . Not that we might be changed into what we were not, but that we might be renewed with glory to that which we were.'

heaven and the descending again are actions of a circumscribed body, for 'he shall so come to you,' it is said, 'as you have seen him going into heaven.'[99]

This recognition of the danger of a heavenly priesthood *sine carne* is laudable. But discussion of the ascension throughout this period nonetheless remained trapped by the underlying competition between the divine and the creaturely which the councils struggled constantly to surmount, a competition quite pronounced (as we will shortly see) in the work of Augustine.[100]

We repeat, reminded by *de Fide Orthodoxa*, that the ecclesiastical tradition consistently sided with Irenaeus when the chips were down. In spite of the fact that the humanity of the exalted Christ was regularly reaffirmed, however, the logic of that affirmation was never other than thoroughly obscure. Received cosmological frameworks underwent little serious modification to accommodate any such incongruous claim, though other important adjustments were being made.[101] Even in the likes of Chrysostom the upwards call was just that – upwards. The union of heaven and earth was therefore a rather uncertain affair after all, as the iconography of the ascension also suggests. In the early western tradition artistic representation was literal to the point of absurdity, showing a very ordinary-looking Jesus stepping up into the heavens from the mountain, aided by a helping hand from above. In the east, and increasingly in the west from the fifth century, a more symbolic approach prevailed – heavily influenced, it has to be said, by motifs borrowed from the apotheosis of emperors – in which the eternal world above and the temporal world below were sharply demarcated. In neither case was there much insight into the eschatological relation between the earthly and the heavenly which the doctrine of ascension in the flesh requires.[102]

* * *

[99] *Orth.* 4.1. John also wrote a hymn on the ascension, glorifying the God man in his offering of a redeemed creation to the Father.

[100] Davies' research shows how heavily affected by the see-saw debate over the two natures was discussion of the ascension at this time. As we will see, the Nestorian/Eutychian problem is very much connected to that of the presence and the absence. Separation of the natures leads to the distancing of Christ's departed humanity, which may then be sought out through liturgical anamnesis or some other artificial means; confusion of the natures leads to a doctrine of ubiquity and a failure to recognize his absence as a problem.

[101] Witness Basil's *Hexaemeron*, e.g., or the work of John Philoponos (cf. C. Kaiser 1991: 12ff.).

[102] See E. Dewald 1915:279ff., noting especially figs. 2 and 5, which illustrate the two contrasting styles from different panels of a 5th C. door (St Sabina, Rome); cf. A. Grabar (1968:35, 117) on the influence of imperial art. It is interesting to observe how western literalism, as it merges once again with the eastern dualist type after a return to roots in the Carolingian period, yields an oddity we might call the 'partial eclipse of Jesus,' leading eventually to the famous dangling feet renditions (e.g., St Mary's, Fairford). A much happier but most unusual stylistic compromise between east and west can be found in the 6th C. fresco of the church of SS. Cosmas and Damien (Rome), which looks to the parousia of the ascended one.

We have already indicated that the backing away of the conciliar fathers from the bold eucharistic worldview of Irenaeus cannot be explained simply by appeal to theological circumstance, that is, to their preoccupation with the Arian problem and its aftermath. Yet circumstance did have a lot to do with it, and the main political circumstance ought now to be mentioned as well. To say the least, the attenuation of eschatology was not discouraged by the exchanging of emperors who were deified in the old sense for those who were being deified in the new! Before turning back to Augustine we must acknowledge the changed climate in which theology was being done, and show too how an ambiguous doctrine of the ascension played a role in securing that changed climate.

With the conversion of Constantine, the edict of toleration, and the elevation of Christianity to an established religion the church's sense of its eucharistic precariousness naturally began to fade. Traditional eschatological commitments were squeezed by a powerful pincer movement. On the one hand, there was a conscious attempt to reclaim or sanctify temporal history just as it is. The invention of the daily office and the growth of a liturgical calendar – including of course a special feast to honour the ascension – marked this change of perspective. So too did the general displacement of interest in the parousia with interest in the afterlife.[103] On the other hand, given the increasingly obvious limitations of the effort to create a godly form of life in society at large, there was a mushrooming of the monastic communities, which were often open to the more radical aspects of Origenist spirituality.[104] On both sides, then, people were busy translating a faith that had once involved a conflict *between* histories into a correlation of history (the now common history of church and world) with eternity.[105]

At the same time the theological weakness on which we have remarked became a window of opportunity for those whose ecclesiastical interests were ruled by socio-political ones. 'God descends, man ascends' was a partial truth which, in the context of the Arian struggle, did just enough violence to the history of Jesus to leave the symbol of the cross a prey to ideological piracy. Which is to say, in the fourth century the glory of the ascended one was being attested in such a way as to emphasize his divinity at the expense of his humanity, and this had two significant side-effects.

---

[103] Dix (305ff.; cf. 263ff.) observes that the political changes which led to the church's reconciliation to time also shifted its liturgical emphasis from eschatology to 'the representation, the enactment before God, of the *historical process* of redemption' (i.e., of Jesus-history). But we should consider too the influence of Platonist ideas about the mimetic relation between time and eternity.

[104] It was in the monastic communities that the daily office evolved, of course, but this qualified affirmation of time was matched by a turn towards mysticism and a rejection of much that belongs to temporal existence (marriage, procreation, material pleasures, etc.).

[105] In what Pelikan (1/131) calls a 'decisive shift from the categories of cosmic drama to those of being'.

First, it made the problem of the presence and the absence less pressing; second, it left room on the stage of human affairs for an icon of grand proportions, *viz.*, the Christian emperor.[106] Ascension theology should not be overlooked in rendering an account of the strange new partnership between church and state which was then forged, a partnership in which the precariousness of ecclesial being would for a time be all but lost to view.

It is tempting here to point to the bishop of Caesarea in particular, that great admirer of Constantine and *de facto* court propagandist, whose Origenist view of the ascension (as of much else) made possible an unusual degree of collusion in providing a rationale for the new order. As others have noted, the Christ of Eusebius – that is, the Christ who fights with and for Constantine, the Christ who can be used to sanction imperialism and, within a generation, the use of the sword for the sake of the gospel – is the heavenly Christ whose humanity and whose humiliation are well behind him.[107] In his Tricennial Oration in praise of the emperor, having already gloried in God's mastery over the present creation and over the ages upon ages which have preceded it, Eusebius turns to christology and thence to Constantine himself:

> Lastly, he who is in all, before, and after all, his only begotten, pre-existent Word, the great high priest of the mighty God, elder than all time and every age, devoted to his Father's glory, first and alone makes intercession with him for the salvation of mankind. Supreme and pre-eminent ruler of the universe, he shares the glory of his Father's kingdom: for he is that Light, which, transcendent above the universe, encircles the Father's person, interposing and dividing between the eternal and uncreated Essence and all derived existence: that Light which, streaming from on high, proceeds from that deity who knows not origin or end, and illumines the super-celestial regions, and all that heaven itself contains, with the radiance of wisdom bright beyond the splendor of the sun. This is he who holds a supreme dominion over this whole world, who is over and in all things, and pervades all things visible and invisible; the Word of God. From whom and by whom our divinely favored emperor, receiving, as it were, a transcript of the divine sovereignty, directs, in imitation of God himself, the administration of this world's affairs.
> . . . [B]ringing those whom he rules on earth to the only begotten Word and saviour [he] renders them fit subjects of his kingdom. And as he who is the common saviour of mankind, by his invisible and divine power as the good shepherd, drives far away from his flock, like savage beasts, those apostate spirits which once flew through the airy tracts above this earth, and fastened on the souls of men; so this his friend, graced by his heavenly favor with victory over all his foes, subdues and chastens the open adversaries of the truth in accordance with the usages of war. He who is the pre-existent

---

[106] Cf. Eusebius of Caesarea, *Vita* 1.28–32, 40, 42, 2.48; *Orat.* 1.6, *passim.*
[107] See Gunton 1983, chap. 9 (esp. 195f., which takes up the criticism of Werner Elert). That Eusebius (*Demo.* 6.9) followed Origen in his view of the ascension should not go unnoticed.

Word, the preserver of all things, imparts to his disciples the seeds of true wisdom and salvation, and gives them understanding in the knowledge of his Father's kingdom. Our emperor, his friend, acting as interpreter to the Word of God, aims at recalling the whole human race to the knowledge of God; proclaiming . . . with powerful voice the laws of truth and godliness to all who dwell on the earth. Once more, the universal saviour opens the heavenly gates to those whose course is thitherward from this world. Our emperor, emulous of his divine example, having purged his earthly dominion from every stain of impious error, invites each holy and pious worshiper within his imperial mansions, earnestly desiring to save with all its crew that mighty vessel of which he is the appointed pilot.[108]

This naked correlation of the man Constantine with the divine Logos (whose own humanity is nowhere to be seen) requires no further commentary, except to say that those who would implicate the doctrine of Nicea in the Eusebian error should first take stock of his Origenist and Arian sympathies.

Let us not be content with the most tempting of targets, however, but point also to the bishop of Alexandria, Eusebius' sometime opponent, who at that very hour would begin proving that his own quite different convictions were by no means subject to the interests or claims of the state. For Athanasius' commendable resistance to theological prostitution should not induce us to pass over the fact that his influential *de Incarnatione* takes a small but dangerous step in the same direction. This occurs as he attempts to defend the divinity of Christ by way of the works achieved in his resurrection. After beginning with the evidence that can be found in the witness of the martyrs, he goes on to argue his point from the successful expansion of the Christian church and its profound impact on the gods of this world, concluding as follows:

> Behold how the saviour's doctrine is everywhere increasing, while all idolatry and everything opposed to the faith of Christ is daily dwindling, and losing power, and falling. And thus beholding, worship the saviour, 'who is above all' and mighty, even God the Word; and condemn those who are being worsted and done away by him.[109]

Athanasius certainly shows no tendency to put the emperor, or anyone else, in the place occupied by the human Jesus. But by following this line of thought he too shifts the focus in the doctrines of the resurrection and ascension from the question of what happens to Jesus to the question about his superior nature. What is more, he again implies (while retaining a traditional reference to the last things) that history is a process by which

---

[108] *Orat.* 1.6—2.5 (capitalization altered). We have taken the liberty of quoting at length because the movement of thought here illustrated must not be dismissed as the mere flattery of an obsequious cleric, who was after all 'the most learned Churchman of the age' (A. Robertson) and a centrist figure of enormous influence. It is a pattern of things to come.
[109] §55; see 26ff.

absence is converted into presence by degrees. In short, he himself concedes too much to the spirit of triumphalism.[110]

Athanasius liked to point out to the Jews that in choosing Caesar over Christ they had 'the penal reward of their denial; for their city as well as their reasoning came to nought.'[111] What, we wonder, might Eusebius have said of the distant fall of Constantinople to the armies of Islam? In the west, of course, the fall of Rome was already on the horizon, a momentous and shocking event that would inspire the writing of *The City of God*, and in it some distinctly Irenaean noises made by Augustine, so to speak, at the end of the day. But in turning to the father of western theology we must not be content to hear only what suits us.

***

John Rist describes Augustine as standing at the frontier between ancient and medieval thought, passing judgment on the classical heritage while preserving and redirecting its spent energies.[112] Where the doctrine of the ascension is concerned he is also something of a transitional figure, whose frequent sermons and comments on the subject did much to bring it into focus in the western church.[113] Any judgment of that doctrine on our part, however, requires us to take account of the transition in his own thinking towards the end of the first decade of the fifth century, and of the influence of his earlier as well as his later view.

It is plain enough that the Augustine of the *Confessions* shared the erect, anthropomorphic cosmology of Origen and of educated Greeks generally. Though perhaps somewhat less interested in cosmology for its own sake and more interested in its anthropological core – hence the well-known existentialist flavour of his work – by the time of his conversion he had come to see the world with cultured neoplatonist eyes: visible cosmos and invisible heaven, like corporeal body and incorporeal soul, vertically arranged under God in the hierarchy of being; the outer pointing to the inner, the lower to the higher, the many finding stability in subjection to the one. On such a view the rational soul of man belongs to heaven as his body belongs to earth, and is at odds with itself until it escapes from

---

[110] Whatever his later success, even 'in a setting of increasing social legitimacy for Christianity,' at 'casting Christian identity in starker form over against the larger world or its history,' as Lyman (159) helpfully puts it. Lyman, we note, appears more than a little suspicious of that success and seems to prefer Eusebius, whose 'broad, sweeping vision of the public triumph and dominance of Christianity rested on the unmistakable signs of divine power and social progress' (163) as seen through the lens of his Origenist optimism.

[111] *Ari.* 2.42; cf. *Inc.* 40.

[112] 1994:1.

[113] He returns regularly to four related concerns, notes Davies (136): the meaning of John 3:13; the *totus Christus* concept and the ascension of believers; the nature of bodily ascension; the significance of the forty days.

earthly distractions into an uninterrupted *visio dei*. Its affinity for heaven (or rather for God, of whose divinity the heavens partake) puts it in competition with the body, whose dissipating tendencies must be mastered for the sake of higher aims. All of this Augustine brought with him into Christianity, and though important elements of it were to be profoundly modified in the course of his pastoral and theological labours, and in disputation with stubbornly pagan neoplatonism such as that of Porphyry, his doctrine of the ascension would be made to count *for* it before being turned against it.

Not surprisingly, the relation between creation and redemption in the thought of the earlier Augustine shows signs of the old confusion. In the *Confessions* we learn that to come into being is to go forth from God, and that to sin is to go astray. These concepts are difficult to distinguish, as von Balthasar observes, and Augustine makes no consistent effort to do so. Though he later insists on an historical fall (a fall *in* the body rather than into it) the distinction between creation and fall is at first not a sharp one; both describe the human creature at some remove from the Creator and as the recipient of a summons to return to him.[114] Creaturehood is already a problematic condition, and salvation is not only redemption from the debilitating effects of sin but also from the 'straits of space and time.'[115] In other words, the hamartiological problem can be separated from the ontological only with difficulty. Diversity and dissipation run together, so that the biblical optimism about our creaturely world is missing from Augustine at this stage, as it was from Origen. Ascension theology is again about the purification and advance of the soul. To 'ascend steps within the heart' is the believer's goal; the historic ascension of Jesus is not a matter on which Augustine dwells, though he affirms it in *Faith and the Creed*.[116]

Things have changed considerably when we get to *The City of God*, of course. Guided by a more literal interpretation of Genesis, and by new attention to *creatio ex nihilo* and to the church's belief in resurrection and ascension in the flesh, his affirmation there of the goodness of the material world is quite lyrical. It is made plain that the problem with human beings is not related to their lower or bodily nature but strictly to

---

[114] *Conf.* 11.4ff.; cf. Plotinus, *Enn.* 5.1.1. Balthasar (1967:5ff.; cf. 2/105f.) observes a 'dangerous' proximity to Maximus, who 'sees creation and the Fall as simultaneous, though not identical.' 'To move out from God, to wander away from God: one is creation the other is sin. But who can, in terms of our concrete consciousness, distinguish between the two?'

[115] Time and things temporal 'tend towards non-being' (*Conf.* 11.14). That which is ontically stable belongs to the realm of the eternal Logos, who restores us to our source in God *via* the incarnation and the sacraments. Rist (55; cf. 205) notes that in *Reconsiderations* 1.3.2, however, Augustine withdraws the claim that the kingdom which Christ said is 'not of this world' may be identified with the intelligible world of the Platonists (*Ord.* 1.11.32).

[116] Cf. *Conf.* 13.9ff., *Fid. Sym.* 13. In the latter, he wisely adds: 'But the question as to where and in what manner the Lord's body is in heaven is one which it would be altogether over-curious and superfluous to prosecute.'

the corruption that has entered into them through sin; and there is room now in his eschatology for a physical and social dimension which had been lacking.[117] The heavens to some extent have been humbled and the earth exalted, making it easier for Augustine to defend more vigorously the teaching of scripture against that of the philosophers and cosmologists, even on an apparent absurdity such as the opening of heaven to corporeal bodies. Though his deviation from the common physics is not uninteresting, in the end he simply dismisses opposing arguments sarcastically as being more ponderous than the human body itself, as Jesus' ascension demonstrates. The new cosmological construct falls well short of the revolution which ascension in the flesh calls for, nor indeed does it pretend to be revolutionary.[118]

We are left nevertheless with two very different perspectives on our doctrine. But there is a crucial feature of Augustine's treatment of the ascension which relativizes the difference, limiting the impact of the later emphasis on ascension in the flesh. That feature becomes visible when we examine the way in which the original event is linked to the believer's own experience, that is, to its repetition for us through the exercise of faith. His mentor, Ambrose, had already forged the link in an anti-Arian context,[119] but Augustine turns it into a principle of spiritual theology to which he attaches the prescriptive maxim, *per Christum hominem ad Christum deum.*[120] This maxim rests on the assumption that the humanity of the Word has no greater purpose than to lead us to his divinity, an assumption equally well-suited to an Origenist agenda as to the Nicene. And now the feature in question comes into focus, for no such result is possible unless and until *the humanity is withdrawn from our view.* That indeed was a primary objective of the ascension, suggests Augustine, for the disciples' minds

> were concentrated on his human nature, and they were unable to consider him as God. In fact, they would then think of him as God [only] when his human nature would be removed from their eyes, so that, with the intimacy

---

[117] CD 22 (cf. 13.17; *Retr.* 1.16, 2.3). See Rist, chap. 4, who suggests that Augustine eventually 'became almost as hostile to "spiritual" reductionism as . . . to "material" reductionism' (101). We should not suppose, however, that the earlier perspective disappears entirely. Heaven, after all, is the natural abode of pure angelic spirits, and were the saints not chosen to make up the number of the fallen (CD 22.1; cf. McDannell and Lang 1988:54ff.)?

[118] CD 22.11.

[119] 'It is expedient for thee that thou shouldest believe that he has ascended and is sitting at the right hand of the Father; for if in impious thought thou detain him among things created and earthly; if he depart not for thee, ascend not for thee, then to thee the Comforter shall not come . . .' (*Fide* 4.24; quoted Davies 105).

[120] 'Through the man Christ you go to the God Christ . . . Where you are to abide, he is God; on your way thither, he is man' (*Ser.* 261). E. Przywara (1936:277ff.) supplies a number of excerpts on this theme, which according to Marrevee 'summarizes the whole process of the Christian life' (99; cf. e.g. *Io. Ev.* 13.4, 121.3).

which they had formed with his human nature thus severed, they might learn to consider his divinity in the absence of his humanity.[121]

In short, the inferior nature of Christ again gives way to the superior, if only on the subjective level. Bodily ascension, though affirmed, is for the first time assigned an essentially negative value or function. Moreover, there is a disturbing psychologizing of this climactic moment in salvation history. As William Marrevee observes:

> Although Augustine does not deny the objective Ascension of Christ as man, he maintains that this objective event loses its significance for men, if they are not able to believe in Him as God. The Ascension then takes place again, every time we accept Christ's divinity: 'Therefore He has ascended for us, when we rightly understand Him. At that time He ascended once only but now He ascends every day.'[122]

The ascension, seen from this angle, is no longer the joyful occasion of man's presentation to God but the removal of a stumbling block to faith. It has been made over into a retraction of the human Jesus for the sake of the divine – this is what renders it repeatable – lest in overstaying he should undermine his own purpose. 'I am removing myself from you exteriorly,' Jesus is made to say, 'but I am filling you with myself interiorly' (i.e., divinely).[123] In effect, then, it is a drop-in theory of the incarnation that we meet in Augustine, who in fact dismisses Christ's human nature as being necessary only 'for our weakness.'[124]

---

[121] Ser. 264; cf. Trin. 1.18.

[122] Ser. 246. Marrevee (103) does not make our criticism. Earlier he explains: 'It is therefore in view of the function of the Incarnation, which was to bring man to God, that the Ascension of Christ as man must be considered, for this objective event indicates that in each believer the same must take place subjectively' (101).

[123] The human Christ does not enter us physically, but 'admonishes from without;' the divine Christ 'dwells within us so that we may be interiorly converted, so that we may be quickened by him and formed after his pattern, for he is the uncreated form of all created things' (Ser. 264). 'You will indeed cease from being carnal, if the form of the flesh be removed from your eyes, so that the form of God may be implanted in your hearts' (Ser. 270).

[124] 'Thus, the manifestation of the human nature of Christ is necessary for the faithful in this life so that they make their way toward the Lord. However, once they have come to the vision of the Word, an entirely human manifestation will not be necessary' (Ser. 264). Cf. Doc. Chr. 1.38, which assures us that the Lord himself 'wishes us rather to press on; and, instead of weakly clinging to temporal things, even though these have been put on and worn by Him for our salvation, to pass over them quickly, and to struggle to attain unto himself, who has freed our nature from the bondage of temporal things, and has set it down at the right hand of his Father.' Or En. Ps. 110(109).5: 'There is, I say, one thing that is transitory in the Lord: another that is enduring. What is transitory is the Virgin's delivery, the incarnation of the Word, the gradation of ages, the exhibition of miracles, the endurance of sufferings, death, resurrection, ascent into heaven . . . For Christ is no longer in birth, or dying, or rising again, or ascending into heaven. Do ye not see that these acts . . . exhibited to those on the way something transitory, so that they should not abide on the path, but reach their country?' In the same place (7ff.) ascension and parousia in the flesh are declared, but with the goal that he who has appeared in the form of a servant should afterwards appear in the form of God, when 'at some time we shall reach what is not time.'

We hasten to say that there are yet other angles from which Augustine views the ascension, and that his firm confession of resurrection, ascension and parousia in the flesh rules out any retraction of the incarnation on an ontological level. But it is hard to deny that he furthers, rather than checks, the dangerous process (begun by Clement and Origen) of interiorizing our relation to the ascended Lord.[125] The impact on ecclesiology, namely, a deepening of the drive towards individualism on the one hand and institutionalism on the other, is predictable enough. And while other factors do come into play here, a second striking feature of Augustine's treatment of the ascension is that he makes a more deliberate attempt than any of the fathers to correlate that doctrine with his view of the church.

* * *

As the condition of a penetrating faith in Jesus' divinity, Augustine regarded the ascension as a point of departure both for the process of personal sanctification and also for the diffusion of the church among the nations. This latter (Lukan) theme he provided with a theoretical basis having a biblical ring but pronounced neoplatonist overtones. The spread or increase of the gospel means the decrease of human fragmentation, as our ascending head brings his entire body under control. Christ 'diffuses himself through all his members' in every age and place in order to draw them with him, as one man, into heaven.[126] Joined to Augustine's subjectivist interest in the ascension, in other words, is a complementary teaching about the *totus Christus*, based on the universal presence of the ascended one and on his power to reassemble the dissipated fragments of temporal man in order to introduce them into the timeless cohesion of the Jerusalem above. This teaching is fundamental to his ecclesiology. Again and again he stresses the identity of head and members as *unus homo, una persona.*[127] The pneumatological note struck by Irenaeus is not forgotten here, nor his *communio* motif; yet so strong is the emphasis on oneness that the distinction between Christ and the church begins to blur. 'Let us rejoice and give thanks that we are made not merely Christians but Christ.'[128] If the church is also the bride of Christ, Augustine

---

[125] There is an attendant narrowing of pneumatology to its revelational component, another Origenist feature connected with the downgrading of Jesus' humanity (but cf. e.g. *Prae. Sanc.* 15.31).

[126] *Ser.* 263. See Marrevee 104ff., 138ff.

[127] 'The poignant sense of the need to regain some lost unity is perhaps the most distinctive strand in Augustine's mystique of the Catholic Church' (P. Brown 1967:224; see Davies 136ff., Marrevee 120ff., McGinn 1/248ff., Przywara 211ff.). Cf. *Conf.* 13.28.

[128] *Io. Ev.* 21.8.

tells us, there are plainly 'two in one flesh,' but these two are the divine Word and the one corporate Man.[129]

Now the *totus Christus* idea obviously serves as a powerful brake on individualism; likewise, it would appear to mitigate against any abstract or merely institutional understanding of unity. But there is something going on here which we must be careful not to miss, namely, that the humanity of Jesus, having been sublated by Augustine's treatment of the ascension, comes back into play ecclesiologically. The church begins to be seen as a prolongation of the incarnation, and to attract to itself more and more of the essential functions of Jesus. It, not he, serves presently to mediate our faith in the divine Word. A new line of thought thus emerges, seemingly at odds with the former one:

> The church is spread throughout the whole world: all nations have the church. Let no one deceive you; it is the true, it is the catholic church. Christ we have not seen, but we have her; let us believe as regards him.[130]

The cynic might be forgiven for replying that if it were easier for Christ's disciples to believe in his divinity after the withdrawal of his humanity, how much more so for us today could we only remove the opaque barrier of an all too human church! Augustine however did not start from the church's opacity, nor did he recognize an inconsistency here. By virtue of its supernatural growth and marvelous catholicity, the church makes visible in the world the otherwise invisible glory of its exalted Lord.[131] Indeed, as the church increases in stature, so too does the compulsion to believe in him as the exalted one; such is the triumphant spiral of faith set in motion by the ascension.

The obvious danger in this turbo-charged construction, of course, is the likelihood of its running away with itself. When the earthly church is seen as a mirror of heavenly triumph, when its success on the horizontal axis is thought to display the dizzying heights to which its Lord ascends, it is difficult to set limits to the glory which should accrue to it:

> The Lord, glorified in his resurrection, commends the church; about to be glorified in his ascension he commends the church; sending the Holy Spirit from heaven he commends the church.[132]

---

[129] 'The "two" you must refer to the distance of his divine majesty from us' (*En. Ps.* 143 [142.3]). See Kelly 413f. on Christ's 'triple mode of existence' as eternal Word, as God-man, and as the *totus Christus*. Does the last of these not invite some critical questions about the encroachment into ecclesiology of the notion of a universal man, and of neoplatonism's diversification/unification scheme (cf. Gregory Nyssen, *Hom. Op.* 16.16ff.)?

[130] *Ser.* 238. 'Their faith was made complete by the sight of the head; ours is made complete by the sight of the body' (*Ser.* 116 [*Scr. N.T.*], quoted Przywara 223).

[131] '"Be thou exalted, O God, above the heavens: and thy glory above all the earth." Let him who does not grasp the second part not believe the first part. For what is the significance of "And thy glory above all the earth," except that thy church is above all the earth, thy lady is above all the earth . . .' (*Ser.* 262; cf. Marrevee 120f.).

[132] *Ser.* 265.

A powerful inflationary factor is thus introduced at the institutional pole of Augustine's ecclesiology after all. The *totus Christus* notion combines with a Nestorianizing analysis of the ascension to allow what belongs to Jesus to pass more or less directly to the church. This Nestorianizing is already evident in the misleading maxim *per Christum hominem ad Christum deum*, which obscures the biblical and liturgical movement *per Christum ad Patrem*. Jesus' human particularity is marginalized by a misconstrual of his earthly priesthood in the narrow terms of an epiphany, and by a corresponding neglect of his heavenly priesthood.[133] Under these conditions both his hard-won glory and his mediatorial role are easily transferred to the church without proper regard for their eucharistic qualification. There even arises the backwards notion that the world is to serve the church, rather than the church the world.[134]

Augustine's epoch-making innovation known as amillennialism encouraged this dangerous line of thought. The moment of truth in the notion that the millennial kingdom is *now* is the assurance that the church, like Jesus, gains its victory over the world precisely by walking with him on the way of the cross; that the martyr really does reign with Jesus through his or her martyrdom. That moment of truth (often emphasized by Augustine) is lost as soon as we overlook the eschatological reserve, the 'not yet' of the kingdom, the real absence of the Lord. Unfortunately on the bishop's scheme it is possible to do just that, as his construction of the eucharistic problem demonstrates:

> In respect of his majesty, his providence, his ineffable and invisible grace, his own words are fulfilled, 'Lo I am with you always, even to the end of the world.' But in respect of the flesh he assumed as the Word, in respect of that which he was as the son of the Virgin . . . 'you will not have him always.' And why? Because in respect of his bodily presence he associated with his disciples for forty days; and then . . . he ascended into heaven, and is no longer here. He is there indeed, sitting at the right hand of the Father; and he is here also, never having withdrawn the presence of his glory. In other words, in respect of his divine presence we always have Christ; but in respect of his presence in the flesh it was rightly said to his disciples, 'Me you will not have

---

[133] But cf. *Retr.* 1.23.1, where Augustine interprets his expression, 'Jesus Christ now wholly God after his resurrection' (*Gal.* 2), as follows: 'Accordingly, because of his immortality the Christ God is now no longer man, but because of the substance of human nature in which "he ascended into heaven" is now, in truth, "Mediator between God and men, the man Christ Jesus," for he will come as those saw him who saw him "going up to heaven."'

[134] Cf. Matt. 20:28. In Augustine this transference is only preliminary and many passages may be adduced against it, but D. Ritschl (1967:123ff.) not unjustly fingers him as 'the theological architect of the "Constantinian" Church' (post-Constantinian would be more accurate). Ritschl also discerns the beginnings of a utilitarian streak: 'For this Catholic Church, vigorously spreading far and wide throughout the whole world, uses all who are in error to her own advancement . . . She uses the heathen as material on which to work, heretics as a test of her teaching, schismatics as a proof of her stability, Jews as a comparison to show her beauty' (*Ver. Rel.* 6.10).

always.' In this respect, the church enjoyed his presence only for a few days; now it possesses him by faith, without seeing him with the eyes.[135]

At first glance this appears to be carefully balanced and quite unexceptionable. But it is not at all clear, as it should be, that one and the same Jesus is both present and absent. Rather what is relatively unimportant about Jesus (his humanity) is said to be absent while his divinity is said to be present.[136] And when we recall that the latter is meant in any case to be the real object of our faith, we can see that the door has been left ajar to an over-realized eschatology. A church backed by an invisible but fully present Christ may easily forget its own eucharistic ambiguity.[137]

We will not turn aside to consider Augustine's problematic sacramental theory, which rests on a creative reworking of the relation between *signum* and *res* in the Platonist tradition.[138] In passing, though, we may observe that to affirm the divine presence at the expense of the human is to reintroduce inflation at the other pole as well, loosening the brake against the individualism inherent in every theology which turns on the relation between God and the soul. It makes possible the famous claim, *crede et manducasti* – 'believe and you have eaten'[139] – which in its radical inwardness necessarily places a question mark beside the social, corporate, and corporeal nature of the eucharistic event. Other atomizing influences might be pointed out, but we want instead to show how Augustine did develop a doctrine of the church's ambiguity, one built on the *corpus permixtum* concept rather than on the doctrine of ascension in the flesh or on the eucharist. The difference we think instructive.

It was under the pressure of Donatist rigourism that Augustine began referring to the *corpus permixtum* as a means of rejecting any naïve identification of the church in sociological or sectarian terms.[140] To do so was certainly to insist on an eschatological qualification, but in a way that effectively nullified its application to the institution as such. How

---

[135] *Ioh. Ev.* 50.13; quoted in Heron, 1983(b):72, who does not fail to notice the 'sharp distinction between Jesus' physical presence and that of his divine power' which here befuddles eucharistic theology.

[136] It is usually the divine presence Augustine has in view: 'The absence of God is not absence' (*Ser.* 133). 'When he ascended into heaven, we were not separated from him' (*Ser.* 263). Cf. *Ser.* 395 (which Davies flags as pseudepigraphal): 'He is the Head: we are the members. He is in heaven: we are on earth. Is he, as it were, far from us? If you ask space, he is far away; but ask love, he is with us.' Anticipating later controversies, however, he does lean on the hypostatic union to claim that the flesh of Christ is also present eucharistically, as he wills.

[137] Cf. Wainwright 1967:12.

[138] An eternal reality is hidden in, and revealed by, a temporal one. The relation between them is based on *similitudo* rather than *commutatis* or *conversio*; it is more pedagogical than eschatological. (Augustine is thus closer to Origen than to his mentor Ambrose; cf. Heron 1983b:69ff., W. Crockett 1989:88ff.)

[139] *Ioh. Ev.* 25.12.

[140] The *corpus permixtum* idea was taken over from Tyconius (see R. Markus 1970:115ff.) but goes back to Clement and Origen.

so? Taking up Origen's 'κόσμος of the cosmos' perspective, he too employed an allegorical reading of Genesis 1:1 to speak of the church's spiritual and carnal parts.[141] As an empirical phenomenon the church is to be found in a dynamic of descending light (the truth of the gospel) and ascending matter (repenting sinners). As such it is always a mixture of good and evil, indeed, a 'standing betrayal' of its heavenly foundation.[142] Which is to say, such purity as it can and must claim is a purity grounded not in the decisions and actions of specific persons or communities here below, but in what comes to them from above; not in the earthly stuff *of* which the church is built, but in that from heaven *by* which it is built. It is in that sense a formal rather than a material purity, belonging to the scriptures, doctrines and sacraments through which the catholic church, just because it is catholic, reduces the chaos of 'our disordered parts.'[143]

The church's ambiguity resides in its members, in other words, not in the church *qua* church. Even Augustine's doctrine of predestination (an atomizing force) underscores our need to find repose in the latter, as Jaroslav Pelikan notices.[144] To be sure, the true church is the eternal church, and the eternal church is simply the sum of the elect; but that is a reality hidden from us in the inscrutable will of God. The visible institution therefore becomes vital to us during our temporal pilgrimage. Like Christ's humanity it is necessary for our weakness: *per ecclesiam carnalem ad ecclesiam caelestem*, we might say.[145] This distancing of the church from the sins and errors even of its own functionaries, which was the immediate aim, had merit as a response to Donatism. Nevertheless it helped to entrench a damaging dichotomy between the church as institution and the church as the people of God, a dichotomy which still troubles us today.[146] While cooling sectarian fervour it facilitated a false security about

---

[141] *Conf.* 13.13.

[142] Markus 180.

[143] *Conf.* 13.34, 49 (cf. Book 12). The Donatists also had a formal view of the church, as a ritually pure rather than a truly righteous people (Brown 221f.); but on their view care had to be taken not to contaminate the clean with the unclean. Augustine rightly rebuked that pretension. Words he liked to put in the mouth of Christ took on new meaning if there were schismatics within earshot: 'If you wish to ascend, be my members!' (*Ser.* 263)

[144] 1/302f.

[145] Kelly (415f.) overlooks the unity this brings to Augustine's ecclesiology, which we may represent as follows:

heaven	divine Christ	*totus Christus*	*ecclesia caelestis*
earth	human Christ	*corpus permixtum*	*ecclesia carnalis*

[146] It is difficult to agree with A. Dulles (1987:36) that the church was 'relatively free of institutionalism' until the end of the Middle Ages. The fact that bishops in east and west alike were already having to plead with people to share in the eucharist along with the clergy is a poignant witness to the fact that this dichotomy was deeply felt.

Mother Church herself. But before commenting further on that we need to consider Augustine's response to the other main challenge he was called on to face, namely, the changing situation of the church as the western empire crumbled. For in this connection a different and quite dangerous concept of ecclesial ambiguity would be introduced, compounding the problem.

That Luke, and for that matter Paul, saw in the ascension a guarantee that the gospel would be preached to all nations cannot be doubted; that either would have subscribed to the growing speculation of the fourth century about an 'ineluctable course of history'[147] in which the church was fated not only to spread to the four corners of the world but to become more or less co-extensive with human society, certainly can be. Yet some such vision was what Augustine at first set over against the sectarianism of his opponents. The universal display of Christ's heavenly glory implied that the struggle for a holy people would eventually take place *inside* the church, rather than in competition between the church and the world.[148] So optimistic a view of history, if not of the church, he had occasion to modify as the knocking of the barbarians at the gates grew ever louder. The Constantinian myth of progress, or at least of a new golden age (the *tempora christiana*) in which church and state would be the 'twin roots' of divine blessing, was quickly being shattered. There could be no return to apocalypticism, however, which was tainted by association with extremists. A new conception of the ecclesial situation was needed.

Robert Markus argues that Augustine's response was to confront both Constantinian triumphalism and Donatist separatism with a more truly eschatological perspective.[149] Christians were neither at home in the world in the way the former suggested, nor could their homelessness be marked out quite so concretely as the latter supposed. What then? Human society and human history were in fact 'secular' or neutral, suggested the bishop of Hippo, neither promising nor setting at risk the kingdom of God. The church could reside in the world without inviting abuse as something subversive, while yet regarding it with a certain indifference as something wholly provisional. Suspicion of regress and belief in progress were both replaced by Augustine's notion of the homogeneity of time,[150] a notion quite in keeping, it may be said, with his understanding of the Christian life. Paraphrasing Acts 1:6 with considerable sermonic licence, he chides his listeners: 'What are the times to thee? Thy concern is to escape from time, and thou askest the time!'[151]

---

[147] Brown 221.

[148] See ibid. 212ff.; cf. e.g. *Ep.* 93.31, *En. Ps.* 147(146).19.

[149] See p. 167.

[150] The time of revelation, covenant time, is an exception; cf. Markus 62f., 157ff.

[151] *Ser.* 265 (cf. Plato, *Theae.* 176b; Brown 244f., 323f.). 'The life of the church is like walking on the spot,' says Balthasar (1967:38), and elsewhere remarks (2/143): 'It is a constant astonishment to find how much *The City of God*, which laid the foundations of

Within this hypothesis room was made for something, at first glance, not unlike the Irenaean conflict of histories. *De Civitate Dei* speaks of a struggle between two cities that has been going on since Cain and Abel. The invisible or eternal church is one of those cities; alienated, reprobate humanity, with its lust for power and its various parodies of divine unity, is the other. Neither can ever be fully identified as such, for they are too closely interwoven in the fabric of the *saeculum*.[152] But in the train of Christ's ascension the visible church has emerged as a *signum* of the city of God in the midst of the city of man, a *vestigium gloriae* testifying to the former's ultimate victory over the latter.[153] Precisely as a sign, however, it belongs to the *saeculum* and shares its ambiguity – a secular rather than a eucharistic one, which would have been inconceivable to Irenaeus.

A strain, perhaps even a contradiction, now appears in Augustine's ecclesiology itself. On the one hand, the catholic church with its doctrine and sacraments is regarded as a fixed point of reference, that is, as an institution divinely ordained to redeem the time by functioning as a check upon human dissipation and disorder. On the other hand, it too is provisional, relative, open to compromise insofar as it really does belong to the present age. Indeed, from the standpoint of the *saeculum* Augustine sometimes seems ready to grant the worldliness of everything to do with the church, except of course the hidden reality of the elect in their unity with Christ as members of the heavenly city. This leaves him open to the Donatist criticism that he believes not in one church but in two, a criticism to which he offers no entirely satisfactory answer.[154] The eucharistic tension, and the church with it, appears to have broken down into vertical and horizontal, interior and exterior, components.

Now any such breakdown produces a hazardous state of affairs, as the Donatists discovered, since the eschatological reserve implicit in the eucharist no longer operates effectively in either direction. Not only was the great church free to follow the path of assimilation to the pattern of other institutions, taking its place as a full member of the *saeculum*. It was free to use secular means to achieve its divine purposes, drawing men and women into its embrace even by coercion, if need be. What is more, it could be confident that in using those means it still remained holy, because it was not itself subject to the same process of self-questioning

---

the western philosophy of history, is an essentially unhistorical work, original and creative only in those places where it abstracts the eternally unchanging existential conditions of historical existence from the historical process.'

[152] The *saeculum* is 'the sphere of temporal realities in which the two "cities" share an interest,' says Markus (133); 'it is the sphere of human living, history, society and its institutions, characterised by the fact that in it the ultimate eschatological oppositions, though present, are not discernible.'

[153] 'As *res* the Church is lost [i.e., hidden] in the "world"; as *signum* it has distinct being as the world's pointer to the Kingdom' (ibid. 185).

[154] See ibid. 120f., 181ff.

and self-doubt to which its individual members were subject.[155] As a matter of fact, Augustine had taken the fateful step of supporting the coercion of dissenters even before he had fully worked out his new understanding of the *saeculum*. The triumphalist logic of his doctrine of the ascension already made it possible for him to countenance the church lending its divine sanction to actions devised and exercised under the non-eucharistic conditions of the state.[156] As the western empire disintegrated, this line of thought only hardened. His later theology contained little to hinder the church from becoming in due course a fierce competitor for the levers of social control, or indeed from making a habit of calling the earthly sword to the service of the heavenly keys.[157]

The dark places to which all of this would lead are too well marked to need rehearsing here. The ex-Donatist Tyconius, from whom Augustine borrowed a good deal of weaponry for his theological assault on the schismatics, recognized what Augustine did not, *viz*., the antichrist capacity of the church insofar as it intended to pursue such a course. He refused to join the official church, a church which no longer knew how to criticize itself effectively in the light of the cross and of its own post-ascension precariousness, a church which thus failed to answer the question posed by the Donatist movement. Whether or not Tyconius could foresee the way in which the successors of Augustine would turn the bishop's 'eschatological' alternative into an even more dangerous triumphalism than that of the Constantinians, what he did see – Christians persecuting Christians – was enough to convince him that his lonely stance was necessary.

Unfortunately his was indeed a lonely stance. With its millennial advance on the saints' post-parousia authority as operating capital, the church bravely and ambitiously took on a formidable role in the reconstruction of western society. No doubt this was a gift, often a generous and costly one. Before long, however, the ecclesial *res* (if we may re-employ this term in our own frame of reference) became well and truly hidden under the welter of secular interests occupying the church as *signum*, and abuses of power multiplied. That was only the negative side of an often very positive performance, of course, and the positive no less

---

[155] Cf. Rist 239ff. Two dichotomies are operative here: that between the eternal church of the elect and its temporal sign (the *corpus permixtum*); and, on the temporal level, that between the institution and its membership.

[156] His defense of that support to Vincentius only serves to reinforce our impression that the trajectory of Acts (which, not insignificantly, leaves off with *Paul* in prison) has been falsified by plotting the doctrine of the ascension on the wrong grid. See *Ep.* 93 (AD 408), the opening section of which makes appeal *via* Psa. 108:5 to the ascension and to the present glorification of the church (cf. §§9, 23, and 28; also *Ep.* 185, *Retr.* 2.5).

[157] Markus (154ff.) claims that Augustine's theology of history was misread and became 'the very thing it was designed to undermine: the theological prop of a sacral society, of a Christian political establishment in which the divine purpose in history lay enshrined.' But perhaps Augustine himself provided a basis for the 'misreading'?

than the negative frequently had its roots in Augustine. Yet we think it fair to conclude that the contribution of Augustine, his indisputable place as a father of the church notwithstanding, represents a second backwards step in the matters that concern us. Once again a cosmology favouring discontinuity over continuity inclined Christian theology towards a subjectivizing approach to the ascension, with telling results in ecclesiology. Ascension 'in the flesh' was affirmed as Origen could not affirm it, but in such a fashion that the church's gradual substitution for the marginalized humanity of Jesus was actually encouraged the more. Might it even be the case that this second step, by virtue of being the less obvious, proved the more dangerous of the two? Of the subsequent lengthening of the church's reverse stride throughout the Middle Ages we will speak a little in the next section.

Dualist Ecclesiology

With Origen and Augustine the die was cast. In the shadow of these two giants a truce was struck with dualism that would hamper any further wrestling with a worldview based on Jesus-history, or with the eucharistic ecclesiology that must accompany it. We are not surprised, then, though we think he has overlooked some important material, that J. G. Davies should discover a dearth of intelligent references to the ascension 'throughout the whole of the next millennium.'[158] Nor is it any wonder that the expanding church – which, in Augustine's phrase, 'got up by degrees'[159] – should have produced layer upon layer of baptized secularity in the process. While we cannot hope to offer anything like a full account of the flowering of ecclesiastical self-assurance, a few general observations from our own point of view are in order, touching both the Latin and the Greek churches.

It ought to be said first of all that the marginalization of the human Jesus, which lies at the root of the problem, was often keenly felt during the Middle Ages, as various pietist movements attest. Yet on the whole, and sometimes even there, any sense of his absence lacked poignancy inasmuch as his presence was no longer thought of as a worldly concern. He belonged to another and very different existence, a distant heavenly one not quite so human as our own. The hungry soul did not seek Jesus, then, but at best (in the image of the later mystics) the elusive Sacred Heart of Jesus. The man himself was not absent enough, since his absence was by now held to be something quite natural.[160]

On a dualist foundation the eucharistic question could not be properly framed, in other words; neither then could an ecclesial identity turning

---

[158] p. 147.
[159] CD 18.54 (trans. J. H.).
[160] But cf. G. Buccellati 1998:69ff.

on a truly eschatological axis be maintained. With the easing of both political and philosophical estrangement the church grew bolder in offering itself as a substitute for the absent saviour, and as a link to the higher realm he now inhabited. The problem of the presence and the absence became less a question about the church's peculiar footing at the border between two ages, or two histories, than about its task of dispensing on earth a useful heavenly commodity called grace. A sense of self-importance set in, as the ecclesiastical scaffolding went up so that grace might trickle down. What began as a precarious community of the Spirit became ever more conscious of its own paracletic role.[161]

Too many factors were at work here to grasp easily their relative weight, but it is not hard to fix upon a single image which effectively captured the new sense of identity: This is the period of the ascendency of the Virgin Mary. Already in Ambrose and Zeno of Verona we have Mary, quite rightly, as a type of the church. But there were other developments as well. After the triumph of the Theotokos title at the Council of Ephesus the practice of praying to Mary and affording her a unique veneration was widely embraced.[162] These two facts are not unrelated, for the honour and function ascribed to the type belongs also to the antitype. The church itself, as we have seen, was assuming an intercessory role and an exalted status distinct from that of its members. It too had an air of unassailable purity about it, in spite of its participation in the agonizingly difficult world of political responsibility. By appealing to its offerings on their behalf (and by now the cult-oriented sacrificial theory of Cyprian and Cyril of Jerusalem, e.g., had gained ascendency over the Irenaean view)[163] individuals or an entire people might hope to gain favour with God.

It can be argued that belief in a heavenly church as the original cosmic reality naturally came to expression in this way; that it required just such an image, the a-historical and non-eschatological image of a perpetual virgin, as its proper reflection; that Marian dogma is really nothing more than a mirror of ecclesial self-consciousness evolving within a dualist framework. Admittedly this can be pressed too far. But if the precise

---

[161] Our argument here largely parallels that of Heron 1983b:80ff., who attributes the marginalization of Jesus and the process of ecclesiastical substitution to the combined effects of anti-Arianism, the church's changing role in society, and liturgical adjustments (e.g., praying *to* a divine Christ rather than *with* a human one). Cf. 1983:87ff. for his discussion of the marginalization of the Spirit in connection with the *filioque* and with the reification of grace. We are contending, however, for recognition in both cases of an equally important factor, namely, that the discontinuity problem was again being perceived in cosmological rather than christological terms.

[162] It was Augustine, conceding a point to Pelagius, who introduced the idea of Mary's sinlessness into mainstream theology. Theodore of Studios went so far as to claim that she participated in the angelic nature (*Or.* 6.9, Pelikan 2/140f.; cf. *ODCC* 882f., Kelly 494ff.). Aquinas eventually reformulated the doctrine of *hyperdouleia* so as to clarify Mary's status as falling between that of the angels and that of her divine Son.

[163] See Heron 1983b:74ff.

relationship between ecclesiology and mariology is a matter of speculation, the mariological dimensions of ecclesiology plainly suffered distortion from the outset. Cosmological predilections cultivated an idealized view of the church, setting it up to function as a bridge to God in its own right.

At all events, both Mary and the church rapidly took on elevated features. The impact on the way in which they were subsequently conceived was profound. It is often pointed out that Mary offered a more tangibly human face as a focal point for faith and piety than did a Christ who seemed now to stand mainly on the side of God, but as she substituted for her receding Son her story increasingly paralleled his in an artificial way. There was talk of an immaculate conception (rejected in the east), of bodily assumption, of a Queen in heaven, of Mary the ladder to heaven. Each of these notions had its correlate in ecclesiology, which made of Mary its central myth. The church may have had its feet on the ground but its upper parts stretched ever further into the clouds, as it continued to attract to itself the mediatorial function belonging to Jesus.[164]

This false mariological shift, this spatializing movement in which the church abandoned its painful place alongside Jesus at the rupture of diverging histories – where the heart, as Mary was forewarned, is exposed to the sword – for a more comfortable cathedral-building enterprise, began in the east but was only fully realized in the west.

East

Hagia Sophia in Constantinople was built by Justinian, the greatest of Constantine's successors. Here 'the worship of God and the cult of the Theotokos . . . received their fitting artistic statement,'[165] in a triumphant investment of architectural space with the heavenly qualities of a luminous expanse. As it rises towards its great dome all 'is fitted together on high with extraordinary harmony,' wrote Procopius. 'If anyone enters to pray . . . his mind is lifted up and he walks in heaven.'[166] Church buildings indeed emerged during this period as gateways to another world, as symbolically significant structures having (together with the art they contained) an almost sacramental power. About the same time the liturgies

---

[164] See Pelikan 3/160ff. (cf. Rev. 10). Medieval notions of Mary, taken together with teaching about angels and saints and ecclesiastical princes, can rightly be seen as a Christian form of the late neoplatonist mythologization of the principle of mediation, though of course the latter's immanentism was inconsistent with official dogma.

[165] Pelikan 1/342f. The emperor too had his monument, then – appropriately enough, since 'God had given Christians "two gifts, the priesthood and the empire, by which affairs on earth are healed and ordered as they are in heaven"' (ibid. 2/144, quoting Theodore of Studios, who spoke thus in a moment of peace between the two gifts).

[166] Quoted H. Wybrew 1984:74. See H. W. Janson 1986:217ff. for further discussion of Hagia Sophia.

performed in them were becoming increasingly ritualistic; allegorical representations of the life of Jesus grew more complex as a way of making present the benefits of the redemption wrought in him.[167] These actions shared the sacramental potency, for both temporal and spatial structures were meant to be translucent with an eternal light, like the incarnate one himself on the mount of transfiguration.[168] At the material level, it is important to notice, icons began to proliferate as the preferred means of contact with kingdom personages and realities, gradually replacing reception of the eucharistic elements where the laity were concerned. Sacerdotalism grew apace, strengthened not only by a cultic view of the eucharist but by a notion of the hierarchical transmission and appropriation of divine light. Monasticism, through which most systems of spiritual gradations entered Christianity, flourished alongside. Presiding over all was the image of the Virgin, which soon came to dominate the apses of Christendom's grand churches as well as the dingy cells of the monks.[169]

All of this represented a huge if gradual alteration to the ethos and traditions of earlier times, an alteration which found its voice and its justification in the religious genius of Denys the Areopagite. Just as the condemnation of Origen was being made official under Justinian – a condemnation made necessary, ironically, by the fact that his followers were causing disunity in the church and hence in the empire, which now depended upon the church for moral and social stability – Denys revived certain aspects of early Alexandrian theology in a more acceptable form, ensuring them a long afterlife in both east and west.[170] There is also a good deal of controversy about the interpretation of Denys, of course.

---

[167] Wybrew (60ff.) points to the Antiochene influence which, in drawing attention to the successive stages of Jesus' life, undermined the notion of participation in a present reality in favour of a commemoration of past events. But the real problem is in the fact that for the Greek mind imitation *was* (or could be) participation.

[168] Janson speaks of the 'illusion of unreality' lent to flat surfaces by early Christian mosaics, which contributed to the strangely ethereal effect of buildings like Hagia Sophia; in this sense Christian architecture was 'antimonumental' (p. 203). Yet both the architectural and the liturgical developments of this period reflect the assimilation of things ecclesiastical to the imperial dignity.

[169] See Pelikan 2/139ff. In the liturgies of Basil and Chrysostom the Virgin was lauded as 'our all-holy, immaculate, supremely blessed Queen, the Theotokos and ever-Virgin Mary;' to introduce her praises into various nooks and crannies of the liturgical tradition, so that she was verbally as well as visually well represented, became a common preoccupation. According to Nicephorus, Mary was appointed by God in connection with her Son as 'mediator and secure patron,' overseeing the welfare of church and empire.

[170] This second irony has been noted by many. Pelikan (1/348) opines that 'most of the doctrines on account of which the Second Council of Constantinople anathematized Origen were far less dangerous to the tradition of catholic orthodoxy than was the Crypto-Origenism canonized in the works of Dionysius the Areopagite.' Balthasar (2/207f.), who mounts a spirited defense of Denys, reminds us that his theology 'was seen and used for a thousand years and longer as one of the basic forms of the Church's theology. He remains, with Augustine, *the* classic representative of theological form in the West' (*sic*).

Doubtless his strong apophatic emphasis and his far more positive view of creation set him at a safe distance from Origen. So does the much sturdier communal dimension, which Andrew Louth has recently defended. Balthasar even goes so far as to claim that it 'belongs to the Areopagite to have caught up the whole spiritual energy of the Alexandrines and the Cappadocians in his work and at the same time to have banished definitively their tendency to threaten the Incarnation, the visible Church and the resurrection of the flesh.'[171] Whatever we make of that, it remains the case that Denys stood quite consciously 'at the point where Christ and Plato meet,'[172] which is where Origen had also stood to take his bearings. Luther's judgment in *The Babylonian Captivity of the Church* that Denys 'platonizes more than he Christianizes' is not easily dismissed.[173]

His resistance to rationalism (including Origen's) and 'relentless pursuit of the transcendent'[174] were in part an outcropping of, and in part a response to, the late neoplatonist tradition. Preoccupation with the problem of the one and the many persisted, answered now in the fashion of Iamblichus and Proclus by means of a theurgic system of processions and returns, differentiations and unions – the latter holding pride of place over the former.[175] Trinitarian commitments told, however. In the threeness of God Denys found a principle of 'transcendent fecundity,' of a positive going-forth in creation and revelation that left no room for polytheism or for a loveless deity; in the oneness, a principle of the recovery and maintenance of unity.[176] This translated once again into a cosmological programme of descent and ascent, but one in which the doctrine of pre-existence and a fall into diversity was rejected, along with the natural divinity of the soul and other Greek tenets at odds with a Nicene faith. Like most everyone else, Denys did subscribe to a graded scale of being in which higher creatures mediate the light and power of God according to the degree of simplicity proper to them, and attained by them. The ascent of the soul or mind, whereby it achieves a likeness to the 'supra celestial spirits' in their pure concentration on God, was still the chief object of his anthropology, though the pinnacle of this ascent was now understood in terms of ἔκστασις and unknowing rather than in terms of

[171] 2/184.
[172] Louth 1989:11.
[173] See McGinn 1/158. 'The student of Dionysius has every right to be confused regarding what appears to be the central underlying issue: Christian or Neoplatonist?' (D. Carabine 281)
[174] Carabine 299.
[175] 'In the divine realm unities hold a higher place than differentiations,' says Denys (*DN* 2.11).
[176] Cf. *DN* 1.4f., 2.4f., 5.2, 11.6, 13.2f. God himself, who is ultimately beyond oneness and threeness, Denys styles τὴν τριαδικὴν ἑνάδα (cf. Lossky 1974:23ff., who argues that the principle supplied in the previous note applies to God only economically and not immanently).

the refining away of material existence. Removal of the world was necessary epistemologically but not ontologically, at least not in Origen's sense.[177]

One of his interesting innovations was to provide a systematic outline of the angelic and ecclesiastical orders through which the divine light is refracted, and divinization realized. These hierarchies (one of many Dionysian neologisms) are the cosmic backbone, so to speak, transmitting the impulses of the knowledge of God to the lower extremities of creation.[178] To understand the role of the churchly hierarchy in particular, it is important to observe that it functions symbolically by pointing to a higher, more unified truth.

> [T]hose beings and those orders which are superior to us are also incorporeal. Their hierarchy belongs to the domain of the conceptual and is something out of this world. We see our human hierarchy, on the other hand, as our nature allows, pluralized in a great variety of perceptible symbols lifting us upward hierarchically until we are brought as far as we can be into the unity of divinization.

Holy men, especially the bishops 'standing erect before the holy altar,' thus wield in word and sacrament the temporal and material signs of our salvation, assisting us as we strive to ascend inwardly to that which is ultimately unspeakable and unknowable. They achieve this both through their personal proximity to Jesus (a point of essential agreement with Donatism) and by re-enacting the descending and ascending movement, from the One to the many and back to the One again, which lies at the heart of his work.[179]

But what about Jesus himself? How far is this worldview christologically grounded? Denys calls Jesus the source and summit of every hierarchy. He is not referring exclusively or even primarily to Jesus of Nazareth, however, but to 'Jesus who is transcendent mind, utterly divine mind, who is the source and the being underlying all hierarchy, all

---

[177] 'Since the union of divinized minds with the Light beyond all deity occurs in the cessation of all intelligent activity, the godlike unified minds who imitate these angels as far as possible praise it most appropriately through the denial of all beings . . . And yet, to praise this divinely beneficent Providence you must turn to all creation. It is there at the centre of everything and everything has it for a destiny.' (*DN* 1.5; cf. 1.1f., 7.3, *MT* 1.3.)

[178] A hierarchy, he explains (*CH* 3.1f.; cf. 8.2, 10.1ff., 13.3f.), 'is a sacred order, a state of understanding and an activity approximating as closely as possible to the divine. And it is uplifting to the imitation of God in proportion to the enlightenments divinely given to it.' 'Their function is to "bring God down out of silence," to initiate the lower orders into the science of the higher ones, and in this way to serve as a channel to the descending procession of God and also to the ascension of the being toward the transcending Good' (Meyendorff 102, quoting R. Roques). They do not mediate being itself, however, which is the immediate gift of God; they have rather a *theophanic* character, which is the character of creation as such. This distinction separates Denys from the neoplatonists (see Louth 84ff., McGinn 1/ 169f.).

[179] See *EH* 1 and 3.3.10ff. Denys' consistent focus on the clerical is significant, but it should not be forgotten that the ecclesiastical hierarchy includes a threefold ordering of the laity.

sanctification, all the workings of God, who is the ultimate in divine power.' This is the one who assimilates the members of the heavenly hierarchy, as far as can be, to his own light. As for their human counterparts,

> with that yearning for beauty which raises us upward (and which is raised up) to him, he pulls together all our many differences. He makes our life, disposition, and activity something one and divine, and he bestows on us the power appropriate to a sacred priesthood. Approaching therefore the holy activity of the sacred office we come closer to those beings who are superior to us. We imitate as much as we can their abiding, unwavering, and sacred constancy, and we thereby come to look up to the blessed and ultimately divine ray of Jesus himself.[180]

In other words, the Dionysian Jesus is more akin to the cosmic Christ of Origen than to that of Irenaeus. He is the eternal Logos who mediates creaturely being, unfolding it in its diversity and renewing it again in unity. In the liturgy we are indeed called to 'give our full attention to his divine life in the flesh,' by which he 'beneficently accomplished for us a unifying communion with himself,' but ultimately it is to 'the simple, hidden oneness of Jesus, the most divine Word,'[181] that Denys would have us look. Seeking the divine in Jesus remains the operative principle, for the incarnate one is at once the most fully articulated moment in God's self-revelation *and* the point of greatest hiddenness.[182]

What do we mean? In the incarnation God comes to meet us, suddenly and directly. Here 'the transcendent has put aside its own hiddenness and has revealed itself to us by becoming a human being.' On the other hand, says Denys, 'he is hidden even after this revelation, or, if I may speak in a more divine fashion, is hidden even amid the revelation.'[183] As a rejection of any rationalization of the incarnation, or any false kenoticism, this qualification is entirely necessary, of course; but there is more to it than that. It is not simply a matter of God maintaining his freedom and sovereignty in his revelation, as trinitarian theology insists. It is not simply a way of pointing to the irreducibly (tri)personal nature of revelation, which defies any reductive objectification. It is also a matter of the underlying dialectic of differentiations and unions, immanence and transcendence, presence and absence, which governs Dionysian thought. The incarnation, though 'sudden' and unique, belongs to the former pole and as such is only a beginning of the knowledge of God. Real knowledge,

---

[180] *EH* 1.1 (*pace* Balthasar 2/200). The doctrine of Aristotle that what is below is moved by desire and love to emulate what is above obviously exerts an important influence here.

[181] *EH* 3.3.12; cf. *Ep.* 4, *DN* 2.10, 7.4, *CH* 4.4.

[182] 'Jesus, who is above individual being, became a being with a true human nature' (*MT* 3): This belongs to affirmative theology, to kataphasis; it is indeed 'the most evident idea in theology' (*DN* 2.9). But there is an apophatic counterpoint in which 'every affirmation regarding Jesus' love for humanity has the force of a negation pointing towards transcendence' (*Ep.* 4). Cf. Balthasar 2/192f.

[183] *Ep.* 3.

the knowledge that is had only through unknowing, requires us to make a kind of turn (with and around the incarnate one as God's self-articulation) back towards the unarticulated Source. For the incarnation does not so much discover the hidden God to us, as enable *us* to discover the hidden God. To do that we must eventually go beyond everything creaturely, following Jesus in the movement of his ascension. We must turn from the human to the divine.[184]

What actually becomes of Jesus is not made clear in the extant works. Does the controversial monenergism of the fourth letter leave room for some form of eschatological docetism? How shall we interpret the comment that 'because of his generous work for our salvation he himself entered the order of revealers and is called "the angel of great counsel"'?[185] Why is there no treatment of the parousia? Perhaps we do not need to press Denys in this way, since he confesses the resurrection of the whole person. Jesus 'generously snatches from the old swallowing pit of ruinous death anyone who . . . has been baptized "into his death," and renews them in an inspired and eternal existence.'[186] The bodies of the righteous will share with them in that existence, for 'their whole being will be granted the peace which will make them Christlike.'[187] At the same time, however, he does not want us to entertain any this-worldly ideas about the next, where we shall be absorbed 'in most holy contemplation,' with 'our minds away from passion and from earth,' marvelously conformed to 'those in the heavens above.'[188] In other words, Denys (like the early Augustine) is not quite comfortable with biblical and credal eschatology, which introduces a foreign element into his vertical and essentially

---

[184] This does not mean letting go of the incarnation, which as a 'theandric' work is both a temporal and an eternal one, the fixed centre of all creaturely history and the hinge of all true knowledge of God. The question must be asked, however, why we are not offered the long treatise on the incarnation which Denys' method would lead us to expect. Instead we have only the exceedingly brief, sharp comments on Christ in the third and fourth letters, and in *Ecclesiastical Hierarchy* a thorough discussion of the eucharist (cf. Balthasar 2/162ff., 177). Surely the dangerous climate of christological controversy cannot account for this. Could the explanation be found in a combination of two factors? First, the territory proper to the incarnation – as an imparting of God to the world which genuinely coincides with God and with the world, which declares them in their difference and in their unity – is territory that has *already* been covered in the doctrines of creation and providence. Second, as the sudden completion of that impartation the incarnation compels us to move decisively from immanence to transcendence, and thus from a particular event to a universally repeated one. The particular event itself is a point of pure transition, about which it is difficult to speak directly.

[185] *CH* 4.4 (cf. *Ep.* 9.5).

[186] *EH* 4.3.10f. (cf. 3.3.11). This passage goes on to speak of Jesus having 'received the sanctification of the divine Spirit for us,' and arranging now 'for the gift to us of the divine Spirit.'

[187] *EH* 7.1.1f., 7.3.9.

[188] *DN* 1.4. Note that the hierarchies are not going to be overturned (cf. 1 Cor. 6:3, *AH* 5.36.3); humans will simply be conformed to the lower rank of the heavenly hierarchy. Hence whoever becomes 'truly indifferent to the realities of the flesh . . . will have arrived at the highest possible measure of divinization' (*EH* 3.3.7).

a-historical worldview.[189] His *Grundmotif* is ascension of the mind, not ascension in the flesh.

Here we may question Balthasar's judgment that Denys has taken the transcendence of God to the point of denying that there is any 'direct opposition between him and anything created; and therefore the latter is set forth in its limitedness and finitude, and as such affirmed and sustained.'[190] That he has attempted something very like this can be admitted and admired. It is doubtful, however, whether he has done so in the only way possible, that is, christologically. His apophaticism suggests that he has begun instead with the problem of creation as such, and a secret opposition already lies behind his construal of the creative act in terms of procession and return. God is not free to be our creator simply as the one who speaks; his going forth in that address always requires a reconciliation to himself.[191] The same opposition (which appears more starkly in Hegel's attempt to Christianize neoplatonism) can be detected when the incarnation comes into the picture. Though God is free to become incarnate, it is not *as* incarnate that he perfects communion with us. The Christ-event, as a critical moment within the divine ἔκστασις, serves only to make possible an answering movement of human ἔκστασις which surpasses and supersedes all creatureliness, even God's own. That is why it is unnecessary and unhelpful for Denys to develop too robust an eschatology, despite the fact that there is no question of creation disappearing.

Now on such a scheme the eucharistic question about the presence and absence of Jesus is bound to be conflated with a quite different question – arguably a misleading one – about the presence and absence of God. It will be perceived in similar terms, as one of epistemic distance, and resolved in the same way, by reference to the hierarchies which span the firmament created by gradations in that distance. That is, appeal will be made to the towering conduit of revelation, impressively arranged in its sacred ranks, which God has bestowed 'as a gift to ensure the salvation and divinization of every being endowed with reason and intelligence.'[192] From this falsification of the eucharistic question, and of its answer, at least three closely related consequences follow.

First is the rearranging of the church's corporate life along the lines indicated by the principle of symbolic imitation, which is an aesthetic rather

---

[189] On Denys' view of history, see Balthasar 2/152, 176f.

[190] Bathasar (2/194; cf. 166) refers us to *DN* 11.1, e.g., that marvelous passage on the harmony of the manifold.

[191] The incessant flow of πρόοδος and ἐπιστροφή, which has κατάφασις and ἀπόφασις as its epistemological counterpart, is transcended by God in his self-abiding (μονή), of course. God's complete freedom in and for creation is nonetheless called into question by it. So too is creation's own liberty, for the panentheistic implications of the neoplatonist construct cannot be avoided. (Is Denys working in fact with an *ex deo* rather than an *ex nihilo*? Cf. *DN* 10.1.)

[192] *EH* 1.4; cf. 5.2. Angels form 'the missing ontological link' to the invisible world (Pelikan 2/141f.). The higher ones dwell 'in the neighbourhood of the Deity;' for those beneath them, God 'concentrates his clear enlightenment for the unknown union with his hiddenness in proportion to the degree of distance from conformity to God' (*CH* 13.4).

than a sacramental one.[193] The case for charging Denys with nominalism can be overstated; the claim that he presents the sacraments 'in complete separation from the central mystery of Christianity, the incarnation,' is erroneous. But imitation rather than intervention, elevation rather than transformation, communion of 'one-like' minds rather than communion in an eschatological reality, these *are* his fundamentals.[194] They lead to a doxological structure far removed from that of the early church, not least through the multiplication of the symbols to be found in the church's liturgical apparatus. Indeed, they lead inevitably to an arbitrary extension of the church's actual sacramental footing. We are not thinking here of iconography, which offers windows to heaven more opaque than those afforded by participation in the eucharist itself but better situated (as Denys noted) for the average person.[195] We are thinking rather of the so-called sacrament of oil, which on his triadic arrangement perfects that of water, which belongs to the many, and that of bread and wine, which belongs to the few, inasmuch as it remains the exclusive province of the hierarch alone. This extrapolation from two basic sacraments to three is by no means incidental; on the contrary, it is quite decisive. It speaks volumes about the kind of ecclesiology which was now emerging, namely, one controlled not by Jesus-history and the apostolic tradition, but by monastic spirituality and its cosmological presuppositions.[196]

Second is the incorporation into sacramental life of a Pelagian element (already inherent in the neoplatonism on which Denys drew) which no proclamation of divine grace can erase. In the *corpus Areopagiticum* talk of grace and of condescending generosity is prominent enough, but talk of tireless imitation and raising oneself up as far as possible – ἔρως responding to Ἔρως along the arduous path of unions and negations – is even more prominent.[197] Limits are placed on this Pelagianism by the fixed nature of the hierarchies, of course, but that only introduces a more systemic form of elitism. All spiritual beings may desire the same deity, yearning as one after the God who is always present and yet always absent;

---

[193] *EH* 4.3.1. Denys (see Balthasar 2/164ff., esp. 183f.) would not agree with this 'rather;' but we reject any direct co-ordination of the aesthetic and the sacramental, since the latter, and only the latter, is eschatological.

[194] Cf. Meyendorff 105ff., whose complaint that the eucharistic rite 'appears in its very essence as an "image" of intelligible communion' is not fully answered by those who defend Denys. There is some truth in Pelikan's comment (1/346) that his approach threatens – even here! – to make Jesus himself 'no more than a "chief symbol" for the transcendent reality of man's union with God through mystical ascent.'

[195] *EH* 3.3.2

[196] See *EH* 4.3.3, 4.3.12 (cf. Louth 63ff.). Denys is careful to justify all this by an Origenist appeal to secret tradition: Since we 'need perceptible things to lift us up into the domain of conceptions,' human things to lift us up to the divine (*EH* 1.5), 'the sacred iniators of our tradition resorted freely to symbolism appropriate to God, regarding the sacraments of the most holy mysteries' (*Ep.* 9.1). They were shown by the celestial hierarchy how to do this, but knowledge of their reasons 'is not for everyone' (*EH* 1.4f.).

[197] See e.g. *CH* 12.3; cf. *DN* 4.10ff.

but all do not participate in the blessedness of his presence in the same way. The share of each is apportioned according to station.[198]

Third is the more or less successful harmonization, at the liturgical level, of the rigorous spirituality espoused by the monastic movement and the realities of an imperial church. The difficulty here was not restricted to the latter's impulse towards an ever-grander spectacle, through which it vied with the splendour of the emperor's court to display on earth something of the glories of heaven. Above all, it concerned the general loss of discipline amid the increasing throngs of church-goers. The Dionysian vision (such was its genius) addressed both these problems. The ecclesiastical hierarchies, particularly in their liturgical capacities, were an extension of the heavenly hierarchies of the seraphim, the dominions, and the principalities. What further justification of outward glory could be required? But of course it was inward glory that really mattered.[199] Here these same hierarchies, depending on one's vantage point, provided either the necessary access to the divine or several layers of *insulation* between it and the common person. It will be recalled that by now very few of the laity were communicating regularly, and that in the east the most integral parts of the liturgy were gradually being withdrawn from their sight and hearing. The temple veil was being resewn, for what was holy had to be protected from the mob.[200] Yet the mob still had to be serviced. Denys' compelling exposition of the liturgy and its ranks of λειτουργόι helped to ensconce in the wider church the principles of mystical theology (another neologism) that were being developed in communities like his own, while managing to make the necessary allowances for the ritually unwashed.

For the polity and spirituality, indeed, for the entire mindset of the Byzantine church, few developments would prove more significant than these three, which together made possible a transposition of the descent–ascent scheme of Christian Platonism into something institutionally durable and concrete. Naturally that was not Denys' doing alone, but it is difficult to think of anyone who contributed more.[201]

* * *

[198] *EH* 1.2; cf. *DN* 1.2. On κατ' ἀξίαν see Balthasar 2/171f.

[199] More divine minds 'do not gaze after that glory so stupidly praised by the mob' (*EH* 4.3.1) – i.e., 'the profane' (1.5), 'the general crowd' (3.2), 'those uniniated regarding contemplation' (3.3.2).

[200] Wybrew (86f.) notes Justinian's unsuccessful opposition to the silencing of the anaphora, commenting that few changes 'have been so far-reaching in their implications and consequences.' In time an actual veil across the inner sanctuary was introduced in monastic circles, and eventually the iconostasis came into wide use in the churches. Nicholas of Andida, while acknowledging the people's complaints, argued that 'the holy liturgy is celebrated principally for those who have offered and for those on whose behalf they have offered' (quoted ibid. 138).

[201] Meyendorff (102ff.) argues that Denys 'marked forever Byzantine piety.' Leaving obscure the 'corporate, christological, and eschatological' dimensions of the eucharist, he

As it happens, Denys owes his own theological afterlife largely to Maximus the Confessor, who is said to represent Greek theology in its maturity.[202] That maturity derives in part from a creative synthesis between the Irenaean and Origenist traditions, after some further corrective surgery to the latter. Maximus himself was happy to talk about bodily ascension. He even revived the doctrine of recapitulation, if in a modified form.[203] So stern was his resistance to docetic lines of thought that he braved the cruelty of the imperial surgeon rather than recant his objections to monothelitism. Even so, there is reason to doubt that this justly famous monk succeeded at liberating christology from its bondage to cosmology, or eastern ecclesiology from its dualist heritage. Let us look briefly at a cosmic vision which, though quite independent in some respects, was much indebted to 'the true theologian, the great and holy Denys.'

Crucial to Maximus was the anthropomorphic worldview of Socratic and pre-Socratic speculation; the universe was a μακράνθρωπος and each man a microcosm.[204] The Christian way in which he developed this idea can be displayed in a diagram:

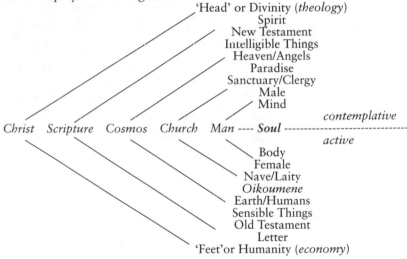

opened the door to a kind of 'magical clericalism' on the one hand, and a private perfectionism on the other. Under his influence the liturgy came to be seen as 'a symbolic drama that the assembly attend as spectators, the mystery of which can only be penetrated by initiated individuals.' (Curiously, Meyendorff also argues that it is only in piety, and not in theology, that Denys made a lasting impact, a dichotomy neither Denys nor many others would recognize.)

[202] It was Maximus (see *Amb.* 5) who delivered Denys from the taint of monophysitism.

[203] God has laid hold of the entire creation from its centre: 'all time and all that is in time has received in Christ its beginning and its end' (*Q. Thal.* 60; cf. *Amb.* 41, *Or. Dom.* 2).

[204] See *Myst.* 7 (cf. L. Thunberg 1965:140ff., 1985:73f.). Gregory of Nyssa (*Hom. Op.* 16.1) criticizes the notion of man as microcosm as 'dignifying man with the attributes of the gnat or the mouse.'

With the advent of the God-man, as the unifying Logos in person, all the dualities which structure our existence are held together. The lower elements are integrated into the higher, generating a unity without confusion or loss of identity. A cosmos (macro and micro) becomes possible.[205]

Also crucial was the patristic notion of *creatio ex nihilo*, which Denys had de-emphasized. Maximus put it to work in a new way, consistent with the above. The mystery of the world is precisely that it has non-being as its own proper ground.[206] Continually faced by the threat of imminent dissolution, it can exist truly only insofar as it allows this very fact to stand forth; insofar, that is, as it is constantly referred back to its creator. Such is the task of man, who by virtue of his microcosmic constitution becomes (in Balthasar's apt terminology) the cosmic liturgist, the mediator of creation. What he fails to achieve here, because of self-centred fascination with material objects, is achieved by the incarnate Word, who binds the world together across the cracks which have opened up in it: Cracks between male and female, paradise and the inhabited world, heaven and earth, intelligible and sensible, God and humanity. Christ puts to death both the flesh and the fleshly mind, while introducing a Godward motion into human nature that carries man beyond himself into communion with the divine. He thus makes possible the repair of every debilitating breach within creation, since by arriving at God (through self-denial) it arrives also at its own integrity.[207]

But what exactly is the role played in Maximus' scheme by ascension in the flesh? In the virgin birth Christ transcended the first major division, that of gender. In the resurrection, and the communion he held with his disciples during the forty days, he transcended the second, that between paradise and this world.

> Then, by his ascension into heaven, he clearly united heaven and earth, and with his earthly body that is of the same nature and consubstantial with ours he entered into heaven and showed that the whole nature that can be perceived through the senses is, by the most universal *logos* of its being, one, thus obscuring the peculiar nature of the division which cuts it into two. Then, in addition to this, by passing with his soul and body, that is, with the whole of our nature, through all the divine and intelligible ranks of heaven, he united the sensible and the intelligible and showed the convergence of the whole creation with the One according to its most original and universal *logos*,

---

[205] See *Myst.* 1ff., *Amb.* 56. What Clement (*Strom.* 2.317f.; cf. Plato, *Tim.* 33f., Plotinus, *Enn.* 2.2.1) ascribes to the Logos, Maximus ascribes to Christ (cf. Irenaeus, *AH* 5.18ff.). Creation, Scripture and Christ constitute a progressive realization of God's will 'to effect the mystery of his embodiment' (*Amb.* 7; Thunberg 1985:75).

[206] *Amb.* 41; but cf. *CT* 1.48ff. For his part, Denys 'prefers to say that we come from (ἐκ) God than from nothing' (Louth 1989:85; cf. Thunberg 1965:427).

[207] See *Amb.* 41, *Or. Dom.* 2, 5. It is in this priesting of man, so to speak, and in man's priestly activity that the hope of creation lies, says Zizioulas (1990:5; cf. Balthasar's *Liturgie Cosmique*).

which is completely undivided and at rest in itself. And finally, considered in his humanity, he goes to God himself, having clearly appeared, as it is written, in the presence of God the Father on our behalf (Heb. 9:24), as a human being.[208]

In these three phases, bodily ascension completed Christ's work of reconciliation and recapitulation, bringing the cosmos into subjection to himself and to God. It laid the groundwork for a new reality that is to be revealed at the parousia.[209]

Maximus thus takes up neglected aspects of the ontology of Irenaeus, and recovers something of his eschatological focus as well. Nonetheless he accommodates everything as far as possible to the spirituality of the intervening period, which is marked by its zeal for the soul's union with God and its distrust of bodily entanglements. It is frequently pointed out that Origen's στάσις/κίνησις/γένεσις account of the present creation is reversed by Maximus, who affirms the world's essential goodness in a more biblical way by speaking instead of γένεσις/κίνησις/στάσις.[210] What is not so frequently noted, however, is that this reversal simply reproduces the latter half of Origen's larger scheme, which is of course στάσις/κίνησις/γένεσις/κίνησις/στάσις. The difference is still significant, since the breaking down of the Alexandrian's symmetry imports a different content (our world!) into the final στάσις. Yet we quickly discover that Maximus does not understand creation's eternal rest as Irenaeus does. It is indeed a perfection of our nature through communion with God, but much of what Irenaeus regards as belonging to that nature Maximus regards as belonging rather to its distorted τρόπος, that is, to its fallen mode of existence. When we hear that all visible things need a cross, all intelligible things a tomb, we may understand this as an existential requirement of that humanity which through the fall has developed in opposition to its unifying vocation.[211] But the simultaneity of creation and fall in Maximus suggests that his correction of Origen is incomplete, that a confusion between ktisiology and hamartiology is still operative, and that behind

---

[208] *Amb.* 41 (Louth 1996:159f., italics omitted).

[209] i.e., for 'a greater and more mystical arrangement in the time of the expected universal consummation, when the world, as man, will die to its life of appearances and rise again renewed of its oldness in the resurrection expected presently' (*Myst.* 7; cf. *Myst.* 24, *CT* 2.28f.).

[210] See Meyendorff 132ff. (cf. Louth 1996:66ff.).

[211] 'All visible things need a cross, that is, a capacity which holds back the participation in what is active in them according to sense. All intelligible things need a tomb, that is, the total immobilizing of the activities of the mind in them. For when this natural activity and movement with respect to all things is taken away along with their participation, the Word which alone exists by itself as if he had risen from the dead is manifested anew, having in outline all which is from him, though absolutely nothing has any kinship with him in any natural relationship. For it is by grace and not by nature that he is the salvation of those who are saved' (*CT* 1.67).

this maxim lies a lingering doubt about the goodness of the temporal and material world. If we hope to be godlike we must wash away our fondness for matter 'like dust from our spiritual eyes.'[212]

In other words, the Maximian vision remains very much a monastic one; *ascensus* and *ascesis* are virtually synonymous.[213] This translates once again into a serious loss of continuity between the old creation and the new. Who would say, he asks us, 'that heaven, the kingdom prepared from the world's foundation . . . for those who are worthy, is in any way identical to the earth?'[214] To enter that kingdom man must attain to a more angelic mode of being, exchanging the active life for the contemplative life. This will not mean leaving the body, but the body 'will become like the soul' when man arrives in the resurrection at that divine realm which is 'above age, time, and place' – at that end which is also the beginning and in which 'no middle shall be contemplated.'[215] Here his only motion will be motion into God, which means a cessation of the natural activities of body and mind alike. Here, where the distractions of our present spatio-temporal modality do not exist, he may hope finally to 'behold with the naked mind the pure Word as he is in himself.'[216] Meanwhile, his task is the pursuit of those transforming virtues which carry him upwards towards a truly passionless existence, following the trail blazed by Christ.

It would appear, then, that Maximus overwrites his correction of the Origenist tradition with something at least of the old error, much as Denys does. Unlike that of Denys, his cosmology is anthropocentric as well as anthropomorphic, and rests in its entirety on the incarnate Jesus.[217] But this further advance against Origenism turns into a retreat. The communion between creator and creature established through the incarnation is based on a dynamic which subtly reintroduces the abandoned

[212] OD 4 (fourth petition). Cf. Q.Thal. 59 (Balthasar 1967.9). 'The moment man comes into being he departs through sin from his true origin.'
[213] See CT 2.32, 2.59, 2.94, OD 2. One must pull out the nails that bind the soul to the flesh, escaping the passions and rationalizing all that is by 'holding it together in its pure relationship with the Logos' (Thunberg 1965:429; cf. CT 1.83, 1.99). Having come thus to 'the border of natural knowledge,' and being 'no more sinfully attached to the world in its manifoldness,' the mind 'is naked and open to mystical illumination' (ibid.; cf. Carit. 1.86).
[214] OD 4 (second petition); cf. Amb. 10.32f.
[215] See CT 1.68ff., 2.86ff., Myst. 7. The excluded middle is the world of becoming in which man 'was once nurtured as a child;' it will give way to 'a settled state of sameness.' (Note that an Irenaean theme is here made to serve an Origenist view.)
[216] i.e., in the original divine simplicity in which he is already 'called flesh,' though not yet incarnate, since he 'possesses the clear and naked forms of the truth of all things' (CT 2.60, 2.73). It is ironic that Maximus accuses the Jews (sic) of despising the visible creation and its Maker, when it is his own teaching that only 'by abandoning his body and whatever is the body's' can a man seek after God (OD 4, second petition).
[217] See Q. Thal. 60 (cf. D. Yeago 1996:163ff.). What is needed, however, is a cosmology that is anthropocentric *without* being anthropomorphic.

symmetry.[218] There is a descending movement towards the earthy and the particular, which amounts to a 'thickening' of the Logos and an expansion of the cosmos through the differentiation of its various λόγοι, followed by an ascending movement in a return to the universal, that is, the 'thinning' of the Logos and the contraction of the cosmos through deification. And this symmetry has its implications for spirituality. It means, as usual, a turning from the earthly Jesus to the cosmic Christ. A strong echo of Origen can be heard when we are told that even *Jesus*, from our perspective, requires a cross and a tomb:

> Those who bury the Lord with honor will also behold him gloriously risen, while to all those who do not he is unseen. For he is no longer caught by those who lay snares, since having no longer the external covering by which he seemed to allow himself to be caught by those who wanted him, and by which he endured the Passion for the salvation of all.[219]

Indeed, Maximus has a good deal to say on our subject that sounds, if not like Origen, then like Augustine, with whom he was also familiar. Since bodily ascension is strictly a function of ascension of the mind, and ascension of the mind is what Christ came to make possible,[220] the temptation to subjectivity is irresistible:

> For those who search according to the flesh after the meaning of God, the Lord does not ascend to the Father; but for those who seek him out in a spiritual way through lofty contemplations he does ascend to the Father. Let us, then, not always hold him here below though he came down here out of love to be with us. Rather, let us go up to the Father along with him, leaving behind the earth and what is earthly . . .[221]

In a claim of great consequence for the eucharistic problem, he even asserts that it is no longer necessary 'that those who seek the Lord should seek him outside themselves.'[222] We follow his trajectory 'if we know him not

---

[218] That dynamic is already hinted at in the epistemological thesis that 'the affirmation of superbeing must be the negation of beings, and the affirmation of beings must be the negation of superbeing' (*Myst.* intro.). But is this thesis compatible with the principle that 'God has no contrary' (*Carit.* 3.27f.)?

[219] *CT* 1.62; cf. 2.37ff., *Amb.* 33. Thunberg (1965:420ff., 1985:173) insists that none of this ever takes us beyond the incarnation; that descending and ascending, thickening and thinning, remain in a dialectical relationship. But is there not in any case a self-cancelling symmetry, and does it not tell in eschatology? See *Myst.* 15ff. (esp. 24), where the closing of the church doors after the liturgy of the Word signifies the passing away of material things.

[220] See again *Amb.* 41. Recapitulation is the work of every person who, with a mind 'genuinely hastening towards God' in the light of Christ, 'passes through all things in search of unity,' until coming to God himself.

[221] *CT* 2.47. With subjectivity goes repetition, of course, not only of the act but of the agent: The soul that rises above the passions belonging to worldly dualities receives 'the full power of knowing the divine nature insofar as this is possible . . . By this power, Christ is always born mysteriously and willingly, becoming incarnate through those who are saved' (*OD* 4, second petition).

[222] *CT* 2.35; cf. 2.29. Simeon the New Theologian drew the conclusion that Christ is always present, and that the responsibility for failing to see him lies with us (Pelikan 2/259).

in the limited condition of his descent in the incarnation but in the majestic splendor of his natural infinitude.' Beginners, says Maximus, may cling to the one who had 'neither form nor beauty,' but the advancing gnostic will climb 'the lofty mountain of his transfiguration before the creation of the world.'[223] Taking leave of the flesh, he will be 'snatched up on the clouds of loftier understandings to the diaphanous air of mystical contemplation, where he will ever be able to be with the Lord.'[224]

Maximus has been praised for weaving together the cosmological interests of the Greeks with the biblical interest in salvation history, but it is not at all clear that the accolade is deserved. Can such teaching do other than cultivate a process of interiorization, favouring the former against the latter? Can it sustain, as it is said to, an ontology which takes seriously the many as well as the one, or support an ecclesiology which elevates κοινωνία over contemplation?[225] To be sure, the deifying unity which Christ inaugurates is not achieved by doing away with creaturely particularity, but by overcoming the dissolute tendency of the particular, manifesting it in relation to the whole.[226] Yet in Christ's own case (to identify just one difficulty) this means the laying aside of his 'external covering' for a cosmic ubiquity. How we are to square this with ascension in the flesh is far from obvious. The ascended one appears rather to take on the role of the universal Νοῦς or 'world-building spirit'[227] which the Greeks believed to be responsible for all motion and order. Maximus is even prepared to speak of him as the Logos incarnate in all things, and so to apply Chalcedonian principles to the entire creation along the lines of his *tantum/quantum* principle.[228] If we are still talking about ascension in the flesh, and hence about the affirmation of the particular, it is increasingly difficult to distinguish from its alternative.

Now the immanentist aspect of his christology could only encourage the general misconception of absence as a form of existential distance.[229]

---

[223] See *CT* 1.97, 2.13, 2.18, 2.27ff., 2.37ff. *Pace* Louth 1996:70f., *Amb.* 10.27 does not suggest 'an ever deepening engagement with the Incarnate Word.'

[224] *CT* 2.50 (modified)

[225] Zizioulas (1985:92ff.) believes Maximus to have achieved his remarkable reconciliation between Greek and Hebrew by way of a Christian ontology of love, to which otherness and communion are fundamental. But we may ask what is meant by communion in a context where contemplation (a word which occurs more than 800 times) is surely the dominant category.

[226] God makes all beings, 'which are by nature distant from one another,' to 'converge in each other by the singular force of their relationship to him as origin. Through this force he leads all beings to a common and unconfused identity of movement and existence . . . This reality abolishes and dims their particular relations considered according to each one's nature, but not by dissolving or destroying them or putting an end to their existence. Rather it does so by transcending them and revealing them, as the whole reveals its parts . . .' (*Myst.* 1).

[227] Anaxagorus; cf. H. Nebelsick 1985:58f.

[228] See Thunberg (1965:80ff., 419ff.; 1985:108ff., 132ff.) on 'Maximus' dominant idea of a universal incarnation of Christ the Logos in the world,' an idea which puts him in close proximity to Origen (cf. *CT* 2.18 with *Princ.* 2.11.6) and, as Thunberg notices, to Teilhard.

[229] See e.g. *CT* 2.57ff., which begins with his own version of *quodammodo praesens, quodammodo absens*. Cf. 2.91.

Given the working assumption that 'the whole spiritual world seems mystically imprinted on the whole sensible world in symbolic forms,' this guaranteed that the ecclesiastical space defined by Denys would be left intact, as would his clericalized view of the church's sacramental life. For according to Maximus the ascended one continues to descend to us in liturgical figures, at holy places,[230] through carefully defined ministrations; 'the beaming ray of ceremonies' guides those who are seized by the desire for divine things safely into 'the secret recesses in God.' It also guaranteed that the main burden of his ecclesiology would rest on the hidden formation of the soul. His treatment of the liturgy, while having a stronger corporate dimension and a more pronounced eschatological thrust than the Dionysian version, is likewise aimed at the centring of the soul on itself and on God.[231]

To that end Maximus develops in the *Mystagogia* an understanding of the church and its rituals in terms of a fourfold image-bearing function. By virtue of its unifying dynamic the church serves as a model of God, of the universe, of man, and of the soul itself. It is a model of God, who is the beginning and end of all things, because it gives new birth to myriad individuals, offering them 'one divine form and designation, to be Christ's and to carry his name.' It is a model of the world and of man, because the harmony of the intelligible and the sensible is signified in the communication between sanctuary and nave. And it is a model of the soul – which conjoins reason and virtue, contemplation and action, truth and goodness in a single life – because in the holy sacrament it gathers together all the preceding signs in both spheres 'for the mystery accomplished on the divine altar.' The marriage of Christ and the church, whereby the two become one flesh eucharistically, is thus made to represent, and to effect, the marriage of God and the soul. 'Whoever is fortunate enough to have been spiritually and wisely initiated into what is accomplished in church has rendered his soul divine and a veritable church of God.'[232]

For Maximus, then, *each soul* is potentially a church, insofar as it allows the dimming and disclosing of every human particularity in the light of the whole. This thesis ought to give us pause for thought. Should we put it down, with John Zizioulas, to a theory of ecclesial perichoresis, and to an understanding of communion rooted in the doctrine of the Trinity? Or do institutionalism and individualism here coincide, as the church itself

---

[230] *Myst.* 24 attaches new importance to church buildings, in which angels are said to remain – noting 'each time people enter and present themselves to God' – and in which the grace of the Spirit 'is always invisibly present.'

[231] 'Gazing with a simple understanding on him who is not outside it but thoroughly in the whole of reality, it will itself understand the principles of beings and the causes why it was distracted by divisive pursuits before being espoused to the Word of God' (*Myst.* 5; see intro., 1ff., 13ff.). This allows it to anticipate its eventual gathering into 'the mysterious oneness of the divine simplicity in the incorruptible age of the spiritual world' (21).

[232] *Myst.* 5.

becomes an instrument of contemplation, not only as κόσμος of the cosmos but as an icon of the inner spaces of the soul? Evidence can be adduced for either view, but the latter may well be the more accurate. In any case, as Zizioulas admits, it was not the former which prevailed in later generations.[233]

Hugh Wybrew credits Maximus much as we have credited Denys. He was first and foremost a monk, he concludes, 'nourished by the ascetical and mystical tradition of the desert, which he integrated, in the *Mystagogia*, with the liturgical tradition of the Church.' To this Wybrew adds the commendation that it was among his great achievements 'to relate Christian mysticism firmly with the mystery of Christ, from which the teaching of Evagrius and of Dionysius ran the risk of detaching it.' Perhaps so, but we are tempted to put it the other way round. The mystery of Christ, and that of the church with it, was pegged more firmly than ever to the monastic framework.[234] Be this as it may, we can say that the Maximian synthesis brought to an end careful thought about the ascension of Jesus as an event of cosmic and ecclesial import, while bequeathing to the eastern church some of its richest resources along the way of its chosen course. Like the Areopagite, the Confessor would later influence developments in the west as well, but we will speak about that in its place.

* * *

What happened over the next couple of centuries did much to settle the eastern course. We speak of the famous iconoclastic controversy, naturally, which degenerated into one of the ugliest of ecclesiastical conflicts before issuing in what is still celebrated today as the Triumph of Orthodoxy. In this hugely complicated and protracted affair a number of matters germane to our present discussion come to a head. We will be able to touch on just a few of them before turning to the western church.

Let us observe straight away that whatever other reasons might be put forward for the proliferation and veneration of images within the church, or for the dramatic attack on this practice and its subsequent

---

[233] We cannot enter into a discussion of what Zizioulas (1985:49ff.) calls the ecclesial or eucharistic hypostasis, though we shall speak of it again later, much less the Cappadocian interpretation of the Trinity to which he appeals (cf. *CT* 2.1). We need only say that the focus in *Myst.* 5 is not, in any obvious way, on a communion of persons. Nor are we convinced that Maximus' microcosm/macrocosm dialectic encourages or even permits a perichoretic model, since it concerns the relation between the particular and the universal, not a relation between human persons.

[234] Pelikan quotes Fedotov's rather harsh judgment in concluding that during this period 'soteriological consistency seems to have been achieved by means of a christological abstraction far removed from the figure described in the Gospels, so that "practically the whole of Byzantine religion could have been built without the historical Christ of the Gospel"' (2/75; cf. Wybrew 94f.).

defense – it is quite plain that the verticalization of salvation history in the Christian Platonist tradition was a major factor on both sides. The argument, after all, was about means rather than ends. Did the use of material images elevate the soul, or drag it down into the idolatrous mire of the 'cult of matter'?[235] It is equally plain, perhaps, that the corresponding verticalization of the church must needs have brought it into conflict with the state, from which the practice of venerating images was initially borrowed.[236] Our main interest, however, lies not in the political sphere but in the theological; not in the curtailing of caesaropapism but in the further weakening (under pressure of dualism) of the sacramental principle, and with it the false expansion of ecclesiastical space.[237]

To explain we must back up a little. The defense of the icons required a defense of the personal particularity of Jesus, a healthy development that nonetheless witnesses to an underlying tendency in the opposite direction. To be more specific, the iconoclasts had complained that their opponents were overturning the universality of Christ, making him out to be a mere individual by circumscribing him in an artist's image.[238] Meyendorff speaks of 'a new phase of Christianization' of Origen and Denys in the iconophiles' response, which (without abandoning the traditions shaped by these men) sought to emphasize afresh the reality of Jesus-history and his distinct human identity, past and present.[239] The validity of making visible portraits of Jesus, to accompany the verbal portraits in the Gospels, was established by reasserting his human particularity against both ordinary and eschatological docetism, and by a reaffirmation of the goodness of creaturely things in general.[240]

---

[235] Cf. Meyendorff 191.

[236] See Dix 422ff. on the influence of emperor-worship, once the occasion of Christian martyrdom, on the development of the cult of images. We should also acknowledge other sources for the practice, however, including perhaps the gnostic tradition mentioned by Irenaeus in *AH* 1.25.6 (a passage L. Ouspensky, 1983:25ff., might have done well to face) and of course the widespread veneration of relics.

[237] 'Was the eucharistic presence to be extended to a general principle about the sacramental mediation of divine power through material objects, or was it an exlusive principle that precluded any such extension to other means of grace, such as images?' (Pelikan 2/94)

[238] The doctrines of *anhypostasis* and the *communicatio idiomatum* were pushed by some of the iconoclasts to a Eutychian extreme; but as Pelikan (2/29) points out, the issue of Jesus' circumscription was a false one in some ways, since it did not apply to other icons.

[239] Drawing on such diverse sources as Aristotle and Cyril of Alexandria, the iconophiles insisted that Jesus was a particular man, and as such describable in his human nature. They in turn were accused, less cogently perhaps, of falling *either* into Nestorianism, by isolating that nature for the sake of the image, *or* into Eutychianism, by supposing the image somehow adequate. See Meyendorff 173ff.

[240] When we ask *why* such portraits, however, we cannot answer simply in terms of the needs of the illiterate, or of those not communicating in the mysteries. The desirability of visible portraits, as well as the doubts about them, owed something, at least, to the ambiguous status of sight in Platonism: On the one hand, sight was sensual and a source of distraction; on the other, it was the *highest* of the senses and took precedence even over hearing as a source of guidance to the worthy soul (cf. Pelikan 2/120ff.).

Now the legitimacy of a portrait and its veneration are two different issues. Yet once the question of christological orthodoxy had been decided in favour of the iconophiles there could be little doubt as to the final verdict on the second issue as well. The reason for this goes beyond the iconophiles' advantage in occupying the doctrinal high ground, enjoying popular support, and benefiting (as it happened) from favourable changes at the imperial palace. Given the common cosmology, and the shared hierarchical worldview of the Areopagite, the icons could not but prevail in the end. For they were a perfectly natural part of a long ladder of signs and images, each more holy than the last, by means of which the soul's ascent to God was deemed possible.[241] The iconoclasts, of course, wanted to restrict the lower end of that ladder to a single rung, that is, to the mysteries themselves, which were said to be unique among material signs by virtue of an identity of essence with their prototype. Yet the bread and the wine were certainly not alone among material things in receiving their devotion. Perhaps the most damaging blow ever struck against them, and it was struck repeatedly, was the charge of inconsistency. How could they venerate the cross or the scriptures and fail to venerate the icons as well?[242]

For their part, the iconophiles were entirely clear about the fact that icons were *not* of the same essence as their prototype. But by emphasizing as far as possible the similarity between the real presence in the mysteries and the spiritual encounter with Christ and his saints achieved through the icons, they turned the tables on their adversaries, making an attack on the latter look like an attack on the former.[243] Afterwards the distinction between the mysteries and the icons had to be reaffirmed in order to safeguard the church's eucharistic centre against rampant individualism and other side-effects. But the most vital distinction of all, *viz.*, the eschatological nature of the mysteries, had long since slipped out of focus together with the human Jesus. Unfortunately, recovery of the one[244] did not lead to recovery of the other. If it had it would have called into question the putative continuity of the icons with the eucharist. Which is to say, the link that was forged between them did not eschatologize the

---

[241] Pelikan (2/115) thinks it 'a matter of great historical significance that one of the favorite technical terms in the Dionysian tradition for this chain of being between the various levels of reality was "image."' John Damascene argued the case right back to the world as image of the eternal forms of God's creative will, and the Son as image of the Father (though this appears to threaten either the ὁμοούσιον or his own concept of imaging).

[242] 'Why do you worship the book and spit upon the picture?', asks John V of Jerusalem. Besides, if Christ can be circumscribed in the eucharistic elements why not in the icons? (Here the iconophiles put the doctrine of the *communicatio idiomatum* to work for themselves; see Pelikan 2/129ff.).

[243] 'The real theological dimensions of the iconoclastic controversy thus appear clearly: the image of Christ is the visible and necessary witness to the reality and humanity of Christ. If that witness is impossible, the Eucharist itself loses its reality' (Meyendorff 190).

[244] The immutability of the incarnation 'is affirmed and demonstrated by the icon' (Ouspensky 34).

icons, as some appear to think; rather it tended to reduce the eschatological mystery of the eucharist to something iconic.[245]

The threat posed to the superior dignity of the eucharist by the quasi-sacramental status granted to icons was met by fortifying the concept of the real presence. If the icons in their own way opened a window to heaven, connecting the worshiper with the person depicted, the consecrated bread actually was the Person. But of course *this* distinction was made at the expense of the real absence, with predictable consequences, including the growth of an unrestrained adoration of the bread and an increasing complexification of the priestly rites attached to it.[246] It cultivated an over-realized eschatology, to which the likelihood of a churchly substitute for Jesus always attaches. The victory of the icons, then, though happily a defeat for the exaggerated dualism and neo-docetism of the iconoclasts, was not so clear a victory for incarnational theology as it is usually made out to be. Given the nature of the argument against icons, the church may have taken the only decision it could have taken, but that is not to say that the issue was properly resolved or the danger to Christ's ascended humanity fully averted.[247] That would have been the case only if the danger had lain entirely on the one side.

The ramifications of our criticism (if it is valid) are enormous, for in the last analysis the problem of the icons is no other than the problem of the church's own existence in the here and now, the problem about the meaning and truth of its eucharistic qualification. We have agreed with Zizioulas that it is not the church which grounds the eucharist but the eucharist which grounds the church. That is because the church has its

[245] Zizioulas (1985:99f.) suggests that icons were understood in a specifically eschatological way. So does Ouspensky, for whom liturgical art is 'also God's descent into our midst, one of the forms in which is accomplished the meeting of God with man, of grace with nature, eternity with time' (36). This art springs from a seeing in the Spirit which anticipates and reveals a future transfiguration. It belongs to the possibilities of sacramental man, as man in the process of deification. It belongs, i.e., to the possibilities of the church, which like the God-man 'is an organism both human and Divine,' combining in itself indivisibly and without confusion two realities, an earthly reality and the sanctifying grace of the Spirit. Like the scriptures, it indicates and mediates a revelation 'that is outside time, contained in a given historical reality.' But all of this only shows that Ouspensky cannot mean by eschatology what we mean. More importantly, it causes us to wonder how far this theology of the icon, and behind it that of the eucharist, depends upon a deviant notion of the church as the incarnation of the Spirit.

[246] See Wybrew 103ff. Two of the most important developments of this period were the addition of the rite of the prothesis and the provision of the antidoron as a kind of lay-substitute for the holy mysteries themselves. Meanwhile, not insignificantly we think, the Old Testament reading had disappeared and the parousia been fixed at 6500 years (ibid. 125). In some of the later commentaries (e.g., Nicholas Cabasilas) the parousia hardly figures.

[247] As late as the 17th C. attempts were still being made to distinguish between honouring icons and *adoring* the mysteries, in view of the 'more real' presence belonging to the latter – in support of which formal appeal was now made to transubstantiation or μετουσίωσις (Pelikan 2/291f.).

being from the Spirit, who allows it to participate in and with the person of Jesus Christ, and hence in a kingdom which does not derive from this world but *transforms* it. When John of Damascus tells us that the term supersubstantial, as applied to the bread of the eucharist, 'either means that which is to come, that is, the bread of the world to come, or it means that which is taken for the sustenance of our substance,' he is not really inviting us to choose between the two. Nor should we, for the consecration of the bread, and the transformation of those who partake in it, is an act which has its *terminus* in the new reality of the eschaton, where Jesus Christ is Lord.[248] But does the granting of quasi-sacramental status to icons not force such a choice, by confusing a Platonic participation and transformation with an eschatological one? Certainly it is less than obvious how objects such as images (or scrolls or relics or buildings, etc.), even those blessed and sanctified by the church, can mediate the communion of the life to come, insofar as they remain in their place as artefacts of this present age. Nor is it clear how the church which blesses them for that purpose is being true to its eucharistic constitution. Is it not implying a reality that simply *is*, rather than one that is newly made with every eucharist?[249]

The sacramentalizing of icons does appear to have contributed to an inflationary spiral of clericalism, dogmatism and other indicators of a self-affirming church, whose reign as official sanctifier not just of icons, but of the societies of eastern Europe, would be challenged effectively only a thousand years later by the mutant caesaropapism of the Marxists. And this reminds us that the political aspect of the controversy is not easily swept aside. Considering the extensive temporal rewards which were among the spoils of the battle for the icons, must we not at least ask whether that long and often unholy war was more about defending the

---

[248] He is Lord here and now too, but in just that way. John, it must be said, does not see the matter quite as we do, see *Orth. qq i ji*

[249] Can protests against a Platonic interpretation address this concern? The icons do their work as the product of, and as instruments for, contemplation of a spiritual reality, as Symeon the New Theologian says. But what is this 'spiritual' reality and should we think of it as something to be accessed by contemplation? Is that not still a dualist conception? We are aware, of course, that the icons are linked (not unproblematically) to the scriptures by the seventh council, but must we concede that scripture too is to be regarded in that way? And may we not insist in any case that the sacraments proper are not sacraments by virtue of lending themselves to the practice of contemplation, but precisely because they constitute an act of communion the ultimate reality of which is something in which they *issue* (the kingdom of God), not something that is 'hidden' in them or which 'interpenetrates' them, to be observed by the worthy eye of the spiritual person? And would we not then be implying – why should we hesitate to say this? – that even the practice of reserving the sacrament for adoration is a misguided one, which underestimates the power of the eucharist in the manner of all so-called realized eschatology, assimilating it to the icons? This much is beyond doubt: Until the question of the eucharist is properly resolved no very satisfactory decision about the icons can be reached. The Victory of Orthodoxy may be an ancient celebration, but it is nonetheless premature.

territorial interests of the church than about defending either the freedom or the veracity of its faith in Christ?[250] Might iconoclasm not be regarded after all as a legitimate protest, however misguided or even insincere, against the fact that the church was busy setting herself up as the new mediator between earth and heaven while her Master tarried on the mountain?

The answer to these questions might be a cautious denial. Nevertheless we cannot overlook the telling array of devices which the church was evolving to help close the gap between God and man. To its domed and partitioned buildings, its clerical hierarchies, its hermits and pole-sitters and relics, its complex and often confusing liturgies, it now approved as well of a whole series of sacred images on a graduated scale: saints lesser and greater, the holy angels,[251] Mary, Christ, the Trinity – a veritable Jacob's ladder with humanity at one end and divinity at the other, and those whom it wished to honour somewhere in between. Chief among these was its own symbol, which prompts one final observation: If there is anything right about iconoclasm, perhaps it could best be expressed by concentrating on icons of the ascension, which rapidly became icons of the Virgin more than icons of Christ. For it is these which provide the most eloquent testimony to a diminishing Jesus and a larger-than-life church.[252]

West

In the candid words of Michael Psellus, an eleventh-century professor at the university of Constantinople, 'the famous Origen . . . was the pioneer of all our theology and laid its foundations, but on the other hand all heresies find their origin in him.'[253] The irony of this admission is striking to one who stands outside the eastern tradition, surveying the damage done to the oriental church through its inability to eradicate Origenism, which displaces Jesus of Nazareth for another cornerstone. There was however one aspect of Origenist thought – the horizontal aspect, let us say – which was not so highly developed in the east as in the west. Various circumstantial factors, including the Muslim phenomenon, have to be taken into account here, but an

---

[250] Photius' comments (see Wybrew 107) at the consecration of the New Church, built in the palace of Emperor Basil I at the close of the controversy and dedicated to Mary, indicate something of the church's positional gain.

[251] Theodore described the angels as a 'precosmic cosmos before this cosmos, who announce to this cosmos a cosmos that is above the cosmos, namely, Christ' (Or. 6.1; Pelikan 2/142). We are inclined to ask in this connection whether the east ever quite got to grips with the query of Luke's angels, 'Why stand ye gazing up into heaven?' But cf. Ouspensky 194ff.

[252] See the telling comments of Dewald (286f.); cf. Anjali D'Souza's recent painting of the ascension.

[253] Acc. Cer. 20 (Pelikan 2/244).

intense concern for that heavenly doctrine and worship of which the icons became the symbol suggests that a more strictly vertical enterprise was in view from the beginning. Angelomorphic aims to some extent outstripped earthly ambitions.[254] Not so in the Roman church, the church of Augustine! In due course it laid claim to heaven and earth alike, constructing an imposing edifice that would dominate the socio-political landscape for more than a millennium. In its shadow many would take refuge, but as that shadow lengthened the fears of Tyconius would prove well founded.

We have already shown how Augustine's dualism led to an ecclesiology in which the church began to appropriate for itself, even in its secular ambiguity, something of the glory of the ascended one that did not belong to it. What we want now to show is how its appetite for that glory grew, expressing itself mariologically in the first instance, though more secular expressions would later follow. A fear of Protestant *cliché* must not prevent us from further exploring this sensitive ground, which no consideration of the doctrine of the ascension can afford to bypass. For one of the main legacies of an insufficiently radical adherence to ascension in the flesh was a quiet rivalry between Mother and Son (just hinted at here and there among the countless portraits adorning the churches) which in the west especially had public consequences.[255]

When the human Jesus disappeared before the apostles' eyes his mantle, the Spirit, fell to his followers. But when his humanity began to disappear in a theological sense, the mantle of his mediatorial office also fell, coming to rest on the shoulders of the Virgin.[256] More and more, she contracted a duty and attracted an honour which were not hers. As she had once

[254] This made possible a relatively peaceful co-existence with the state, in an arrangement sometimes referred to as dyarchy. It also made for a certain comfortable insularity in the autokephalous churches, an insularity still capable of showing a vicious edge when disturbed. It is interesting to note, however, that the last two centuries have produced a cross-fertilization which – in V. Soloviev's notion of 'Godmanhood' and in variations produced by N. Fedorov and S. Bulgakov, e.g. – has introduced into Russian Orthodoxy new forms of Origenist and Dionysian thought mediated in the first instance by Hegel and Schelling (cf. R. Williams [D. Ford 1996] 499ff., P. Evdokimov 1970). These forms contain some of the outward-looking western elements we have in view.

[255] Need it be said that the criticisms we are about to make do *not* imply that Mary should receive no special honour in the liturgy? Neither of course does our previous questioning of icons imply that there should be no place in the church for theological art, or for honouring saints and martyrs.

[256] Evidence for the fact that the human Jesus was being jostled towards the margins of theology may be found in the adoptionist controversy which erupted, by way of reaction, in the 8th C. Unfortunately the Spanish bishops who created the *furore*, Felix and Elipandus, so far from detecting the Nestorian tendency already at work in the Augustinian tradition, opted for an even more pronounced Nestorianism as a solution. They were answered by a renewed stress on Christ's divinity, often expressed in devotion to the cult of the Theotokos, which soon gained a popularity previously unknown in the west (cf. Pelikan 3/52ff., 160ff.). The entire problem was thus exacerbated.

delivered the Son of God to the world, so now she would continue to deliver him and his benefits to the individual believer. She was both 'the ladder of heaven on which God descends to earth' and the one 'through whom we ascend to him who descended through her to us.'[257] Such exalted notions (encouraged by the legend of Theophilus, e.g., which told of her maternal influence in heaven) invited a general reconstruction of her biography. Mary-history, or what soon passed for such, began to vie with Jesus-history in the plagiarist fashion already described.[258]

What was attributed to Mary, as we have said, passed implicitly or explicitly to the church. One of the defining moments here was the fateful eucharistic dispute between Radbertus and Ratramnus, which actually began as an argument about her perpetual virginity (perhaps the earliest example of plagiarism). Radbertus insisted that Mary brought Jesus into the world in a miraculous way, that is, without any painful opening of her womb. He *also* insisted that the elements consecrated by the church become, contrary to our senses, the very same flesh to which she gave birth. In this way he meant both to guard the dignity of the mediatrix and to guarantee the quality of the church's offering.[259] Ratramnus, however, objected to the violence to nature implied by this perfectionism, or rather by the miracles for which it called. The second of these was the more contentious. Like Berengar after him – who insisted that the ascended Jesus could not be 'summoned down' by the church[260] – he opposed any strict identification of the eucharistic body with the historical body and argued for a more spiritual kind of eating, a partaking of 'the power of the divine Word.'[261] But it was Radbertus who prevailed. By a miraculous transformation within the sacramental *species*, the flesh and blood of Jesus were literally present on the altar just as they had once been present in Mary's womb. For the church's task, like Mary's, was

---

[257] Ambrose Autpert (*Nat. Vir.*, quoted ibid. 70) and Bernard of Clairvaux (*Adv.* 2.5; ibid. 165). Ildefonsus of Toledo effectively makes Mary the mediator of the *Spirit* as well as of Christ: 'I pray thee, I pray thee, O holy Virgin, that I may have Jesus by the same Spirit by whom thou didst give birth to Jesus' (*Vir. Mar.* 12; ibid. 69).

[258] It did so on the basis of the premise articulated in the rather tardy promulgation by Pius XII of her assumption into heaven, namely, that she is 'always sharing His lot' (*Mun.* 38) – a premise perfectly sound in itself, whether we are thinking of Mary corporately or *in sua persona*, but unsound in the realized eschatology it embraces.

[259] The parallel was drawn by Radbertus himself, and was natural enough in a context where Marian titles and concepts – even Theotokos – were habitually transferred to the church. See Pelikan 3/72ff. for references.

[260] This was not quite fair to Radbertus, since he held that the eucharistic body was a special creation. But his teaching did appear either to demand such a summons or to introduce a contradictory bifurcation of Christ. Attempts to address this convoluted problem would be made well into the Reformation; cf. W. Walker 1968:36ff.

[261] *Corp.* 49. 'So while Ratramnus is prepared to speak of the elements as being changed into the body and blood, it is not Jesus' physical body that he understands by this' (Heron 1983b:94). His position, in fact, is not far from Augustine's.

indeed to bring Christ down in order that it might offer him up anew in its own time and place.[262]

This decision helped to instil in the church an abiding sense of awe at its own maternal and sacerdotal role, while inculcating an attitude of humble obedience in the laity and a good deal of popular superstition as well.[263] Since both sides in the debate were working within a dualist framework, neither could propose any christological corrective to its basic terms. For Ratramnus, as for Augustine, the Word's humanity remained remote and peripheral; for Radbertus it took on a peculiar form, to say the least. If one and the same Son of Mary really was made present in his humanity, this humanity was no longer recognizable as such, not because of what we have called the ascension–parousia differential but because the claims of Radbertus stubbornly defied that differential, as Berengar later recognized. Of course, even Radbertus and his heirs were forced to allow *some* distinction between the Jesus who ascended and the Jesus who became present at the bidding of the church, but every such contrivance only confused the issue further.[264] In the west, too, theological and liturgical manipulation of the body of Christ grew more and more complex, as abstraction was piled on abstraction, and symbol upon symbol. What was never in doubt was the church's ability to produce it at will.

Now in order to answer the objection of Berengar based on the ascension, various theories were proposed in support of that ability. One prominent approach employed the doctrines of the hypostatic union and the *communicatio idiomatum* to contrive a voluntary body, present not only in heaven but wherever its owner willed, which meant wherever the priests performed their duties.[265] Thomas Aquinas later followed this line

---

[262] For Radbertus the sacrificial aspect of the eucharist was the most important. By articulating the need to bring Christ down, so that the sacrifice offered up might be a worthy one, he laid a double stress on its mariological character. From one point of view this new descent of Christ *was* the ascent of Mary, in her *alter ego* as the church.

[263] An oft-quoted passage from James Joyce (1992.171) seems *apropos*: 'No king or emperor on this earth has the power of the priest of God. No angel or archangel in heaven, no saint, not even the Blessed Virgin herself has the power of a priest of God: the power . . . to make the great God of Heaven come down upon the altar and take the form of bread and wine. What an awful power, Stephen!' Yet we should not forget that this is a modern perspective. St Francis, for one, looked at it the other way round: 'Christ's humble descent into the hands of officiating priests' (Petry 277) became a model for his self-renunciation in obedience to the hierarchy.

[264] Peter Lombard, e.g., distinguished between the exalted man and the 'sacrificial' body which remains on earth; the former is omnipresent and the latter 'multipresent.'

[265] 'After the ascension, "the flesh of Christ, which has been exalted by God above all creatures . . . is present everywhere, wherever it pleases, through the omnipotence that has been given to it in heaven and on earth." Therefore, if Christ willed it, his body could be present, completely and truly, in heaven and in the Sacrament at one and the same time.' (Pelikan 3/194, quoting Hugh of Metellus.) Whether or not such a view strips Jesus of the attributes belonging to creaturely particularity was a matter of some debate (cf. Walker 37f.).

of thought, mixing Greek and Christian concepts to provide the definitive explanation: Christ is indeed absent from earth in his human nature, which through union with his divine nature has ascended to that 'most excellent of places' beyond all confinement of space or time.[266] But, by virtue of his omnipresence in creation, the divine Logos is able to generate a eucharistic version of his humanity by making present under the accidents of the bread and wine, in this world yet non-spatially, the actual substance of his exalted body and blood. This way of reconciling the ascension and the eucharist, while eschewing any crude materialism in defending the real presence, continued to undermine a proper sense of the real absence.

Let us explain briefly. Since the problem of the presence and the absence, like that of the ascension itself, was neither identified nor treated in eschatological terms, but in terms of the traditional cosmological opposition between heaven and earth, a pair of dilemmas was created. How are we to have a Christ who is both here – in many places – and in heaven at the same time? And if he really is here, how can we lay hold of him with confidence? To the first question, de-spatialization was the necessary answer. What is given in the bread is not Jesus himself or even his body, to be precise, but rather the substance of his body, existing for us under foreign dimensions.[267] To the second question, which was more felt than asked, response was made simply by tightening further the ecclesiastical screws that hold together the heavenly and the earthly: The sacrament of the eucharist, unlike all other sacraments, is constituted through the action of the priest quite apart from any consideration of its use by the people; it is a *fait accompli* at the moment of consecration, not of communication. In other words, the eucharistic gift was first abstracted from the absent Nazarene and then pinned down with the greatest possible precision to the worldly dimensions provided for it by the church.[268]

---

[266] Aquinas (*ST* 3/57f.) is not clear what sort of place this might be, but *is* clear that Christ retains his bodily humanity. An Augustinian tension is still operative here: on the one hand, we should 'no longer think of him as a man on earth but as God in heaven;' on the other hand, 'the presence of his human nature in heaven is itself an intercession for us' (57.6; cf. 76.1).

[267] See *ST* 3/75f. A substance cannot be perceived by the senses. It is recognized and received mentally, in this case through faith, though it is also received in some fuller sense by actually communicating. The whole Christ is received with it, according to the notion of concomitance or 'real accompaniment.'

[268] i.e., having first been de-particularized by being considered non-spatially according to substance, Christ was then re-particularized by the liturgical forms of the church; and this latter particularity, since it was tied to the act of consecration, depended upon the power conferred in ordination. Aquinas (who has Christ, not the priest, as the active agent throughout; cf. 74.7, 76.5, 78.1, 80.1, 82.1) would not be happy with our provocative way of putting the matter, however! Nor would Jean-Luc Marion (1991:163ff.), e.g., who has recently made a forceful objection to the kind of analysis we are offering. To Marion's own construction of the doctrine of transubstantiation (see 178ff.) we are in fact sympathetic, but we remain unpersuaded that such a construction prevailed at the time, or that it can defend everything which he wants to defend by it.

This process, justified at each stage by appeal to the miraculous power of God, placed Christ fully in the church's possession. Indeed, it meant that the church now controlled the parousia. At the ringing of a bell the *Christus absens* became the *Christus praesens*.[269] The latter could not but suffer a false and de-personalizing objectification; with equal ease he could be displayed in a monstrance or withheld altogether, and so deployed to political or economic advantage. Conversely, the slimming of an already thin eschatological reserve allowed Augustine's principle, that the heavenly glorification of Jesus is made visible through the earthly glorification of the church, to work itself out in ever more explicit terms. Seated comfortably with the Christ-child on its lap, the church soon became his regent rather than his servant.[270] In short, its Marian ego, already out of control at the beginning of the eucharistic debates, afterwards knew no bounds.

※ ※ ※

If the veneration of Mary is indeed, as Otto Semmelroth puts it, 'the Church's testimony to herself,'[271] that ego is one of the best-attested facts of its history. Mary was lifted up into heaven with Christ and lauded in terms once reserved for God alone. She became 'the fountain from which the living fountain flows, the origin of the beginning.' She was not only Queen of the world but ruler of the universe; there was nothing in heaven itself 'that was not subject to the Virgin through her Son.'[272] Through her the very elements were renewed, and to her succour all people were invited to appeal for their salvation.

Only when it threatened the renewal of full-fledged docetism was a halt called to this orgy of adulation. Meanwhile the glory Mary shared with Christ *in patria* continued to require expression *in via*. This was invested chiefly in the pope, the universal pontiff, who in successive personages grew increasingly jealous of the dividends.[273] Innocent III,

---

[269] Should we be surprised that there is 'practically never any reference in the western texts of the eucharist to the second coming of Christ' (Wainwright 1978:87f.)?

[270] As Pelikan notes, Richard of St Lawrence (*Laud.* 4.19.6) could even rewrite John 3:16 to read, '*Mary* so loved the world,' etc.

[271] *Mary, Archetype of the Church* 174 (quoted R. McBrien 1981:895).

[272] Even there Mary's standing as the Mother of God threatened to outrank that of Jesus. Anselm, e.g., in a statement remarkable for its christological vacuity, indicates that there is 'nothing equal to Mary and nothing but God greater than Mary.' Indeed, God himself was said to be subject to Mary as a son to his mother. (For references see Pelikan 3/16off. and 4/38ff.; for a more sober mariology cf. Aquinas, *ST* 3/25.5.)

[273] The sentiments to which we refer are captured in a mural decorating the papal apartments, in which Mary takes her place as it were in the Holy Trinity, while Jesus stands off to one side, casting his light below on the figure of the pope. According to Giles of Rome (*Ecc. Pot.* 3.12; Pelikan 4/111) the pope himself 'can be called "the church," because his power is spiritual, heavenly and divine, and is . . . without measure.'

under whom the papacy reached the apogee of its power and who was the first to use the title Vicar of Christ, came to regard his office 'in a semi-Divine light, "set in the midst between God and man, below God but above man."'[274] Boniface VIII, who in his infamous bull *Unam Sanctum* not only claimed the power of the two swords but decreed that 'submission on the part of every man to the bishop of Rome is altogether necessary for his salvation,' can hardly be blamed for pressing the point to its logical conclusion. But as the Roman authorities became 'the self-confessed soul of the *Corpus Christianum*,' to borrow Ray Petry's not unkind description, they also became something of an occupying force.

As in the east, radical dualists counter-attacked from time to time, castigating the official church for its lofty aspect. Once again this only obscured the fact that dualism had already triumphed in just this form.[275] Bolstered by what Boniface called the law of the universe – *viz.*, Denys' principle of hierarchy, which had been adapted to a western understanding of catholicity[276] – and backed by Aquinas' delicately formulated theology of coercion, Rome's institutional demeanour grew increasingly triumphalist. Concurrently, encouraged by that very same Dionysian theology and Radbertian eucharistic doctrine, which conspired together to underline the laity's spectator status, a sub-ecclesial fascination with private spiritual experience was also flourishing. This was the beginning of the golden age of western mysticism. Mary and the angelic ranks lent their support to the one as to the other, helping to secure a grand cosmological vision which justifed both the complicated machinery of the church and the other-worldly aspirations of those who followed its spiritual advice.[277]

Christianity's double face, as we have called it, appears quite starkly in a paradoxical figure from the twelfth century. The great Bernard of Clairvaux may be taken as an early representative of the bizarre combination of militarism and mysticism (not to put too fine a point on it) which was being nurtured in the west by the breakdown of eucharistic eschatology. With equal zeal he promoted a passionate commitment to the contemplative life and preached into existence the second crusade, a remarkable feat even for a man who stood at the threshold of what many

---

[274] 'He was, so he affirmed, Melchisedek, the priest-king, who would bring a centralized Christian society into being . . .' (*Oxford Dictionary of the Christian Church* 704).

[275] Since all challengers, along with heretical dualists like the Cathari, were 'lumped together in the minds of churchmen as attackers of the hierarchy' (Petry 317), that very hierarchy became, like the icons in the east, the chief symbol of an orthodox, *non*-dualist faith.

[276] i.e., one which calls for a distribution of grace from the *centre* as well as the top. Cf. Lateran IV, Canon 1: One God and one Christ mean one church and one eucharistic ministry, the guarantee of the latter lying – not in the Holy Spirit, as it does in Eph. 4 – but in a single Supreme Pontiff.

[277] The advent of private chantries testifies to the individualizing and internalizing effects of a eucharistic theology that laid great stress on a sacrifice that was made *for* one by the priest, but promised benefits corresponding to one's own devotion.

regard as an era of contradictions.[278] Along the one path lay the heavily psychologized ascension spirituality of Thomas Gallus, for example, not to mention the *erotica* of Hildegard, Mechthild, Gertrude or Angela.[279] The other gradually descended into the institutionalized violence which reached its nadir, perhaps, during the Spanish Inquisition and the subjugation of Central America. It is the latter path which most concerns us. Though it is fashionable these days to make of such crimes of violence a reason for rejecting the church altogether, that is a ruse exposed long ago by Bernard himself when roundly criticizing abuses of ecclesiastical power. Yet we cannot regard the slide into imperial ways as entirely an aberration. Where the church is seen as the express image of an ascending Christ who is all but absorbed into the divine Reason, ecclesiology is bound to move along an absolutist course.

Bernard, a Cistercian reformer, was also concerned about that course. Did he not warn Eugenius III, at whose request he called for another crusade, about the dangers of being heir to Constantine as well as to Peter? As for the ascension, did he not provide for its feast a new procession and a new prominence? Did he and his friends not speak boldly of King Jesus – *dispositor saeculorum*, yes, and also returning judge – in such a way as to remind both the great and the lowly of their real position?[280] Since we are treating him as a symbol of his times we should not overlook the fact that Bernard, like Francis and Bonaventure after him, has been said to belong to an 'uncompromisingly christocentric' tradition in which the human Jesus was being rediscovered. In much of this tradition, particularly on the Franciscan side, it was the humanity of the crucified rather than the resurrected or ascended one that was restored to view. If anything, the latter came to be even more neglected.[281] But there were

---

[278] 'Bernard disavowed all interest in temporal concerns. Yet no man had more success in controlling what he professed to despise. This little monk, personally shy and retiring, a poet at heart and a recluse by desire and temperament, became under the pressure of events a consummate master of men and virtual dictator over all he surveyed' (W. Cannon 1960:202).

[279] The beatific vision was often conceived in a rather coldly intellectual light. Bernard, expounding the Song of Songs, introduced a more passionate version which was transposed by some of the women mystics into an intensely individualistic 'beatific lovemaking,' reserved for perfect spiritual virgins who were permitted to enter the bridal chamber of Christ (cf. McDannell and Lang 98ff.).

[280] See Pelikan 3/144ff. Cf. B. McGinn 1979:5ff., who points us to *Asc.* 2, e.g., where Bernard (not unlike Augustine) speaks of the ascension as 'the consummation and fulfillment of all other feasts, the blessed conclusion of the whole journey of the Son of the God.' Bernard reads the larger biblical story much as we have done, and is clear about descent and ascent as something undertaken in our human nature (cf. *Asc.* 4, *Div.* 60).

[281] In Bonaventure, as in Francis, much can be found to the contrary (cf. Balthasar 2/315ff.). But descending and ascending serve Bonaventure as a cosmological and an anthropological principle, much as they did Maximus; the cross therefore stands at the centre of his worldview in such a way as to limit the impact of the doctrine of the resurrection (see e.g. *Itin.* 7).

those who saw in Jesus' bodily ascension the climax of salvation history; who were quite clear about the eschatological qualification of the gains and losses of the present time; who sought to hold together the things of the flesh and the things of the spirit. Bernard was a leader among them, yet here too there were tensions and paradoxes. Bernard sounds very like Irenaeus when he says of Christ, 'He offered his flesh to those who knew flesh so that through it they might come to know spirit too.'[282] But he sounds even more like Augustine when he turns Paul's proscription against regarding anyone κατὰ σάρκα into a formula for progressing from the love of Christ's flesh to the love of his spirit, and thence from a merely human love for a man to a divine and divinizing love for the God who comes to us as a man. Bernard's refrain, in other words, is still *per Christum hominem ad Christum deum*, and the feast of the ascension is still seen as the best occasion to learn it.[283]

Perhaps this helps to explain the fact that Bernard, as much as anyone, was responsible for the mariological shift we have been describing. Certainly his sermons *In Praise of the Virgin Mother* were hugely successful at establishing his slogan, 'everything through Mary' – a slogan, by the way, that found architectural expression in the marvelous Gothic cathedrals which became the landmarks of western Europe, 'built partly as trophies for a beautiful woman, forever young, forever kind,'[284] purveyor of eternal light.[285] He appealed to the celestial hierarchy as well, not only to assist the individual soul in its search for the heavenly marital chamber but to buttress the church's escalating clericalism. For he laboured hard, in the spirit of the Cistercian reform, to arrange the church under one earthly head as the angels were arranged under God. All the while Bernard did his best to promote a highly spiritual (almost Clementine?) view of the church without denying its wrinkles and blemishes as a worldly institution. In the end, however, he was unable to prevent western ecclesiology from dissolving into dangerous alternatives.[286]

---

[282] *SCC* 6.3 (quoted McGinn 2/165). Our exile from God, says Bernard (*Conv.* 17.30, ibid. 172f.; cf. *Res.* 1.11), is not the body's fault. Nevertheless he indicates elsewhere (*Dil.* 10) that only when the soul has been relieved of all concern for the body will it be 'immersed completely in that sea of endless light and bright eternity.'

[283] Cf. *SCC* 20, 79.2, *Div.* 101. Thus again: 'Christ ascended once and for all above heaven's height in corporeal fashion, but now he ascends every day spiritually in the hearts of the elect' (*Div.* 61.1; quoted McGinn 2/177). The admixture of Dionysian to Augustinian thought led in time to the apophaticism represented by *The Cloud of Unknowing* and *The Book of Privy Counseling* (see *Priv.* 23; cf. W. Johnstone 1973:16ff., F. Bauerschmidt 1997:86).

[284] C. T. Marshall (Dowley 1977:296)

[285] See McBrien 874ff. Bernard presented Mary as 'our mediator with that Mediator,' that she might assuage all fear of Christ the judge. Bonaventure would later imply that 'Christ reserved to himself the realm of justice while ceding to his mother the realm of mercy' (ibid. 876), a dichotomy with obvious consequences for Christian piety.

[286] If Christ is both bridegroom and bride (*SCC* 27.7), the church is a divine entity; the danger therefore exists that its 'spotted actuality' will be ignored or even denied at the institutional level. Alternatively – and especially where we are invited to think of the divinized

One of these alternatives was constructed by a Cistercian abbot of the next generation, Joachim of Fiore. Deeply troubled by what he saw around him, he attempted to relegate the church as he knew it to a passing age: that of the *ordo clericorum*, which was giving way, he believed, to the *ordo monachorum* and a church whose holiness would be more transparent. After a dreadful cataclysm shortly to come, and the proclamation of a new kingdom gospel, human society would be assimilated into an *ecclesia contemplativa*, there to be governed by the 'more ample grace' of the Spirit.[287] Joachim's elaborate philosophy of history foreshadowed a modern preoccupation, his misguided idealism later utopian yearnings; but his prophecy did not come to pass. The alternative we have been lamenting did, with Innocent III trimming his sails to take advantage of the wind that was blowing in Joachim's direction. In his station as Vicar of Christ, he was quick to present *himself* as the architect of a new age and of a universal Christian society. On his scheme, naturally, the Calabrian's anti-institutionalism had to be eradicated and the apocalyptic element strongly discouraged. A new form of Constantinianism would be cultivated instead.

* * *

There were hints early on that the worldly glory won by the western church was easily tarnished. The combination of grandiose claims and failing powers that characterized the papacy of Boniface (to say nothing of the Avignon *débâcle*) already suggested that Innocent's vision was no more reliable than Joachim's. But the changing fortunes of the papacy did not prevent the 'vicar' principle from continuing to erode the tension between the presence and the absence. John Wycliffe, though his own theology was of a severely dualist sort, managed to put his finger somewhere near the heart of the problem:

> If you say that Christ's Church must have a head here on earth, you say truly; for Christ is the head, who must be here with his Church until the day

---

soul as bride (*SCC* 73.10), interpreting *ascensus* as *excessus* – the danger arises that the institutional church will become incidental, even dispensable. Bernard's Mary, 'as "personified Church" and soul identified with the Church (*anima ecclesiastica*)' (Balthasar 2/262), stood on guard against the latter danger by mediating between the corporate and the individual.

[287] See Pelikan 3/298ff. Joachim lays out history in three interlocking *status*, appropriated to Father, Son, and Spirit respectively. H. Bett (Petry 473) may be right to see the resulting scheme as 'a sacerdotal history of the world, beginning with the Levites, prolonged in the secular clergy, and fulfilled in the Benedictine Order as finally reformed under a more rigorous rule,' but it is also something more profound than that (cf. McGinn 1985:161ff.). His disposal of Augustine's homogeneity doctrine in favour of a coming parousia 'in the Holy Spirit' (*Ev.* 1) struck a chord that is still resounding today, in spite of the censure brought against him by Aquinas (*ST* 2.1/106.4), who claimed on christological grounds that the word preached from the beginning could *not* be surpassed, and that no new spiritual gospel could bring the world any nearer to its ultimate goal.

of doom, as well as everywhere by reason of his Godhead. For since the power of a king must be extended everywhere throughout all his realm, much more is the power of Christ shared with all his children. And if you say that Christ must needs have such a vicar here on earth, you deny Christ's power and place this devil above Christ.[288]

In other words, a Christ whose presence must be thus mediated is a Christ whose power to *be* present is falsely restricted, eucharistic claims notwithstanding. His functions and prerogatives then pass over to the church without remainder, while he himself is excluded.

That Wycliffe reverted to a purely spiritual view of the church, demonstrating that he had not got to the heart of the matter after all, does not invalidate his critique. Indeed his case can be put more strongly yet. Fyodor Dostoevsky does just that in *The Brothers Karamazov*, when he has Ivan's Grand Inquisitor confront Jesus himself with the bald facts:

> 'You have transmitted all Your authority to the Pope and now he wields it. As to You, You had better stay away or, at any rate, not interfere with us for the time being.'[289]

What Dostoevsky understood, and his own apocalyptic streak owed much to this insight, was that western ecclesiology at its one extreme actually comes full circle. It *requires* a completely absent Christ if it is to provide instead that miraculous eucharistic one who will underwrite the programme of the church, a programme always in danger of becoming fully immanentist, and hence absolutist, in nature.[290]

We should notice in passing that this immanentist tendency in Latin ecclesiology was strengthened by continued cross-fertilization from the east. With Duns Scotus, who applied his famous maximalism to Christ and Mary alike, the west began to look towards the idea of the Logos incarnate in all things, and to explore more confidently a ubiquitarian christology. His lead was followed by Nicholas of Cusa, who situated the

---

[288] *Ecc.* 2 (Petry 521). This is something of a watershed in internal western criticism. Dante, for instance – who took Bernard for his last guide, and whose brilliant *Comedia* did for religious cosmology what Bernard's sermons had done for mariology – happily consigned the greedy Boniface to hell (*Inf.* 19), along with several other popes. But his judgment was strictly a moral one, concerned with the person not the office. To be sure, he did seek to limit the power of the office by calling for a world monarch to oversee the temporal happiness of the race while the pontiff attended to its eternal felicity (*Mon.* 3.16). But Wycliffe attacks the office itself, for christological reasons.

[289] K. Mochulsky writes in his introduction to the novel that the Legend of the Grand Inquisitor represents 'the culmination of Dostoevsky's work' (1970:xiv; see Book 5, chap. 5).

[290] This of course is *anti*christ, as the Cardinal confesses: 'We shall tell them, though, that we are loyal to You and that we rule over them in Your name. We shall be lying, because we do not intend to allow You to come back.' A little later, referring to 'that wise and dreaded spirit' whose counsel was rejected by Jesus in the desert but embraced by the church under Constantine, he expostulates: 'we are not with You, we are with *him* – and that is our secret, our mystery!'

ascended Christ in a place that cannot really be defined in terms of place, but is at once 'the centre and the inclusive periphery of all spiritual beings,' and thus also of the cosmos as such.[291] The resurgence of neoplatonism and even of Hermeticism, that *prisca theologia* which the later Middle Ages shared with the Renaissance, must also be taken into account here. It testifies to the tenacity of a pre-Christian sacramentalist worldview, which in Cusanus and others merged with orthodoxy to produce a form of panentheism.[292] That was a worldview naturally resistant to the hard edge of biblical eschatology, but quite comfortable with a hidden Christ who is always ascending and a Mary who is always bringing him down again; with an endless liturgical rhythm in which the parousia (not unlike the philosophers' stone) is always within reach yet forever receding.[293] For in the regularity of ascent and descent there is a divine *stabilitas* similar to that of the heavens themselves; in the rounds of the church year there is a terrestrial reflection of the so-called circles of God, and the consolation of 'an assured presence through apparent absence.'[294]

Now one difficulty with immanentism, in any of its varieties, is that the distinction between presence and absence is difficult to maintain. That is why it is not so big a step as some may think from the piety just described to the more cynical perspective of Ivan's legendary Inquisitor. But we will have more to say about immanentism later; for now let us sum up the western developments as briefly, and as pointedly, as we can. We have noted that Augustine did not follow Origen in employing the doctrine of the ascension to dispense with the concrete humanity of Christ altogether, as the ancient cosmology required, but that he did use it to shift the focus to his divinity. For Augustine the presence of Christ was

[291] From that atopic position Christ could indwell and govern all things, bringing them to harmony by means of the church as it radiates throughout the world. See Balthasar 1967:297f., who credits Scotus with having 'translated the Greek approach to the Ascension into the western world,' where it was taken up by Cusanus.

[292] Among some of the mystics things were now being said which drew the charge of actual pantheism, though Cusanus attempted in response to re-emphasize divine transcendence. See Nebelsick 1985:163ff. on the influence of Hermeticism; also O. Pedersen (Tracy and Lash 1983) 17.

[293] If Hermeticism aimed at 'nothing less than the deification and rebirth of the whole of reality' (Nebelsick 181), this had nothing to do with biblical eschatology, but rather with accessing a transforming cosmic power through 'proper *gnosis* of the world-God.' Its final hope was a familiar one, *viz.*, unification of the One with the many, and the perfection of world harmony. This was Cusanus' own theme (see Pelikan 4/97ff. on 'catholic concordance') though like most in those troubled times he retained something of the apocalyptic.

[294] The phrase is von Balthasar's (1967:295), who speaks of these matters in a different vein! But is there not rather too much here of the old pagan cycle of life and death (witness, e.g., The Birth of Venus) even if elevated by Christian content? We never fail to be impressed by the way in which late medieval and Renaissance art enfolds man's religious experience within its countless Madonnas and crucifixions, annunciations and depositions; the resurrection, ascension, and particularly the second coming of Jesus are by comparison greatly under-represented.

chiefly a divine presence; human absence was not a problem but a solution. This left room, however, for the church to become joined to the divine Christ in such a way as to supplant his humanity with its own.[295] The incarnate one, the mystery of God's presence in the world, was ultimately – the church. Jesus himself had gone, but Mary remained behind to continue his work, still pregnant with his divinity. She was able to produce the Christ, the whole Christ, on demand; less and less did she concern herself with the absence of the son she once bore in Bethlehem's stable. His absence was her presence, and her presence his absence.

Obviously we are not pretending to offer a balanced judgment of medieval western ecclesiology.[296] To some degree we have caricatured the church's self-awareness for the purpose of highlighting the diminution of its sense of eucharistic precariousness, a diminution which even a more charitable sketch would have to admit. What was most needed to correct that diminution, in our opinion, and the mistakes and illusions of the church's mariological construct, was a thoroughly eschatological treatment of the problem of the presence and the absence. That was not forthcoming in part because the dualist assumptions of classical times – and the underlying monist drive which generates that dualism – went largely unchallenged even by the doctrine of the ascension, discussion of which had a habit of trailing away into moralism and irrelevancy when not busy propping up those assumptions.[297]

On the other hand, we have made very little capital out of a widely recognized feature of medieval ecclesiology, namely, the emphasis on human merit that emerged (more or less automatically, if by rather complex mechanisms) in the shift of focus from Jesus to Mary. There can be no doubt that it was this feature, together with an ever more blatant clerical packaging of merits to meet the inevitable shortfall, which finally necessitated that dramatic attempt at self-reconstruction known as the Reformation. We shall come to the Reformation in Chapter 5, but not before we consider the impact of the scientific revolution. For the dualist cosmology inherited by the church, once adapted to its own ends, served to support all those weighty Marian dogmas and ecclesiastical structures that were built up around it.[298] The shattering of that cosmology was therefore just as traumatic as the shattering of the west's religious unity.

---

[295] Dante's Fulk (*Paradiso,* Canto ix) might have paused to consider this, when he observed of pope and cardinals: 'They in their thoughts never to Nazareth come ...'

[296] Or of the church's political vocation, insight and experience; see O. O'Donovan 1996, chap. 6.

[297] Harsh judgment is also passed by Davies (161) on the preaching of the ascension during this period, when he remarks: 'Not even the great Bernard of Clairvaux could escape the prevailing "isms" of his age, viz. archaism, plagiarism and moralism, to which may be added, as a fourth note, irrelevancy.'

[298] Nebelsick (159) notes that Cecco d'Ascoli and others paid with their lives for challenging Dante's 'orthodox' cosmology.

5

Where is Jesus?

From Homer to Stephen Hawking the word 'god' is liberally sprinkled on the pages of human reflection about the universe, indicating that the ancient bond between theology and cosmology is not easily snapped. Yet the modern era has been an era of religious doubt, or at any rate doubt about the Bible and about orthodox Christianity, fostered in part by drastic cosmological revisions.[1] The church, whose alignment with a now defunct world-picture once encouraged the marginalization of Jesus, has itself been marginalized in the society it used to dominate. Its want of rigorous self-criticism has been made up in abundance from elsewhere, such that alternative forms of religious discourse and practice have returned in a flood to press (even in some scientific circles) their ancient claims.

All of this has meant a series of crises in ecclesial identity, crises which owe a good deal to an unexpected radicalization of the problem of the absent Christ. Out of that radicalization new possibilities for ecclesial self-understanding have arisen, however, each requiring some account of the ascension and some way of addressing the question which stands at the head of this chapter. Where is Jesus? An evasive answer cannot be taken seriously, nor one which disclaims any interest in cosmology.[2] What we want to do in the present chapter is to examine the boldest of the options that have emerged, and the manner of their emergence. In doing so we will find that we are still exploring the paths marked out for us by Irenaeus and Origen, albeit in rapidly changing terrain.

The Copernican Factor

From the reverent skepticism of Pseudo-Dionysius (who offered ranks of angels and clerics and holy mysteries as compensation) to the reverence

[1] Cf. L. Gilkey 1961:194ff.
[2] The Where? question must certainly be asked and pursued existentially – e.g., Where is Christ in the face of human suffering? – but it cannot be treated strictly on that or any one single level. An entire worldview is always at stake, and hence the question must be put even quite literally: Where is Christ with respect to space and time?

of skepticism in the heirs of Hume and Kant (who scorned the lot) is a shorter journey than it appears to be. In any case it was dramatically hastened by the sudden collapse of the classical tradition in cosmology, a collapse usually associated with Copernicus. We may, if we like, speak with Harold Nebelsick of the Copernican *non*-revolution, pointing both to his failure to persuade fellow astronomers that the earth was in orbit around the sun, and also to his conservative approach. For Copernicus, as Nebelsick argues, remained committed to an interpretation of the heavens as circles of God, an essentially religious notion which prevented him from discovering the irregularity of planetary motion and thus from arriving at a true heliocentricity. Yet with the help of Kepler and Galileo hallowed schemes were nonetheless undone.[3]

The results were nothing short of revolutionary, not least in those matters directly related to our own inquiry. Where the ascension of Jesus was concerned Augustine's 'little coterie of skeptics' would be heard after all, even if their new argument was the reverse of the old one. Kepler's discovery that celestial bodies shared the defective (non-circular) motion of terrestrial bodies, and Galileo's observation of various irregularities in the sun and moon with that irreverent invention, the telescope, called into question the common logic of the ascension. It was doubtful whether the heavens could any longer be thought of as a stairway to God. This lent an unintended poignancy to the iconography which had been popular from the Gothic period onwards, in which Jesus was depicted as nothing more than a pair of dangling feet disappearing into the clouds; and there was still more trouble to come.

Even before the implications of a celestial realm stripped of its divine attributes had sunk in, or a new way of mediating between God and the material world had been agreed, another momentous change in perspective occurred. Isaac Newton (who with the publication of his *Principia* in 1687 arrived on a chaotic scene in messianic style) recovered the perfectionist vision of the heavens that had been lost. Indeed, he pointed out the godlike simplicity and stability underlying *all* physical phenomena, whether supra-lunar or sub-lunar, namely, the immutable laws of motion. Creation as a whole could now boast a certain divine character, but the final demise of the cosmic hierarchy suggested to many the demise of organized religion too. This aftershock badly shook the tottering remains of a weak and divided Christendom.[4]

---

[3] See Nebelsick 248ff. The undoing actually began just as Denys – 'whose instruction the church now follows,' wrote Roger Bacon (ibid. 132) – was getting properly established in the west. Certainly William of Occam's radical nominalism struck at the very foundations of the old worldview.

[4] After Newton had 'eliminated the barrier between earthly mechanics and celestial mechanics, and established by *empirical and mathematical proof* the existence of *universal* laws,' there came into prominence a worldview on which there was 'no *need* for supernatural guidance, prayer, priests, sacraments, or penance' (T. Greer 1982:361ff.). All of this implied an entirely new social order, for which many were already clamouring.

Newton himself, we should note, was among those who came to the defense of religion, helping to shoulder the burden of adapting the church's beliefs to the new scientific realities.[5] Broadly speaking, this meant a transition (already implicit in the natural philosophy of late medieval scholasticism) from trinitarian to unitarian ideas. The doctrine of the incarnation was set to one side, and the creator was placed in a mainly utilitarian relation to creation, serving only to guarantee spatial and temporal consistency, epistemological integrity, or the soundness of the social order. Critics of such impiety were not wanting, of course, but there were some who did not question the theological utilitarianism so much as the utility of theology. Were these guarantees actually necessary? Perhaps a self-consistent and largely self-explanatory cosmos did not require the God-hypothesis after all? Unitarianism gave way to deism, and deism to atheism.[6]

In this milieu a deep skepticism naturally began to infect biblical scholarship; the interventionist history of salvation recounted in scripture did not fit with the Newtonian worldview. Now at last a concerted effort would be made to recover the lost humanity of Christ, only the Christ in question was the Ebionite one Irenaeus had labelled *homo tantus*. Out of the sulphuric clouds of Reimarus' attack on the divine Christ of the Evangelists, the quest for the so-called 'historical Jesus' was quickly launched.[7] Here the only relevant Where? question concerned his proper contextualization by period scholars. Not that this labour, even if it were to succeed at exposing the enigmatic figure hidden for so long beneath layers of obfuscating tradition, could be regarded as producing something strictly pivotal for the faith of modern man! On the contrary, G. E. Lessing's famous dictum separating the contingent facts of history from the necessary truths of reason shows how diligently the men of the Enlightenment stood on guard against such an error.[8] It also demonstrates the dualism of their age, and their preoccupation with the universal over the particular. As Ernst Troeltsch would later put it – fighting at the turn of the twentieth century for *some* importance to be attached to Jesus' increasingly distant figure – there was a definite 'disinclination to concentrate the measureless totality of life at this single point.'[9]

---

[5] Descartes had already begun this process, but was resisted especially where his views had negative implications for the Catholic doctrine of the eucharist (cf. C. Kaiser 1991:163). M. Buckley (1987:347) argues that both men 'registered their recognition of the theological office fallen to them,' and in their different ways subsumed theology under the mantle of their physics.

[6] Newton resisted these more radical tendencies (see Kaiser 175ff.) but is justly identified with the rise of deism, against which William Blake later directed such a powerful diatribe in his widely read *Jerusalem*.

[7] Parts of Reimarus' *Apology for the Reasonable Worshipers of God* were published posthumously at the instigation of Lessing, under the title *Fragments by an Anonymous Author from Wolfenbüttel*.

[8] See *On the Proof of the Spirit and of Power* (1956:51ff.; cf. K. Barth, *CD* I/1, 146f.).

[9] '. . . when everywhere else it flows through the whole breadth of things' (1990:190).

Yet, and here is the development of greatest interest to us, modern dualism was now able to bring history itself into the service of the universal, having rid it of everything which smacked of supernatural intervention. In place of the upward-looking teleology of the pre-Copernican world, a forward-looking one was substituted. This too was natural enough. Europeans stood, literally and metaphorically, on the brink of a new world. According to Lessing, the prophecies of Joachim about a *tertius status* had not proved wrong but merely premature, their apocalyptic elements aside. Capitalizing on the Calabrian's shift from christology to pneumatology – or, as some would say, from the past to the future – he argued in *The Education of the Human Race* that God is operating immanently in the processes of human social development to prepare the race for its ultimate destiny; that is, for a voluntary brotherhood of man in a worldwide kingdom of peace. This variation on a medieval theme made history generally, as opposed to Jewish or Jesus-history in particular, the locus of divine revelation and human salvation. The maturation of man through a culminating period of inspired self-education became the basic faith of the Enlightenment, and the establishment of a fully rationalized society the focus of its this-worldly optimism.

What consequences this had for the doctrine of the ascension we can begin to see by pausing for a moment with Kant, who took up Lessing's 'philosophical chiliasm,' as he called it, in his own way.[10]

* * *

Immanuel Kant's self-announced Copernican revolution in philosophy offered Newtonian science an epistemological basis. At the same time it stole something of its glory by treating the human mind as the source of all phenomenal order, and the human will as a powerful agent of change in an otherwise tedious causal nexus. In short, it limited the domain of science and put man back at the centre of a world picture which was threatening his own relevance along with that of his God.[11] As for the latter, Kant's distinction between *phenomena* and *noumena*, and between

[10] See Moltmann 1996:184ff., who regards Lessing's treatise of 1780 'as the foundational writing of the German Enlightenment.' (On Joachim cf. Moltmann 1992:295ff., and McGinn 1985:190f., 236.)

[11] Kant renewed man's exemption from the debasement which the rest of nature was suffering under a mechanistic worldview. Here he had one eye on Descartes and another on his hero, Rousseau, whose emphasis on human freedom he appropriated even while rejecting his attempt to return to a pre-scientific relation to nature. But in all of this Kant bequeathed to modernity a version of the nature–freedom dualism which is fraught with peril, a peril heightened by his attempt to resolve the difficult relation between will and intellect *via* aesthetics. (In this light, see Peter Cohen's disturbing film, *Architektur des Untergangs*; cf. A. Bloom 1987:298ff., Prigogine and Stengers 1984:86ff.)

pure and practical reason, allowed him to transfer God-talk from the realm of rational demonstration (whence Hume had recently evicted it) to that of discourse about moral duty. While this brought a temporary halt to the deterioration of theology, it also nudged Lessing's neo-chiliasm even further in a Pelagian direction. For Kant went on to argue that a religion rooted in moral or practical reason does not concern itself directly with what God is doing with man, but with what man may hope to do with himself.[12]

Now in the teleology of the Enlightenment what man may hope to do with himself is to fulfill the law of his own being, rising eventually to his full potential; a doctrine of human perfectibility was in some quarters held with great enthusiasm. Kant's approach was a more sober one, to be sure. He was prepared to acknowledge a radical evil in man. And he made clear that if it is the task of man to shape his own reality, to give meaning to his world and construct a better future, the end which he pursues lies beyond his finite comprehension and capacities. The kingdom of God, though in one sense already immanent in his moral consciousness, can never be represented purely in any concrete state of affairs. History is a story of progress insofar as it embodies a perpetual striving after the *unattainable*. Kant, in other words, regarded the perfectibility of man as a necessary myth, the rejection of which could only mean capitulation to evil.[13] It was still possible, however, for him to claim with Lessing that history is moving towards a day in which humanity will enjoy the ripened fruit both of scientific knowledge and of the right exercise of practical reason. Indeed, since our perfection as individuals is so obviously unrealizable in this mortal life, and since immortal life is beyond all comprehension, hastening that day must be our foremost aim. The perfection of the species as a whole must command our best energies.[14]

In *Religion Within the Limits of Reason Alone* Kant allowed that whatever is actually to be achieved here cannot be made to rest entirely on the 'crooked wood' of which society is constructed. Only an overarching providence can turn reality into something that approximates

---

[12] See *Religion Within the Limits of Reason Alone* and his other late works; cf. *Critique of Judgment* 2.28.

[13] See J. Passmore 1970:215ff. If history is the sphere of hopeful action – for it is hope which drives it forward through a process of perpetual self-criticism – 'God' is the justification of hope and hence the guarantor of the myth. But can we not demythologize God-talk, and the language of hope with it, simply by speaking of the tension between finitude and infinitude? Human beings are uniquely historical in nature because they are painfully aware of their finitude, and make their protest against it. Of course history so conceived can have no *terminus*, other than that forced upon it by the death of the solar system (as the early Kant suggested).

[14] Rousseau, whom Kant dubbed 'the Newton of the moral world,' taught him not to despise human nature but to find in society the main source of human ills (cf. C. Friedrich [Kant 1949] xi, xxiiff.). However, Kant was rather more hopeful about the reformation of society.

the ideal, even if man must proceed 'as though everything depended on himself.'[15] There was sufficient scope, then, in his carefully blinkered synergism, to sneak a glance at Jesus – so long as one did not suppose that Jesus, in any exclusive hypostatic sense, is the Son or Word who proceeds from God. Mankind 'in its complete moral perfection' is that Word, the archetype of which 'is to be sought only in our own reason.' To clarify the role of Jesus Kant took up the traditional language of descent and ascent, which he modified in good Hellenic fashion:

> Now it is our universal duty as men to *elevate* ourselves to this ideal of moral perfection, that is, to this archetype of the moral disposition in all its purity – and for this the idea itself, which reason presents to us for our zealous emulation, can give us power. But just because we are not the authors of this idea, and because it has established itself in man without our comprehending how human nature could have been capable of receiving it, it is more appropriate to say that this archetype has *come down* to us from heaven and has assumed our humanity . . .[16]

Here indeed was an exemplarism more radical than anything yet produced by the Origenist tradition. Jesus provides 'as perfect an *example* of a man well-pleasing to God as one can expect to find in external experience.' In him the archetype has found its clearest expression. Through him we are therefore called to an ascension of the mind[17] that will prepare us, too, to sacrifice ourselves for the common good as we stretch out towards the full stature of man.

Against this rather flimsy christological backdrop, the later Kant joined Lessing in the task of reinventing the medieval vision of a divine kingdom which will gradually unfold on earth through the establishment of a universal church. He referred to it as an 'ethical commonwealth,' a notion he developed by drawing critically on a diverse stock of recent ideas (those of Hobbes, Leibniz, Voltaire, *et.al.*) and on the conventional categories of dualist ecclesiology:

> An ethical commonwealth under divine moral legislation is a *church* which, so far as it is not an object of possible experience, is called the *church invisible* (a mere idea of the union of all the righteous under direct and moral divine world-government, an idea serving all as the archetype of what is to be established by men). The *visible church* is the actual union of men into a whole which harmonizes with that ideal.[18]

---

[15] *Rel.* 3.1.4 (see 3.1.2ff.).

[16] i.e., in that 'godly-minded person' from whom we may learn how 'to become acceptable to God' (*Rel.* 2.1).

[17] Resurrection and ascension in the flesh are explicitly rejected in an extended note (*Rel.* 3.2, 119f.); 'the spirituality of rational world-beings' is 'more congenial to reason' than some form of 'cosmological materialism.'

[18] *Rel.* 3.1.4. The essential features of this 'church' are described in terms of the four credal *notae*, which are adapted to Kant's secular frame of reference.

This was closely co-ordinated with an ambitious political agenda – still very much alive today – namely, 'the progressive organization of the world citizens into a system of cosmopolitan scope.' As the inner and outer face of the ultimate society, an ethical commonwealth and a world state together held out the promise of perpetual peace on earth.[19]

In *Leviathan* Thomas Hobbes had vigorously attacked the medieval scheme while setting out a new mechanistic model of society; not unlike Wycliffe, he had even brought against it the charge that it encouraged mere men to usurp an authority which belongs only to the ascended and returning Christ.[20] Kant, of course, had no longer to compete with the older scheme in quite the same way, or to speak in quite the same terms. Neither then did he see any need to safeguard his vision against that same hybris. The parousia of a peaceful society in which humanity might flourish was, after all, nature's highest goal. Jesus may have effected 'a revolution in the human race' by pointing us towards that goal, but it is perfectly appropriate that we ourselves should press on to achieve it, taking charge of our own corporate destiny. The future belongs to Man, not to *that* man, whose personal name Kant habitually avoided.[21] Man as his own project, his own last end – this was the mutant doctrine of the ascension he embraced. To embrace it was already to ascend. But that meant letting go of Jesus, who could no longer be seen standing either at the centre of history or at its putative end.[22]

It fell first to Friedrich Schleiermacher, who sought to rescue something like an orthodox faith from its Kantian despisers, to find a new and firmer place for Jesus in the evolving post-Copernican world. This stirring preacher developed a comprehensive christology the likes of which had not been seen for some time. To show the significance of his contribution to the doctrine of the ascension, however, or to trace further the relevant legacy of Lessing and Kant, we must first backtrack a little.

---

[19] Kant thus came to the rescue of utopianism: In the last analysis humankind should not be described as evil, 'but as a species of rational beings who are steadily progressing from the evil to the good, striving against hindrances.' Human intentions 'are generally good, but the carrying out [of these intentions] is made hard by the fact that the achievement of the purpose does not depend upon the free agreement of individuals, but upon the progressive organization of the world citizens into a system of cosmopolitan scope' (*Anthropology Practically Considered*, Friedrich xliii; cf. *Rel.* 1, and his highly influential political essay *On Perpetual Peace*).

[20] See *Leviathan*, chap. 41ff., for criticism of what Moltmann (1996:182) aptly describes as 'the ecclesiastical occupation of chiliasm.' This was for Hobbes an argument of convenience, however.

[21] Others have observed the curious fact that Kant could not 'bring himself to pronounce the name of Jesus' (C. Brown 1973:104).

[22] Superstitious attachment to the historic particulars of the Christian faith amounted to a denial of its inner essence as a true religion. It preserved an unfortunate Jewish habit, incompatible with universality and hence with rational thought. From this Marcionite point of view Kant looked for 'a "Newton of history" who would reduce history to a science just as Newton had reduced physics to a science' (Passmore 221). His pupil, Herder, aspired to that distinction.

An Unresolved Question

When the procession of scholars at the University of Königsberg reached the open door of the chapel, Kant would regularly turn aside in order to pass quietly to the sanctuary of his study. Though not averse to Christianity in the manner of the *philosophes*, he regarded its worship (even in Protestant mode) as retrogressive and laden with superstition. A couple of centuries earlier certain other scholars had ventured similar criticisms, and to them church doors had quickly been barred. Yet these men were whole-hearted adherents to the church's creeds. Indeed they were as much troubled by the tide of skepticism that was already rising around them as by the abuses and superstitions which were helping to produce it.

The early reformers (of whom we are speaking) were able to evade the challenge posed by the new cosmology, which had not as yet been proved.[23] But there was another challenge which they could not evade, and it too had cosmological implications. In their struggle with Rome the stubborn eucharistic problem of the presence and the absence emerged as one of their chief preoccupations. It became in fact a great stone of stumbling within the Reformation itself, as immense theological effort exposed, but did not resolve, fundamental disagreements between them. Among these was the question of the whereabouts of Jesus, which was notoriously difficult long before anyone peered into the heavens through a telescope.

Though we need to move quickly here, we cannot bypass entirely the complexities which arise at the junction between the problem of the presence and the absence and that of the eucharist as sacrifice. On the latter subject the reformers were at least united by their strong opposition to Rome, for each in his own way found it necessary to stress that what ultimately matters in Christian worship is not the church's offering, but Christ's. They also agreed (consistently or inconsistently) that the consecration of the host did not entail its actual displacement by Christ's holy body, since that appeared to arrogate to the church a certain power over his offering. That is where their agreement stopped, however, for attempts to answer the following questions provoked volatile disputes: What connection should be made between the bread and the body? How *is* Jesus present in the eucharist?[24] Where is he otherwise? The doctrine of the ascension would play an important part in shaping their various responses.

---

[23] In Calvin's words, Copernican ideas were but another demonic attempt 'to pervert the order of nature' (*Ser.* 8 on 1 Cor.; quoted W. Bouwsma 1988:72). To 'jumble heaven and earth' could only contribute to the general breakdown of social order, a matter of greater pastoral interest than the scientific question. Cf. Kaiser 139ff.

[24] Wycliffe's rather vague '*quodammodo*' (*Ser.* 2.61) would no longer suffice.

Martin Luther made his approach by way of analogy with the incarnation. As God, in becoming man, did not annihilate human nature but rather assumed it to himself, so in the eucharist the consecrated elements received the body and blood of Christ without themselves being unmade or converted into something else.[25] This model allowed Luther to hold together a heavenly reality (Jesus Christ) and an earthly one (bread and wine) without confusion or separation, so to speak: without confusion, that he might emphasize the faith in which the consecrated elements ought to be received rather than the bare fact of their supernatural content, thus avoiding an essentially Roman ecclesiology; without separation, since the realm of faith and the realm of sight must not be permitted to diverge too sharply, an ever-present danger in his own theological dialectic.

The evolution of Luther's model was determined in part by Zwingli, however, who ascribed to faith such a dominant role that the body and blood could be identified with the bread and wine only in the much weaker sense that the gathered community obediently invested the latter with a symbolic significance. For this he was rebuked by the German reformer, who not only saw a great breach opening up between faith and sight, but also feared a new meritorious work on the part of the church, if all the emphasis were to fall on remembering rather than receiving Christ.[26] *Hoc est corpus meum* had somehow to be given a literal interpretation, even if not a Roman one. Zwingli, however, like Berengar before him, appealed to the doctrine of the ascension in order to insist upon the bodily absence of Jesus, that is, upon his departure to heaven, from which none should think to fetch him down again in order to hide him under the consecrated elements. Luther replied with a quite different view of the ascension. Jesus may have gone to sit at the right hand of the Father, but that could hardly mean that he was now confined to heaven as to 'a place in the sky.' On the contrary, it meant that he shared the divine omnipresence.[27] In short, Luther resorted to the doctrine of ubiquity as a way of justifying his sacramental realism.

Here was a fateful decision. Though the great reformer boasted in another connection that he had 'put Origen under the ban,'[28] he produced

---

[25] See *Babylonian Captivity*, part 1. Cf. Pelikan 4/53ff., who notes some anticipation in Wycliffe of this solution.

[26] But how far is this already implicit in Luther's own view that the sacrament depends for its validity on the church's authentic proclamation of the gospel?

[27] The Swiss were arguing that Christ was present '"according to his divinity, majesty, grace and Spirit," but not according to his human nature which was at the right hand of God' (Pelikan 4/159f.). But now it was the German's turn to shun literalism, by pointing out with Berengar's opponents that this phrase merely signifies God's limitless power. Bodily ascension 'occurred as a sign' that Christ 'is above all creatures and in all and beyond all creatures.' 'He is present everywhere,' complete in both natures, 'but he does not wish that you should grope for him everywhere' (*The Sacrament of the Body and Blood – Against the Fanatics*, part 1).

[28] See Trigg 256.

a christology with at least one remarkable likeness to Origen's. In defense of his eucharistic teaching he essayed an answer to the Where? question which had Christ running through everything, at once everywhere and nowhere. Some said that a new Eutychianism threatened, especially when the trinitarian concepts of περιχώρησις and *communicatio idiomatum* were transferred to the relation between Christ's two natures in order to explain and support that answer. Lutherans began to speak of the *genus majestaticum*, or even of deification, meaning thereby to affirm the glory of Jesus in his universal lordship and hence also his ability to be present in the bread. But their Reformed counterparts protested that this supposed glory was purchased at the expense of his human particularity.

T. F. Torrance rightly argues that a faulty view of space and time contributed to the Lutheran ubiquity doctrine, with the consequence that problems deeply rooted in the western tradition were carried over into the Reformation.[29] While making real advances towards a more dynamic way of thinking about the eucharist, and hence about the cosmological and anthropological dimensions of Christian faith, Luther was still trying to fit the ascended Lord spacelessly into our time or (as Torrance would have it) timelessly into our space.[30] The difficulties thus created were exacerbated by a metaphysical opposition between the realms of time and eternity, which on Luther's view meet only at the mathematical point where Christ's will to be present *pro me* invokes and awakens faith. Against the obvious danger here of falling into a dualism even more radical than Zwingli's, Luther simply pounded more vehemently on the *hoc est corpus meum*, says Torrance, as if on 'the ontological nail that held the two kingdoms together.'[31]

In the long run the German's strategy could only backfire. The ubiquity notion put at risk Chalcedon's 'without confusion' in christology itself, while failing to do for eucharistic theology what he intended. It did not support but actually undermined the 'without separation' which guaranteed the uniqueness and indispensability of the sacrament. In Pelikan's words, the presence of Christ in the elements threatened to become 'a mere corollary of [his] massive cosmic presence.'[32] Conversely the distinction

[29] Torrance (1969:30ff.) shows how the 'container' concept of space called for a dialectic of κένωσις and πλήρωσις in interpreting the incarnation, then in the Newtonian era undermined the doctrine of the incarnation altogether.

[30] 'Timelessly' inasmuch as it cuts off the presence of Christ from the actual history of Jesus (ibid. 34f.), but it is perhaps more helpful to put it the other way around. Cf. Heron 1983b:118, who points out the strong similarity between Luther and Aquinas respecting a non-local presence.

[31] Torrance 1969:34

[32] Pelikan (4/202) is describing the Reformed objection, but see below. Heron (118) correctly observes that 'the doctrine of ubiquity, taken by itself, says both too much and too little to establish the identification of the body of Christ with the bread, which it was Luther's primary concern to maintain. Too much, in that it "proves" the presence of Christ's human nature everywhere, not merely in the consecrated elements; too little, in that the special and *particular* connexion and presence in and with the eucharistic bread and wine does not follow from it.'

between the hidden Christ who is always present, and the Christ who wills to be present *pro nobis*, began to focus so much attention on the problem of revelation that all manner of distracting questions arose to obscure also from this side the eucharistic centre that Luther wished to preserve.[33]

It may be that Augustine's stress on the subjective aspect of the eucharist was bound to run amok once the sacerdotalism which served to hold it in check was dismantled; that in any case is what subsequently happened in the German Reformation. Had the humanity of Christ been brought into sharper focus at the same time, things might have turned out differently. Instead, the loss of Jesus' space–time particularity augured the loss of the church's own particularity precisely *as* a eucharistic community. As for Zwinglian circles, their pronounced dualism, coupled with an inclination towards Nestorianism well marked by the Lutherans, meant that resources for a happier outcome were slim. The Reformation thus promised on both sides to produce little more than a repetition, in somewhat altered terms, of familiar debates. But just here Calvin entered the fray.

Calvin basically endorsed Luther's early approach to the relationship between the body and the bread; the maxim *distinctio sed non separatio* well represents his eucharistic teaching.[34] At the same time, he followed Zwingli in firmly rejecting the notion of a ubiquitous Christ, which he regarded as a 'monstrous phantasm.' The very idea of a man who was physically ἄτοπος (without place) was itself ἄτοπος (absurd).[35] The concreteness of the incarnation had to be maintained just as carefully with respect to the mediator's exalted state as it was with respect to his humiliated state. But if among the Zwinglians that conviction led back around to the marginalization of Jesus, and of the sacraments too, it was not so with Calvin. Heaven – understood as a distant place to which Jesus had departed bodily – was the right answer to the Where? question, insofar as that question could be answered at all. Jesus had passed 'beyond the whole machinery of the visible world.'[36] Yet this did *not* mean, as

---

[33] On the *ubiquity/ubivoli* distinction, cf. D. Bonhoeffer 1978:54ff.

[34] Cf. *Inst.* 4.17.5. On Calvin's frequent and varied application of the formula *distinctio sed non separatio*, see B. Milner 1970:190ff., who points out its pneumatological links. In the eucharistic debate it was pneumatology which allowed Calvin safely to stress the *distinctio*.

[35] *Tracts and Treatises* 2/282 (cf. 240). 'Let nothing inappropriate to human nature be ascribed to his body,' urges Calvin (*Inst.* 4.17.19), 'as happens when it is said either to be infinite or to be put in a number of places at once.'

[36] See *Eph.* 4.8ff., where Calvin struggles to prevent misunderstanding by the literal-minded: 'When we say Christ is in heaven, we must not imagine that he is somewhere among the cosmic spheres, counting the stars! *Heaven* means a place far beyond all the spheres, destined for the Son of God after his resurrection. When we speak of it as another place outside the universe, we do so because we must speak of the Kingdom of God using

some of the Swiss appeared to think, that the bread and wine were empty symbols or that the church's actual participation in his flesh and blood should be denied. On the contrary, a true partaking had to be affirmed lest a gnostic view of salvation prevail after all.[37]

'But why,' asked Calvin, 'do we repeat the word "ascension" so often?'[38] To answer in our own words, it was because he found it necessary to reckon more bravely than the other reformers with the absence of Christ as a genuine problem for the church. Negatively, he did not hesitate to spell out the consequences of any attempt to gloss over that absence, to convert it into presence by abusing the doctrine of the ascension: First, an injustice is done to Christ, and to all who depend on him, by making him quite 'unlike himself.'[39] Second, 'a serious wrong is done to the Holy Spirit,' whose role in uniting us to the absent Christ goes unnoticed.[40] Third, the doctrine of Christ's return, not to mention the resurrection of the flesh and the judgment of this world, is effectively overthrown, since he has not so much gone from us as diffused himself in our midst.

> When Scripture speaks of the ascension of Christ, it declares, at the same time, that he will come again. If he now occupies the whole world in respect of his body, what else was his ascension, and what will his descent be, but a fallacious and empty show?[41]

Positively, by looking to the Spirit – not as a substitute for Jesus but as a link to him – Calvin displayed a keener sense of the interpersonal, trinitarian dimensions of human existence *coram deo*. And by introducing the parousia into the debate, as a control on the doctrine of the ascension,

---

the only language which we have . . .' But against the ubiquitarians, who in handling Eph. 4:10 showed a perverse literalism of their own, it was necessary to be equally emphatic: Heaven 'is opposite to the frame of this world' (*Acts* 1.9). Even if 'philosophically speaking there is no place above the skies, yet as the body of Christ, bearing the nature and mode of a human body, is finite and is contained in heaven as its place, it is necessarily as distant from us in point of space as heaven is from earth' (*Mutual Consent* 25, *Tracts* 2/220).

[37] When Calvin (*Inst.* 4.17.17) rejects the spectre of Marcion he perceives behind the ubiquity doctrine, he has already insisted against some of that doctrine's Reformed opponents that 'communion of Christ's flesh and blood is necessary for all who aspire to heavenly life' – i.e., that Christ is not received 'only by understanding and imagination' (4.17.9ff.; cf. 3.1.1).

[38] 4.17.27.

[39] 4.17.29 (see §25–34). Though Calvin attempts on this point to wrest from Luther the support of Augustine, he himself does not follow that venerable father in assigning to the ascension a negative function. The ascension is primarily about the exaltation of a man, not our recognition of that man's divinity (cf. 2.16.14ff).

[40] 4.17.33. A related injury is done to our faith, which is drawn away from heaven and back to earth. And another to the goodness of God, in that Christ (if literally present in the bread) is equally shared by all, yet does not bring salvation to all.

[41] *Tracts* 2/286; cf. *Inst.* 4.17.27. As R. S. Wallace (1953:225) observes, it is one of the merits of his doctrine 'that he leaves room for a more significant eschatology than would be possible on the assumption of his opponents.'

he secured a vital soteriological point. To maintain a real absence is also to maintain a real continuity between the saviour and the saved.[42]

All of this demonstrates that Calvin had a better grasp than his contemporaries on the way in which the Where? question is bound up with the Who? question. That indeed was his critical insight into the whole debate. Calvin saw that neither a Eutychian response (Jesus is omnipresent) nor a Nestorian one (absent in one nature but present in the other) will do, since either way Christ's humanity is neutralized and his role as our mediator put in jeopardy. It is the God-man who is absent and the God-man whose presence we nevertheless require.[43] Against the Lutherans, then, he applied the dogmas of bodily ascension and bodily return as an antidote to Eutychianism. Against *both* sides, he appealed to the power of the Holy Spirit as the proper basis for a robust doctrine of the real presence.[44] In the ascension the mediator has been removed from us by a great distance; yet the Spirit, who 'overcomes distance,' draws us heavenward to participate in him in some mysterious way. A 'species of absence' and a 'species of presence' thus qualify our communion with Christ, who remains in heaven until the day of judgment. It is *we* who require eucharistic relocation.[45]

It appears, in sum, that the Genevan reformer attempted to find a path through the minefield of the eucharistic debates by returning to a much earlier orientation, determined by the trajectory of the ascension and 'the upwards call of God in Christ Jesus.' He worked from the ascension to the eucharist, rather than the other way round, in a bid to get back behind centuries of acrimonious dispute.[46] One of his most impressive moves, as he struggled to preserve the particularity of Jesus without sacrificing sacramental realism, was to reach out towards a relational, christocentric

---

[42] Conversely, to assert Christ's presence at the expense of a real absence is to posit too great a *discontinuity*. We should not allow the 19th C. eucharistic controversy among Presbyterians in America (cf. L. de Bie 1995:431ff.) to obscure this point, which neither J. Nevin nor his opponent, C. Hodge, grasped clearly.

[43] 'Who can be offended when we wish Christ to remain complete and entire in regard to both natures, and the Mediator who joins us to God not to be torn to pieces?' (*Tracts* 2/241) Bonhoeffer (59) takes a similar line when he insists on asking the Where? question only 'within the structure of the *Who*?'; but a closer look at Calvin might have helped him to overcome his preoccupation with the *pro me* dimension of Christ's existence at the expense of the *pro Patre*, and a glaring pneumatological deficiency.

[44] *Inst.* 4.17.12. Augustine speaks of a presence 'in majesty, in providence, and in ineffable grace': 'Under grace,' says Calvin, 'I include that marvelous communion in his body and blood – provided we understand that it takes place by the power of the Holy Spirit, not by that feigned inclusion of the body itself under the element' (§26).

[45] On the one hand, *quadam absentiae specie nos ab eo disjungi* (*Tracts* 2/240). On the other, since Christ 'so raises us to himself,' we may rightly assert a *species praesentiae* (ibid. 2/286; cf. 3/280); for the Spirit 'truly unites things separated in space' (*Inst.* 4.17.10).

[46] Calvin did not want to inquire yet again how Christ can be hidden in the bread, but how we come to share in his body, 'as once for all it was given for us' (4.17.33; cf. Walker 39ff.). This made christology the starting point and invited a fresh look at the ascension, which is 'one of the chief points of our faith' (*Acts* 1.9).

concept of space that would resolve the conflict. The ascended Lord is not everywhere, that is, ubiquitous and hence atopic, but he *is* everywhere accessible. The 'infinite spaces' that we cannot leap are effectively compressed for us by the the the Spirit. In other words, Calvin's insistence on keeping the human Jesus sharply in focus forced him to seek a pneumatological solution to the problem of the presence and the absence.[47]

Unfortunately it has to be said that his solution was just that – somewhat forced and not altogether convincing, being restricted by his worldview. On the one hand, Calvin sought to penetrate as far as possible into the unique logic of the ascension and the eucharist, avoiding any false tribute to natural philosophy in these matters.[48] On the other hand, his resistance to Copernicus speaks loudly of the hold that the old vertical cosmology had on his thinking; as others have noticed, the 'jumbling' of heaven and earth in nature was scarcely more acceptable to him than the mixing of the divine and the human in Christ, and his pneumatology did little to correct that. We need not explore the various dualistic features that crop up in his work, nor decide whether he himself had Nestorian tendencies, in order to discover the root of the problem.[49] We need only notice that his vertical orientation made it difficult for him to factor time into the equation, that is, to subject temporal relations to the same pneumatological reinterpretation with which he experimented in spatial relations. Calvin handled the dialectic of presence and absence almost exclusively in spatial terms, and hence (what has already been said about the parousia notwithstanding) in a non-eschatological fashion.

The immediate result was to put in doubt his sacramental realism, which to this day has been disputed by would-be friends as well as by

---

[47] Quenstedt (*Theo.* 3.3.1.2.14; Pelikan 4/357) later put the question thus: 'Is Christ, according to the humanity that is united with his divine and infinite person and that is exalted at the right hand of the Divine Majesty, present, in this glorious state of exaltation, to all creatures in the universe with a true, real, substantial, and efficacious omnipresence?' While Calvin never doubted Christ's freedom in the Spirit to make his kingly power felt anywhere he liked (*Inst.* 4.17.18, 28ff.; cf. *Tracts* 2/558), for him the question was rather: Are fallen creatures really made present by the Spirit with and to Christ? The Lutherans, like the Romans, did not understand 'the manner of descent *by which he lifts us up to himself*' (4.17.15f., emphasis ours; cf. H. Heppe 1978:507ff.).

[48] 'I pay no regard to physical arguments,' says Calvin (*Tracts* 2/557; cf. *Inst.* 4.17.24), though T. F. Torrance (1969:29f., 1988:81) thinks that his exposition of the ascension 'in relation to questions of space and time' owes something to advances by John Major and Duns Scotus.

[49] Calvin too could sound much like Origen: 'Shut up as we are in the prisonhouse of the flesh, we have not yet attained to angelic rank,' he says; hence our need for tangible aids like the sacraments (*Inst.* 4.1.1, 4.14.3). His austere eschatology, and his rejection of the idea that the incarnation belongs to creation as well as redemption (2.12.4ff.), also betray his dualist heritage. As for the Nestorian tendency, how else are we to read his argument in 1 Cor. 15.27 (unless with J. Moltmann, 1974:258f., as 'docetic') that the mediation of the mediator will come to an end when his kingdom is finally transferred 'from his humanity to his glorious divinity'?

opponents.[50] Calvin knew that to preserve the continuity between Christ and ourselves the discontinuity had also to be of a kind relevant to human beings. That is why he insisted on spatial opposition rather than spacelessness or ubiquity, and treated the eucharist as a ladder for our ascent not Christ's descent.[51] But if we do not speak of a *temporal* as well as a spatial opposition, the reality of our putative union with Christ is confined to the hidden sphere of the soul. The body itself is not involved. This helps to explain why the marks of inwardness are everywhere present in Calvin's sacramental writings, belying (if that is not too strong a word) the 'true partaking' he nonetheless believed and preached. It helps to explain why some find it easy to reduce his eucharistic teaching to the *sursum corda*, that is, to the invitation to 'feed on Him in your hearts by faith with thanksgiving,' as the prayer book has it. Indeed Calvin himself could invite such a reduction:

> What then is the sum of our doctrine? It is this, that when we discern here on earth the bread and wine, our minds must be raised to heaven in order to enjoy Christ, and that Christ is there present with us while we seek him above the elements of this world.[52]

Insofar as he did so, however, he failed to point the way towards the church concord for which he hoped.

One other result of his failure to think eschatologically requires mention, for it will occupy us further in the next section; it concerns the heavenly session as such. Calvin's attention to Christ's heavenly priesthood, which was furthered by Knox and by the divines of various traditions influenced by Calvin, was in many respects salutary. Indeed there is little of real significance in the Reformation that can be sustained in a wholesome way without reference to that concept.[53] But the corresponding emphasis on heavenly *kingship* was more problematic. Since Calvin understood Christ still to share our time, to have a history that continues to run more or less parallel to ours, it was open to his followers to introduce an artificial separation between Christ's priestly

---

[50] See B. Gerrish 1993, chap. 1.

[51] The latter would bring us into judgment prematurely. Cf. Wallace 225f.

[52] Ibid. 229 (*CR* 12:728). Were Calvin's eucharistic logic fully eschatological the '*ac tum praesentem nobis esse Christum*' could be given more weight, but as things stand it is not hard to see why he has been accused of reducing the eucharist to 'a noetic moment.' (K. McDonnell 1967:376ff. rejects this charge, but candidly remarks: 'It is not at all clear, nor even tolerably unclear, as to how the Spirit makes present the body of Christ. There is much one could praise in Calvin's pneumatology but one has the impression that the Holy Spirit, to put it bluntly, is used.')

[53] Cf. e.g. W. Milligan 1892. A debt was owed here to Socinian reaction against a strict *theologia crucis*, but of course heterodox associations also discouraged this line of thought (cf. Heppe 505f.). In any event, it did not shape Calvinist ecclesiology as much as it ought to have, for the latter rested more fundamentally on a doctrine of predestination and remained highly pedagogical (see *Inst.* 4.1).

and kingly work. Attention to the latter was not controlled (as in Irenaeus) by the doctrine of recapitulation, but by speculation as to the effect of Christ's new lordship over the ongoing process of history. 'He does not now sit idle in heaven':[54] This belief did not serve so much to inhibit that ecclesiastical substitution for Jesus which is characteristic of the western tradition, as to prepare the way in Reformed circles for the general swing to the horizontal, and indeed for the revival of Pelagianism, which was just around the corner. If Calvin himself was of two minds about temporal progress, his reservations gave way – in John Owen, for one – to a new confidence in the power of Jesus, working through the church, to mould from human affairs a 'latter-day glory' in advance of his eventual return.[55] Here and there post-millennialist enthusiasm began to produce a Christian optimism that would gradually coalesce with its secular counterpart (Kant's 'philosophical chiliasm') into a new form of triumphalism even more beguiling than the old.

William Bouwsma's recent biography of Calvin concludes that he 'was much like Copernicus: unable to abandon traditional modes of thought, partly because of temperament but above all because he depended on them to make sense of the world; yet he undeniably was fumbling toward a new culture.'[56] In the narrower sphere of our own interests this broad judgment certainly rings true. But if, as William Walker thinks, Calvin was in the end 'unable to give a clear and logical answer to the question, Where is Christ now?', it was not the where but the *now* (or rather the relation between them) that was the deepest difficulty for his changing paradigm.[57] This in due course would come to light.

Discourse on the Dead Christ

Now the Reformation stalemate made it all the more difficult for the church to grapple successfully with the drastically altered worldview that emerged from the successive triumphs of Copernicus, Newton and Kant. A master mediator eventually appeared, however, in the person of the Reformed preacher who headed the theology faculty in Berlin. Friedrich Schleiermacher laboured hard to redeem faith and piety from the embarrassment of living off the 'metaphysical and ethical crumbs' falling from

[54] *Acts* 1.11; see *Inst.* 2.16.14ff. There is much more to be said about the separation in question than can be said here; we hope to treat this matter in another place.

[55] Milner (194) indicates that already with Calvin we must think of the church dynamically as 'the history of the restoration of order in the world.' Owen, at any rate, had something like that in view (see *Works* 1/235ff., and vol. 8, Sermons 5–12; cf. the Savoy Declaration of 1858, §26, and P. Toon 1971:82ff.).

[56] p. 233.

[57] Calvin (*Inst.* 4.17.26; cf. *Phil.* 3.20) echoed Augustine's warning against 'prying and superfluous' inquiries into Christ's exact location in heaven. He ought, however, to have inquired a little further into the matter of Christ's *temporal* location. Walker (124ff.) also observes this, but his analysis differs widely from ours.

Kant's plate. He did this not by flouting the canons of contemporary science or epistemology but by turning (with other Romanticists) to the affective domain as theology's true ground. Since the notion of a special salvation history was now *passé*, and direct speech about God suspect, Schleiermacher proposed that the believer's own self-consciousness, together with that of the church corporately, should afford the immediate subject matter for theological reflection.[58] Only within that domain would he attempt his own answer to the Where? question, which could no longer be asked in the same way, but among Christians could not simply be dismissed either.

We may preface our discussion of his answer by observing that what appears in retrospect to be an impossible restriction for the theologian presented itself to Schleiermacher rather as a liberation from the even tighter straitjacket which Kantian epistemology must otherwise impose. The downgrading of christology and the reduction of religion to ethics need not, he believed, be the end result of Kant's revolution. For Christians are indeed aware, at the very foundations of their human subjectivity, of a vital relation to God, and that precisely in connection with Jesus. Such being the case, religion is something more profound than morality,[59] and Jesus something more than an exemplar from the distant past. Theology as christology is a legitimate enterprise after all. Kant and Calvin walk together in Schleiermacher.[60]

His way forward, however, left almost nothing unaltered in the faith he sought to defend. There were heavy concessions to be made in eschatology especially, for the data provided by Christian subjectivity does not extend into the beyond.[61] On Schleiermacher's view doctrines such as the resurrection, ascension and parousia do not speak of things that happened to Jesus, but of things that happen in us; that is, they articulate in various ways our recognition of his 'peculiar dignity' and our longing to be united with him in his perfect God-consciousness. Internalizing these doctrines was not a new thing, of course, but for the first time we

---

[58] See the Second Speech §§3f.,15,50. The Romantic critique of Kant's modified rationalism was coupled with a move from deism back to panentheism, apart from which such a proposal would make no sense.

[59] 'Neither metaphysics nor ethics is the home of religion,' comments Heron (1980:24), which 'has to do rather with the infinite universal wholeness of all things, of that all-embracing totality which may or may not be labelled "God", but which includes and enfolds everything within itself.' Of this wholeness the religious person is conscious at 'another level of being which lies deeper than knowing or acting.' See *CF* §4.

[60] In the famous thesis of *CF* §11, 'Christianity is a monotheistic faith belonging to the teleological type of religion, and is essentially distinguished from other such faiths by the fact that in it everything is related to the redemption accomplished by Jesus of Nazareth.' Jesus' sphere of influence, however, is 'the inner life;' it does *not* include 'the governance of the whole world' (§105; cf. 91).

[61] §157ff. The objective pole of Christian doctrine is everywhere weakened, but here in particular (see 159.1). When confronted with eschatological texts in his sermons, remarks Barth (1982:43), 'he hardly knows what to do but give urgent warnings against enthusiasm.'

encounter from within systematic theology the really quite astonishing contention that the Easter events and the parousia 'cannot be laid down as properly constituent parts of the doctrine of his person.' That is, they have no organic connection with belief in the redeemer *qua* redeemer. So far from being 'one of the chief points of our faith,' then, as Calvin thought, the ascension 'is not directly a doctrine of faith' at all! From one perspective it is merely 'an accidental form' for effecting Christ's heavenly session.[62]

The immediate impact on the Where? question was to collapse the spatial distance on which Calvin had insisted into something radically Lutheran, that is, to render it in strictly existential terms.[63] But at the same time it opened up the temporal dimension to Christ's absence which the reformers had largely ignored. Jesus' contemporaneity could no longer be taken for granted. For the new christology to work, a bridge between past and present was required, rather than a bridge between heaven and earth. Schleiermacher set out to build it, spanning Lessing's 'great ugly ditch' with an attractive Romanesque structure: In the society of his followers Jesus' unique God-consciousness (which is also his true self-consciousness) has survived and indeed widened with the advance of history; his personality and spiritual activity have been prolonged in the common life of the church.[64] Here was Protestantism's own mariological turn, modestly performed yet even more decisively. The church itself was now the τόπος of Jesus, the only possible answer to the Where? question.

Without a realistic conception of the ascension and the parousia to support it, the much-disputed heavenly session of Christ was thus conflated with his earthly life, or rather with its ecclesial consequences.[65]

---

[62] See §99 (cf. 29.3, 158.1). The only warrant for accepting the resurrection and ascension as real events for Jesus is the apostolic witness, which offers meagre attestation for the latter in particular. Walker (141ff.) has chronicled the subsequent decline of attention to the ascension, but it must be said that this decline owed far less to its supposedly 'meagre' attestation than to a changed understanding of God and his relation to the world. If God is simply the absolute Unity which underpins the relative unity of the cosmos, if his will may therefore be identified with 'the nexus of natural causation' (H. MacKintosh 1937:81), if there is nowhere 'any action of God which we are justified in calling *special*' (ibid. 71; see §46f.), then the ascension is but one of a long list of casualties from the biblical witness. Need it be said that this is Marcionite? (Cf. F. Watson 1997:127ff.)

[63] By describing our relationship with Jesus as a 'mystical' one, Schleiermacher (§100) moves the whole issue of distance and nearness back into Lutheran territory, so to speak. In effect, it becomes an hamartiological question, related to the waxing and waning of the God-consciousness.

[64] Schleiermacher's construct allows us to speak of an *ongoing* incarnation that passes from Jesus to the church: 'And so, since the Divine Essence was bound up with the human person of Christ, but is now (his directly personal influence having ceased) no longer personally involved in any individual, but henceforward manifests itself actively in the fellowship of believers as their common spirit, this is just the way in which the work of redemption is continued and extended in the Church' (§124.2; cf. 122.3).

[65] The Gordian knot of the Lutheran–Reformed debate on the *status exaltationis* was thus cleanly cut: Christ's 'enduring influence' or spiritual presence 'may well depend upon his sitting at the right hand of God – by which, however, since the expression may be strictly

For Schleiermacher the second or glorified phase of Jesus' existence not only secretly sustained the church, it *was* the church, to which his high priesthood had passed and which itself now 'appeared before God' as representing the human race.[66] Embarrassing disputes about Jesus' physical dimensions or heavenly whereabouts could therefore be forgotten; what mattered was his 'total effective influence' in the community he founded, as the 'self-perpetuating organism' of the divine presence once embodied in him.[67] So understood, of course – and this at the time was a bone of considerable contention – the church was once again situated to offer leadership to the world in the quest for God's kingdom. By mediating the impulses flowing from Christ, by receptively cultivating the feeling of absolute dependence so wonderfully realized in him, it could hope to correct the imbalance of Kantian synergism and hasten the advent of a truly spiritual Man.[68] Origen's idea of Christ as the soul of the church, which becomes an extension of his unifying activity in the world – the κόσμος of the cosmos – was here translated into the modern context to good effect.[69] For Schleiermacher happily embraced the evolutionary utopianism of the Enlightenment, while making 'the hidden moving force' that drives history forwards more definitely Christian.[70]

Schleiermacher, then, was certainly not without a doctrine of the ascension altogether. He merely forsook the internecine church struggle to fight a larger battle. Lessing and Kant had already tipped the doctrine of the ascension onto its side, so to speak, making it natural to think in terms of 'an endlessly progressive work of the Spirit that reveals himself in all human history.'[71] Schleiermacher was concerned to ensure that its

---

an impossible one, we must understand simply the peculiar and imcomparable dignity of Christ, raised above all conflict – but not upon a visible resurrection or ascension, since of course Christ could have been raised to glory even without these intermediate steps' (§99.1; cf. 105, postscript).

[66] §104.6. We put the matter bluntly, ignoring the nuances introduced by his Platonic conception of Christ as the 'ideal' or universal man (§93; cf. Bonhoeffer 43f.).

[67] §100 (cf. M. Redeker 1973:137ff.). Lutheran revelational subjectivism and Calvinist christological objectivism thus converge in Schleiermacher's ecclesiology, which, as Barth observes, forms the real nerve-centre of his work.

[68] Christ 'sleeps in the soul' of man, requiring only to be roused (Trinity 2, 1931). That is the work of the church, which in Barth's well-phrased summary 'is a free society of like-minded people founded on common love for Christ with the aim of the common contemplation, fructification, and extension of the stimulus received from him' (25).

[69] 'But the share of the Redeemer in the common life, viewed as continuing, we are fully justified in calling soul-bestowal (*Beseelung*) . . .' (§100.2).

[70] That one should allow oneself to be carried along by this force is what Paul learned on the Damascus Road, and what all non-Christian 'fellowships of faith' are destined to learn (Trinity 9, 1832; cf. CF §117). Barth (47) is again trenchant in describing Schleiermacher's Christian 'as the ideal civilized man who is distinguished from others only by knowing what is the goal of civilization, namely, the divinely willed mastery of nature by spirit . . .'

[71] Fifth Speech (1958:214).

theological potency continued to flow into the Christian religion first of all, and only thence into the broader channels of an historical world-plan (to use Fichte's expression). In keeping with that aim he had to recast the reformers' doctrine of election to fit a universalist framework, and open up their ecclesiology by arguing that 'the absolute integrity of the church is only to be seen in the totality of the human race.'[72] The converse was also true, however, since the unity of the human race was bound up with the advance of Christianity as its organizing principle. Not that we should look for complete religious uniformity, or expect a consummation in time that belongs only to eternity. Nevertheless,

> faith in the Christian Church as the Kingdom of God not only implies that it will ever endure in antithesis to the world, but also . . . contains the hope that the Church will increase and the world opposed to it decrease. For the incarnation of Christ means for human nature in general what regeneration is for the individual.[73]

History, in other words, will afford a resolution of the dialectic of church and world, as near as may be, in favour of the church. For 'the activity of the Redeemer is world-forming, and its object is human nature, in the totality of which the powerful God-consciousness is to be implanted as a new vital principle.'[74]

This was Schleiermacher's doctrine of the ascension, and with it he met squarely the efforts of the Enlightenment to secularize history as well as science, time as well as space. At the very end of *The Christian Faith* he pressed boldly his bid to christen the new theory of progress:

> The divine wisdom, as the unfolding of the divine love, conducts us here to the realm of Christian Ethics; for we are now confronted with the task of more and more securing recognition for the world as a good world, as also of forming all things into an organ of the divine Spirit in harmony with the divine idea originally underlying the world-order, thus bringing all into unity with the system of redemption. The purpose of this is that in both respects we may attain to perfect living fellowship with Christ, both in so far as the Father has given him power over all things and in so far as he ever shows him greater works than those he already knows. Hence the world can be viewed as a perfect revelation of divine wisdom only in proportion as *the Holy Spirit makes itself felt through the Christian Church as the ultimate world-shaping power.*[75]

---

[72] §125 (cf. 117ff.).

[73] 'And just as sanctification is the progressive domination of the various functions, coming with time to consist less and less of fragmentary details and more and more to be a whole . . . so too the fellowship organizes itself here also out of the separate redemptive activities and becomes more and more co-operative and interactive. This organization must increasingly overpower the unorganized mass to which it is opposed' (§113; cf. 1958:250ff., where in the Fifth Speech he assures us that 'the religion of religions' is one which scorns autocracy).

[74] §100.2.

[75] §169.3 (emphasis ours).

The main agenda for theology in the modern period was established just here. Schleiermacher's hopeful vision of an emerging world church, thoroughly oriented to its civil duties, liberated from all distasteful divisions, eventually triumphant in its task of redeeming 'human nature in general,' caught on widely in both Protestant and Roman circles. More than anyone else (save perhaps Hegel) he contributed to the coalescence of Christian and secular optimism mentioned above, which has not entirely failed even in our more pessimistic post-modern era.

Schleiermacher, it has been said, focused Christian thought onto the figure of Jesus with 'a new and peculiar intensity.'[76] His attempt to confess Jesus without the resurrection and ascension, however, brought him to the brink of a great precipice, towards which theology had been straying since the beginning of the third century. Pursuing Augustine's line, he argued that it was altogether necessary for Christ's visible presence to come to an end, that his invisible and spiritual work in human society might succeed.[77] But now it was far less clear whether anything more could be said that was not, properly speaking, pneumatology or ecclesiology rather than christology.[78] The constraints of a rigorously subjective method, compounded by that prejudice against the particular which marks the idealist tradition even in its Romantic form, conspired against the latter. In the *Speeches* Schleiermacher held forth a Christianity that stood for the victory of God over 'the universal resistance of all things finite to the unity of the whole.'[79] In *The Christian Faith* he presented a Jesus who in his human concreteness was finally a distraction which had to be removed for the sake of the church – not so that men might believe in *his* divinity, as Augustine had taught, but that they might believe also, *mutatis mutandis*, in their own.[80]

Must we not agree with Karl Barth, then, that it is doubtful after all how important Jesus really is for Schleiermacher?[81] Indeed, it is hard to

---

[76] K. Clements 1987:40. As Troeltsch (184ff.) notes, Schleiermacher has thus been criticized for offering only a half-way house between an outmoded Nicene Christianity and a Christian principle that is properly detachable from Jesus. Troeltsch himself criticizes Schleiermacher in this connection, while recognizing the indispensability of belief in the historical Jesus for a renewed flourishing of Christianity, which is the highest form of religion likely to be produced by our Mediterranean culture.

[77] §§115.2, 122.2 (cf. Barth 102, who refers also to an ascension sermon of 1795).

[78] Between pneumatology and ecclesiology no sure distinction can be drawn, for the Holy Spirit has become 'the common Spirit' of the church (§§116.3, 121ff.).

[79] See MacKintosh 56. Christianity sees this victory only in relation to Jesus; he is the essential particular, the window on the *universum*. Yet it cannot entirely exclude the possibility that, for the sake of wholeness, there might be 'a redemption *from* him as well as . . . through him' (CF §11.4).

[80] If it is said that Jesus goes to the Father to become for us the source or path of the Spirit, for Schleiermacher this means rather that he might not *obstruct* the Spirit. 'For the more a common life depends on an individual life, the less is it an existence in common.' See §122 (cf. 115f., 144.1).

[81] 1982:103ff.

avoid the conclusion that his is a theology in which ecclesial substitution for Jesus is finally perfected. We may add that there is nothing on Schleiermacher's horizon to qualify or call into question that substitution. Since so little can be said of Jesus' own destiny as a particular human being, since his afterlife (his 'ascension' in that sense) remains like ours a matter of baffling obscurity, it will have to be conceded that he no longer stands before us but only behind us. Or rather, that he stands before us only as an ideal which has yet to be realized among us, and as a reminder that the potential to achieve it is strictly a hidden one. And here is another of Schleiermacher's little ironies: Augustine's homogeneity notion now restricts, not our expectation of historical progress, but our expectation of Christ's return.[82] No stern Inquisitor forbids it; far less a theologian's patiently reasoned contention that of the parousia no coherent picture can be formed. It is forbidden rather (in Barth's phrase) by 'the smiling march of the lofty world-spirit,' and by an eschatology that is resolutely irresolute.[83]

***

If Schleiermacher hesitated to let go of Jesus entirely, prising from ecclesiology a new lease on life for him after his 'disappearance,' his more famous rival in Berlin, G. W. F. Hegel, dispensed with the euphemism and came to the point with characteristic boldness:

> Christ dies; only as dead is he exalted to Heaven and sits at the right hand of God; only thus is he Spirit. He himself says: 'When I am no longer with you, the Spirit will guide you into all truth.'[84]

With Hegel the very obverse of the biblical and credal doctrine openly appeared; it was he who willingly leapt over the precipice. The ascension was regarded in time-honoured fashion as a retraction of the human Jesus so that his divinity might appear, but here at the nadir of the Origenist–Augustinian tradition that retraction was complete. Nothing remained but the impact of the cross on subsequent history. Christology had become a discourse on the dead Christ.

---

[82] §160. In a similarly ironic echo of Aquinas, he asserts that 'to point forward to anything new which is still to occur would necessarily be to preach another gospel' (for which reason he rejects the Apocalypse, §103.3). This alone ought to make it evident that J. Hick has erred in linking Schleiermacher to Irenaeus rather than to Origen.

[83] Except insofar as it is resolutely Greek rather than Hebrew! See §159ff., which misconstrues the continuity/discontinuity problem in terms of an irresolvable tension between the personal and the corporate, the many and the one. The decision, if it may be called that, is for discontinuity, and having substituted 'the efficacious activity of Christ for his bodily presence,' Schleiermacher (§160.2) points in the direction later pursued by Teilhard.

[84] 1956:325. Hegel was dismissive of Schleiermacher's attempt to ground God-talk in *Gefühl*. To the latter's left-wing Hegelian opponents he was 'the man who disguises (*verschleiere*) the naked truth' (Redeker 131).

To combine an ascension theology with a *theologia crucis* was Irenaeus' achievement against the gnostics; to make them one and the same thing was the achievement of Hegel, who did much to translate gnosticism into a modern idiom. 'The history of the resurrection and ascension of Christ to the right hand of God,' he insisted, began at the point where the history of the crucified received 'a spiritual interpretation.'[85] Which is to say, it began where people saw in Christ, especially in the yielding up of the human element through death, the appearance of the divine glory; where in consequence they began to be conscious of the fact that finite human being 'is a moment in God himself,' albeit an alien and disappearing one.[86] Though this fact at first presented itself only to the religious imagination, which brought it into focus (and also corrupted it) by way of objectifying dogmas about one particular man, it presents itself now as the basis for a rational interpretation of man *qua* man, and for a history of the human race that is at the same time a history of God.[87] To expound that history in a definitive way, showing man his own emerging divinity in the mirror of the crucified, was Hegel's sacred task. In fulfilling it, he himself would be instrumental in bringing the ascension to its goal.

How shall we overlook the sheer hybris of such a claim, or of the principle behind it? By glorying in the cross *we* cause Christ to ascend.[88] But to grasp better the implications of Hegel's position we must notice the changed meaning of the cross itself. Hegel viewed all temporal process, internal or external, as the positing and sublating of the finite for the sake of the infinite, of the particular for the sake of the universal, of what is not God for the sake of what is or will be God.[89] The self-realization of

---

[85] 1988:468. A. Galloway (1951:169f.) thinks that Hegel turned to christology to combat Kantian dualism just as Origen, e.g., did to combat gnostic dualism. But if Origen charted a course far too near to his opponents – recall here the liberties of his 'sanctified perspicuity' – then Hegel even nearer.

[86] 'The truth to which human beings have attained by means of this history, what they have become conscious of in this entire history, is the following: that the idea of God has certainty for them, that humanity has attained the certainty of union with God, that the human is the immediately present God. Indeed, within this history as spirit comprehends it, there is the very presentation of the process of what humanity, what spirit is – implicitly both God and dead' (1988:468; cf. 465f., n. 199).

[87] Here Hegel adroitly commandeered trinitarian as well as incarnational language, something Schleiermacher failed to do; but by allowing world-history to stand in for Jesus-history he brought western trinitarianism to its inevitable monist end (see R. Jenson 1982:134f.).

[88] Such is the final outcome of Augustine's shift to the subjective pole, i.e., to a Christ who ascends daily if we allow him to: the ascension depends upon us; the subjective *is* the objective. And in keeping with this it is no longer enough to say with Augustine that *we* know God though the ascending Christ. We must also say that God knows himself – indeed, becomes himself – through us. This opens up the whole western tradition to Feuerbach's critique. It also means, as we shall see, that the heavenly session of Christ can be identified with *Zeitgeist*.

[89] Concisely put, 'it is from the special and determinate, and from its negation, that the Universal results.' Or more forcefully: 'The particular is for the most part of too trifling a value as compared with the general: individuals are sacrificed and abandoned' (1956:32f.).

Spirit, understood as absolute freedom, was for him the holy cause 'to which the sacrifices that have ever and anon been laid on the vast altar of the earth, through the long lapse of ages, have been offered.'[90] Among these the death of Jesus turned out to be the most crucial, for through it the divine wrath against finitude and otherness (which at their extreme are evil) somehow found its voice and was properly articulated.[91] The cross therefore became the wheel or hinge on which history turns. It opened up an era in which the natural limitations of finite existence began to be annulled and transcended.[92] In Dionysian terminology differentiations began to give way to unions, for the divine Spirit flowing out from the cross is self-consciously a World Spirit, a Spirit of 'beautiful unification,' which must lead us into ever-greater appropriations of freedom.

Hegel's contemporary, Jean Paul, included in his *Siebenkäs* a 'Discourse of the dead Christ from atop the cosmos: there is no God.'[93] Hegel himself was not an atheist, at least not in the ordinary sense, but his treatment of the cross and the ascension did complete the *Aufhebung* of classical Christian theology. To make the ascension merely a hermeneutic of the cross, while continuing to regard it as the unveiling of deity, was to assert in principle the deity of every man, the universalization of the incarnation. Conversely, to make the cross into an instrument of human advance was to affirm that the Spirit emanates from a point on earth not in heaven, from a point within history not beyond it. Hegel's pneumatology did not support the worshiping community as such, then, but modern Germanic society, and more specifically the Prussian state. But how did Hegel see the church itself? That is a matter of more direct concern to us.

Hegel, like Schleiermacher, spoke of the church as a society formed by the friends of Jesus after his death for the purpose of participating in the spiritual kingdom which was his legacy. Yet he had something else to say as well, which he set out under the banner of Lutheran insight into the eucharist.[94] The medieval church, he argued, had generated a distorted version of the kingdom by 'isolating the sensuous phase' of salvation from the spiritual, confusing the holy with the external, the local, the particular – above all by making the host, as a mere *thing*, into an object of adoration. In this way it had mistakenly carved up the kingdom into sacred and secular. From that error the Lutheran Reformation had effected a liberation, abrogating externality by making 'faith and spiritual enjoyment' the essential elements in Christian worship.[95] A principle of

---

[90] Ibid. 19.

[91] Cf. Balthasar 5/578.

[92] Salvation is conceived in terms common to the mystical tradition, Greek and German, as the liberation of spirit through the overcoming of nature. 'Man realizes his spiritual essence only when he conquers the natural that attaches to him' (1956:377; cf. 318ff.).

[93] 1991:51 (cf. C. Brown 139 n. 5; Moltmann 1967:168).

[94] We quite agree that here 'the whole question is concentrated' (1956:415; cf. 328ff.).

[95] See 376ff., 412ff. Christ himself is set aside, says Hegel, if his presence is identified with the consecrated host rather that the 'mental vision and Spirit' of the faithful.

inwardness was now at work breaking down false dichotomies in society, freeing humanity from the church's artificial constraints and releasing the Spirit into all areas of human life. Thus on the wreck of ecclesiastical unity the foundations of a greater worldly unity were being laid, in which everyone might share the task of mediating between God and nature, and God become all in all.

For Hegel, then, the church required to be buried along with the earthly Jesus if it hoped to be taken up into the glory of the new age of the Spirit. Its mission was already essentially complete. Through its recent great controversy it had made the painful discovery that spirituality is 'the common property of every man.'[96] It had therefore served well the dialectic of history's march to freedom, if only by first resisting that march in a narrow and static determination of its inheritance. Like Jesus, it had now to learn to deny itself for the sake of freedom. It could continue as a conduit of the Spirit only through self-abnegation, only by accepting the fact that the church is or can be the world, and the world the church.[97] Here was a theology of convergence *par excellence*. Where the church had once thought to stand in for the absent Jesus, Kant had put forward his ethical commonwealth to stand in for the church; thereafter various efforts had been made to achieve an acceptable synthesis between the two. After Hegel, however, such a synthesis could only mean an attempt to absorb the church into a religious version of the state, leading to the demonization of both. Witness especially the German Christian Movement and the great *Kirchenkampf* it precipitated.

With Hegel, then, we appear to stand in close proximity to the end of a long and troubled tradition of immanentism. Not because the problem of the absence has been faced squarely but because it has been resolved yet again, and even more arrogantly, into a putative presence. To exalt the dead Christ is simply to transform an ecclesiological immanentism into an even more dangerous anthropological version, by substituting a principle for a person. Hegel's disciple, D. F. Strauss, was fluent in defence of this move and understood its implications. He took it as read that the whole story of Jesus, and all the dogmatic convictions that go with it, must be transferred to humanity as such:

> Mankind is the unity of the two natures, the Infinite Spirit depotentiated in finitude, and the finite spirit mindful of its infinity; it is the child of the visible

---

[96] *Pace* Maximus, Hegel (318ff.) believed that what liturgical man could *not* finally unite, *viz.*, heaven and earth, the man of science would. Having learned from the church something about the task of conquering nature with Spirit, and having in turn conquered the church itself, this new man stood at the dawn of a bright new day, 'the day of Universality' (411).

[97] As 'all that is special retreats into the background,' to use Hegel's own phrase, the ecclesiological idea must inevitably be transmuted into a socio-political one, yet without abandoning its religious force. 'The process displayed in History is only the manifestation of Religion as Human Reason – the production of the religious principle which dwells in the heart of man, under the form of Secular Freedom' (334f.).

mother and the invisible father, of spirit and nature; it is the miracle-worker, for in the course of human history the spirit ever more fully takes control of nature; it is the Sinless One, for its progressive growth is blameless, and impurity clings only to the single life but disappears in the race; it is the Dying, Rising and Ascending One, for from the negation of its merely natural qualities there springs an ever higher spiritual life, and through the abrogation of its finitude as personal, national and secular spirit it is exalted into unity with the Infinite Spirit of heaven.

And he boasted, 'it is that carrying forward of the Religion of Christ to the Religion of Humanity to which all the noblest efforts of the present time are directed.'[98]

The optimism represented by Strauss sustained heavy damage in the two great wars, of course, for which its purveyors must themselves bear some responsibility.[99] Even before the dramatic failures of our century there were unbelievers, however, among which the most remarkable was Friedrich Nietzsche. Nietzsche recognized the end of a tradition when he saw it; indeed he wondered why so many others could not.[100] The manipulation of Christian theology in support of contemporary notions of cultural advance he took to be a sign, not of that religion's regenerative power, but of the stubborn failure of imagination that had dogged a whole civilization from its pre-Christian days. Christianity became his *bête noire*, since to make a god out of the crucified one, whether in the old way or the new, was to testify to the worst sort of decadence: the apotheosis of

---

[98] 1879 §100. For the long quotation (cited here in the form given it by McKintosh, 119) see 1973 §151. Cf. D. Jamros 1995:278ff.

[99] Etienne Gilson (1937:243ff.; cf. K. Popper 2/25ff.) is damning in his indictment of Hegel. The path of his God, he says, and of his state – for Hegel claimed that war is a law not an accident, indeed, that 'the military class is the class of universality' – is strewn with ruins. Is it an accident, we may ask, that the shift from Marian to Aryan optimism was accompanied by spectacles far more appalling than anything witnessed in the 'terrible night of the Middle Ages'? Or by an unprecedented assault on the Jews, as that stubborn speciality which refuses to retreat into the background? (Cf. Walker Percy's *The Thanatos Syndrome* 130ff.; on Hegel's anti-semitism, see Balthasar 5/579ff.)

[100] One who did, and who commented on it with a prescience greater than Nietzsche's, was Heinrich Heine: 'It is to the great merit of Christianity that it has somewhat attenuated the brutal German lust for battle. But it could not destroy it entirely. And should ever that taming talisman break – the Cross – then will come roaring back the wild madness of the ancient warriors of whom our Nordic poets speak and sing, with all their insane Berserker rage. That talisman is now already crumbling, and the day is not far off when it shall break apart entirely. On that day the old stone gods will rise from long-forgotten wreckage and rub from their eyes the dust of a thousand-year sleep. At long last leaping to life, Thor, with his giant hammer, will crush the Gothic cathedrals! . . . And laugh not at my forebodings, the advice of a dreamer who warns you away from the Kants and Fichtes of the world, and from our philosophers of Nature. No, laugh not at a visionary who knows that in the realm of phenomena comes soon the revolution that has already taken place in the realm of spirit. For thought goes before deed as lightning before thunder . . . There will be played in Germany a play compared to which the French revolution was but an innocent idyll' (cited and translated by J. Satinover 1996:236; see *Works* 5/207ff.).

one's own impotence for life in this world.[101] Thus, just at the point where the suppression of the living Christ was virtually complete, Nietzsche strove to suppress the dead one as well, in order that a moribund tradition might be allowed to die properly. With Nietzsche there is at last a sense of sheer absence, the burden of which will not be refused. The answer to Where? is simply Nowhere, for Jesus and for God alike.[102]

Return of the Cosmic Christ

One of the miracles of our time is that Hegel lives on in spite of everything; among artists and the literary community, Nietzsche perhaps, but elsewhere Hegel, if in a variety of disguises.[103] The tragedies of the twentieth century, and the prospective calamities of the twenty-first, have conspired to suppress most utopian dreams, but the idea of progress (however cold and hard) remains 'the working faith of our civilization,' our necessary myth.[104] Among Christians attempts to prop up the cult of progress with a doctrine of the ascension, and so somehow to re-establish the mission of the church, are not uncommon. While the result is sometimes labelled Irenaean, it generally entails a return (via Hegel and Luther) to Origen. That is a point of confusion we must try to clear up as we sketch further the option we are exploring.

The origin of the confusion can be traced back to Denmark, in the period of Hegel's ascendency. There Professor Hans Martensen, later Bishop Martensen, sought to reinterpret the Lutheran tradition in a manner consonant with modern reason. We cannot pause to outline the development of his thought, which was increasingly drawn towards theosophical speculation,[105] but his attempt to show the 'cosmical significance' of Christ deserves our attention. Martensen found evidence for this in Paul and Irenaeus, but more importantly he belonged to something of a Scotist revival.[106] In view of our earlier criticism of Scotism's immanentist tendency, we hasten to add that Martensen defended the

---

[101] See especially *The Anti-Christ*, which in one sense is what he also regarded Christianity to be (§36ff.), in *all* its permutations, including those of the Enlightenment and of Hegel. Strauss, meanwhile, had also turned to atheism.

[102] 'God' dies with Jesus, if only we will let Jesus be quite simply dead, and nothing more. We prefer Nietzsche's candour to Hegel's sophistry; nevertheless the tragedies Heine foresaw owe as much to the one as to the other. (See *Ecce Homo* 2.4 for Nietzsche's praise of Heine; cf. E. Muir 1987:128 for a curious but profound insight into Nietzsche.)

[103] In fact, the Nietzschean crisis of absence – 'Do we not feel the breath of empty space?' – has been largely domesticated, not least by the covert metaphysics of postmodern immanentism. See C. Pickstock 1998, chap. 2f.

[104] See C. Lasch 1991:40ff.; the quoted phrase is Christopher Dawson's.

[105] Like Hegel he was attracted to the German mystical tradition, writing works on Eckhart and Jacob Böhme.

[106] See *Christian Dogmatics* (1849) §129ff. on Christ as the centre and crown of creation. Martensen's friend, I. A. Dorner, was influential here; cf. Lyons 11ff.

particularity (*haecceitas*) of Christ against runaway ubiquitarianism.[107] Yet he still attached descending and ascending to the divine and the creaturely respectively, by emphasizing what he called the double life of the mediator: his world-creating 'Logos energy' in which he goes forth from God, and his world-perfecting 'Christ energy' in which he returns to God.[108]

This certainly had implications for the interpretation of cosmic dynamics and the shape of history. Quite crucially, it led Martensen to propound the notion of a progressive advent. The resurrection and ascension of Jesus Christ, who is 'the beginner of the world's perfection,' have established a brand new economy through which our world is being replenished 'with the energies of the future,' enabling it to advance with Christ towards God.[109] The parousia should not be sharply distinguished from this as if it were a separate movement.[110] For the Spirit is now at work in history converting absence into presence:

> The presence of Christ in the universe must be looked upon, not so much as actual *being*, but rather as an essential *becoming;* it must be treated as a progressive advent, a continual coming, in virtue of which, by the growing development of his fulness, he makes himself the centre of the whole creation; and the creation itself is thus being prepared and created anew as a living, organic, and growing *temple of Christ.*[111]

This shift from being to becoming in framing an answer to the Where? question presaged momentous changes to church theology. Spurred on by the appearance of Darwinism, the idea of the risen Christ who by virtue of his ascension gradually penetrates and perfects every sphere of

---

[107] CD §177 warns against 'that error, which has so often appeared among Mystics and Theosophists, which loses sight of a personal Christ,' and which among Lutherans too has led in the direction of a 'pantheistic Christ of nature.' For 'even a glorified individuality, a spiritual body, cannot be conceived of without limitations.' At the same time, the Reformed are criticized for ackowledging 'only the moral, religious, and spiritual influences of a Christ who has gone up to heaven,' making the rest of creation 'wholly impenetrable by Christ' (§178).

[108] See §134, §180. The world-perfecting movement was still seen as the spiritualization of matter, only there was greater emphasis on matter's inherent goodness.

[109] See §131, §170ff. A parallel may be drawn with Bonaventure, for whom Christ was the beginning of the perfecting of creation in history: 'As both Ratzinger and Fischer have argued persuasively, the theology of ascent is identical [here] with the theology of history. The collective history of humanity moves to a future point at which the possibility of a supra-intellectual, affective-mystical contact with God will be granted to all' (Z. Hayes 1981:208f.).

[110] 'When we say that he *sits* at the right hand of the Father, that he *intercedes* for us with the Father, that he *comes* again into the world, we express only different aspects of his exaltation,' says Martensen (§175). Nevertheless, the ascension was a real departure to a sphere 'above the limits of time and space,' from whence 'for the first time' Christ was able 'perfectly to unfold and display his organic relations to the children of men' (§173).

[111] In constructively addressing the ubiquity debate Martensen distinguishes the power of Christ's heavenly session from the creator's 'direct omnipotence,' finding it instead to be 'a world-perfecting power, penetrating in *progressive* development all ranges of creation in nature and history' (§179).

creaturely existence quickly evolved into a kind of cosmic maximalism rivaling the Marian maximalism of old. And as ascension and parousia were conflated into a single movement – as God, to use the language of our own century, became the Future of the world – any thought of two distinct histories (Christ's and ours) was decisively set aside. What was left was a concern only with the ongoing sacralization of the world.[112]

The 'reconsecration of the whole universe' by Christ was precisely what J. R. Illingworth focused on in the historic volume, *Lux Mundi*, in his contribution entitled 'The Incarnation and Development.'[113] By then evolution was in the air, as he said, especially in England. With a backwards glance at the Copernican revolution, Illingworth claimed that history had repeated itself by showing the supposed opposition of science and faith to be no such thing. Indeed, science had this time brought about a significant theological advance by recalling our attention from the narrow confines of the doctrine of the atonement to the broader places of belief in the incarnation as the consummation of creation. The natural expression of the life-giving Logos, he argued, is 'the perpetual development which we are learning to trace throughout the universe around us.'[114] Moreover, the enfleshing of that Logos

> introduced a new species into the world – a Divine man transcending past humanity, as humanity transcended the rest of the animal creation, and communicating His vital energy by a spiritual process to subsequent generations of men.[115]

With Christ creation has turned a corner, in other words. With the resurrection and ascension (here Illingworth too appealed to Irenaeus) new vistas have opened up before it. From now on, he concluded, 'we can conceive of no phase of progress that does not have the Incarnation for its guiding star.'[116]

Lux Mundi, like Henry Drummond's *The Ascent of Man*, may to some extent represent 'a phase of easy optimism' native to the atmosphere of

---

[112] Already in Martensen the two histories are so closely identified that we can say 'even of him who has gone up heavenward that he grows and advances, not indeed in wisdom, but "in favour with God and man"' (§176). Yet a progressive advent does not make a final advent redundant; see §278ff.

[113] See 183, 211. *Lux Mundi* was published in 1889 under the editorship of Charles Gore, with intent 'to put the Catholic faith into its right relation to modern intellectual and moral problems.' Once again Hegel stood in the background, providing the philosophical underpinnings, as he did for Soloviev and his followers, who were undertaking a parallel enterprise in Russian Orthodoxy.

[114] p. 196. This is closely connected to his insistence on 'the importance of restoring to its due place in theology the doctrine of the Divine immanence in nature' (192), a subject to which he later devoted a volume of his own.

[115] p. 207. In *Divine Immanence* the incarnation is seen 'not merely as an event in the history of man, but . . . in the history of matter,' an event which marks 'the appearance of a new order of being in the world' (see 114ff.; Lyons 27). A fruitful comparison can thus be made with Soloviev's own notion of 'Godmanhood.'

[116] pp. 213f.; cf. 184.

Victorian England.[117] Certainly the lone apocalyptic note weakly sounded in its final essay is drowned out by a sustained chord of triumphalist expectations.[118] Yet the task of adapting Christian beliefs to an emerging cosmology will always have an aura of urgency about it, in good times or bad. Illingworth, at all events, had one eye on a very real enemy. In his programmatic essay he was seeking to establish a secure place for Christian faith – for what the book's subtitle called the Religion of the Incarnation – over against the dangerous relativism inherent in any concept of perpetual development. To that end the Logos was identified as the secret source of evolution, and its incarnation as an infusion of power capable of bringing the whole process to consummation. Martensen's idea of a progressive advent suited this agenda nicely, and would gain much ground in the next half-century.

After the war, L. S. Thornton took up Illingworth's agenda with undiminished enthusiasm, using the tools provided by process philosophy to expound the incarnation as the initial event of a divinely achieved evolutionary climax.[119] More influential, perhaps, was William Temple, who also interpreted the incarnation along these lines, and saw in the ascension the inauguration of an age of consummation. Temple's tone was by no means triumphalist, however, and his work took more account of the cross. History as we know it cannot produce the kingdom in its fullness. Indeed it might even lead to the passing away of our species and our planet. Hope for a new order of being lies ultimately in resurrection; which is to say, history must find its fulfillment in eternity.[120] But Temple regarded the present age as an age of consummation nonetheless, and even attempted to equate the parousia with the events between Calvary and Pentecost. The church ought not to look for a so-called second coming, he said, but rather get on with its task of realizing the two unities (the outer harmony of the race and the inner harmony of specific human beings) which the incarnation has made possible.[121] The church should recognize in *itself* the earthly body of the ascended Lord; and not only in itself, but also in the world, it should recognize the work of the Spirit drawing all things to God.[122]

---

[117] Cf. J. Hick 1968:245.

[118] As Troeltsch remarked, eschatology was now 'closed for repairs' (Wainwright 1989:343). In the main it was being refashioned along Joachimite lines, as R. L. Ottley's concluding essay on Christian ethics illustrates.

[119] 'With the aid of A. N. Whitehead's process philosophy, Thornton described the universe as an ascending cosmic series which requires for its completion God's intervention through the Incarnation' (Lyons 28).

[120] See 1960:427ff., 1962:viiiff., 75ff., 187ff., 253ff., 271f.

[121] The incarnation is 'the natural inauguration of the final stage of evolution,' impelling human nature towards its goal, i.e., towards this inner and outer unity (1962:139, 154ff.; cf. 1912:35ff., A. E. Baker 1946:148ff.). It was this conviction which energized Temple's ecumenical efforts.

[122] 1962:229ff. 'Democracy and Evolution have together made the thought of the Indwelling Spirit, urging us onward and upward, so natural that in fact many people accept it in a manner much too facile' (169f.).

Temple's creative blend of doctrines new and old, eastern and western, Protestant and Catholic, left a lot of fuzzy edges. He was, after all, an Anglican archbishop and leading ecumenist as well as a philosopher. Though we cannot afford him the space he deserves, we may at least observe how his (basically Lutheran) view of the ascension underwrote the christological immanentism to which he subscribed:

> The ascension of Christ is his liberation from all restrictions of time and space. It does not represent his removal from the earth, but his constant presence everywhere on earth.[123]

With Mary Magdalene, then, the followers of the resurrected one must learn not to cling to him in the limitations of his body, but to look for him in a post-incarnate form:

> So He taught her the meaning of that last Appearance, the final withdrawal of His physical presence, which we call the Ascension. It was separation in one sense, for it closed the period of the first form of intercourse. But in a profounder sense it was the inauguration of a fuller union. In the days of His earthly ministry only those could speak with Him who came where He was. If He was in Galilee, men could not find Him in Jerusalem; if He was in Jerusalem, men could not find Him in Galilee. But His ascension means that He is perfectly united with God; we are with Him wherever we are present to God; and that is everywhere and always. Because He is 'in Heaven,' He is everywhere on earth; because He is ascended, He is here now. Our devotion is not to hold us by the empty tomb; it must lift up our hearts to heaven so that we too 'in heart and mind thither ascend and with Him continually dwell'; it must also send us forth into the world to do His will; and these are not *two* things but one.[124]

The physical absence of Christ was thus made over by Temple into a spiritual presence which rendered the whole world a sacramental affair. The answer to Where? was once again Everywhere. But the episodic nature of the incarnation, to the same degree that it made easy this answer to the Where? question, left room for serious doubts as to who or what the Christ who inhabits our unfolding cosmos really is.[125]

A quite radical answer, though hardly a new one, had already begun to appear in the writings of another influential churchman, W. R. Inge, who contributed a great deal to the twentieth-century rehabilitation of Origen. Dean Inge, though somewhat cautious on the subject of

---

[123] Quoted in *The Tablet*, 30 May 1992.

[124] 1947:382 (emphasis ours). No one, says Temple (1962:248), objecting to the ancient preoccupation with space, 'now thinks of Heaven as a place "elsewhere," and exclusive of "here."' As for the glorified or ascended body, it is 'so transmuted as to be no longer a physico-chemical entity at all.'

[125] Temple (ibid. 144) criticized the kenoticists on this very point, but his response is quite inadequate: 'The Incarnation is an episode in the Life or Being of God the Son; but it is not a *mere* episode, it is a *revealing* episode.'

progress,[126] attempted to bring christology into touch with science's rediscovery of the connectedness of all things. Calling for a 'cosmocentric view of reality,' he presented Christ as a cosmic principle, and the church as an extension of the incarnation; he even toyed with the notion of panpsychism.[127] Various efforts to find a more precise answer would be made, but the direction taken by Illingworth, Inge, Thornton and Temple indicates a common tendency on the part of some British theologians to see in Christ, beyond his divinity and humanity, 'a further aspect, which is cosmic' – a third nature, in fact.[128] That tendency (*viz.*, to revise the church's answer to the Who? question in light of a popular answer to the Where? question) would appear even more potently in the French scientist and theologian, Pierre Teilhard de Chardin, to whom we must shortly turn.

Another British theologian who should not be overlooked, however, is Allan Galloway, whose book *The Cosmic Christ* contributed to the confusion by attacking dualism in the name of this Christ, even the attenuated dualism of Origen or Augustine. According to Galloway it is necessary to 'stand by Irenaeus' in affirming christologically the latent value of the natural order. His rather involved argument turns on the problem of the subject–object relationship and merits a separate discussion, but it is possible to abstract the pertinent results, which fall into a familiar pattern: Galloway invites us, first, to let go of Jesus in his bodily particularity, while affirming the profoundly personal and personalizing nature of our encounter with him. Second, to see that in this encounter we are brought into a new relationship to the rest of reality, such that God is actually encountered in *all* things.[129] Third, to allow the cosmos itself, in that light, to become sacramental in the fullest sense (the sacraments of the church being but illustrations of a wider truth, just as Hegel argued). Fourth, to catch the vision of a universalist ecclesiology. 'The ultimate destiny of the church is to become the whole cosmos, so that there shall be no more church,' he concluded. 'So Christ shall be truly "the fulness of Him that filleth all in all."'[130]

---

[126] 'Personally, I hope for it, as a matter of reasonable faith . . . But the progress of humanity, if there is any, is always slow and precarious; and it cannot go on forever' (1924:84f., after the death of his young daughter).

[127] A notion he rightly believed would become more popular. See Lyons 35f., who notes Underhill's observation, about the same time, that for the mystic the incarnation is not only the life of Jesus 'but also a perpetual Cosmic and personal process,' of which the 'essential constituents' are dramatized by Jesus (1911:141).

[128] Lyons 36. Cf. H. Clark 1943:150ff.

[129] 'When we have encountered Him as "Thou" nothing is added to His Meaning by our being able to grasp him as an "It" within experience. But once we have been brought face to face with the complete ascendency of meaning over existence, of "Thou" over "It", nothing can ever be meaningless for us again in the ultimate sense . . . That is to say, once we have encountered God in Christ we must encounter God in all things' (p. 250).

[130] p. 259. 'When the sacramental principle is thus freed from its distortion in Roman Catholicism, we see that we cannot place any limit upon it. For when we limit it, we bind it to a particular existent and in doing this we contradict the "mystery" which is Christ –

Galloway's ascending cosmic Christ has as his task the completion of creation by the personalizing of nature, beginning with man. This thought, and the book which contains it, directly influenced the Lutheran theologian Joseph Sittler, who at the New Delhi congress of the World Council of Churches in 1961 delivered a famous address entitled 'Called to Unity.'[131] Sittler's concern was the growing ecological crisis, a point of obvious stress for evolutionary optimism. The main target of his criticism was a theology of redemption dislodged from 'the larger orbit of a doctrine of creation': in short, that spiritual inwardness which has rightly been said to signal a massive loss of nerve among western Christians in the face of post-Copernican realities.[132] He argued that it was high time to do for nature as a whole what had already been done for the soul, and more recently for history, namely, to claim it for Christ. His plea was for 'a daring, penetrating, life-affirming christology of nature' which would root out the vestiges of gnostic dualism (whether rationalist or pietist) that threaten to bring about the damnation of nature. Against every effort to restrict grace to the interior life should be set 'the imperial vision of Christ as coherent in τὰ πάντα.' And that, he repeated, will require us to take Irenaeus as mentor rather than the more popular Augustine.[133]

Since the New Delhi congress references to an Irenaean type of theology have become commonplace. Much more frequent as well are references to the cosmic Christ. But discussion of such themes has been characterized by one of the noteworthy features of Sittler's own address – its strange silence about Jesus of Nazareth. At the outset we are referred to 'this concrete Man who is God with us and God for us,' but after that to the Christ who coinheres with nature, or to the 'Christic energy and substance' which permeates nature. *All* is Christic, to redeploy the author's own phrase. In other words, what Sittler presents as the beginning of an ecological theology does not appear to be based on the Jesus-centred vision of Irenaeus after all, but rather on a doctrine of ubiquity which is intended to recapture the latter's much needed affirmation of the material world.[134] This synthesis has proved attractive, both for the ecologically minded and for those whose concern is with universal history. But of course it hides

---

namely the complete ascendency of Ultimate Meaning in Him over His particular existence' (256). Not only in every person, then, but 'in every encounter with the material world we meet the same claim upon our ultimate concern in terms of the sacramental principle.'

[131] Published in the *Ecumenical Review* 14:2 (Jan 1962) 177ff.

[132] Cf. O. Dilschneider, *Gefesselte Kirche, Not und Verheissung* (Lyons 58).

[133] Sittler's text was Col. 1:15–20, though to say that Christ 'coheres' in all things is actually to reverse that text.

[134] Moltmann (1990:276ff.) offers a more positive reading of Sittler over against Lutheran criticism, but do we not find here a Lutheran concept of Christ's glorification and heavenly session, still situated somewhere between Origen and Hegel? It could not have served Sittler's agenda to appeal directly to Origen, whose dualism is even more pronounced than Augustine's, but he has drawn Irenaeus into an orbit not his own.

the fact that we are dealing here with two very different answers to the Where? question, and with two dissimilar conceptions of the cosmic Christ.

On close inspection the Christ whose background we have been recounting is anything but Irenaean. He proves instead to be yet another device for resolving the problem of the one and the many, constructed in various ways with various good intentions, but always at the expense of the human Jesus. The universal redemptive power of his exalted personality depends upon his and our liberation from a prior space–time particularity. As Paul Tillich put it in the 1950s: 'The finality of his separation from historical existence, indicated in the Ascension, is identical with his spiritual presence as the power of the New Being but with the concreteness of his personal countenance.'[135] This sleight of hand, in which bodily absence becomes concrete personal presence, betrays the fact that neither dualism nor pietism have really been overcome. On the contrary, they have been established. What is more, the supposed evolution of nature towards the personal comes out much as it did in Origen, as a look at Teilhard will demonstrate.

***

'If Teilhard had not existed,' wrote John Passmore in *The Perfectibility of Man*, 'it would almost have been necessary to invent him, in order to weave together our diverse themes.'[136] We might have said something similar here. It is not just that we find in Teilhard a more complete (if highly adventurous) sketch of the answer to the Where? and the Who? questions which we have begun to trace. We also find a powerful synthesis of speculative interests ancient and modern, formulated as a theology of the ascension which aims to reconcile 'faith in God and faith in the World,' or 'the cult of progress and the passion for the glory of God'[137] – what Teilhard called *l'En-Haut et l'En-Avant*.[138] The cosmic Christ is the instrument of that reconciliation and as such one of his dearest subjects.

Already in 1916 the young Jesuit priest spoke in his journal of 'surrender to the cosmic Christ' as the option that would secure what is best both in classical spirituality and a more world-affirming kind.[139]

---

[135] 1957:162. In Tillich the symbolic theology of Origen which moves through and away from the historical Jesus finds a thoroughly modern expression, as an inverted mysticism of 'descent' rather than 'ascent,' accompanied by an inverted kenoticism in which the human Jesus empties himself into the divine Christ-principle.

[136] p. 258.

[137] Quoted by D. G. Jones (1969:13) from N. M. Wildiers.

[138] Lyons 148, to whose research we continue to be indebted in the present section.

[139] Lyons 37. We must pass over the direct influences on Teilhard's cosmic christology, which others have already explored. For a concise statement of his programme see 'The Heart of the Problem' (1949), published in *The Future of Man* (1964:260ff.), a collection of key essays chronologically arranged.

Behind this positive concern, however, lay an anxiety that never left him, an anxiety with roots in the Copernican era, renewed in our own century by discovery of the expanding universe and the fact that the cosmos itself has a history. A loss of bearings in the vastness of the universe; a sense of the futility of human endeavour in a world subject to the law of entropy; the 'malady of space-time' which manifests itself as a 'fundamental anguish of being,' a 'sickness of the dead end,' a feeling, strangely enough, of confinement: All this deeply impressed itself on Teilhard.[140] So too did the spreading fear of submersion in the whirlpool of modern civilization, of the crushing of one's individual life under the steadily increasing weight of man's world-building project.[141]

> As the years go by, Lord, I come to see more and more clearly, in myself and in those around me, that the great secret preoccupation of modern man is much less to battle for possession of the world than to find a means of escaping from it. The anguish of feeling that one is not merely spatially but ontologically imprisoned in the cosmic bubble; the anxious search for an issue to, or more exactly a focal point for, the evolutionary process; these are the price we must pay for the growth of planetary consciousness; these are the dimly-recognized burdens which weigh down the souls of christian and gentile alike in the world of today.[142]

He made it his aim to address this anxiety, to restore confidence in progress, and so to make the Christian faith relevant once again.[143]

To that end Teilhard undertook a 're-cosmologization of our religion' on a scale rarely seen, commandeering evolution as the vehicle not only of creation but of salvation. The way out, he was convinced, could only be the way forwards,[144] through the sea of seeming futility, which under the staff of his capable imagination parted to reveal something called Omega – that final issue our hearts desire, a point of complete cosmic convergence that quells all fear of perpetual, meaningless becoming.[145] This combination of evolution and eschatology provided the nucleus of Teilhard's response to the challenge of post-Copernican science and to the spiritual crisis of the modern world.[146] Around it the themes on which

---

[140] 1970:249ff. Cf. Jones 11f.; also Prigogine and Stengers 213ff.

[141] 'There can be no doubt that the burden of continuing the World weighs more and more heavily on the shoulders of Mankind' (1964:42; cf. 262f.).

[142] 1965:138f.; cf. Henri de Lubac 1967:143ff. This 'great secret preoccupation' is by no means peculiarly modern, of course, even if it has been intensified by first embracing, then doubting, the idea of progress. Nor are scientific discoveries its chief source.

[143] See 'A Note on Progress' (1920) 1964:11ff.

[144] 1964:44.

[145] 'Essentially the Universe is narrowing to a centre, like the successive layers of a cone: it is *convergent* in structure' (1964:46). It reaches its tip when it arrives at God and is united with him in the Pleroma (*sic*).

[146] 'To our clearer vision the universe is no longer a State but a Process. The cosmos has become a Cosmogenesis. And it may be said without exaggeration that, directly or indirectly, all the intellectual crises through which civilisation has passed in the last four centuries

we have already touched find something like their proper orbit. Its christological dimensions, and what answer it affords the Where? question, we will discover by expanding just a little.

For Teilhard evolution is not an impersonal process but one with which we ourselves have a great deal to do. As the head of creation, humanity stands today at the crossroads. Cosmological, religious and social doubts are forcing us to face the question: 'Is the Universe utterly pointless, or are we to accept that it has a meaning, a future, a purpose?'[147] Shall we attempt to go forwards into that future or shall we turn back? *Can* we still go forwards? The answer he gives is that we can and we must – unless we wish to rebel against the most obvious evidence that the evolving universe is not a mindless affair, namely, ourselves! Our own existence as thinking, questioning beings is the clearest possible proof of a marvelous 'noogenesis rising upstream against the flow of entropy,' as he puts it.[148] But how shall we go forwards, how shall we co-operate with evolution and direct it to its proper end? Not by seeking to withdraw from the material world that spawned us, as both Christian and pagan spirituality encourages us to do, nor yet by pursuing our own fulfillment or private aspirations in this world. The one course is premature, a kind of self-abortion in fact, since it is hardly conceivable that the Mind or Spirit that is emerging from the play of matter is already fully formed. And both are falsely individualistic. To move forwards can only mean to press on, whatever the cost, towards a truly cosmopolitan society. 'We can progress only by uniting,' says Teilhard, by concentration around a common centre; that, he argues, is 'the law of life' and the very essence of noogenesis.[149]

A common centre is just what he sought to provide by promoting these ideas. The *theory* of noogenesis furthers the process of noogenesis by breaking down the disastrous barriers between devotion to God above or to worldly progress here below. These 'rival mysticisms' must not be allowed to divide mankind any longer; the 'or' must give way to an

---

arise out of the successive stages whereby a static *Weltanschauung* has been and is being transformed . . . into a *Weltanschauung* of movement' (1964:261f.).

[147] 1964:42 (see also 67ff.). 'The Grand Option,' written on the eve of WWII and published at its conclusion, is one of his most important essays.

[148] 1970:318. Noogenesis – the universe in the process of 'psychic concentration,' of 'acquiring a personality,' of coming to life – offsets entropy. The two are 'complementary expressions of the arrow of time,' one moving backwards or downwards and the other forwards and upwards 'towards zones of increasing improbability and personality' (1964:48f.; cf. 78f.).

[149] 1964:74. The individual mind can be fulfilled only through growth of the collective mind, since it is the nature of mind to con-centrate. There is a 'continual heightening of consciousness in the Universe' through a tightening or contraction produced by increased organization. Having passed through its biological or cephalization phase, this organization is now a 'technico-mental process which . . . has been irresistably causing Mankind to draw closer together and unite upon itself' (301).

'and.'[150] Recognizing in evolution 'a cosmic genesis of the Spirit' makes sense of that 'and.' It introduces a forwards into the upwards and an upwards into the forwards, linking advance towards God with social progress and furnishing social progress with a truly compelling motive.

Here indeed is the real significance of Teilhard. Between the verticalism of classical theology and the faltering horizontalism of the Enlightenment he attempted to fashion a third alternative, an ascension theology for our time.[151] For want of a better term we may call it diagonalism. In an article entitled 'The Heart of the Problem' Teilhard himself offers the following diagram, in which O^Y represents 'Christian Faith, aspiring Upward;' O^X 'Human Faith, driving Forward;' O^R 'Christian Faith, "rectified" . . . reconciling the two':[152]

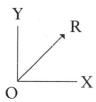

Mankind, as he says elsewhere, 'is to achieve a breakthrough straight ahead by forcing its way over the threshold of some higher level of consciousness.' All who share this conviction, whether Christian or not, can 'advance unequivocably side by side.'[153]

Teilhard's unifying diagonalism amounts to a synthesis between ascension in the flesh and ascension of the mind – only the flesh in question is not that of Jesus but our own, and its ascent means precisely its increasing animation or assimilation by mind. The 'ascent of the Universe towards consciousness,' 'the general "drift" of matter towards spirit,' was

---

[150] See 1964:76ff., 268f. 'The Higher Life, the Union, the long dreamed-of consummation that has hitherto been sought *Above*, in the direction of some kind of transcendency: should we not rather look for it *Ahead*, in the prolongation of the inherent forces of evolution? Above or ahead – or both?' That, he says, is 'the vital question, and the fact that we have thus far left it unconfronted is the root cause of all our religious troubles' (263).

[151] 'Faith in God and faith in the World: these two springs of energy, each the source of a magnificent spiritual impulse, must certainly be capable of effectively uniting in such a way as to produce a resulting upward movement' (ibid. 77).

[152] Ibid. 269. In pointing the way to human unity O^R points also towards Omega, a vectorial sum representing the ascent of the universe, with man at its helm, into the absolute unity of God.

[153] 'The *union sacrée*, the Common Front of all those who believe that the World is still advancing: what is this but the active minority, the solid core around which the unanimity of tomorrow must harden?' (ibid. 80)

his entire theme.[154] The Hellenic character of the underlying cosmology is difficult to disguise, in spite of Teilhard's characteristically modern concern with the temporal axis. Noogenesis means the gradual 'liberation of consciousness' from the more primitive or crudely material layers of cosmic reality, the triumph of the interior over the exterior.[155] Time itself is defined 'as precisely the rise of the Universe into high latitudes where complexity, concentration, centration, and consciousness grow and increase, simultaneously and correlatively.'[156] What results is a *conical* outline of the universe, whose spatio-temporal dimensions finally reduce to a vanishing-point when the emergent consciousness, satiated on 'the whole divinisable substance of matter,' breaks away 'to join up with the supreme and universal focus Omega' (i.e., with God).[157]

All of this invited expression in christological terms, however. Like Schleiermacher, in fact, Teilhard saw himself as making a place for Christ in the modern world. Unlike Schleiermacher he was quite prepared to speak boldly of Christ's physical or cosmic primacy. That was something the church had always confessed but had never been able to explain convincingly, in consequence of which our Lord's ascendency had been treated too narrowly in moral or juridical terms and his influence confined to 'the extra-cosmic sphere of the supernatural.'[158] The situation only worsened, he said, with the arrival of modern science. The expanding cosmos (in which even the planet that hosted the incarnation lost its centrality) rendered Jesus Christ virtually irrelevant. On this point, Père Teilhard's defense of the faith was little more than a concession. Jesus, he suggested, was only a face (one among many) on the cosmic Christ, a subdivision appropriate to the needs of our particular planet and race.[159] But the primacy of the cosmic Christ he never tired of celebrating.

---

[154] Cf. 1964:18, 1960:110. All matter has a 'within' as well as a 'without.' The latter is of dubious ontological status, however, since to be is to unite, and to unite is precisely a process of interiorization: 'In the perspectives of cosmic involution, not only does consciousness become co-extensive with the universe, but the universe rests in equilibrium and consistency, in the form of thought, on a supreme pole of interiorization' (1970:338; cf. 322 n. 1).

[155] The newest layer is a layer of *thought* which surrounds the whole and determines its destiny: 'Far from being swallowed up by Evolution, Man is now engaged in transforming our earlier idea of Evolution in terms of himself, and thereafter plotting its new outlines' (1964:87), *viz.*, a 'laborious communal ascent towards the summit of consciousness' (1965:106). On this ascent the cruder bottom layers slough off and 'redescend' (1964:93).

[156] 1964:88.

[157] 1960:110, 1970:338. 'If it is to be adjusted to Man, the high point and effective spearhead of evolution . . Space-time must be given whatever form is most appropriate. Caught within its curve the layers of Matter . . . tighten and converge in Thought, by synthesis. Therefore it is as a cone . . . that it can best be depicted' (1964:88).

[158] Teilhard (1964:94f.) did not deal with Schleiermacher's option.

[159] *Journal* 24.2.1918. A basic problem 'which cosmic Christology has to face is the effect of the Copernican revolution in dislodging mankind, together with the Saviour . . . from the mid point of creation to an obscure corner of the universe' (Lyons 69; cf. T. Hall 1982:122ff.).

To secure that primacy Teilhard set out resolutely down the path the Anglican theologians were also beginning to explore. Beyond the traditional two natures of Christ, he claimed, we must reckon today with his third nature – with his relation to the universe rather than the Trinity – as our most pressing theological problem.[160]

> Hitherto the thought of the faithful explicitly distinguished in practice hardly more than two aspects of Christ: the Man-Jesus and the Word-God. Now it is evident that a third face of the theandric complex remained in the background. I mean the mysterious super-human person everywhere underlying the most fundamental institutions and the most solemn dogmatic affirmations of the Church; the One in whom all things have been created – the One 'in quo omnia constant' – the One who, by his birth and blood, restores every creature to his Father, the Christ of the Eucharist and the Parousia, the consummating and cosmic Christ of St. Paul.[161]

In his third nature Christ cannot be marginalized. Rather he turns out to be the all-pervasive, attractive force that overcomes the natural rivalry of individual beings and binds them together in the holy unity of noogenesis. He is, in short, the motive power of the world's ascension. But for Teilhard he is also its goal and its product. There is a sense in which he does not yet fully exist.

> Since Jesus was born, and grew to full stature, and died, everything has continued to move forward *because Christ is not yet fully formed*: he has not yet gathered about him the last folds of his robe of flesh and of love which is made up of his faithful followers. The mystical Christ has not yet attained to his full growth; and therefore the same is true of the cosmic Christ. Both of these are simultaneously in the state of being and becoming; and it is from the prolongation of this process of becoming that all created activity ultimately springs. Christ is the end-point of the evolution, even the *natural* evolution, of all beings; and therefore evolution is holy.[162]

To discern in evolution the ongoing work of forming Christ was Teilhard's special intellection.[163] Christ's place is certainly at the centre, as Christianity teaches, but the centre is at the end. That is where we can expect to find him: 'In a Universe of "Conical" structure Christ has a place (the apex!) ready for Him to fill, whence His Spirit can radiate

---

[160] *Journal* 8.7.1945. Teilhard, as Lyons (190ff.) reminds us, actually thought of his project as an attempt to deal with some of Nicaea's 'unfinished business.'

[161] Quoted Lyons 189f. ('Christianisme et Évolution,' *Oeuvres* 10:209f.). Teilhard is quite right, of course, to intuit a persistent gap in the tradition between 'the Man-Jesus and the Word-God.'

[162] 1965:13. See also 1970:294ff.; cf. Lyons 203, on Omega as prime mover and final cause.

[163] If evolution is noogenesis, noogenesis is christogenesis: 'Quite specifically it is *Christ whom we make or whom we undergo in all things*' (1960:123).

through all the centuries and all beings . . .'[164] Towards that apex he, and we, continue to ascend.

Who then was Jesus? In him the Christ appeared pro-actively, so to speak, as a particular man. He did so in order to infuse into human nature a grace essential to evolution's 'hominization' phase. That phase is the critical one, for in it what has hitherto been a process of ontological diversification is turned back on itself and becomes, through the centring effects of human self-consciousness, a process of unification. By his supreme sacrifice on the cross Jesus provided the impetus to self-transcendence without which unification (incorporation into one infinite person) is ultimately impossible; in his resurrection he anticipated our liberation from 'the temporal zones of our visible world' into the oneness of the Pleroma.[165] Having thus demonstrated 'a law common to *all* life,' he began to draw the whole world after him as the body of his ascension: 'Towards the peaks, shrouded in mists from our human eyes, whither the Cross beckons us, we rise by a path which is the way of universal progress.'[166] In the vanguard on this climb is the church, that 'portion of the world which has reflexively become Christ' already. Little by little it harnesses 'the world's expectancy and ferment and unfolding,' sacrificially gathering together mankind's spiritual energies 'in their most sublime form' so as to focus them on the Omega-point.[167]

For Teilhard the incarnation was a decisive but temporary affair, then. The Christ 'appeared for a moment in our midst' that we might see and touch him, 'before vanishing once again, more luminous and ineffable than ever, into the depths of the future.' His withdrawal – both a going up and a going ahead, an ascension and an advance – means a going beyond the humanity he once shared with us.[168] But these two radii provide a grid on which we can locate and track the post-incarnate Lord. His ascension, spatially interpreted, means that he has become ubiquitous, 'an immense and living force' to be encountered already, and worshiped,

---

[164] '. . . and because of the genetic links running through all the levels of Time and Space between the elements of a convergent world, the Christ-influence, far from being restricted to the mysterious zones of "grace," spreads and penetrates throughout the entire mass of Nature in movement' (1964:94).

[165] Like those who follow him he 'pre-adheres to God' (1960:119; cf. 101ff.) through the self-denial of the cross, and so anticipates the consummation. Jean Danielou (1988:351) testifies that he finds no trace of Kant or Hegel in de Chardin; a less perceptive judgment would be hard to imagine, unless one were to fail to see Origen here.

[166] 1960:103.

[167] Ibid. 153f. 'Across the immensity of time and the disconcerting multiplicity of individuals, one single operation is taking place: the annexation to Christ of his chosen; one single thing is being made: the mystical body of Christ, starting from all the sketchy spiritual powers scattered through the world' (143).

[168] That is what creates the vital sense of expectancy which is Christianity's unique contribution to evolution; for evolution itself is now fuelled by the creative tension between the upwards and the forwards that is propelling all of us towards the *superhumanitie* of the Pleroma. See 150ff. (cf. 1965:32ff.).

in all creatures. This is his physical primacy.[169] Temporally interpreted, on the other hand, it means that he has preceded us into the future, from whence he is already returning to meet us, exciting in us an enthusiasm for progress. By way of synthesis we may say that his presence is 'silently accruing in things,' until in the parousia, as if at a kind of flashpoint, it will suddenly break forth in all its splendour. For as the twin vectors of our rectified faith 'veer and draw together' they point us to the consummated Christ, the divine soul of a divinized creation.[170]

Such is Teilhard's resolution of the Where? question, so far as our rather crude outline (in which are many *lacunae*, some his and some ours) allows it to emerge. But has he really provided a place for Christ, or has Christ been pressed into the service of his cosmological compromise? To meld two opposing worldviews requires a powerful bond. Since Jesus of Nazareth could not supply that bond Teilhard turned to the cosmic Christ.[171] There is something too convenient about this substitute, however. His lineaments are established in no other way than by the forwards and the upwards which he is asked to reconcile. Is he something more substantial than a diagram, an invented metaphysic, an empty guarantee that forwards is upwards? And if so, can we follow Teilhard in addressing him as 'Jesus'? For this much is clear: the first task of the cosmic Christ is to dispose of the scandal of particularity with which Christianity has hitherto been burdened. Jesus of Nazareth is retained only as a reference point on our evolutionary chart, stretched out on the cross that is constructed for him by the intersection of Teilhard's twin axes; to expect belief in him today, as a living man, would not unite but divide. The resurrected Christ, whose strength bends these axes until they touch again at Omega-point, is someone quite different. He is no longer the incarnate one, with his own human and bodily specificity, but the immanent one.[172] And the place he is securing for himself is, quite literally, no place for Jesus. Teilhard's diagonalism is a retraction theory on a cosmic scale.[173]

* * *

[169] 'Because you ascended into heaven after having descended into hell, you have so filled the universe in every direction, Jesus, that henceforth it is blessedly impossible for us to escape you' (1960:127). It should be noted that Teilhard understands omnipresence in terms of *action*, an action which conducts us into God's presence by effecting that 'unitive transformation' which ultimately undoes our space.

[170] See 1960:122f., 150; cf. 1964:268.

[171] Cf. G. Maloney 1968:206. Lyons (192, following J. Laberge) notes the entry for 30.8.1946: 'Neo-Christianity saves and exalts the 3 *Christs*: (1) *historical* (nuclear seed) (2) *cosmic* (Hominizing) (3) *transcendent* (irreversible).'

[172] In an apologetic passage this immanent Christ (who is 'incarnate in the world,' 1965:28) is described as 'an expansion of the Christ who was born of Mary and who died on the cross' (1960:117).

[173] Here is a Eutychianism in which the cosmos itself is absorbed into God; the universal Christ is realized in direct correlation with the contraction of spatio-temporal reality.

A full critique of Teilhard would be a large and onerous task, complicated not only by the criticisms of fellow scientists but by the fact that the power of his prose far outstrips the clarity of his reasoning in matters theological. If it is tempting, then, for these or other reasons, simply to dismiss his ideas, his enormous influence in and beyond the church dictates otherwise.[174] Fortunately it will suffice to show that his alternative ascension theology brings us virtually full circle to Origen, while recapitulating in itself the major problems of the intervening tradition. Afterwards we will comment briefly on his ecclesiology.

Like both Origen and Hegel, Teilhard sought to counter the materialist streak in western culture while at the same time upholding the goodness of creation against radical dualism. But he also shared their attraction to monism. He himself pointed to the problem of the one and the many as the key to his work,[175] and to a life-long quest 'for the Necessary, the General, the "Natural," as opposed to the Contingent, the Particular and the Artificial.'[176] In that light it is not surprising that his theology was for all practical purposes unitarian. Or that he thought evil to be a necessary by-product of creation, requiring some kind of self-cancelling dynamic,[177] which is just what we discover: Teilhard's evolutionism consists of a twofold process of descent into multiplicity (divergent evolution, which is subject to entropy) and ascent into unity (convergent evolution, which is not). There is first a spreading out of material forms and then a regathering through the perfection of inwardness. The spreading out can rightly be regarded as a fall, just as the regathering is a redemption. 'The multitude of beings is a terrible affliction,' he avowed; or in the plain words of his Journal, 'there is only one Evil = disunity.'[178] In short, Teilhard shared the pagan antipathy towards temporal and material existence.

The evil of disunity is what his cosmic christology was designed to rectify, of course.

> The principle of unity which saves our guilty world, wherein all is in process of returning to dust, is Christ. Through the force of his magnetism, the light of his ethical teaching, the unitive power of his very being, Jesus establishes again at the heart of the world the harmony of all endeavours and the convergence of all beings.[179]

---

[174] i.e., in the academically sophisticated western churches – those, it seems, who provide the clearest evidence for the law of entropy! Witness, e.g., the prayers (particularly those after the Psalms) in the Anglican Church of Canada's *Book of Alternative Services*.

[175] Jones 26 (following C. Cuénot). The Christ he worships, and the Pleroma which he regards as the goal of creation, are precisely the 'ineffable synthesis' of the one and the many (1965:75f., 1960:122).

[176] From the autobiographical essay 'Le Coeur de la Matière' (*Oeuvres* 13:26; Lyons 148).

[177] 1970:339ff.; cf. D. Kim 1976:81f.

[178] See Passmore 252, H. de Lubac 1967:251; cf. Origen, *Princ.* 2.9. 'At the exact opposite to God, pure multiplicity is Teilhard's notion of absolute nothing' (Lyons 178); hence 'the final victory of good over evil can only be completed in the *total* organization of our world' (1960:85) and the cessation of 'regression into plurality.'

[179] 1965:147

Hamartiological and soteriological presuppositions thus determine the kind of saviour that is needed and the form he must take. 'Christ is loved as a person; he compels recognition as a world.'[180] Curiously, Teilhard complained that modernist theology 'evaporates Christ, dissociates him in the world.' For his part, he wanted rather 'to concentrate the World in Christ.'[181] But could such a project hope to come out any differently? 'Why should we go searching the Judaea of two thousand years ago?' he says to his Jesus; for 'you do truly appear to me as that vast and vital force which I sought everywhere that I might adore it.'[182]

The notion of divergent and convergent evolution, with the crucified Jesus as the limit of the former and the cosmic Christ as the goal of the latter, is simply the thickening-and-thinning dialectic all over again.[183] Teilhard's angelomorphic anthropology bears out this conclusion. What he called '*Homo progressivus*, that is to say, the man to whom the terrestrial future matters more than the present,' might not at first glance appear a suitable candidate for the ethereal spheres, but that is precisely what he is.[184] The cosmic school has been re-conceived, the curriculum changed, but the objective is the same: that through intellectual and spiritual exertion man should transform himself completely, advancing by degrees into union with God.[185] Do we not think it conceivable, Teilhard asks,

> that Mankind, at the end of its totalization, its folding-in upon itself, may reach a critical level of maturity where, leaving Earth and stars to lapse slowly back into the dwindling mass of primordial energy, it will detach itself from this planet and join the one true, irreversible essence of things, the Omega Point? A phenomenon perhaps outwardly akin to death: but in reality a simple metamorphosis and arrival at the supreme synthesis. An escape from the planet, not in space or outwardly, but spiritually and inwardly, such as the hyper-concentration of matter upon itself allows.[186]

---

[180] Ibid. 153.

[181] H. de Lubac 1988:366 n. 5.

[182] 1965:140f.

[183] In the background stand Denis, Maximus and Bonaventure, but in the foreground Hegel, Rothe and Blondel; note that it is the *crucified* Jesus who represents creation re-ascending 'the slopes of being' (1960:104).

[184] 'They are scientists, thinkers, airmen, and so on – all those possessed by the demon (or the angel) of Research' (1964:137). 'There can be no place for the poor in spirit, the sceptics, the pessimists, the sad of heart,' he says (72).

[185] It is 'through the medium of education that there ensues, directly and indirectly, the gradual incorporation of the World in the Word Incarnate' (1964:35); 'to *be* more is in the first place to *know* more' (19).

[186] 1964:122f. 'Thus from the grains of thought forming the . . . indestructible atoms of its stuff, the universe – a well-defined universe in the outcome – goes on building itself above our heads in the inverse direction of matter which vanishes . . . All round us, one by one, like a continual exhalation, "souls" break away, carrying upwards their incommunicable load of consciousness,' until the noosphere is complete (1970:299). And then? What else but 'the overthrow of equilibrium, detaching the mind, fulfilled at last, from its material matrix, so that it will henceforth rest with all its weight on God-Omega' (1970:316)?

It is worth recalling that Origen once remarked that it was not easy to say whether the heaven to which the Christ-like soul ascends should be understood as lying above, or within, the visible world; and it is well known that he regarded the total process of ascension as requiring a great succession of ages and worlds.[187] If we opt for the 'within' rather than the 'above,' while focusing relatively more attention on the progress of the race and of the ages than on the advance of the individual soul, we approach very nearly the ideas of Teilhard de Chardin.

Just here we find ourselves in unexpected agreement with his foremost defender, Henri de Lubac, who thought it ironic that Origen should be charged with too great a discontinuity in eschatology and Teilhard (as he often is) with too great a continuity, when in fact they are saying more or less the same thing. They are indeed, and neither achieves either the proper continuity or the proper discontinuity.[188] Both link the fall with creation, and both resolve their monist prejudice against matter by a process of incremental change. One obvious difference, of course, is that Teilhard was inclined to downplay the fall while he restored the parousia to a place of prominence. Some passages even lend the impression of a biblical urgency about the latter:

> We persist in saying that we keep vigil in expectation of the Master. But in reality we should have to admit, if we were sincere, *that we no longer expect anything*. The flame must be revived at all costs.[189]

His occasional diatribes against those 'dangerous' folk who hold to an imminent return of Christ speak volumes, however.[190] The Christian hope must not be spoiled by hasty expectations! The day towards which we must look and labour so eagerly is literally aeons away. 'Only twenty centuries have passed since the ascension,' he chides. 'What have we made of our expectancy?'[191]

If there is a truly modern element in Teilhard's scheme, it is not his eschatology but the notion that Christian hope invites us to take up the

---

[187] See *Princ.* 2.3.6, 3.6.6.

[188] De Lubac (1967:30) suggests that Teilhard's thought is 'essentially eschatological;' that he actually restores, at least in principle, the balance between continuity and discontinuity in eschatology which many are in danger of losing in the fog of materialism; that he represents the tradition well (140ff.)! Perhaps he does, if we are willing to accept Origen and the mystics as its legitimate representatives.

[189] 1960:152. 'The whole future of the Earth, as of religion, seems to me to depend on the awakening of our faith in the future' (1964:7).

[190] Those who doubt that the parousia depends on human progress, or are not easily reassured by the claim that 'the vast industrial and social system by which we are enveloped does not threaten to crush us' (1964:183), seem to worry Teilhard. 'It would be criminal or insane to attempt to resist the great explosion of the innate forces of the Earth that is now beginning,' he says (187). And we may take 'explosion' literally – for even the atom bomb, as a triumph of human ingenuity and co-operation, proclaims 'the coming of the *Spirit of the Earth*' (147). Cf. Lyons 208, Passmore 255, de Lubac 1967:30.

[191] 1960:151.

project of perfecting or 'personalizing' the species.[192] By placing greater emphasis on the parousia than on the fall, on the end rather than the beginning, the Origenist tradition easily accommodates itself to this project. It becomes quite natural to focus on corporate rather than individual advance. The parousia, says Teilhard, will coincide with the moment of man's collective maturation.

> We have gone deeply into these new perspectives: the progress of the universe, and especially the human universe, does not take place in rivalry with God . . . To look with longing to the Parousia of the Son of Man we have only to allow to beat within our breasts – and to christianize – the heart of the world.[193]

Here is Teilhard's message in a nutshell. It may, he allows, require a 'simple readjustment' to orthodox beliefs – *viz.*, the rejection of imminency for immanence,[194] of 'the man who lived two thousand years ago' for one who 'shines forth from within all the forces of the earth.'[195] But by way of compensation for the loss of these (Irenaean!) elements Christianity itself is born again as a catholic faith in a new sense of the word: a faith 'containing and embracing all others,' a strong and attractive faith that must eventually 'possess the Earth.'[196]

Teilhard's double apologetic, to be successful, could come to no other conclusion perhaps, yet we cannot help expressing our surprise at the baldness of its expression. Some minor tinkering and nothing of substance separates church and world; indeed, Christianity's central symbol, the cross, now represents 'the deepest aspirations of our age'![197] What is this if not the vision of Hegel, Origen's greatest western heir, falsely christened in a Roman font? But there is a profound lesson here for the whole church: If in his resurrection, ascension and parousia Jesus is not allowed to stand over against us as a man with his own distinct history (for that is the effect if not the object of the tinkering), then on the cross he is not allowed to do so either. To turn it round the other way, on the cross he is made to identify not so much with our sin as with our thirst for righteousness; he does not die outside the camp. The salvation he brings, then, the life he

---

[192] 'Some say, "Let us wait patiently until the Christ returns." Others say, "Let us rather finish building the Earth." Still others think, "To speed the Parousia, let us complete the making of Man on Earth."' The last proposal is Teilhard's (1964:260) but it could be Bergson's or Renan's or Drummond's.

[193] 1965:149 (1960:153f.). Neither Irenaeus nor Origen would ever have spoken thus. Yet it is the latter's heirs who say it, for in Origen's own scheme of things the forwards and the upwards were already united in principle.

[194] 1964:267f.

[195] 1965:33. It also requires an adjustment to Enlightenment orthodoxy, which shares with Judaism and naïve Christianity what Teilhard calls 'a childishly timid outlook that can conceive of nothing greater or more vital in the world than the pitiable perfection of our human organism' (25).

[196] 1964:268f.

[197] Ibid. 94f.; cf. 1960:103f., 1970:342.

offers us, is no other than our *own* life, as Teilhard liked to say.[198] In that case Christianity may well possess the earth, for it surely belongs to it already.

***

Before leaving Teilhard behind we must look a little further into the impact of his diagonalism on the doctrine of the church, for it is here that the main lines we have followed in our last two chapters converge. The first thing to be said is that the imprint of Origen is not effaced by the modern component. Augustine's mark also remains visible. The universalist and triumphalist tendencies of their respective ascension theologies are uniquely combined by Teilhard, lending new force to a most familiar theme: that of the church as κόσμος of the cosmos. Teilhard's equivalent of that doctrine is his description of the church as a phylum, as a kind of genetic pattern that has emerged to govern the future unfolding of evolution. At the heart of this governance is its catholic drive, the fruit of a heightened consciousness Teilhard identifies with love (*super-charité*).[199] Since the ascension itself is precisely a process of synthesis, to grasp its truth can only mean to foster convergence, to strive towards a planetary synaxis, to demolish all barriers to social unification – religious barriers in particular. The function of the church is 'to Christianise all that is human in Man,' cultivating in the name of God 'a huge and *totally human* hope.'[200] That is how it builds up Christ.[201]

No heir to the tradition we have been describing could fail to expound this in sacramental terms! In a revealing passage in *Le Milieu Divin*, Teilhard speaks of 'the onrush of the cult of the Holy Eucharist.' Has the church not been busy all along transforming creation, little by little, into an extension of the body of Christ through its daily masses? Not in some crass physical sense, of course, but by the steady assimilation of humanity into the one communion of him who (underlying the visible institutions of the church) ultimately transcends space and time?[202] Here again is the dialectic of divergence and convergence, of *descensus* and *ascensus*:

> As our humanity assimilates the material world, and the Host assimilates our humanity, the eucharistic transformation goes beyond and completes the transubstantiation of the bread on the altar. Step by step it irresistably invades

---

[198] See e.g. 1965:142f., 148f.

[199] 1970:326; cf. Maloney 208ff., Danielou 356f., and especially de Lubac 1988:369f.

[200] See 1964:265, 1960:151ff. For the sake of this 'common great hope' (1964:72) it is no doubt *necessary* that the way of the cross should become 'no more nor less than the road of human endeavour supernaturally righted and prolonged' (1960:104).

[201] Cf. 1960:122ff. Without the Church, said Teilhard (de Lubac 1988:370), 'Christ evaporates, or crumbles, or disappears!'

[202] 1960:121ff.

the universe . . . [For] in a secondary and generalised sense, but in a true sense, the sacramental Species are formed by the totality of the world, and the duration of the creation is the time needed for its consecration.[203]

The church, then, is engaged in effecting the consecration of *everything*. It is knitting together for Jesus, out of the stuff of creation, an immense body 'worthy of resurrection.' It is fulfilling its Marian task of bringing forth the Christ.[204] Through its co-operation with the world, the one who has hidden himself in the womb of the world will reappear. And what is that labour? It is the 'sanctification' of matter through the adoration of the holy offspring it is expecting, namely, Unity.[205]

In the theology of Teilhard de Chardin ecclesiastical self-idolization is complete. His famous Mass on the World (what some regard as the offering of strange fire in the Ordos desert) gives ample testimony to the elevation of catholicity, and the power of christogenesis on which it is based, into a god to be worshiped.

'Lord.' Yes, at last, through the twofold mystery of this universal consecration and communion I have found one to whom I can whole-heartedly give this name . . . Glorious Lord Jesus Christ: the divine influence secretly diffused and active in the depths of matter, and the dazzling centre where all the innumerable fibres of the manifold meet . . . it is you to whom my being cried out with a desire as vast as the universe, 'In truth you are my Lord and my God.'[206]

For this it is altogether necessary, as we seen over and over again, that the man of Nazareth withdraw, allowing 'our love to escape from the constrictions of the too narrow, too precise, too limited' image of God he represents.[207] But there are other victims on the altar of universality as well. Next in line, ironically, is the church itself.

---

[203] Who, he asks (124f.), 'can tell where the diffusion of Christ, with the influence of grace, stops, as it spreads outward from the faithful at the heart of the human family?' For it is 'one of the most certain points of our faith' that 'the human layer of the earth is wholly and continuously under the organising influx of the incarnate Christ.'

[204] 'The greater man becomes and the more humanity becomes one, conscious of its power and able to control it . . . the more Christ will find, for the mystical extensions of his humanity, a body worthy of resurrection' (1965:149). Thus in one very striking passage *the eucharist is fully reversed*: 'To allay your hunger and slake your thirst, to nourish your body and bring it to full stature, you need to find in us a substance which will truly be food for you. And this food . . . I will prepare for you by liberating the spirit in myself and in everything' (134).

[205] Christ will 'come to us clothed in the glory of the world' (1960:128).

[206] 1965:33f.; see 19ff., and note N. M. Wildiers' introduction (13ff.).

[207] 'How strange, my God, are the processes your Spirit initiates. When two centuries ago, your Church began to feel the particular power of your heart, it might have seemed that what was captivating men's souls was the fact of their finding in you an element even more determinate, more circumscribed, than your humanity as a whole. But now on the contrary a swift reversal is making us aware that your main purpose . . . was to enable our love to escape from the constrictions of the too narrow, too precise, too limited image of you which we had fashioned for ourselves' (ibid. 34).

According to Teilhard the (Roman) church has become 'the principal axis of evolution,' the hub of 'a perennial act of communion and sublimation' by which Christ 'aggregates to himself the total psychism of the earth.'[208] But it cannot be this sacrament of universality if it is not prepared to grow and change with the world, to embrace the world in its own advancing humanity, to be fulfilled by the world. We might say that the church's 'Jesus' identity must give way to its 'Christ' identity; that is, it must allow its faith and praxis to be rectified by the pull of society at large. If it will not thus transcend itself it can hardly hope to lead others in the quest for God, who is the centre of all centres.[209] But the same problem arises in ecclesiology as in christology: To assimilate the world, the church must first be assimilated *by* the world; to christianize, it must first be humanized. Who then is consecrating whom? Which is really the critical phylum? Is it not more likely that the church will be absorbed into the world than the world into the church?

A further and related victim is the human person as such, whose needs and whose value also appear to be too narrow, too precise, too limited, when compared with the interests of the whole. In the universal Mass the individual is consumed, transubstantiated, totalized – becoming 'one and the same person' with the cosmic Christ. Teilhard denied that this meant any loss of distinct identity or any diminishment of personhood. 'Union differentiates,' he was fond of saying.[210] Totalization must not be confused with eastern pantheism, as if it meant absorption of the human spirit into a god with no face. God is person, and whatever is united to God is thereby personalized.[211] Against the rampant individualism of our times he wished to set, not the annihilation of the individual, but his or her 'hyper-personalization.' Did he not consider it his holy vocation to personalize the whole world in God?[212] But there, of course – and quite apart from the messianic pretensions of such a claim – is the rub. When we begin to speak of a universal person, or of a world that is slowly acquiring a personality,[213] what is happening to the meaning of these terms? Can a passion for the One, the All, the Absolute, offer any foundation for the personal? Can it prevent the merely particular (the artificial!) from being regarded with a utilitarian

---

[208] See 1970:320ff. (cf. Maloney 214, de Lubac 1988:369). It is most often in a eucharistic or ecclesiological context that the ascension is used to set Jesus aside for 'a God to adore' (1960:127; cf. 123ff.).

[209] 1964:265f.

[210] We must not 'confuse individuality with personality,' he rightly insists (1970:288f.).

[211] See de Lubac 1967:143ff.

[212] '"I really believe," he wrote to a friend in 1917, "that my vocation has never seemed so stark and clear: to personalize the world in God," and to that vocation he always remained faithful' (ibid. 145).

[213] 'A Universe that is in the process of psychic concentration is *identical* with a Universe that is acquiring a personality' (1964:79).

eye?[214] Does transubstantiation not mean just this: that when the consecration is complete there is no longer bread, only Body?[215]

By working without recourse to the trinitarian insights from which the idea of the person arose, Teilhard does indeed produce, as Colin Gunton observes, a suffocating pantheism that leaves little room to be human.[216] By universalizing the incarnation, we would add – turning God with us as a particular Jewish man into God with us as a christic force hidden in the cosmic dust – he sets the stage for a grotesque parody of the personal, with features shaped by the world's homogenizing forces, especially death. John Passmore, who documents the darker side of his thought, makes a telling point when he observes that Teilhard substitutes love of the world for love of one's neighbour as the second great commandment.[217] That is entirely consistent, of course, since he has already substituted love of the world for love of Jesus: 'Always from the very first it was the world, greater than all the elements which make up the world, that I was in love with; and never before was there anyone before whom I could in honesty bow down.'[218]

This brings us back to ecclesiology, for all talk of charity as the church's essential feature, as its special personalizing contribution to evolution, must be seen in this light. The loss of Jesus in his human concreteness – the confusion of christology with pneumatology and of anthropology with cosmology – makes itself felt just here. The universal 'amorization' presaged by the church is not a matter of κοινωνία but of tightened social organization. That is why de Chardin could describe, not only Roman Catholicism, but also fascism and communism as being 'in line with the essential trend of cosmic movement.'[219] It is true that after the Second

---

[214] 'I do not attribute any definitive or absolute value to the varied constructions of nature. What I like about them is not their particular form, but their function, which is to build up mysteriously, first what can be divinised, and then, through the grace of Christ coming down upon our endeavour, what is divine . . .' (1960:93).

[215] 'When Christ, extending the process of his incarnation, descends into the bread in order to replace it, his action is not limited to the material morsel . . .: this transubstantiation is aureoled with a real though attenuated divinizing of the entire universe' (1965:14). 'Before passing into the Beyond, the World and its elements must attain what may be called their "point of annihilation." And it is precisely to this critical point that we must ultimately be brought by the effort consciously to further . . . the movement of universal convergence!' (1964:56).

[216] Gunton 1991:106ff. Note that Teilhard finds in eugenics and social engineering and computer technology 'liberators of the spirit' (1970:336 n. 4; see 310f., 1964:144f., 230ff.).

[217] Passmore 254.

[218] This substitution gives new meaning to the way of the cross: 'My God, I deliver myself up with utter abandon to those fearful forces of dissolution which, I blindly believe, will this day cause my narrow ego to be replaced by your divine presence. The man who is filled with an impassioned love for Jesus *hidden in the forces which bring death to the earth*, him the earth will clasp in the immensity of her arms as her strength fails, and with her he will awaken in the bosom of God' (1965:32f., emphasis ours; see also 1960:130f.).

[219] 1964:46.

World War he paddled harder against the current of his own ideas, criticizing faceless and de-humanizing collectives. However, his cosmic Christ (neither fully human nor fully divine but itself a faceless *tertium quid*) pulled him steadily towards the reefs of the impersonal. 'Even as late as 1946,' notes Passmore, Teilhard 'was still prepared to write that it was too early "to judge recent totalitarian experiments fairly", to make up our minds whether "all things considered, they have produced a greater enslavement or a higher level of spiritual energy."'[220]

We do not judge him too harshly, then, if we conclude that Teilhard's synthesis of the forwards and the upwards only reproduced in heightened form that combination of militarism and mysticism we have met before, that disquieting double visage of the Christianity shaped by Origen and Augustine. There is a visible tilt, though. The Mass on the World, conceived and conducted in solitude on the feast of the transfiguration, 1923, displays as perhaps nothing else could the distorted individualism of Teilhard's thought; but the more powerful pole, and the more worrisome, is always his collectivism. Is not the whole of his work, like the Mass, an urgent expression of that 'unquenchable thirst for universal unity' which Dostoevsky's Grand Inquisitor identified as 'the third and last ordeal of man'?[221] Like the Inquisitor, by the way, Teilhard was not blind to the fact that the unification (christification) of human society seems to be producing not harmony but turmoil among the nations – what Irenaeus called 'minglings without cohesion.' But he had a kind of chaos theory by which to account for this. 'Incoherence is the prelude to unification,' he said; harmony will come in due time.[222] Meanwhile, we must 'look for our essential satisfaction in the thought that by our struggles we are serving, and leading to salvation, a personal Universe.'[223] Such was Teilhard's understanding of suffering as an ecclesial vocation.

In brief, the ascension theology of Teilhard de Chardin represents a total collapse of the tension between Jesus-history and our own, and so

---

[220] p. 246. 'When an energy runs amok, the engineer, far from questioning the power itself, simply works out his calculations afresh to see how it can be brought better under control. Monstrous as it is, is not modern totalitarianism really the distortion of something magnificent, and thus quite near to the truth? There can be no doubt of it: the great human machine is designed to work and *must* work – by producing a super-abundance of mind.' (1970:282; cf. 1964:118f.)

[221] 'Men have always striven to be organized into a universal whole,' says the Inquisitor.

[222] See 1970:293f. 'As the end of time approaches, a terrifying spiritual pressure will be brought to bear on the limits of the Real, born of the effort of souls desperately straining in their desire to escape from the Earth. This pressure will be unanimous. But the Scriptures teach us that at the same time it will be rent by a profound schism between those who wish to break out of themselves that they may become still more masters of the world, and those who, accepting Christ's word, passionately await the death of the world that they may be absorbed with it into God' (1964:307).

[223] Quoted de Lubac 1967:151. This echoes Renan's words (Passmore 251), 'let us console ourselves, poor victims: a God is being made with our tears.'

also of that between the church and the world. Christology has become mariology, and mariology cosmology, virtually without remainder.[224] In varying degrees we are all incarnations, and we are all ascending together. Together we will 'force the bars' of our earthly prison and realize for ourselves (in Sittler's words) 'the imperial vision of Christ coherent in τὰ πάντα.' The church, of course, does not disappear. It is made over into the visible sacrament of social progress, the place where our own divinity is acknowledged.[225]

***

We will shortly meet a few of the troublesome characters who have refused to travel this path, which appears to be the broad way in theology today. But one conspicuous figure who has travelled it, if only for a limited distance, is Karl Rahner.[226] Rahner, let it be noted, differs sharply from de Chardin at crucial points. He insists that the festival of the ascension is a 'festival of holy pain,' since Jesus has truly parted from us. And he has not done so 'in order to destroy his identity, in order to escape from the state which was his when he was here among us.' On the contrary, he will be manifested in due course just as he was and is. About the future of the world no such theory as Teilhard's can be entertained, says Rahner; if we are materialists we are crass materialists, for we believe that matter 'will last forever, and be glorified forever.'[227] Yet Rahner also adopts an evolutionary worldview as the starting point for christology. He too insists that the driving force of history is the world's natural attraction to God in his self-communication – that is, to Christ – and that 'the world as a whole flows into his resurrection and into the transfiguration of his body.'[228]

> Jesus' corporeal humanity is a permanent part of the one world with its single dynamism. Consequently Jesus' resurrection is the beginning of the transfiguration of the world . . . [T]he risen Lord, freed by resurrection from the limiting individuality of the unglorified body, has in truth become present to the world precisely because risen (and so by his 'going'), and . . . his return will only be the disclosure of this relation to the world attained by Jesus in his resurrection.

---

[224] 'In their respective treatments of the cosmic Christ – a Platonizing treatment and an evolutionizing treatment – Origen and Teilhard are both putting, so to speak, the face of Christ on the Logos of the World.' That is Lyons' not unfavourable conclusion (218).

[225] To that extent Teilhard answers the atheistic Hegelians, and those who would make science their substitute for religion: 'Evolution has come to infuse new blood, so to speak, into the perspectives and aspirations of Christianity. In return, is not the Christian faith destined, is it not preparing, to save and even to take the place of evolution? (1970:326; see 311ff.).

[226] See *Theological Investigations* 5/157ff.

[227] See 7/177ff., 181ff. (cf. G. McCool 1975:358).

[228] 4/353 (McCool 360f.); cf. 5/171ff.

The tendency to conflate resurrection, ascension and parousia is still evident here.[229] No real distinction can be drawn between the way of Jesus Christ and the way of the world, in the ascension of which we ought also to have 'the courage to believe.'[230] Eschatology is chiefly futurology, then, and so indeed is theology proper. God is identified as our absolute future, while the incarnation 'appears as the necessary and permanent beginning of the divinization of the world as a whole.'[231]

To be sure, the term *absolute* is meant to guard against still more errors of the type to which Teilhard is prone, and especially against modernity's temptation to allow the future to become 'a Moloch before whom the man existing at present is butchered for the sake of some man who is never real and always still to come.' Rahner's approach, as usual, is heavily nuanced.[232] But the effect of the above commitments on his ecclesiology – still the subject of intense debate in and beyond Roman circles – is substantial. Ἐν Χριστῷ the world has become the church 'implicitly,' and is in its way an authentically Christian affair, just as anyone who accepts their own humanity is an 'anonymous' disciple. The church and the world can therefore discern their God-directed future together, as partners in dialogue; each is oriented towards the other in mutual dependence, even if the former may expect to be 'a controversial and rejected institution until the dawn of the absolute future itself . . .'[233] Hans Urs von Balthasar (for whom openness to the world was axiomatic, but who also recognized the church's proclivity to 'paint her cheeks with the changing colours of the world') has pointed to the loss of the distinctively Christian element in much of this dialogue.[234] More recently Walter Kasper

---

[229] 1978a:333 (cf. D. Edwards 1991:11). The problem begins with the way Rahner relates the resurrection to Jesus' death, on the one hand, and to faith on the other (see 1961:66, 7/184f., 17/16ff.). He is too much influenced by Hegel and Schleiermacher, and too quick to connect finitude with death. Cf. W. Pannenberg 2/267ff.

[230] 1978:191 (5/172). Cf. J. Ratzinger: 'Finally, there is only one single all-embracing world-history, which for all the ups and downs, all the forwards and backwards it exhibits, nevertheless has a general direction and goes "forward"' (1979:245; but see also 1988:212ff.). J. R. R. Tolkien offers a quite different perspective: 'Actually I am a Christian, and indeed a Roman Catholic, so that I do not expect "history" to be anything but a "long defeat," though it contains . . . some samples or glimpses of final victory' (*Letters* #195; similarly, B. Horne 1991:168ff.).

[231] 5/161. 'Christianity is a religion of the future. It can indeed be understood only in the light of the future which it conceives as an absolute future gradually approaching the individual and humanity as a whole . . . Absolute future is just another name for what is really meant by "God"' (6/60ff.).

[232] See ibid., and McCool chap. 14.

[233] Ibid. (McCool 347). This is a long way from Teilhardian triumphalism. But cf. P. T. Forsyth 1948:324, who argues that 'the saving faith that makes a Church' does *not* view Christ 'as the pledge of our human future.'

[234] See 1975:199ff. (quotation 1979:111), which contains a powerful description and indictment of 'the broad way' traveled by Rahner and company.

has charged Rahner with 'a complete reversal' of the church's eucharistic foundations, and with ignoring the fact that the Bible's apocalyptic vision

> starts from a continual struggle between the kingdom of God and the kingdom of the world, a conflict which does *not* gradually come to an end with the progress of history, but which, on the contrary, reaches a climax and is intensified as history draws to a close.[235]

On the Protestant side Jürgen Moltmann has broken much more decisively with Teilhard while seeking to recover such a vision.[236] Before we fall in with new companions, however, let us mention two other examples, both from the Americas, of those who have chosen to travel in Teilhard's direction. The main link between them is a shift of allegiance (encouraged by the British scientist, Gregory Bateson) from the cult of progress to the cult of survival, and a willingness in that connection to render the church itself anonymous. When we have remarked on this development we will be in a position to sum up.[237]

'The sacred everything.' That is what Matthew Fox's widely read popularization of Teilhard, *The Coming of the Cosmic Christ*, claims to be about.[238] Fox is not at all shy regarding the change he thinks necessary in Christian faith today: 'I believe that the appropriate symbol of the Cosmic Christ who became incarnate in Jesus is that of Jesus as Mother Earth crucified yet rising daily.'[239] A familiar doctrine of the ascension (owed in part to his *bête noire*, Augustine) helps to accommodate his recommendation. It has a spatial vector, which turns us away from Jesus as a mere man to the ubiquitous divine Christ, and a temporal vector, which gives him back to us in altered form as the one 'who can change history once again and ground that change in a living cosmology.'[240] What is new here, besides the feminine imagery, is concern with the ecological crisis, to which Fox offers the same solution as Sittler: participation in the Christ who is incarnate in all things. He defines this Christ, in words borrowed from Bateson, as 'the pattern that connects.'[241]

---

[235] 1989:125ff. *Veritatis Splendor* (1993) represents in moral theology the very same concern, namely, that today's church is at risk of becoming (in Kasper words) only 'a religiously solemn elevation of the world.' It is noteworthy that the encyclical calls for a return to a distinctly Christian morality in the spirit of *martyrdom*.

[236] This in spite of the fact that he too is a universalist, and working with a symmetrical emanationist cosmology; see 1990:292ff., and 1996 §10f. (cf. Farrow 1998b).

[237] We must pass over the process theologians such as John Cobb, e.g., all of whom contribute in their own way to an 'ascending christology' and an ecclesiology committed to a universal commonwealth of faith communities. See M. Suchoki 1982:93ff. for an overview (on Cobb cf. M. Garascia 1988, G. Boelhower 1988).

[238] 1988:8.

[239] p. 145.

[240] p. 162. Fox (140ff.) tries to correct the cult of progress, on the one hand, and other-worldly mysticism on the other, with a diagonalism of his own.

[241] See 133ff.; cf. Bateson 1980:8f.

The connection that is foremost for Fox is that between the paschal mystery and the suffering planetary ecosystem. Backed by a chorus of mystics ancient and modern, he reminds us that we are *all* Christs,[242] and invites us to recreate the paschal mystery, and indeed the birthing of the church, by sending the Spirit onto the earth for its healing.[243] Teilhard thus stands corrected on one important point. Enthusiasm for the subjugation of the material world over the course of many millennia must give way to something like a full-orbed nature worship, the imminent advent of which may be seen as the longed-for parousia. This lends itself in turn to what Fox calls 'deep ecumenism,'[244] for the sake of which he asks the church to repent of the sin of exclusivism. Christianity must rid itself of oppressive claims to special revelation, for the church of the cosmic Christ is a church which does not allow religion to divide. 'Christ,' says Fox, 'is a generic name' (a thesis which may perhaps serve as a gloss on his recent conversion from Roman Catholicism to Episcopalianism).[245]

While Fox's book frequently borders on self-parody, Juan Luis Segundo's *An Evolutionary Approach to Jesus of Nazareth* requires to be taken much more seriously.[246] Segundo is more interested in the human crisis than the ecological, though he is heavily indebted to theories generated by the latter. Criticizing Teilhard for a linear approach that places too much emphasis on negentropy – that is, for a one-sided view of evolution and a correspondingly shallow anthropology – he seeks to give entropy and death their proper due.[247] The result is a curious synthesis between existentialism and a doctrine of bodily resurrection, which at first glance seems quite promising. In his own search for a christology

---

[242] 'Ironically a commitment to the full spirit of Jesus today requires that we let go of the quest for the historical Jesus and embark on a quest for the Cosmic Christ . . . When this historical Jesus is balanced by the Cosmic Christ, then *we* – and not only Jesus – will be resurrected. We will follow Jesus in becoming true to our vocations as mystic/prophets, as "other Christs"' (161).

[243] 'The issue is survival, and indeed the thriving of Mother Earth. Christianity can assist by, among other things, lending the rich symbolism of the Paschal mystery to the survival of Mother Earth' (149). This lending, admits Fox, means the end of Christianity as we have known it. His book 'names the paschal mystery for the third millennium of Christianity: matricide, mysticism, and the Cosmic Christ reveal anew the paschal story we have understood as the death, resurrection and second coming of Jesus the Christ. The death of Mother Earth (matricide) and the resurrection of the human psyche (mysticism) and the coming of the Cosmic Christ (a living cosmology) name the mystery of the divine cycle of death and rebirth and sending of the Spirit in our time' (3).

[244] See 228f. Origen and Teilhard were both fond of the prefix ὑπέρ, but Fox seems to be fond of ὑπό.

[245] p. 235. From Dorothee Sölle (1982:xvi) he borrows a name for those who insist on something more specific; they are not only fundamentalists but 'christofascists' (7).

[246] Vol. 5 of *Jesus of Nazareth Yesterday and Today*. It is not only the north/south divide which sets Segundo apart from Fox, but his sustained scholarship. He has tempered Teilhard with Bateson in a significant way.

[247] 1988:93ff.; but cf. Teilhard 1964:306ff., 1965:32, 1970:339ff., and our exposition above.

sub specie evolutionis Segundo rejects both the classical tendency to abstract from Jesus a timeless, divine Christ and the modern tendency to allow him to recede into a distant, meaningless past.[248] But in the face of the Where? question he retreats to a position not far from Hegel's. Bodily resurrection does not indicate the restoration of human persons but the definitive manifestation of the value of human projects, a manifestation that takes place in eternity not in time. Jesus, he argues, recapitulates history by lending it meaning precisely *as* a figure of the past.[249]

We cannot turn aside to discuss Segundo's scheme in detail. We do want to notice, however, that there are two things he achieves ecclesiologically by reining in the cosmic Christ and attending to entropy. One is to call the church to a less pretentious form of existence, that is, to a greater participation in the suffering of humanity; the other is to call for its liberation from eccesiastical rigidity so that it may carry out that mission.[250] We might well applaud both these achievements but for the effect of Segundo's christological alternative, which reduces the person to the project.[251] By a parallel logic the church is said to err, not only in entertaining universalist ambitions, but also in seeking to preserve its own identity. If in fact it means to survive at all it must learn 'the lesson taught by evolution' and make flexibility its byword. More specifically, it must not resist 'the hazardous but inevitable immersion in history that takes place through limited, contingent ideologies.'[252] It must be prepared to die and rise constantly, to be stripped of every appearance of continuity. Only so can it effectively 'continue Jesus.'[253] But the church, we respond, is not meant to continue Jesus; it is meant rather to love and serve him.

If Matthew Fox represents an increasingly desperate christological tradition pronouncing its *mea culpa* to a post-modern culture, Segundo

---

[248] 18f., 40f.

[249] ie., as one who 'combined negentropy and entropy in the richest way he could,' and whose own values will in the end prove to be definitive for the meaning of the whole. (This also is his divinity, it seems, for 'God coincides with the meaning of human world,' 103f.) Note that the end in question requires 'the abolition of time,' which Segundo more or less equates with entropy. Here and elsewhere (cf. 98ff., 117ff., 1985:166ff.) he is closer to Teilhard than he lets on.

[250] According to Segundo (106) Teilhard 'prematurely deifies *the Church* along with Jesus;' both are de-historicized by being loosed from the conditions of entropy.

[251] Like his mentors he shares the western tendency to substitute relations in the abstract ('circuitry' to use their own term) for *persons* in relation. Might there also be a distorted trace of Melanchthon's famous dictum, 'to know Christ is to know his benefits'?

[252] See 106f. These contingent ideologies may represent the lesser of two evils in a given situation, which cannot be assessed from afar (Rome). Segundo's theological project is avowedly an experiment in contingency.

[253] Establishing 'the meaningfulness of Jesus' in a given situation does not necessarily entail speaking or even thinking 'in the categories reserved to small groups already united by a particular creed,' concludes Segundo (121f.). Can we not 'encounter the meaning of what happened in the life of Jesus of Nazareth' under other idioms?

can surely be commended for attempting to restore to that same tradition a more profound eschatological tension. In this he fails, however, for the tension he introduces is still not determined *by* Jesus-history but read back into Jesus-history from the examination of cosmic processes. His effort to renew appreciation for the contingent and the particular also fails, and for a similar reason. The naturalization of death in the name of evolution and ecological circuitry, and the correlative revision to the doctrines of resurrection and ascension, still lead to the sublation of the human Jesus and to a domestication of the eucharistic vocation. That the domestication is local rather than global, contingent rather than absolute, only makes the temptation more subtle.[254]

* * *

It is time now to look back, and to assess the situation. In our first main option for a modern doctrine of the ascension a brave counter-claim is made against the threat of pure absence. The course set by Martensen in the wake of Kant, Schleiermacher and Hegel, when fully adjusted to an evolutionary worldview, produces something like the following response to the Where? question: Christ is risen into human history *via* the church, and continues to rise into the entire universe as its unifying principle. His ubiquity is an unfolding ubiquity, his own ascension an ascension by degrees. He is present as one who is coming, as one who is making himself present in a yet grander way than in the incarnation, for he is carrying out the transformation of all nature from dead matter into living spirit. The history of the universe (its ascent from matter to spirit) is the bodily history of the cosmic Christ, who is the real mediator between God and creation. Revelation and redemption must not be fixed in the short history of the human Jesus, even if they are somehow centred there. They entail a process co-extensive with time itself, which, having made its turn round the cross, is now steadily resolving transcendence into immanence, otherness into identity.

For most of its proponents this answer restores to the church something of its dignity as κόσμος of the cosmos. At the same time it lays on the church the obligation to pursue unity *with* the world as well as the unity *of* the world. Its chief theological characteristics are to be found in its universalism, its synergism, and its panentheism, all of which justify us in

---

[254] Segundo, we note, thinks that we should not trouble ourselves over our lack of contemporaneity with Jesus; we can decide well enough what our vocation requires. But it seems to us that contemporaneity with Jesus *is* our vocation. Consider in this light the poignant question posed by *The Mission*: Which missionary domesticated the gospel? The one who died taking up arms to defend the natives against the economic imperialism supported by the church for the sake of its wider 'catholic' interests, or the one who died leading the eucharistic procession?

labelling it as Origenist rather than Irenaean. As for its peculiarly modern features, it should not be overlooked that many of these prove illusory on closer examination. Take the professed appreciation of material and temporal existence, for example, which in Teilhard's case especially is belied by his conicalism and restless grasping at the future.[255] Take too the related observation that theologians today tend to idealize the future, whereas the ancients idealized the past. This distinction, while true, is a trivial one, since in both cases past and future meet and merge in timelessness.[256] Even more illusory, of course, is the notion that the modern version of the Origenist option is somehow legitimized by the science of Copernicus and of Darwin. On the contrary, it neither needs their support nor can claim it. That it owes little or nothing to recent biology in particular is evident from the fact that its fundamentals were already well established in Martensen.[257]

Good reasons for pursuing this option further others may venture to suggest. We have not tried to disguise our own judgment. To perpetuate a discourse on the dead Christ by renaming him the cosmic Christ, bold though it may be, gives every appearance of being a bluff – an evasion of Nietzsche's challenge, not an answer to it. It looks, that is, like an attempt to excuse ourselves from any direct encounter with the real absence. Either that or it hints at something much worse, namely, an attempt to use the church for ends other than those of its founder, in the cynical fashion of the Inquisitor. But we may set this last thought aside. It is already damning enough to point out that the ascension theology which yields the cosmic Christ refuses to allow the Word to remain a man, creation to remain properly distinct from God, or the church to be anything other than a religious expression of the world. Where the ascension is universal there can be no ἐκκλησία.[258] Nothing could be more urgent, then, if indeed we have the welfare of the church at heart, than to put Jesus back into the picture. That is what the other main option attempts to do.

[255] '[I] like the pagan I worship a god who can be touched,' says Teilhard (1965:26f.), 'but to take hold of him as I would wish . . . I must go always on and on through and beyond each undertaking, unable to rest in anything . . .'

[256] Cf. Gunton 1993:85ff. Since the common object is to overcome nature rather than sin, what appears on the modern scheme to be a straight line proves to be but the arc of a great circle. In the words of the ancient collect with which Illingworth finished his essay in *Lux Mundi*, 'all things are returning to perfection through him from whom they took their origin,' and that is a process that will be complete only when growing consciousness 'can peek over the barrier now placed in its way by time' (Segundo 120).

[257] What we have called the Copernican factor could not have arisen in the form that it did were it not for the fact that theology had *already* strayed so far from its christological foundations by the end of the Middle Ages as to render sterile such dialogue with science as it was wont to attempt. See Buckley 341ff.

[258] Insofar as that may be the case, it can aptly be described as a sin against the Holy Spirit, whose own personal identity and activity is also at stake in the question as to the nature and whereabouts of Jesus.

This Same Jesus

There was another Dane, a student and staunch opponent of Martensen, who refused to follow Hegel's rising star. For Søren Kierkegaard the crisis of absence was already urgent in a society where the church still had considerable influence. The reason was not cosmological or epistemological but spiritual, an intuition of fraud: Christ was absent just where he was supposed to be most obviously present, namely, among Christians. Kierkegaard put his finger on the main instruments of the deception, however. 'Incessant talk about world-historical views' and the like had encouraged men 'to start making capital of Christianity' at the expense of its own truth. By converting Christianity into 'a development within the category of the human race,' the uniqueness of the God-man was being sacrificed to the general divinization of the species.[259] Not Jesus himself, but only his lasting influence, was now regarded as important. The great 'calamity in Christendom,' argued Kierkegaard, is that Christ is 'neither the person he was when he lived on earth nor the one he will be at his second coming,' but a 'fantasy God-figure' decked out today in the garb of historical progress.[260] Around that idol was gathered a host of admirers and hangers-on, a false church virtually indistinguishable from the world at large.

Kierkegaard, who is better known for making himself the enemy of the abstract epistemology that allowed for this exchange of theological currency, was also and especially the enemy of an abstract, malleable Christ. To reassert the concrete particularity of Jesus as the object of faith, and so also the costly particularity of anyone who would be Jesus' disciple, was vital. And that required him to deal with the doctrine we are studying. *Practice in Christianity* (which he regarded as the best and truest of his works) shows that he recognized the 'recasting' of the saviour into an object fit for the approval of the masses to rest in part on a triumphalist misreading of the ascension. The book concludes with a series of seven expositions on John 12:32,[261] in which Kierkegaard strives to hold together what others wished to separate: Christ in his humiliation and Christ in his exaltation. The doctrine of the ascension does not permit us to exchange the lowly one for the lofty one, he insisted. These are 'one and the same' and there can be no choosing between them, no letting go of the Jesus who

---

[259] 1991:221; cf. 82. Recognizing in Jesus the intersection of man and God, time and eternity, does indeed make him the central individual, to use Hegel's term, but it also establishes his 'essential heterogeneity' not only to other individuals but to the race.

[260] 'History may be an excellent branch of knowledge, but it must not become so conceited that it undertakes what the Father will do, to array Christ in glory, clothing him in the glittering trappings of results, as if this were the second coming' (1991:31).

[261] The first of these discourses, preached at a communion service in his traumatic and decisive year, 1848, 'substantially determined the whole book' (1991:338; cf. 287).

causes offence in favour of some more winsome Christ – or, worse yet, some pantheistic hallucination about becoming Christ ourselves.[262] Christ's lowliness, the ambiguity of his countenance, the scandal of his suffering, is not merely a fact belonging to the past! It is the form, the only form, his glory takes in a fallen world. Conversely, in his new liberty with the Father he is none other than the one we know in his humility.[263]

Kierkegaard understood, in other words, that Christ's two states could not be set out in a strictly sequential way, since such a scheme would nullify rather than establish the question his life poses to us. Like Irenaeus he refused to interpret the ascension as marking a triumphant new phase in *our* history. The ascension did not signal the beginning, but the boundary, of Jesus' association with fallen humanity. It did not cancel, but confirmed, the possibility of taking offence at him.

> Christ is the only one who can make his life a test for all people. The examination period begins with his ascension; it has lasted for eighteen hundred years and may last eighteen thousand. But (and this belongs to the intervening period as an examination) he is coming again.[264]

To take up such a position was of course to repudiate *inter alia* the whole view of history which had been evolving in the neo-Joachimite tradition of Lessing. His alternative was a stark one:

> From now on the human race will no longer be led on by prophets and judges but forced back by martyrs, who will run headlong against that human discovery, progress. Otherwise there can be no progress: in intensity. The problem is set, once and for all; there is nothing further to add . . . The result of human progress is that everything becomes thinner and thinner – the result of divine providence is to make everything more inward.[265]

The positive aspect of this alternative, which is bound up with the question of inwardness, can be comprehended only if we take account of his

---

[262] 1991:160ff.; cf. *JP* 2/2004 (Hong and Hong).

[263] See discourses IV and V (1991:181ff.). Kierkegaard attends to both aspects of the Son's descent – i.e., in becoming a man, and then in going out into our distorted world as a servant. At his ascension Jesus 'begins a second time from on high,' exalted above that distortion. This compels those who wish to follow him here and now to 'begin at the very same place, from the beginning,' *viz.*, with his abasement (209). Cf. Bonhoeffer 106ff.

[264] 1991:202. For now, the ascension binds us to the cross – not, as in Hegel, to the *idea* of the cross but to the actual scandal of the cross. For the one who will return in glory will be 'the same Jesus,' 'the lowly man' (9, 24).

[265] Dru #787. 'Is this Christianity's view of the present world: it is an evil, sinful world, but for that reason Christianity has come into the world to transform the world, and therefore God's purpose and aim is to get a nice, congenial world out of this world and let it stand? Or is not Christianity based more upon the following view: This present world has come into existence through a fall away from God, exists against his will, and every day it exists it is against his will; he wants to have it back again?' (*JP* 2/1940)

remarkable notion of contemporaneity – what Kierkegaard called 'the central thought of my life.'[266]

'Out with history,' came his protest of 1848, 'in with the situation of contemporaneity.'[267] This was not merely a hermeneutical proposal, an invitation to leap Lessing's ditch in pursuit of a more primitive form of Christianity. Nor was it a flight from historical existence as such. On the contrary, it was a choice *between* histories, an assertion about the ontic priority of a particular history:

> It is indeed eighteen hundred years since Jesus Christ walked here on earth, but this is certainly not an event just like other events, which once they are over pass into history and then, as the distant past, pass into oblivion. No, his presence here on earth never becomes a thing of the past, thus does not become more and more distant – that is, if faith is at all to be found upon the earth; if not, well, then in that very instant it is a long time since he lived.[268]

For Kierkegaard, contemporaneity was at once an act of faith and a genuine co-existence with Jesus of Nazareth, predicated not on the powers of the human intellect or imagination, much less on any supposed extension or prolongation or repetition of the incarnation, but on the absoluteness of Jesus-history *per se*. It meant the real human proximity to him of every true disciple in spite of the march of history. Properly understood, history itself could serve no greater purpose than to provide the occasion for this proximity. Properly understood, time (i.e., time for being human) was governed by this proximity or at least by its possibility, and so by the question of inwardness.[269]

Kierkegaard's concern with contemporaneity and with inwardness was not a form of 'acosmism' or of fideism, though he rejected all *a priori* cosmological and epistemological controls on Christianity.[270] It is therefore fair to observe that a host of questions cry out for answers which, in his passion for the paradoxical nature of faith in Christ, he made little attempt to give. We will not try to speak for him, except to repeat that it is only by way of pneumatology that we can hope to lend coherence to the various

---

[266] 1956:242

[267] *JP* 1/691. See G. Malantschuk (1974:251ff., 348f.) on the development of this concept.

[268] 1991:9. In this light cf. Rom. 10:5ff.

[269] Contemporaneity with Christ is a *relational* possibility, actualized on our side through personal choice and 'prodigious exertion' (*JP* 1/695). Those who were Jesus' historical contemporaries may therefore have lacked true contemporaneity, while those who live at a distance historically can still obtain it, though precisely not at second hand: 'That with which you are living simultaneously is actuality – for you. Thus every human being is able to become contemporary only with the time in which he is living – and then with one more, with Christ's life upon earth, for Christ's life upon earth, the sacred history, stands alone by itself, outside history.' (1991:64; see 23ff.) It is important to add that the sacred history stands alone not because it *negates* time, or is somehow a-historical, but because here and only here time is linked with eternity, the life of man with the life of God.

[270] Cf. 1968:305, *JP* 3/195 (also M. Rae 1997:123ff., 148 n. 21). The case was otherwise with modern heirs like Bultmann; see J. Moltmann 1996:259f.

levels on which his doctrine of contemporaneity appears to operate. Pneumatology, of course, is less evident in Kierkegaard than in Calvin.[271] Yet it was from this highly unusual Lutheran that the latter's abortive effort to address the Where? question finally received the fresh impetus it required. Our *time* as well as our space was made relative to Jesus' own. Obviously Kierkegaard was not much concerned with the Where? question for its own sake, or even for that of the eucharist.[272] It was in correcting the faulty answer to the more important Who? question (Who is Jesus, and who then are his true disciples?) that he made the breakthrough. Yet he it was who turned most decisively from the whole western enterprise of trying to fit Jesus spacelessly into our time, who indeed turned the Where? question inside out.

Let us explain as far as Kierkegaard allows us to. Christ, as the ascended one and the coming one, puts himself as a question to each of us. It is we who must be fitted into him, our history that is being judged by his. The one who has ascended on high is the absolute; the rest can only be understood in relation to him.[273] To take seriously the fact that Christ has ascended to the Father is not to say that he is everywhere, or nowhere, or somewhere else, but that he is with us in this twofold way: He is there, in first-century Palestine, and there again, at the parousia. Because he is with the Father, he is before us and after us; only so is he with us.[274] He is with us precisely as a question put to our very existence, so that we too must decide with Pilate – and under essentially the same circumstances – 'What shall I do with Jesus, who is called the Christ?'[275]

---

[271] But see Rae 168ff. on Kierkegaard's appeal to the Spirit for the epistemological revolution that enables conversion. Perhaps the same appeal is in order when the discussion is broadened beyond epistemology?

[272] We note, however, that his view of the eucharist is remarkably close to Calvin's in some respects (cf. 1991:155f.), and that his contemporaneity doctrine is set over against the notion of ubiquity. Echoing Calvin's language about a 'fantastic Christ-figure,' he remarks: 'But now we must really cross out Christendom's fantasies. We proceed to the situation of contemporaneity' (99; cf. 274).

[273] 'Christ as the absolute explodes all the relativity in which we human beings live' (1991:332). He is in 'the context of completion,' we are not: 'Let us talk altogether humanly about it; he has passed his test, has developed the prototype [*Forbillede*], is now on high; it is just the same as when someone has passed his test and now as one who has finished is occupied in guiding others' (183f.).

[274] This 'is' cannot be reduced to a 'was' and a 'will be,' though these expressions are also true (cf. Rev. 1:8, 17:8). Likewise, it is true that Christ, since he has departed to the Father, is not here but elsewhere; or again, that 'invisible on high, he is also present everywhere, occupied with drawing all to himself' (1991:155). But this activity on high is not a *separate* activity. It is to and through his own earthly history that he draws us: 'His life on earth accompanies the human race and accompanies each particular generation as the eternal history' (64).

[275] Matt. 27:22; cf. 1991:203ff. We should observe here that the 'before' and the 'after' are much more than temporal concerns; in keeping with Kierkegaard's relational ontology, they are the 'behind' of Christ's abasement and the 'ahead' of his glory (238f.), which transcend and transform our temporal categories. But we should also notice the implications

Now when this line of thought is pressed the outlines of a eucharistic cosmology begin to re-emerge, as Kierkegaard himself may have realized. 'If I dare to put it this way,' he said, 'this form of existence makes the Church's whole existence here upon earth into a parenthesis or something parenthetical in Christ's life . . .'[276] But his most urgent task was to apply his insight directly to the struggle with the Church of Denmark, over which Hans Martensen was soon to be presiding bishop. He saw immediately that the concept of contemporaneity demanded 'neither more nor less than a revision of Christianity,' a sweeping revision that meant 'getting rid of 1800 years as if they had never been.'[277] His famous *Attack Upon Christendom*, in intensity leaving nothing to Nietzsche, testifies to the seriousness with which he could make such a statement. If contemporaneity with the despised and crucified One were the real truth of Christianity, then the comfortable legacy of the established church was a lie, and had been from the beginning. Christianity was impossible under the conditions of universality and worldly success for which it yearned, which amounted to contemporaneity not with Christ but with the rabble who murdered him.

Kierkegaard's response was to underscore both the eschatological qualification of ecclesial being that belongs to its parenthetical situation, and the principle of particularity.[278] A century before Teilhard, he too announced that Christianity stood at the crossroads, only the path to which he pointed led in the opposite direction. Any thought of 'marching forward triumphantly *en masse*' makes a mockery of the church.[279] 'Christianity does not join men together – no, it separates them – in order to unite every single individual with God;' and having done so it brings

---

for his philosophy of history. Kierkegaard held to the *homogeneity* of the present age in this sense: that it provides the 'element' in which we are tested and our answer to Christ is elicited. We are 'situated between his abasement . . . and his loftiness' (153), neither moving away from the one nor towards the other. The world 'is going neither forward nor backward; it remains essentially the same, like the sea . . .' (232).

[276] 1991:202.

[277] Quoted Malantschuk 348. Kierkegaard found proof in the fruits of Lutheranism that Luther 'did not go back far enough, did not make a person contemporary enough with Christ' (*JP* 1/691; cf. Dru #1298).

[278] The way these ideas are combined is problematic. So far does he carry the principle of particularity that he can even suggest that the problem with the church that led to 'Christendom' began with the mass conversion at Pentecost (*JP* 2/2056; cf. 2/1997, 1989:8f., 1956:34f.). This should be seen, however, in the context of his war with the Danish church and especially with Hegel, for whom (a) the 'universal divine human' supplants the 'individual divine human,' making the church even more divine than Jesus, and (b) eschatology is the very thing that must be overcome in passing from the religious imagination to pure philosophy. See Jamros 285ff.

[279] 1936:91; cf. *JP* 2/2004, 3/2712, 1991:81. Balthasar (1975:203) begins an account of his disillusionment with the broad way by remarking, 'To my misfortune, however, I had read Kierkegaard in my youth . . .' It is a pity that Teilhard apparently did not share this misfortune.

them into *collision* with human society.[280] That, he said, is a problem Christendom attempts to solve 'in the following utterly simple manner: it makes being a Christian into a qualification of the species so that all collisions fall away.' But for Kierkegaard (and this is what most distinguishes his ecclesiology from the tradition we have been considering) the only path towards genuine ecclesial existence leads rather to a clear break with the species.[281] Passing as it does through the narrow gate of *den Enkelte*, the single individual, it forbids every attempt to find comfort in numbers, in 'the collective, the association, the community, the parish,' even in the church as such.[282]

His was a call to isolation, not to unity. The parenthetical situation is a time of testing and testing belongs precisely to the individual: to the solitary, abandoned individual. The church militant can never truly be a social reality, then; 'the congregation does not really come until eternity.'[283] Here of course we must ask whether Kierkegaard really had an alternative. Since he opposed to the 'bewildering multiplicity' not the homogenous whole but one heterogenous part, namely, Jesus of Nazareth,[284] he quite rightly repudiated every 'leveling' or homogenizing tendency. But his analysis shares with that of his opponents a quite basic flaw. By associating the individual with time and the ecclesial congregation with eternity, he shows that – in spite of his loyalty to the human Jesus and his war against monism – he has not entirely overcome his heritage. For the most part Kierkegaard fights Luther with Luther, if not Kant with Kant; thus in rejecting the collectivist error he apparently falls back into its individualist counterpart,[285] preparing the way for that radically un-ecclesial misappropriation of his thought by modern existentialism.

It would not be fair to part company with Kierkegaard on this note, however, for he does not intend to do away with the notion of a temporal Christian community altogether. Rather, the category of the single individual serves as 'a middle term in order to make sure that "community" and

---

[280] *JP* 2/2052, 2080ff. See 1989:153f. for an indication of his dialectic here; *both* sin and salvation 'split people up into individuals.'

[281] *JP* 2/2080. Kierkegaard (2/2054) attacks the notion that Christ came to save the race: '"Race" is a category of corruption and to be saved means to be saved out of the race.' As for 'Christendom,' whether in Roman or Protestant form (1956:xvi, 34) it comes to a false synthesis with society that actually abolishes Christianity.

[282] *JP* 2/2044 (cf. 2038, 2074).

[283] Struggling, he says, 'is always done by single individuals, because spirit is precisely this, that everyone is an individual before God, that "fellowship" is a lower category than "the single individual," which everyone can and should be.' The congregation 'does not belong in time but belongs first in eternity, where it is, at rest, the gathering of all the single individuals who endured in the struggle and passed the test' (1991:223; cf. *JP* 2/2011).

[284] 1991:152, 157, 223f.; cf. *JP* 2/2010.

[285] See e.g. *JP* 2/2008: 'The task is precisely to work oneself out of sociality more and more, but genuinely and truly, to be able to maintain longer and longer the thought of God-present-with-me.' But here see Rae 144ff.

"congregation" are not taken in vain as synonymous with [the] public, the crowd, etc.'[286] It allows him to place the stress on the church's eschatological nature and orientation over against the givenness of merely temporal institutions[287] – and to make the crucial point, much needed in our time, that in the species of which *God* is also a specific member the whole is not, nor ever can be, greater than the part.[288] Kierkegaard, moreover, does post signs pointing in a more promising direction than sheer individualism. As Michael Plekon observes, he even criticizes the Augsburg Confession for failing to grasp the nub of the ecclesiology of the Apostles' Creed, which is to be found in the notion of the *communio sanctorum*.[289] That is quite in keeping with his rejection of an abstract ecclesiology in which the church is regarded as a person, a third party so to speak, rather than as a fellowship of persons.[290] It may also be connected to his early conviction (never consistently followed up but never abandoned) that the eucharist, dynamically understood as a relational act, provides the proper starting point for ecclesiology.[291]

For all that, Kierkegaard's ecclesiology certainly suffers from the weakness noted, and from his failure to think more deliberately in trinitarian terms. Did he himself not desire another and better way, an escape from the polarization between the individual and the collective?

> How dreadful it is when everything historical vanishes before a diseased probing of one's own miserable history! Who will show us the middle course between being devoured by one's own reflections, as though one were the only man who ever had existed or ever would exist, and – seeking a worthless consolation in the *commune naufragium* of mankind? That is really what the doctrine of an ecclesia should do.[292]

---

[286] *JP* 1/595; but cf. 2/2008.

[287] Cf. *JP* 1/593, 2/2011. See especially 1991:201ff., where for christological reasons he rejects all false anticipations of eternity.

[288] Kierkegaard treated the central problem of the human race as a conspiracy to cover up the peculiar honour it derives from Christ: i.e., that here the part is indeed greater than the whole; that one is of infinitely more value than a thousand. This we would learn, he says, if we allowed ourselves to be questioned – contemporaneously, as martyrs are questioned – by that Single Individual who took his stand *for* the race by standing over against it. But we will not. Instead we band together, as if to intimidate God by our numbers, and crucify Christ anew (*JP* 2/2004, 2006, *passim*).

[289] *JP* 1/600; cf. Plekon 1992:220.

[290] Kierkegaard (*JP* 1/603) points to the tendency 'to get an abstraction between God and oneself' as a kind of buffer. 'Such an abstraction today is "the Church." Men have hit upon making it into a person . . .'

[291] *JP* 5/5089, 28 May 1835 (Plekon 219). 'Even in the late years, 1850–55, during the attack on the Danish Church and society, there is no criticism of the sacraments themselves, but only of their abuse,' argues Plekon, who points to a number of passages which suggest a 'rich and nuanced theology of the eucharist.' (These include *JP* 1/450, which refers to a brotherhood with Christ 'which is the condition for our brotherhood with men.')

[292] Dru #163; cf. *JP* 1/586 for another pointer, in eucharistic terms, towards this middle course.

In order to find it we must take up a yet more robust eschatology than Kierkegaard's, one less tainted by the remnants of dualism, while pursuing a trinitarian foundation for thinking Christianly about human being. That will require, *inter alia*, allowing the doctrine of ascension in the flesh to fill out the content of the doctrine of the incarnation, something Kierkegaard only began to do rather late in the day. Towards these goals we may hope to make some progress by turning to Karl Barth.

* * *

'We begin with Jesus Christ.'[293] The works of Barth breathe a loyalty to the Man of Nazareth that none can mistake. To begin again at the beginning was what Kierkegaard, in the end, called on us to do. Barth made that call his vocation. Indeed he turned it into a method which guided the dogmatic enterprise back towards its historic roots.[294] After the heady days of the *Romans* rebellion, there followed a more concerted effort 'to understand Jesus Christ and bring him from the periphery of my thought into the centre.'[295] And that led in the climactic fourth volume of the *Church Dogmatics* (unquestionably the greatest of modern theological enterprises) to an extensive treatment of descending and ascending.

Before we come to that, however, we want to take stock of Barth's preoccupation with the problem of contemporaneity. From the first edition of *Romans* to the last sections of the unfinished *Dogmatics* it crops up again and again, this feature or that appearing in a fresh light.[296] Since the issue is at bottom a relational one, it has always to be confronted existentially and even hamartiologically. Barth therefore followed Kierkegaard in superimposing on the cosmological question a more personal one: 'how will it stand with us when we are alongside Jesus Christ and follow him, when we are in his environment and time and space?'[297] Yet he was quite prepared to speak to the cosmological question as well, not only because he wished to avoid anything that smacked of mere psychologism, but for the sake of his monumental struggle to proclaim Jesus as the one Word of God.

---

[293] CD 4/3:1.
[294] 'Dogmatics is possible only as *theologia crucis*, in the act of obedience which is certain in faith, but which for this very reason is humble, always being thrown back to the beginning and having to make a fresh start' (1/1:14; see E. Jüngel 1986:18f.). Cf. Kierkegaard 1991:201ff.
[295] Quoted E. Busch 1976:173. See the preface to CD 1/1, which expresses a concern to get beyond Kierkegaard, of whose own evolution Barth took little notice in his effort to overcome both historicism and psychologism.
[296] A decisive turn was taken early on, when Barth repented of the fact that in *Romans* 'play was made and even work occasionally done with the idea of a revelation permanently transcending time, merely bounding time and determining it from without' (CD 1/2:250).
[297] 4/1:293 (capitalization altered here and elsewhere); see 286ff., 348.

There is no need for us to recount that struggle, which has distinguished Barth as a modern Irenaeus. Its most famous front, to be sure, is not the issue of contemporaneity or even the controversial 'hermeneutics of contemporaneity,' but the broad assault launched on natural theology. Here more than anywhere, as if the lessons of the *Kirchenkampf* were already forgotten, critics have tended to neglect Barth's primary objective. The repudiation of any breach between the Word and Jesus (of docetism and its political consequences) is what led him to refuse to every other constituent part of creation, or to creation as a whole, the dignity of being called revelation in its own right:

> Not the cosmos is the Son or Word of God, but the unique One whom he sends into the world as his Son and therefore his Word. Not every man is a Christ, but Jesus of Nazareth alone.[298]

But if Jesus is truly God's self, as the church confesses, no genuine communion with God can be had outside of his company; in fact, outside of his company the integrity and viability of every other creature is put in doubt.[299] Contemporaneity thus becomes crucial. Barth's regard for the church's answer to the Who? question led him to the twofold conviction 'that we have no other time than the time God has for us, and . . . that God has no other time for us than the time of his revelation,' namely, Jesus-history.[300] To uphold that conviction it was necessary to think creatively about the most basic structures of our existence in christological terms, and to give answer to the Where? question from within christology's own resources.[301]

According to Barth, if Jesus is the eternal Lord (*vere Deus*) in time and for time (*vere homo*), he is also the Lord *of* time. He is not merely an occupant of time but also its master; not merely a recipient and as such a co-creator of his own time, but also the mediator, redeemer and consummator of our times.[302] The twofold relation that constitutes his

---

[298] 'Not all peoples are Israel. Not all societies are the community of the Lord. Not all writings are Holy Scripture . . .' Indeed, 'theology is not a universal science' (4/3:222). If then there are penultimate words, and there are, that is *what* they are; they have their truth from him who is the truth (122f.).

[299] 3/2:148f. 'At no level or time can we have to do with God without also having to do with this man' (4/2:33). There is 'no knowledge of God . . . no single movement towards him, which on any pretext or in any way can escape his humanity . . . There is, therefore, no natural religion, no natural theology, no natural law' – where '"natural" means apart from Jesus Christ.' (101)

[300] 1/2:45. The same can be said of space, but Barth viewed time as the more fundamental category, since the content of revelation seemed to suggest that.

[301] 'We must not let ourselves be told what time is,' he says, 'by revelation itself' (ibid.; cf. 2/1:611ff.). *Pace* R. Roberts (Sykes 1979:88ff.) this programme does not have its weakness in Barth's rejection of natural theology, but in his partial succumbing to the same; see below.

[302] 3/2:437ff. Major discussions of time can be found in each volume; see e.g. §§14, 31.3, 41.1, 47, 59.3, 69.2. Notice that the relational dimension requires distinctions between creation time, fallen time, and fulfilled time – i.e., Jesus-history, which consummates the first while dissolving the second (cf. 1/2:49, 2/1:623ff., 3/1:71ff.).

own existence – his radical openness to his Father and also to us – 'makes the barrier of his time on every side a gateway.'[303] Here is Barth's version of the doctrine of recapitulation, which he refused to convert into an Omega-point theory. Jesus-history, as the life of God in time, is 'the centre, beginning and end of all the times,' which derive their own possibilites from him and his time.[304] So thoroughly was Barth convinced of this that he could even claim that our present age has its final term *behind* it, in the cross of Jesus. So much for the cult of progress![305]

Barth's reworking of temporal categories to accommodate the enormous implications of the incarnation is a worthy subject of study in itself. But in the first instance it was intended to bar the door against any attempt to establish a relationship with God apart from Jesus, to find God behind Jesus, or to abstract from Jesus an immanent divinity of another sort – including and especially a λόγος ἄσαρκος, which Kierkegaard had already rejected and which Barth regarded (together with its corollary, the *analogia entis*) as an invention of antichrist.[306] It was also intended to declare in no uncertain terms the unity of creation and redemption:

> By the Word the world exists. A marvellous reversal of our whole thinking! Don't let yourselves be led astray by the difficulty of the time-concept, which might well result from this. The world came into being, it was created and sustained by the little child that was born in Bethlehem, by the Man who died on the Cross of Golgotha, and the third day rose again. *That* is the Word of creation, by which all things were brought into being.[307]

In short, Barth confessed the human Jesus, in his own space-time concreteness, to be the cosmic Christ.[308] Here indeed was 'a decisive turn

[303] 1/2:45; cf 3/2:440: 'The two-fold answer which he gives, to God on the one hand and to men on the other, makes him the Contemporary of all men . . .'

[304] The time of Jesus Christ is 'the time of man in its whole extent.' And yet: 'It is as a man of his time, and not otherwise, that he is the Lord of time. We should lose Jesus as the Lord of all time if we ignored him as a man in his own time' (3/2:440f.).

[305] 'The last time is the time of the world and human history and all men to which a term is already set in the death of Jesus and which can only run to this appointed end' (4/3:295). More positively, and with the resurrection in view: 'When we say Jesus Christ, this is not a possibility which is somewhere ahead of us, but an actuality which is already behind us. With this name in our hearts and on our lips, we are not laboriously toiling uphill, but merrily coming down' (4/2:46).

[306] 'Under the title of a λόγος ἄσαρκος we pay homage to a *Deus absconditus* and therefore to some image of God which we have made for ourselves' (CD 4/1:52; cf. Kierkegaard *JP* 2/2088, 4/4794). This really is *the* insight expounded, not only by §57, but in the whole of the *Dogmatics*, namely, that 'in Jesus Christ we really have to do with the first and eternal Word of God at the beginning of all things,' and at their middle and end as well (4/1:50; cf. 2/2:94ff.).

[307] 1949:57f.; cf. CD 3/2:456: 'There is no god called Chronos. And it is better to avoid conceptions of time which might suggest that there is.'

[308] His own word is *concretissimum* (cf. Dalferth [Sykes 1989] 27ff.). Not until CD 4/3:756 does Barth speak directly of 'a third form of existence of Jesus Christ' as the cosmic Lord. This may be a weakness that requires correction (Gunton 1992:95). But the point to be made here is that this third form is *not* a third alongside his divinity and humanity, but

in the direction of the particular,' to use Eberhard Jüngel's expression.[309] If we do not wish to make it we must part company with Barth almost straight away. For him Jesus-history is 'the history which overlaps all others,' and without that overlap God's address to man, which constitutes man as man, disappears without a trace; so too does God's word to the rest of creation and the very possibility of the church.[310] Of his massive theological output hardly anything compelling remains if on this point there is simply incredulity or outright rejection.

It may be doubted, of course, whether Barth had a clear map of the difficult terrain he was opening up. Even his most conscious conceptual adjustments (his actualism, e.g., or his evolving account of eternity) are far from being unproblematic. The same must be said of the pneumatological exposition offered in support of so bold a christology. But what especially interests us is the fact that the whole burden of Barth's doctrine of contemporaneity, and of his witness to Jesus as the one true and sufficient Word of God, comes to rest on eschatology. For the message of the resurrection and ascension which runs throughout the New Testament 'is the mainstay of everything.'[311] To his handling of that message we must now give our close attention.

* * *

Barth's eschatological interests were stimulated by Nietzsche's friend, Franz Overbeck, and by the two Blumhardts.[312] Overbeck had fearlessly denounced the confusion of Christianity with cultural progress and the substitution of human optimism for eschatology, which he regarded as the very essence of Christianity. Reading Overbeck after the Great War helped to sharpen the focus of Barth's own disillusionment with the consequences of that confusion and substitution. In the second edition of *Romans* he broke publicly with the prevailing academic approach to dogmatics, which could only treat biblical eschatology as a kind of foreign body.[313] Here was a decision about the ground of theology itself. If

---

alongside his self-existence and his relation to the church. In his relation to the cosmos, as to the church, he remains the God-man, ruling both through the Spirit. Cf. Lyons 57.

[309] Jüngel 1986:19. See Hunsinger 14ff., who, drawing on R. Jenson, points up the connection between Barth's particularism and the matters we have been discussing: 'Veiled behind Barth's appeal to the particularity of Jesus (veiled perhaps even partially to himself) is the extent to which all dimensions of "temporality" are subjected to radical reinterpretation according to christological and trinitarian modes of thought' (see also 236ff.).

[310] See CD 4/3:223ff.; cf. H. Hartwell 1964:109.

[311] CD 1/2:23.; cf. 4/1:324. There is no *theologia crucis* without a *theologia resurrectionis* (4/2:355).

[312] See Jüngel 54ff.

[313] See e.g. 1968:314f. (cf. D. Migliore's introduction to *The Göttingen Dogmatics*, LVIIff.).

theology was to be done at all, Barth decided, it must be done in and for the church; criticism was to derive from confession of the risen Lord, not confession from criticism.[314] And theology, like all things human, *could* be done (even if Overbeck did not appear to think so) precisely because of the resurrection. The resurrection made contemporaneity possible, and contemporaneity made theology possible.

A new and very different kind of optimism thus began to permeate Barth's own work. It was fed by the Blumhardts, whom he had already encountered, and from whom he learned in word and deed to reckon with the living Jesus as Lord.[315] Barth now aimed at a theology that would 'dare to become eschatology,'[316] indeed, a theology that would think Christianly on the basis of the fact that in and with Jesus of Nazareth our human nature has been exalted to God. In that sense his entire project moved in the direction of a theology of the ascension, one quite different than those we have been examining.[317]

Overbeck had accused liberal theologians, who were unable to confess the risen Lord or to live in expectation of his return, of living with a corpse: the corpse of Christianity.[318] Barth, for his part, grew increasingly bold about testifying afresh to the Easter events and to their dogmatic implications:

> The knowledge which the apostles acquired on the basis of Christ's resurrection, the conclusion of which is the ascension of Christ, is essentially this basic knowledge that the reconciliation which took place in Jesus Christ is not some casual story, but that in this work of God's grace we have to do with the word of *God's omnipotence*, that here an ultimate and supreme thing comes into action, behind which there is no other reality.[319]

In other words, the ground of the church's conviction about Jesus as the Son of God is the Easter revelation that here is a specific human life that exists purely out of divine possibilities. It is a life that in and through the resurrection has 'the power of divine *presence*,' and in that way declares itself as divine.[320]

Barth recognized, of course, that besides an outright denial of the resurrection there is a way of treating it which more or less discreetly reopens the breach between Jesus and God that he was determined to close. It does so by introducing a breach between Jesus and Jesus. That is

---

[314] Theology 'from above' was really theology 'from inside' (Jüngel 59).

[315] See *CD* 4/3:168ff. Barth (1979:22) described the younger Blumhardt, whom he first met in 1907, as a 'priestly person.'

[316] Quoted Jüngel 62.

[317] For Barth the doctrine of the ascension is the whole work of reconciliation as seen from the side of man; it is the subject in particular of *CD* 4/2. Interestingly, both he and Teilhard (cf. H. de Lubac 1967:244) regarded their own work as potentially 'a piece of the "last things."'

[318] Jüngel 60.

[319] 1949:126.

[320] Ibid. 131; see *CD* 3/2:447ff. (esp. 463f.), 511ff.; cf. 4/1:324.

the way of Teilhard de Chardin (whose *Milieu divin* Barth once described as 'a giant gnostic snake')[321] and indeed of all who deny resurrection and ascension in the flesh. Provoked by Rudolf Bultmann in particular, but also by more moderate figures such as Emil Brunner, Barth mounted an assault on what he rightly regarded as eschatological docetism. The resurrection and ascension took place 'in the body.' If the identity of Jesus was not to be left indeterminate, that had to be insisted upon.[322] Barth's view of the resurrection and ascension was not a naïve one, however, of the sort that Bultmann loved to complain about. Jesus did not just get up and carry on, so to speak, then float away into the heavens. The resurrection was an event with 'retroactive force.'[323] Employing a logic we will examine later, Barth interpreted it as a process of exaltation *identical* with, and yet transcending, the course of Jesus' earthly life from conception to cross. It was, so to speak, the very same personal history and reality all over again in a new way. As such it involved a transfiguration of Jesus-history rather than an addition to it.[324] Barth went so far as to divide Jesus' life into two corresponding 'sides,' the thirty years and the forty days of resurrection appearances, insisting that each is really the whole under a different (and, in the latter case, refracted) aspect. The one history has its climax on the cross, the other in the ascension, yet they are a single event. On no account must ascending be torn away from descending and made over into another Christ who is something other than 'this same Jesus.' In thus rejecting the notion of two successive states Barth did not mean to deny sequence altogether, of course. Life follows death, exaltation humiliation, just as the forty days follow the thirty years. But what follows *is* what precedes, in a new way.[325] Resurrection time is not our time, time which merely continues as before. And for that reason it does not add or subtract anything from Christ's identity; rather it engages with our time as the time of the *revelation* of that identity.[326]

---

[321] 1981:116.

[322] CD 3/2:448, 4/2:143. 'Every kind of Docetism is impossible and forbidden' (4/2:36).

[323] Barth (CD 4/3:298) uses this expression to indicate that the impact of the resurrection on the *world*, as the announcing and effecting of its reconciliation to God in Christ, includes the whole scope of history. But we may use it also, and analogously, to speak of the relation between Jesus' life before the cross and afterwards, of the fact that his pre-history participates in his post-history and *vice versa* (4/1:313). That is not to say with Pannenberg (1968:135ff.), however, that the resurrection 'realizes' Jesus' divinity (cf. 4/3:314).

[324] It is not *another* someone, nor is it simply a further set of events in the same someone's life. It is 'an absolutely new coming of the One who came before' (CD 4/3:308). There is sequence and correspondence, but neither extension nor mere repetition. See 4/1:309ff., 4/2:150, 4/3:310ff. (cf. M. Hoogland 3f.).

[325] Cf. CD 3/2:441f., 4/1:309ff., 342f., 4/2:150. Barth (4/1:132ff.) explains his rejection of two consecutive states in favour of 'two sides or directions or forms' in connection with his actualist interpretation of the doctrine of the two natures; see below.

[326] See CD 4/2:132ff. In resurrection time the *man* Jesus is manifested in the mode of God (3/2:448). 'The resurrection and ascension of Jesus Christ are the completed revelation of

Barth thus attacked eschatological docetism with a dialectic of continuity and discontinuity that doubled as a theology of revelation. The resurrection, if not mere resuscitation, was certainly something more than a subjective faith experience or a purely spiritual encounter with Jesus. It was a new coming of Jesus himself with his humanity intact and his divinity no longer veiled. It was the time in which God was clearly seen and known to live as this man, and this man as God. It was *parousia* time: the time of Jesus made contemporaneous with all times, the time of 'his manifestation in effective presence in the world.'[327] Nor did the final episode of that time – the ascension which set a definite limit to it, preserving its particularity – negate his presence. On the contrary, it signaled that his presence, though now hidden, is hidden with God; that his time, his human living and dying, belongs to God. And by fixing it with God, it fixed it at the heart of every time.[328]

This brings us to the Where? question, to which Barth gave a response not unlike Kierkegaard's. In one sense Jesus remains right where he was, since his resurrection life is not an extension of his life with us, but rather its vindication and manifestation. That is why the question must indeed be turned around, becoming a question about *our* whereabouts in relation to his. Barth went so far as to claim that it is we who belong to the past, not Jesus, since we are the ones whose time and space are still slipping away from us:

> Jesus Christ's having come . . . would answer to what we term the past. But how inappropriate it would be to say of that event that it was past. What Jesus suffered and did is certainly not past; it is rather the old that is past, the world of man, the world of disobedience and disorder, the world of misery, sin and death . . . Sin and death *did* exist, and the whole of world history, including that which ran its course *post Christum*, right down to our day, *existed*. All that is past in Christ . . . But Jesus Christ sitteth beside the Father, as He who has suffered and has risen from the dead. That is the present.

It is we who belong to the past. That is why, from our vantage point, Jesus is absent as well as present; why this is 'in a certain respect' the

---

Jesus Christ which corresponds to his completed work' (4/2:141). 'His coming again as the Revealer of the reconciliation effected in him includes this sphere or time of ours within itself' (4/3:333). In doing so it alters our time too; for it is a real coming and not merely the 'noetic converse' of his first coming (4/1:304).

[327] *wirksame Gegenwart* (CD 4/3:293; cf. 4/1:316). For Barth the parousia, though a single event (3/2:490), has a threefold form – the resurrection, the outpouring of the Spirit, and the final coming.

[328] CD 3/2:454f., 4/1:316ff. Limits belong to the creaturely, whether in time or eternity, though in eternity limits are not *barriers* (3/2:438f., 463f.). As birth and death delimit Jesus' time ἐν σαρκί, so the empty tomb and the ascension delimit his time ἐν πνεύματι, we might say. Barth's inclusion of 'natural death' (3/2:639) as proper to the creature is, however, a warning signal that the position he is taking is not entirely Irenaean.

time of the church's loneliness on earth.[329] That is why we must not give to the Where? question an answer of our own, which could never be anything but a false answer. Rather we must wait (*warten und eilen!*) for Jesus himself as the one who will come again. His present is our future.[330]

On the other hand, Barth's response had a more optimistic thrust than Kierkegaard's. Grounding contemporaneity in the resurrection (which for Barth signified the concord of time with eternity and hence the participation of the resurrected one in every time) meant that all of us simply *are* in Jesus' environment, and he in ours. The overlap between his history and ours is not something to be striven for. Contemporaneity is 'not a problem' in Lessing's sense or even in Kierkegaard's, nor yet in that of the sacramentalists. It is a given.[331] To make such a claim is really only to say with the creed that Jesus is in heaven; that he alone has entered that side of creation on which its true potential is realized; that he alone has secure and concrete reality; that he himself is the *concretissimum*, whose presence is in fact more real than our own.[332] Of course, to say 'he alone' is also to insist with the creed that Jesus is with God absolutely, that in the resurrection and ascension God has laid claim to Jesus-history as his very own act and declared this man to be his one definitive Word. With Barth that is always the crux of the matter.[333]

Like Kierkegaard, then, Barth was determined neither to abandon the universality of Jesus nor to universalize him at the expense of his particularity.[334] We will have occasion later to question his success. Meanwhile, we may notice affirmatively that he takes a middle way between those in the tradition of Schleiermacher who allow no ontological weight to the resurrection and ascension as events that are real for Jesus

---

[329] 1949:128f.; see also *CD* 4/1:319f.

[330] *CD* 4/1:115; see 318ff., 4/3:72ff. Barth turns the Where? question around by arguing that the answer is too great for the question, or rather for those who ask it, since they still inhabit the time of Holy Saturday (cf. G. Steiner 1989:232). But if in Christ this time is already altered, those who know that wait joyfully for the one who himself *is* the answer. They do not proceed to establish an answer of their own – i.e., to seize upon a future which is only an extrapolation of their fading present.

[331] *CD* 4/2:112f.; cf. 4/3:362f.

[332] *CD* 3/2:466ff. Heaven 'is the sum of the inaccessible and incomprehensible side of the created world . . . the throne of God, the creaturely correspondence to his glory;' it is to 'the God-ward side of the universe' that Jesus disappeared in the cloud (453f.; cf. 4/2:153f.). Yet he remains present with us, since as man he exists and acts 'in the mode of God' at the heart of every time, turning its pastness into his present, converting our time into his time, making himself our 'absolute and final future' (4/1:324; cf. 2/1:623ff.).

[333] This was 'true and actual before,' i.e., that this man was with God absolutely; *that* it was true 'is the hidden thing which is revealed in the ascension of Jesus Christ' (*CD* 4/2:153f.). Likewise, then, he who is present even now is *not* an altered, ubiquitous, or 'divinized' Christ, or one who is present only in his deity; he comes to us as the one he was and is and will be, the mediator, the God-man. But he comes in the hiddenness of one who has exited from the sphere of death into the mystery of God; he comes in the form of 'the promise of his Spirit' (4/3:356f.).

[334] *CD* 4/1:313.

and those whose doctrine of the ascension seems rather like the space travel of science fiction. At the same time he avoids the path of those who regard these events as a part of Jesus' own experience but disallow the participation of his body.[335] Against the first it is made plain, as Hans Frei puts it, that Jesus 'owns his own identity;'[336] his history is not reduced now to the history of faith. Against the last, it is made clear that this identity is not another but the very same:

> Since Jesus Christ exists as the person he was, obviously he is the beginning of a new, different time from that which we know, a time in which there is no fading away, but real time which has a yesterday, a today and a tomorrow . . . His time is not at an end.[337]

And this means that even in his contemporaneity, or rather because of it, a breach has indeed opened up, not between Jesus and Jesus, but between Jesus and us.[338]

The breach to which we refer is not that between man and God generally, which in every age has tempted the gnostic mind to search for a cosmological solution, making christology parasitic on the literary or scientific imagination. It is a gap between one particular man and all others, a gap in anthropology and so in cosmology itself.[339] In the end it has but one possible solution, *viz.*, closure from the other side: 'He shall come again in glory to judge the living and the dead.'[340] Barth was very

---

[335] See e.g. E. Brunner 1952:363ff., who argues that here 'theology must have the courage to be ready to abandon the ecclesiastical tradition.' But in doing so he does not set aside 'speculative or mystical theology' for the 'historical' Christian message, as he claims. (Notice that the *church* becomes the one and only 'body' of the risen Lord, a position which tends back to the ecclesiasticism we have criticized.)

[336] 1975:32. 'Luke, in climaxing the resurrection with the ascension story, highlights the fact to which the mysterious veiledness of the resurrection appearances had already pointed. Jesus has a location of his own, and only as he is able to withdraw from a common location with men to one distinctly his own, does he turn to share his presence with them in the Spirit' (49). Barth (1949:125) guards against the naïve view of that location by saying that 'Jesus is removed in the direction of the mystery of *divine* space, which is utterly concealed from man.'

[337] 1949:130. Jesus' human participation in God's eternity is not timelessness. That is what our *fallen* time is becoming by rejecting its God-given limits and ends. The time of Jesus is time in which there is a simultaneity or *perichoresis* of beginning, middle and end, of yesterday, today and tomorrow – a time with movement and depth (CD 4/1:117). It corresponds in a creaturely way to divine time, and thus reveals it.

[338] CD 4/2:27f.; cf. 4/1:290f.

[339] That is why our time is 'the time between the times' (CD 4/1:323) of Jesus' appearing: not, as in the Barth who helped to found *Zwischen den Zeiten*, a time that is no time, a time to be annulled by way of an existential encounter with a timeless God; not, as in Origen and Teilhard, a time to be compressed and overcome through cosmic evolution; but a time for *witness* to Jesus, a time for confessing a real distance between him and us precisely because of his lordly proximity (289ff.; cf. 4/3:313).

[340] Jesus' existence at the right hand of God 'is real existence and as such the measure of all existence,' a measure that will be taken when he rends the heavens to stand before us once more as the same one he is and was (1949:130ff.). Meanwhile, the Spirit provides a bridge (CD 4/2:345).

deliberate about restoring to a place of prominence what Origen had long ago trimmed away, the doctrine of the personal return of Jesus Christ. Nor did he shy away from its implications. For both Barth and Kierkegaard the present age stands under judgment; we have already learned that the term towards which it is moving is the cross.[341] But if the heavenly session of Jesus speaks of a distinction, and hence of a confrontation, between his history and ours, denying any attempt (false comfort!) to suggest that our time as such is already resurrection time, it speaks also and more affirmatively of a parenthesis, of the room created by God *for* our histories. It speaks especially of the church. Before attempting an evaluation of Barth's contribution, we must do likewise.

Christian community, says Barth, is the goal of Jesus-history.[342] Without the gap of which we have spoken, however, there could be no such community, for all history would already be at an end. Indeed, and this is an important point, it could never have been in the first place. For creaturely reality, by conformity to God's own trinitarian being, is ultimately a perichoresis of times and places and the persons who shape and inhabit them, realized 'enhypostatically' in God through the mediation of the incarnate Son.[343] But mediation requires both nearness and distance. Barth did not set himself against an eschatology that left no room for the mediator with the intention of establishing one that left no room for us. He did not repudiate a view of the risen Master that denies his human substantiality in order to take up one that assigns man *qua* man to the margins. Bodily resurrection and ascension may mark Jesus off and set him over against us as the *concretissimum*, but they do so for our sake. In preserving *his* otherness they preserve ours.[344] They do so specifically by inviting a new and positive response to him. It may be that our time is seen in the light of his exaltation to be merely the time between the times – to be only something parenthetical – but it is not true to say that it therefore counts for nothing and comes to nothing. On the contrary, in the dialectic of descent and ascent our time is given back to us in the form of a question about communion, and so as a genuine *possibility*.[345]

---

[341] Teilhard, we may recall, can and does say something similar. But Barth is speaking quite literally of the cross and of the man who hung on it. To hasten towards that term is *not* therefore to embrace the 'death forces' at work in the world (with a view to the separation of the world soul from the world body) but to wait in hope for the crucified and resurrected one.

[342] CD 4/2:337. Conversely, the church is made up of those who confess him and his otherness during this interval (4/1:353).

[343] Just as Jesus' own times are 'perichoretically' related; cf. Dalferth 27ff., Hunsinger 236ff.

[344] 'The interval between the first and the final parousia of Jesus Christ is that of the existence of man' (CD 4/1:333); it is grounded in the affirmation of man in the bodily resurrection of Jesus and in the distance which his exaltation as a man introduces (351ff., cf. 3/2:455f., 4/2:35f.).

[345] See CD 3/1:74, 4/3:326ff. In this light consider the following insightful remark (4/1:121): 'If man does not seriously wait for Jesus Christ, he will not wait for anything else.'

The appearance of 'something ultimate and supreme' is aimed, not at the exclusion, but at the inclusion of something parenthetical. To that the existence of the church here and now bears witness, for it too is 'marked off from the race, from others, in order that it may make "a provisional offering of thankfulness for which the whole world is ordained by the act of the love of God."'[346]

Barth's ecclesiology is too complex for us to examine here, but it is certainly shaped by the tension he establishes between the No and the Yes of Jesus' exaltation.[347] The latter (as always in Barth) is the word that must be heard first. The distance that opens up *between* Jesus and us is really the room he makes in himself *for* us; the time between the times is his own time in the form it takes as he extends it to us. Barth differed from Kierkegaard in emphasizing the gift-nature of this time: The parenthesis is definitely not a void; it is filled with the active self-revelation of Jesus.[348] Contemporaneity, as we have already said, is not something we must achieve, as Kierkegaard sometimes seemed to think. It does not point first of all to the heroic journey of the solitary man or woman finding their own way to the cross. The Christ who stands at a distance from us, the *Christus absens*, is also the Christ who in the power of his resurrection and ascension comes forward to meet us, the *Christus praesens*. If he gives us room to respond, he certainly does not leave us to our own devices. All are summoned, here and now, 'with supreme realism,' to share a common life with him.[349]

We will suggest later that Barth over-corrects Kierkegaard on this point, but for now it is enough to observe that our time, as the time Jesus gives to us, is indeed ecclesial time. For Barth, Christian community is not an unattainable ideal or perhaps even a hindrance to spiritual authenticity. Since the contemporaneous Christ is also the risen Christ, the eschatological 'already' comes back into prominence. This means that Christianity cannot be equated with the pious individual under any definition. Nor yet is it to be equated with 'a pure fellowship of persons' without institutional dimensions or other traces of definite form.[350] Ecclesial time is in every way human time, or rather time that is being humanized. It is corporate and social and socially responsible. 'Has the community been first and foremost human in all that it has done?' Barth can ask this question because of his conviction that Jesus has cleared a

---

[346] *CD* 4/2:511.

[347] The 'No' is in the first place his exaltation on the cross, but in his resurrection and ascension there is also a 'No' to this sphere of sin and death.

[348] See e.g. *CD* 3/2:467f., 4/2:112f., 4/3:356ff.

[349] Barth makes this statement in a liturgical context. He proceeds: 'Why with such realism? Because and as he is among us today, and will be among us tomorrow, in his then act. Did any living Christian or Christian community ever live except on this presupposition?' (*CD* 4/2:112).

[350] Thus Brunner; see Hartwell 143.

space in which we can become human through our encounter with him.[351] He stands behind us so that we may put down roots, and before us so that we may grow. In the Spirit 'that double proximity is actual presence,' a presence more substantial than our own yet gracious in every way.[352] It is a presence that enables us to exist in this world, and for this world, with something of Jesus' own liberty during the forty days – that is, as 'man on the way from here to there,' as those who live already, right where they are, in the light of the kingdom of heaven.[353]

But just here the counterpoint is also heard. Kierkegaard and Overbeck are not forgotten, nor the warning implied by the gap itself. Ecclesial time, as a time of invitation and response to Jesus, is definitely not worldly time. The cross and the ascension speak their combined No! to the idea that the church is on the way along the same way as the world.[354] Barth saw the origins of that idea in the faulty notion that the church is an extension of the incarnation, a notion he attacked with equal ferocity in its Roman and Protestant forms. The doctrine of bodily resurrection and ascension exposes that audacity for what it is, a usurpation of Christ's own place and a denial that the church lives only by encounter with its Lord. Only a 'de-eschatologized Christianity' could take up such a posture! On Barth's view, nearness remains distance. The contemporaneous Christ, as a living human person who has ascended into heaven, cannot be confused with the church – or, for just that reason, the church with the world. In the parenthesis between the ascension and the parousia, the church

> comes from the revelation of the man Jesus as it moves towards it, and it moves towards it as it comes from it . . . This is what determines the whole logic and ethic of the community of the end.[355]

---

[351] CD 3/2:508. See 4/1:343ff., where Barth stands Kierkegaard on his head by arguing that 'in every age, *post Christum* means *post Christum crucifixum et resuscitatum*,' and that we can and must move *forward* on that basis. Elsewhere (1986:3) he asks: 'Where with Kierkegaard is God's people, community, the Church? Where is the deacon's ministry and the task of mission? And where are man's social and political tasks?' (Cf. 4/2:354f.)

[352] CD 3/2:467, 509; cf. 4/3:333f.

[353] R. Wood (1988:69) observes that 'Barth is untiring in his insistence that the church is set in distinction from culture only in order to stand first and last for it. Christians must always acknowledge how deeply they belong to the world even as they refuse to put their trust in it.'

[354] See e.g. CD 1/1:48 (where Barth begins his massive project by standing against Tillich's theology of correlation) or 4/2:511: The church is fundamentally a 'separated and gathered' community, and so a 'holy' community. It does not seek after the future but after 'the *Person* who is coming' (1991:LVIII; Busch 166).

[355] See CD 3/2:508ff. So far from being a prolongation of the incarnation, the church continues in the relationship of the disciples to their Lord as established in the forty days, only in a new form of dependency through the Spirit, who coordinates 'Christ in the heights' with Christ in the depths, i.e., the exalted Jesus and his ecclesial co-humanity, which exists enhypostatically in him (4/3:760; cf. 4/1:317ff., 4/2:51ff., 4/3:327, 754ff.).

In other words, the church has a defining direction all its own, since it is aware that it is bracketed by the presence of Christ. In its encounter with the resurrected one it too is 'pure event,' existing out of divine possibilities, which means that it cannot even be contained within its own earthly forms much less take its direction from the world. Rather it can and must look away from itself and the world in order to take its direction from Christ.[356]

At the outset of the final part-volume of the *Church Dogmatics* Barth pauses to take stock of the church's marginalization in the modern era. He sees in that marginalization a great benefit to the church, namely, the painful rediscovery of its own true relevance. A new path has been opening up: neither justification of the world nor retreat from it, but a Christ-like service to it. In being freed *by* the world and thus from it, the church is slowly becoming free *for* the world once more, conscious of the fact that its solidarity cannot rest on the 'illusory' assumption that it forms a unity with the world, but that it belongs to it precisely 'in its antithesis to it.'[357] Barth knew something about this precarious tension from his own experience. When in the Germany of the 1930s the church was still wanted by worldly powers for their own purposes, when many in the church were only too willing to render service to the state by once again justifying its imperialist ambitions, the Barmen Declaration (drafted by Barth) declared plainly that the church can only serve the world by serving its own Master. The Yes includes and sustains a No. Or to put the matter another way: The stand of the Confessing Church against the German Christian Movement demonstrates the truth of one of Barth's later *dicta*, that only by knowing the real presence of Jesus is it possible to discern his real absence.[358]

* * *

If Kierkegaard began turning the retraction theory inside out, and the practice of theology with it, we might say that Barth came in behind him to complete the job. In support of his attack on eschatological docetism he reversed Augustine's way of appropriating the resurrection and ascension to expound the twofold reality of Jesus Christ. Here it is the *former* that attests Jesus' divinity, while the latter restores our focus on his humanity.[359] This reversal by itself effects already a quite radical

---

[356] This is the message of the *Dogmatics* from beginning to end (see e.g. 1/1:41; cf. 1949:141ff.).

[357] CD 4/3:19ff.

[358] See CD 1/2:28f. Here is Barth's answer to Nietzsche. Here too is the right and necessary footing for our own claim that the real absence must on no account be glossed over. See below.

[359] *Methodus est arbitraria*, of course, and since resurrection and ascension are regarded as a single process it is only a question of relative emphasis. Precisely as a process, however, the ascension – which is or includes Jesus' earthly life – demands that we reckon with his humanity, whereas the event of his resurrection and reappearance discloses his divinity (cf. CD 4/1:300f., 4/2:7, 71f., 154).

correction of the western tendency towards a drop-in view of the incarnation. The humanity which God determines for himself, says Barth,

> in its very creatureliness, is placed at the side of the Creator, πρὸς τὸν θεόν ... It is a clothing which he does not put off. It is his temple which he does not leave ... He is God in the flesh – distinguished from all the idols imagined and fashioned by men by the fact that they are not God in the flesh, but products of human speculation on naked deity, λόγοι ἄσαρκοι.[360]

In other words, the ascension is no longer a device for the undoing of Jesus' humanity, but for its establishment. That, from our standpoint, would appear to be Barth's premier accomplishment, particularly when seen in the light of the new perspective on ecclesial identity to which it led.

On the other hand, among those who have concerned themselves directly with his anthropology, it is often argued that Barth has by no means solved the problem of a theological tradition that affords too little attention to genuine human being, and indeed to creaturely being in general. Inasmuch as he had first of all a quite different problem in view – namely, the widespread substitution of a false anthropology for a true – there are already grounds for entertaining such a charge.[361] Yet we must not fail to remark that the difficulty is inherent in the task of facing up to the tradition itself, both in its ecclesiastical and its secular forms. For the burden the tradition places upon us, as Barth rightly saw, is the burden of fighting first of all to say this one thing: that *this* man, the foremost and fundamental Man, had and has a name; that he not only was, but is and will be, a man; that he is not an abstraction. Everything else, says Barth, depends on this.[362] The doctrine of the ascension itself rebukes a general anthropology and demands a much more specific one. An anthropology that does not concern itself first of all with Jesus of Nazareth is an anthropology without regard for the unique act of God with respect to this man, and hence (here the charge may be thrown back) for the redemption of real people.[363] Likewise a church in which his name is not

---

[360] CD 4/2:101. 'What the New Testament says about Jesus Christ is all said in the light of Easter and Ascension, that is, in the light of the union, achieved once for all, between the eternal Word and the human existence assumed by him ... Is the name of Christ, is Christ the Son of God, really Jesus of Nazareth? Yes, [Christian proclamation] replies; and so with all its might it must maintain that this and no other is his name, that such he is and not something else.' (1/2:165)

[361] In volume 4 it is the ascension which (thrice over) provides the point of departure for the transition from christology and soteriology to ecclesiology and anthropology. If the charge is justifiable, must there not be implications here regarding his doctrine of the ascension?

[362] CD 4/2:31ff.

[363] 'The attempt at a general anthropology, however complete and established, will always founder on the particularity in which he is a man' (CD 4/2:26f.).

the first but only 'the third or fourth word' to be heard is the church, not of the new man, but of the old.[364]

Where then does the problem lie, if there is one? It lies, apparently, in the place of strength. The charge is that Barth has spoken the name of Jesus so loudly that other names cannot even be heard; that the problem of abstraction thus reappears in another form; that once again humanity is being swallowed up, if not by God directly then by 'the humanity of God.'[365] This accusation is sometimes put much too strongly, but in our own look at Barth we have now arrived at the point where a warning signal is sounding. For in the reversal just mentioned we have identified the first of a number of appropriations (and that, to be sure, is all they are) which carry a high degree of risk. Can we afford, even occasionally and as a purely formal device, to use one element in the story of Jesus to speak primarily of divinity and another primarily of humanity? Does that not endanger the story itself, not to mention a sound theology of the incarnation? Is a reversal of emphasis enough, or is an even more radical correction required? It is time to go over the territory we have already covered with a more critical eye.

In our judgment the systematic strength of Barth's position is in the inter-connection (as he puts it) of descending and ascending, or more specifically, in the rejection of a λόγος ἄσαρκος and of a 'basically formless' ascended Christ.[366] But just here a second and far more damaging appropriation appears that we can no longer evade. It is the very thing we have had to contend with right along, namely, the notion that God is the one who descends and man the one who ascends. That notion, which Barth uses to structure his climactic volume on the doctrine of reconciliation, is not mistaken in itself. Certainly it is true that God descends and man ascends. It is true soteriologically, and therefore ontologically, but unless the distinction between the *way* it is true soteriologically and ontologically is carefully noted and preserved the old troubles are sure to surface. And in Barth they do indeed surface. Let us explain as best we can, for our whole criticism reduces to this one point, even if other points must also be made.

Why does Barth fight so tenaciously against any 'tearing apart of the unity of descending and ascending'? To defend the unity and integrity of the God-man, that is, the doctrine of the incarnation? Yes. But why is it that, in spite of his actualism and the primacy he wants to give to the biblical story, he is so widely accused of having produced a strangely static theology, against which the charge of christomonism is in one way or another brought forward again and again? Most often people look to his

---

[364] Indeed it is the church of antichrist (*CD* 4/3:231, 258f.).

[365] *CD* 4/2:72.

[366] See *CD* 4/2:110f. Here we must disagree with David Ford (1981:183), though we shall shortly be drawing on a central aspect of his criticism of Barth.

doctrine of election, with its overemphasis on the pre-temporality of God. Or to his doctrine of the Trinity, which still appears to tilt in the direction of unity over plurality. Or, putting these together, to the pneumatological deficiency which he himself recognized.[367] All of this can, and sometimes should, be disputed. But we may point also to the matter the present study brings into focus. Our suggestion is that Barth did not look as far as he might have into the source of the docetic streak that has plagued theology from the beginning. Continuing to work with the descent of God and the ascent of man as a basic paradigm (old habits die hard, even in a theologian of such immense creativity) meant that the only way to attack docetism was to clamp the two movements tightly together: *so* tightly that it is sometimes unclear how, or how far, the resurrection and especially the ascension really do represent new events for Jesus – the very point at issue with Schleiermacher, Bultmann and the rest, and the very thing necessary to an open, dynamic worldview that respects creaturely reality as such.

Our criticism is connected to those of David Ford and Colin Gunton,[368] though it begins with Irenaeus. Barth puts forward a position which represents only a partial recovery of that early father's vision. Though he reckons courageously with the double aspect of the descent of the Son, that is, with his assumption of fallen humanity,[369] he fails to wrestle with two related facts: first, that in the biblical story itself it is primarily the descending and ascending of a man (the God-man) with which we have to do; second, that any appropriation here risks investing a soteriological pattern with an ontological significance it does not have. At the outset of volume 4 Barth disposes of this line of thought as tautologous. The only thing unique about Jesus' descent is that it is God who is undertaking it.[370] This was not a reaction to Irenaeus, whose position he did not consider, but to the disastrous results of the unresolved disputes left over from the Reformation. Barth's own proposal is at once innovative and obvious. He unites the doctrine of the two states and that of the two natures into a unified theory of the incarnation, such that the being of 'the one Jesus Christ' is understood in terms of two simultaneous and mutually qualifying movements – the humiliation of God and the exaltation of man. In short, he seeks to correct the tradition's tendency to undo the incarnation by translating Chalcedon into actualist terms.[371] To

---

[367] Cf. Busch 494. Barth (CD 2/1:631ff.) did struggle to find a balance between pre-, supra- and post-temporality.

[368] Both Ford (1981) and Gunton (1992) argue that Barth brings premature closure to the story of Jesus.

[369] CD 1/2:151ff.; cf. 4/1:130f., 4/2:27.

[370] 'To say that he is lowly as a man is tautology which does not help us in the least to explain his humiliation. It merely contains the general truth that he exists as a man in the bondage and suffering of the human situation . . .' (CD 4/1:134).

[371] Witness especially his substitution of a *communicatio operationum* for a *communicatio idiomatum* (CD 4/2:104ff.). We may note here with Jüngel (1986:37; cf. B. McCormack

put the results as simply as possible, Jesus is who he is as he does what he does. He does not exist first as the God-man so that he might then accomplish something called atonement; as the incarnate one he *is* atonement, in that he is God happening for man and man happening for God. Any inclination to dispense with his humanity after the fact, so to speak, is thus inconceivable. Descending and ascending are not only interconnected, they are one and the same event.[372]

Barth here does something quite unusual, which if not altogether new is at least an improvement over much of what we have seen thus far. But it is fraught with difficulties. To keep his doctrine of the incarnation from coming apart at the seams, he is compelled to reject any history-related distinction between the humiliated Christ and the exalted Christ. No 'new qualities or further developments' in Jesus can be contemplated after the cross.[373] A total identification of act and being (of soteriology and Chalcedonian ontology) means that Jesus-history is entirely complete at Calvary, for the nadir of the divine descent necessarily coincides with the pinnacle of human ascent.[374] All that remains, says Barth, is that we should see and hear and share in what has already been done. Jesus-history from the standpoint of the Emmaus Road is pure revelation, pure unveiling, pure contemporaneity. Nothing is added to it except our histories. Eschatology, then, has become a theology of revelation pure and simple: In the fullness of his actualized self, the God-man, the crucified-ascended One, becomes and *is* revelation, much as the Holy Spirit in Barth's western trinitarianism *is* the love of the Father and the Son. Since Barth wants to avoid any compromising third movement in the being of Jesus – a third nature such as Teilhard postulated – he cannot allow that what happens in the forty days is anything other than the 'effective manifestation' of a life lived once for all. What is new about this life is chiefly its universal reach and relevance, its accessibility. The outcome of descending and ascending, dying and rising, is precisely sovereign presence, the contemporaneous

---

1995:391ff.) that Barth (1962:230) points to Luther's confusion on this matter, and on the doctrine of the real presence, as leading directly to the confusion between man and God that is characteristic of modern theology.

[372] CD 4/1:122ff., 4/2:35f., 106; see Jüngel 135. In what follows we will not be disputing that Jesus is who is as he does what he does, but only the particular way in which this is construed.

[373] CD 4/2:132ff., 4/4:24. 'Where and when is he not both humiliated and exalted . . . the Crucified who has not yet risen, or the Risen who has not been crucified? . . . We have to do with the being of the one and entire Jesus Christ whose humiliation detracts nothing and whose exaltation adds nothing.' (4/1:133)

[374] Shall we agree that Christ's descent is also his ascent, or even that it becomes such in the 'definite newness' of the forty days (cf. CD 4/2:100, 4/3:323)? Might this not bring us full circle to Hegel, overruling Barth's objection that the resurrection is bodily and historical (4/1:298)? Would we not do better to settle instead for the Irenaean maxim that Christ's descent is *our* ascent?

Christ.[375] But the contemporaneous Christ has become an ambiguous figure after all, just because he is rather too definite. His history is already finished.[376]

Barth's struggle to articulate all this in terms of his doctrine of time has led some to suppose that that doctrine, especially the idea of pure duration, is the source of the problem to which we are pointing. The confusion works mainly in the other direction, however. Since he retains the classical appropriation of descending and ascending, his translation of Chalcedon from substantialist to actualist terms only perpetuates the problem – the swallowing up of time by eternity – he meant to overcome. God and man, despite fine passages to the contrary,[377] are still defined by their opposition to one another, an opposition which can only be resolved by the death of man (which belongs already to the determination of his finitude) and by his reconstitution as a moment in God's eternity.[378] That is why it is hard to distinguish in Barth between the doctrine of election and the doctrine of resurrection, between the beginning and the end. Resurrection, as the revelation of the concord of God and man, is God's free decision, hence a new decision; yet that new decision is simply a confirmation of the decision made in the beginning.[379] The history sandwiched between these decisions – the road to the cross – is not free, except in the sense that it is free to be exactly that. In other words, Barth's eschatology is more Greek than he admits, and it is no surprise that the determinism that mars the dogmatic tradition begins to reassert itself. Is that not also the case with Jürgen Moltmann, for example, who presses beyond Barth in just the wrong direction, confusing ontology with soteriology to the extent that suffering and the cross (and, we are forced to conclude, evil) take their place in the doctrine of creation, leading once again to a determinist eschatology of ἀποκατάστασις?[380]

In *Barth and God's Story* David Ford has suggested that his whole project cries out for integration with a more traditional substantialist

---

[375] Reconciliation includes revelation, in other words, for Jesus now encounters us in the double character of human apprehensibility and divine presence (CD 1/2:110ff., 3/2:451, 463ff., 4/3:8). He exists in spite of death and against death as the same man he was – still within his own proper form and limits, his beginning, middle and end – yet sovereignly alive and *unlimited* (4/1:308, 313).

[376] J. Webster (1997:64) thinks Barth's view preferable to Jüngel's, but are there not common shortcomings?

[377] See e.g. McCormack 246f.; cf. 262ff.

[378] See CD 4/1:8ff.; cf. 3/2:587ff., 625ff. This is the kernel of truth in Richard Roberts' critique, and it stands in contradiction to Barth's claim (4/2:106) that he has 'left no room for anything static.'

[379] Indeed, it *is* the first decision (cf. CD 4/1:44ff., 296ff.). R. Jenson's dictum (1982:182) that 'to be is to rise from the dead' is not an advance on Barth, or a correction of him.

[380] As Moltmann tries to correct Barth's narrowly anthropocentric doctrine of creation he winds up with an ἀποκατάστασις that includes everything that ever was or will be; in Christ resurrection has become 'the universal "law" of creation' (1990: 256ff.). His position is shaped by his panentheism, of course, and hence by a theology Barth (cf. 1981:175f.) consistently rejected. But does Barth's own christology not pull in just that direction?

analysis, and indeed it does.[381] That, in fact, is the only way to preserve the dynamic of Jesus-history, whether before or after the cross. But no such integration is possible on the classical scheme. Where soteriological verticality (descent into hell and ascent into heaven) is confused with ontological verticality (the divine–human dynamic that is proper to man in Christ) some form of 'thinning' is the inevitable result. Descending into hell and ascending into heaven, as we pointed out in Chapter 4, are but one contingent form of a history of communion between God and man, the true possibilities of which eye has not yet seen, nor ear heard; which is to say, Jesus-history does not end with his ascension but only really begins there. Is that not the whole point of insisting on bodily ascension? Barth appears to agree.[382] But when the soteriological reference to Jesus-history and the ontological inference from it are run together, a transference occurs which yields the static quality for which Barth is criticized. Salvation history begins to turn back into myth again:

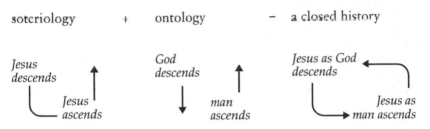

Where can such a history go, except around in circles? The point at which the turn is made is always Holy Saturday, eschatological docetism in one form or another being the consequence. Of the docetic pull Barth was well aware; that is why he attempted to apply his clamp. But inasmuch as he did not reject the whole scheme, the main effect was to run his otherwise brilliant experiment in narrative theology off the rails, with serious consequences indeed.[383]

Ford has rightly argued that Barth's account of the forty days of resurrection appearances forces them to carry a freight not evident in the Gospels. The reason for this is that one effect of his Chalcedonian clamp – which requires a strict correspondence between Jesus-history in its two versions – is to compress the *status exaltationis* into the forty days. Ascension time is really the time that leads up to the ascension; as such it is one with resurrection time, to which the ascension itself brings

[381] 1981:131. See CD 2/1:260 for a place to begin, though the difficulty in christology is already evident (262).
[382] CD 4/1:109ff.
[383] Though with nothing quite like the wreckage imagined by Roberts (Sykes 1979:146)!

closure.[384] This conflation of resurrection, ascension and heavenly session means, as we have seen, that the resurrection already establishes Jesus' lordship over all things, already renders his history universally inclusive, which means in turn that the ascension becomes something of an anti-climax (a common feature in modern theology!) even for Jesus. It is only a sign, like the empty tomb, not something decisive in itself.[385] But that runs directly counter to the 'not yet' of John 20:17, one of the few resurrection passages Barth is content to ignore in his extensive exegetical notes. It also calls into question his talk about distance and room for free participation, contributing to what Ford describes as the 'monism of the Gospel story.' Resurrection time is not only ascension time, it is already the parousia in the first of its three forms.[386] How far the whole construction downgrades the role of the Spirit, a feature to which Colin Gunton points,[387] and whether it leads necessarily to a doctrine of ἀποκατάστασις,[388] may at first be difficult to decide. What is perfectly clear is that it shifts the focus away from what happens to and for Jesus, in his own humanity, to the question of his revelation to us. And with the loss of attention to his humanity goes a loss of attention to ours. The biblical story itself begins to peter out.

The appropriation of the two states or histories of Jesus to God and man respectively thus raises a 'suspicion of docetism' even in Barth. As resurrection time becomes revelation time, it becomes predominantly *divine* time after all, as no less a proponent of Barth's theology than T. F. Torrance concedes.[389] If the humanity of the risen Jesus is fully affirmed against a long history of docetism, it nonetheless remains

---

[384] Cf. Balthasar 1963:84, in whom the echo of Barth is to be heard: In the forty days, the Church learns to see 'the glory of his divinity, the presence of eternity in time. And since it is not possible that the mode of time belonging to the risen Christ should have altered with the ascension (this being rather in the nature of a signing-off gesture, purely for our benefit), it is necessary to grasp that the mode of time revealed during the forty days remains the foundation for every other mode of his presence in time, in the Church, and in the world.'

[385] CD 3/2:452ff.

[386] The notion of a threefold parousia, which to some extent continues the conflation of resurrection, ascension and parousia we have already rejected, imports into the resurrection events a kind of finality, and into the ascension an act of closure, that belong only to the parousia proper (cf. CD 4/3:292ff.; Ford 13, 149f., 165f.). It also invites the very important question as to what our *own* resurrection can possibly mean (cf. Davies 170f.).

[387] 1992:48ff., 65ff.; cf. 1986:329. See CD 4/2:129, 323ff., 4/3:296.

[388] Barth (CD 4/3:477f.) denies this, of course, while also denying its denial. But cf. W. Künneth, e.g., who also makes the resurrection 'the Archimedian point for theology,' denies to the ascension *per se* any distinct significance as a saving event, and winds up defending an ἀποκατάστασις (1965:90 n. 37, 289ff.).

[389] D. McKim 62f. Indeed, since contemporaneity is a quality or prerogative of divinity, and since the one thing that is accomplished in the resurrection is precisely that, it is difficult to see how his view does not amount to divinization after all (cf. CD 3/2:455). To Torrance, whose own reasons for criticizing Barth on this score are given somewhat cryptically, we will also return later.

trapped in the circle we have indicated. We cannot help noticing that Barth's attempt to get back on track only deepens his difficulty. Asking how it is that resurrection time is not immediately the time of judgment and fulfillment – a question he is certainly forced to ask – he appeals to the willingness of Jesus to make time for us.[390] And when he tries finally to say what this means for Jesus himself, what can he do but expound the forty days as a repetition of his sighing and weeping and praying and fighting, as the conducting of a battle not yet fully won? In the resurrection as in his earthly life, Christ is again on the way from here to there, even if this time the victory that lies ahead is assured. Is this not the raising of a history rather than a person? Barth objects to the 'rather,'[391] but it is doubtful whether his objection can be sustained. And here is another question: Is this not Christ as man going over the territory won by Christ as God, that as man he (and we) may see that it is really God who has done it? If so, is the suspicion of docetism not also retroactive, so to speak?[392] A final question combines the previous ones: If Jesus' pre-history terminated in the cross, can his post-history go further than the ascension, or must it simply repeat or re-establish itself in ever-widening spheres of influence? Again Barth denies it, but his doctrine of a threefold parousia and his universalist leanings suggest otherwise. 'What happened still happens, and as such will happen.'[393]

The only way to break out of this circle and get back on track with the biblical story is to repudiate altogether the identification of states with natures, returning to the more primitive notion of the descent and ascent of the God-man. This would open up the envelope of eternity in which Barth's doctrines of election and resurrection have conspired to seal Jesus-history from conception to cross. The resurrection and ascension would then take on real significance not only *for* his history (retroactively) but *in* his history, and the forty days would not be required to bear so much weight. Instead we would be invited to think more carefully about what it means for Jesus to have gone from us to the Father's right hand; to think about his heavenly session in terms of the pneumatological dimensions and

---

[390] See *CD* 4/3:316ff. If in Jesus-history all of history is directly involved, how is it that the actual appearance among us of this new life did not 'at once engulf the whole world like a tidal wave'? Barth's answer is less than convincing. Jesus himself, he suggests, is 'surprised and startled' (328), but it turns out that his power is simply *too* great to be realized in a single day. Cf. *CD* 4/1:734ff.

[391] Ibid. 40; cf. 329.

[392] Cf. Torrance (McKim) 62f. The Nestorian/Eutychian oscillation which Barth hoped to avoid by his actualism thus does not completely disappear.

[393] 1949:131; cf. *CD* 4/1:313. Barth reproves Kierkegaard for a gospel that begins to look something like a doctrine of eternal recurrence, but it may be that he himself is in more danger of falling into that trap. His understanding of sin not only as an episode in human history but 'as the original of all episodes, the essence of everything that is unnecessary, disorderly, contrary to plan and purpose' (4/1:46; cf. 345), does not prevent but encourages such a mishap, since it fixes Christ's own nature in opposition to everything episodic.

possibilities of his new existence, and to take up with even greater seriousness the prospect of his return. In such an enterprise what is good and right about the idea of contemporaneity (its concern for the universality of Jesus) might be set on a safer footing, for surely it is in the ascension and *not* merely in the resurrection as such that his lordship over all things is established.[394] At the same time the temptation to fill up Kierkegaard's parenthesis with the ἐφάπαξ of Jesus-history, undermining both the need for pneumatology and the particularity of Jesus as a freely acting subject, would fall away. And just here we must speak further, and less positively, about Barth's doctrine of the church.

'Anthropological and ecclesiological assertions arise only as they are borrowed from christology,' writes Barth,[395] and of course it follows that they are no sounder than the christology from which they derive. What is the effect of the Chalcedonian service into which he presses the U-shaped story of Jesus? What in particular is the effect of making resurrection time into ascension time, and thus into the ground of ecclesial time? What, in other words, is the impact of a notion of contemporaneity with Jesus that is not properly qualified by his departure? Is it not to misconstrue the problem of the presence and the absence, in short, to undermine the very thing for which we commended Barth in our first look at his ecclesiology?

Not to put too fine a point on it, the effect is simply too much real presence. In Barth, as in the Origenist tradition, the eucharistic possibility is generalized. The universalizing of Jesus already in his resurrection means that our time is contained or bracketed by his in such a way that his absence is more apparent than real:

> We may rightly point out . . . that what really oppresses the world and us in spite of the Easter event, or rather in the light of a true appreciation of it, is not really a lack or failure or absence of its efficacy but simply the fact that this is not evident to us, and therefore its apparent absence.[396]

In other words, it is still a matter of Christ's hidden co-existence in and with the world, which must be proclaimed and celebrated and brought out into the open.[397] But that means, conversely, that in the *church* there is too little real presence. The distinction between church and world gravitates once again towards the noetic. The church is marked off from the world as the place where what is true everywhere and always – because

---

[394] Where in Barth is there a serious discussion of the ascension *per se*? His conflation of resurrection and ascension, systematically and in key biblical passages (see CD 4/2:153f., e.g.), warns us not to expect it.

[395] CD 2/1:148.

[396] CD 4/3:317; cf. 4/1:328.

[397] CD 4/3:323ff., 360ff.; cf. Balthasar 1979:83f. Here we find just a hint of justification for Hans Küng's otherwise groundless and indeed irresponsible suggestion (1988:271ff.) that were Barth to begin again at the beginning today he would write his theology more or less backwards.

true in eternity! – is known and confessed to be true. Everyone belongs in principle to the *communio sanctorum*, though only some know and act upon that fact.[398] Christianity as a qualification of the species is still an operative idea in Barth.[399]

That is not the whole picture, of course. Barth did believe in the real presence of Jesus in the church in a way distinct from his presence in the world.[400] It is quite revealing, however, that this is developed, not sacramentally, but chiefly as an epistemology and a (pneumatological) theory of language. It is developed mainly with respect to the liturgy of the word. Barth's insights here are often profound, as we have tried to notice elsewhere; what we did not notice is the dislocation of the whole discussion from the eucharistic ground of ecclesial life.[401] But Barth – for all his own insistence even in later years that the Lord's Supper should be central in the worship of the church and therefore in its theological reflection – could hardly have countenanced any such recontextualization. For he was not moving towards, but away from, a sacramental understanding of the church.[402]

Why did Barth, a modern ecumenical theologian *par excellence*, not pursue the significance of the eucharistic liturgy as a decisive event in the becoming and being of the church? Was it because he wanted to establish Jesus-history as 'the one and only sacrament' from which the church draws its life? Though we cannot quarrel with this as a motive, it fails completely as an explanation, for the question of the sacraments *is* the question of the church drawing its life from Christ.[403] We may point out that had Barth pursued the sacramental way he might have run into considerable difficulty, since he too inserted a comforting 'even now' into the eschatological tension between the 'already' and the 'not

---

[398] See CD 4/3:363f. Both the church and the world derive from Jesus Christ and his work. 'But the Church is the place where one knows that, and that is indeed a tremendous difference between the Church and the world' (1949:132; cf. 4/1:317, 353). From this perspective the idea of an 'anonymous Christian' makes no sense, yet everyone is a 'designated Christian.'

[399] At one point Barth asks whether we are not forced to approximate 'very closely to the concept of the body of Christ including and uniting all men' (CD 4/1:665). Behind this lies the notion that in Christ 'it is not merely one man, but the *humanum* of all men, which is posited and exalted as such to unity with God' (4/2:49). In short, something of the old idea of a Universal Man continues to war with his particularism. (See also Hartwell's criticism, 185f., and Gunton 1992:46ff.)

[400] CD 4/1:20; cf. 3/2:467f. See P. Molnar 1996:262ff.

[401] 1987:9ff. Barth developed his elaborate doctrine of the Word of God (CD 1) in such a way as to secure the dependency of the church's knowing, and hence its being, on Christ's own sovereign act of self-proclamation. In doing so he treated the liturgy of the word as a kind of substitute sacrament (but cf. 4/3:761, Busch 474).

[402] Cf. Jüngel 47, C. O'Grady 1969:113f.; see also Busch 142f., 184.

[403] i.e., of 'the giving and receiving of this one sacrament,' to use Barth's own words; see CD 4/2:55 (cf. 1/2:228ff., 4/1:295f.).

yet.'[404] But to admit such a thing is really to say that his controversial slide into a non-sacramental ecclesiology cannot be explained as a reaction against abuses ancient or modern, that it is bound up instead with the logic of his position. To the extent that neglect of the ascension as a distinct episode in the story of Jesus weights his christology in favour of presence (that is what we had in mind when we spoke of overcorrecting Kierkegaard) a eucharistic understanding of the church eludes him. So too does a full appreciation of Christ's priestly office, as Torrance has observed,[405] which is in fact the more fundamental point. Both these effects are easily demonstrated by referring to a third and final appropriation, or rather, set of appropriations.

In Barth's beautifully structured fourth volume Jesus Christ is considered in the light of his threefold office as priest, king, and prophet. The first of these is made to correspond to the descent of God, the second to the ascent of man, and the third to the God-man in his revelation as such. The structure is also an ecclesiological and indeed a liturgical one, presenting the church in the light of its call to gather, to grow up in Christ, and to go forth into the world. At first glance this suggests a quite dynamic view of the church, since the accent naturally falls on the going forth. But the dynamic in question is very much in danger of breaking down into a vertical component (listening for the Word in the words) and a horizontal one (Christian mission), for its eucharistic centre is missing, consigned to ethics.[406] This is directly related to the want of any adequate discussion of Christ's priesthood. It is no accident, nor is it a small matter, that Barth's exposition of the same turns out, for all its innovation, to be a basically juridical affair.[407] The divine descent/human ascent scheme simply cannot accommodate the wholeness of priestly action. The very attempt at appropriations guarantees that each office will undergo some distortion through abstraction from Jesus-history, these distortions being passed on to the church. But above all it guarantees that Christ's priestly office, which by nature is a complex movement of descending and ascending and returning with a blessing, will be overshadowed by his kingly and prophetic offices, and particularly by the latter.[408]

---

[404] The doctrine of a threefold parousia – which is forced on Barth by his association of states and natures, and elaborated in terms of Christ's lordship over the three tenses of human time – necessitates this. The middle form of the parousia cannot be any *less* a parousia than the first and third forms; the 'is' cannot be anything less than the 'was' and the 'will be' (CD 4/1:318, 4/3:356ff.).

[405] McKim 62f.

[406] His intention, unfulfilled with respect to the Lord's Supper, was to give to it and to baptism 'their appropriate and worthy place as the basis and crown of the fourth and *ethical* section of the doctrine of reconciliation' (CD 4/2:xif., emphasis ours; cf. 1/2:231f.).

[407] Though the judicial metaphor, as Gunton (1988:113) observes, is modified in the direction of relationality, and thus towards the priestly, it is a mistake to equate the two in the way that Barth (CD 4/1:277) does.

[408] Since the God-man himself, considered as such, is the one who becomes and is revelation, it is really the prophetic office with which Barth has been concerned all along.

The arrangement of volume 4, though it has many compensating merits, betrays Barth's too-narrow Protestant conception of the church as *creatura Verbi*. But the real reason for his failure to rediscover the priestly ministry of Christ, and with it the eucharistic nature of the church, is the undermining of real absence through the ordering of eschatology to prior ontological interests. Ironically that problem is just the sacramentalist error in another guise, which may help to explain why the *totus christus* doctrine reappears in such a way that the church once again becomes the 'earthly-historical' form of Christ's humanity. Though not a repetition or extension of the incarnation, says Barth, the church *is* the incarnation in this secondary form. And here it is plain enough that the gap between Jesus and us looks rather a lot like the gap between God and man after all.[409]

All of this is especially unfortunate in a theologian who sought to make eschatology his mainstay. Barth had many of the tools in hand to correct the weakness we pointed up in Calvin, and to capitalize on his strengths and those of Kierkegaard as well. By falling back into a Zwinglian position on the sacraments, however, he revealed that his worldview was actually less dynamic than Calvin's and his ecclesiology – in this one crucial respect, where the whole matter is concentrated, as Hegel said – less tenable than that of his Danish mentor. Barth's systematic repudiation of individualism and institutionalism, and of a church that knows lords other than its own, still stands. The spirit of affirmation, of joy and thanksgiving, that pervades his theology and belongs to his very sense of the church is much to be prized. But can we, dare we, follow him in reducing εὐχαριστία to ethics?[410] Would that not breathe new life into the gnosticism, Pelagianism, and constructivism he so despised?[411] Would it not leave the problem of the presence and the absence hanging in the air?

If we would not part from Kierkegaard on a sour note, however, then not from Barth either, whose further efforts towards a reversal of the

---

[409] 'To his heavenly form of existence as Son of God and Son of Man he has assumed this earthly-historical – the community as his one body which also has this form . . . And these two elements of his one being are not merely related to each other *as* he himself as Son of God is related to his human nature. But, in this second form, his relation to his body, the community, *is* the relationship of God and man as it takes place in this one being as Head and body. Thus the community of Jesus Christ can be that which the human nature of its Lord and head is' (4/2:60; cf. 4/1:661, and see also N. Healy 1994:258ff.).

[410] As Migliore (Barth 1991:LIV) points out, the later Barth finds it necessary to show that God's sovereign grace is not 'totalitarian.' But surely to treat the sacraments as a human response to a prior divine act (*CD* 4/4 90) is only to compound the error by which the overlap between Jesus-history and ours threatens to become overbearing. And is it not the case that in all this he is closer to Schleiermacher, even to Bultmann, than he wants to admit? (Cf. 4/1 656, 665ff.; Redeker 137, Webster 1995:125ff.)

[411] See Barth 1981:346f., noting that of the seven points in the draft version of this eucharistic confession no less than six refer to what *we* do (cf. J. Torrance 1ff.; but see also *CD* 4/1:682). Unfortunately we cannot stop to follow up this point by engaging with Webster's and Molnar's worthy studies.

Where? question and an alternative ascension theology are by no means to be despised. In his loyalty to the Man of Nazareth he struck a great blow at the head of the 'giant gnostic snake' coiled at the roots of docetic theology, even if in doing so he bruised his own theological heel. Yet in the last analysis his helpful interpreter, Herbert Hartwell, is quite right to describe him as a theologian of the forty days, since Barth does stop short of the full-fledged theology of ascension in the flesh we require.[412] A more radical correction of the tradition *is* needed, and that can only come by way of restoring our attention – not first of all to our own stories – but to that of Jesus. For as Barth himself said, it would be tragic if we were to look away from Jesus just at the last moment.[413]

---

[412] 'His theology is like a vision dating from what may be termed the resurrection-period. It is as if he had walked with Jesus and His disciples during the forty days between Jesus Christ's resurrection and His ascension . . .' (98) Precisely between! Emmaus not Damascus.
[413] CD 4/1:116.

6

Church at the Crossroads

Our age demands to be led in Christology to the idea in the fact, to the race in the individual: a theology which, in its doctrines on the Christ, stops short at him as an individual, is not properly a theology, but a homily.   D. F. Strauss

Looking away from Jesus has become a natural reflex; it is raised here by Strauss to the level of a methodological principle.[1] Our journeying has shown us that the principle is not peculiar to our age, however. Ancients and moderns are allied in misconstruing the alienation between God and humanity in terms of epistemological or ontological distance. Consequently they are allied also in constructing systems of mediation which, even where christological, operate by denying the Christ's particularity. For the only way to overcome alienation, thus understood, is to eradicate distance and otherness: to unite, to homogenize, to divinize; in effect, to universalize the incarnation. And there is no way to do that without turning away from the human Jesus, or indeed from what makes *us* human.

> The fleshless word, growing, will bring us down,
> Pagan and Christian man alike will fall,
> The auguries say, the white and black and brown,
> The merry and sad, theorist, lover, all
> Invisibly will fall:
> Abstract calamity, save for those who can
> Build their cold empire on the abstract man.[2]

No doubt this calamity is what the serpent had in view from the beginning, when it first invited humans to introduce alienation by coveting equality

---

[1] 1973:781. Kant (*Rel.* 3.1.6f.) had already done so, of course, by calling for a religion 'freed from all empirical determining grounds.'

[2] Edwin Muir, from 'The Incarnate One' (1963:228f.). It is a pity that leading feminist theologians such as E. Johnson (C. LaCugna 1993:128ff.) seem not to grasp the danger here, but instead faithfully follow the Straussian lead.

with God.[3] At all events, it is the predictable outcome of the kind of thinking which wars against divine transcendence by inventing a general theory of immanence, a theory which is not really christological but cosmological, a theory which plays itself out politically and culturally as an attempt to slake the 'unquenchable thirst for universal unity.'

It was against all of this that Kierkegaard first raised the flag of resistance – homiletically, yes, and theologically too – by way of his particularism. It was against all of this that Barth protested with his determination to begin again at the beginning, that is, with Jesus. Theologians today who wish to follow up the new start which they represent will do so only by looking *for* Jesus rather than away from him, which is to say, by exacerbating still further the scandal of a particularist christology where a universalist one is demanded. That will mean choosing even more decisively than Kierkegaard or Barth against ascension of the mind and in favour of ascension in the flesh. It will also mean wrestling anew with the ecclesiological and cosmological consequences of that choice. How far we may already have come in clarifying what is at stake the reader may judge, but our destination (a vantage point, not a place to settle) is nearly in view. We will reach it when, with some assistance from the scriptures and from one of Barth's disciples, we have sharpened a little further the contrast between the two lines of thought we have been tracing.

In the Shadow of Sinai

For much of the last two chapters we have been occupied with variations on the theme of ascension of the mind. The Copernican divide notwithstanding, these variations are bound together by the priority they grant to cosmology in their speculation about the ascension, and by a need to make of 'Christ' something other or more than Jesus. From Origen onwards little has changed here. One way or another Jesus-history has been made over into the manifestation of a universal principle or pattern, Jesus himself becoming the dispensable element.[4] The knock-on effect in ecclesiology has been to render the church the κόσμος of the cosmos, domesticating the eschatological tension and making possible the advent of that incorrigible 'man of the world' who today is happy enough to be called such. Who is this man? Not so much the straightforward secularist as the man who thinks that he has 'resolutely to grasp the divine as it presents itself to us in our time,' that is, 'in history and in the connexion

---

[3] How does Hegel (1956:321) put it? 'Paradise is a park, where only brutes, not men, can remain. For the brute is one with God only implicitly . . .'

[4] 'Thus if we know the incarnation, death and resurrection, the *duplex negatio affirmat*, as the eternal circulation, the infinitely repeated pulsation of the divine life; what special importance can attach to a single fact, which is but a mere sensible image of this unending process?' (Strauss 1973:781)

of the individual's subjectivity with the substance of an overarching totality of historical life.'⁵ Here, in our opinion, is a profound falsification of the eucharistic moment, one that perpetuates the error of the western church in particular, from which the putative man of the world has taken his cue.⁶ For its part, the doctrine of bodily ascension neither invites nor allows any such grasping. That is because it cannot admit the reduction of Jesus Christ to a principle or pattern, or the merging of his history with our history in a general synthesis, but instead insists on maintaining his distinct human identity even in his departure. On this view 'the divine as it presents itself to us in our time' is the Holy Spirit, who does not in fact present himself but the absent Jesus. This is the Spirit who convicts the world 'about sin, because they do not believe in me; about righteousness, because I am going to the Father and you will see me no longer; about judgment, because the ruler of this world has been condemned.'⁷ This is the Spirit who through word and sacrament also unites us to the absent Jesus, so that it is we who are grasped or seized, ἐκ τοῦ κόσμου. The Spirit's work is an infringement on our time, an eschatological re-ordering of our being to the fellowship of the Father and the Son, and to the new creation. That gracious infringement is what the man of the world, and the church which has become worldly, falsify with talk of grasping the divine as it presents itself to us in our time.

Now in keeping with this falsification, as if in parody of the eucharistic tension, another has emerged to trouble the church: the tension between past and future. Many today mistake this for *the* ecclesiological issue, though it is nothing of the sort. It belongs to the historicism which is the bastard child of Christianity and the Enlightenment, and which first arises as a problem for the church in connection with the programme set out for it by Kant's *Religion Within the Limits of Reason Alone*. In Book 3 of that work Kant explains that a 'pure religious faith' (i.e., one properly oriented to the universal) cannot be contained in the husk of an historical religion; through perpetual criticism of the latter's facts, legends, liturgies and dogmas, the former must continually be liberated and reinvented.⁸ The church's co-operation with this programme is a sure sign that it has taken its eyes off Jesus and begun to sink like Peter into the abyss, a sign that it no longer knows or comprehends its own peculiar vocation.

⁵ Thus Troeltsch (1990:206), who adds immediately by way of caution that 'the picture of Jesus' must remain for the foreseeable future 'the rallying-point of all God's testimonies to himself found in our sphere of life.'

⁶ By 'western' we obviously do not mean merely, or especially, 'Roman.' Indeed it is fitting enough that the man of the world (inside and outside the Catholic fold) should be questioned so pointedly about his credentials and success as he is by the current pope.

⁷ John 16:9ff., NRSV. O'Donovan (1986b:105f.) correlates these three ministries of the Spirit, during 'the age of Christ's exalted absence,' with the christological events of crucifixion, resurrection/ascension, and parousia.

⁸ 'The gradual transition of ecclesiastical faith to the exclusive sovereignty of pure religious faith is the coming of the kingdom of God,' suggests Kant (3.1.7).

Following Kant's guidance has made it less and less an anomaly to the world, more and more an anomaly to itself. Internecine warfare between progressivist and traditionalist forces has been the inevitable consequence.

The editorial to which we referred in our opening pages belongs to that warfare. It is worth mentioning again because it manages – almost – to set the problem in its correct doctrinal context. 'What would it mean,' asks Mr Kerr, 'to explore the *theological* significance of the hiatus between the first and second coming?' What would it mean to wrestle with the fact that the one who ascended 'is no longer present but absent'? That is the right question. The proffered response fails, however, because it is not theological. It merely argues the toss on the past/future dilemma. The significance of our Lord's 'disappearing act,'[9] we are told, is that we may now appeal to the Spirit to 'free us from traditional theological and cultural restraints for a new openness to the future.' Indeed we may appeal to the Spirit to lift our gaze from the historical Jesus, whose contemporaries (*pace* Kierkegaard) we are not and cannot be, to the more exciting horizons of the cosmic Christ, who will show us greater things than these. Kerr's candour may be admirable, but an *aggiornaménto* of the sort recommended implies a complete abandonment of the eucharistic tension. For the eucharist, if it is anything more than an exercise in subjectivity, means precisely that we who are not contemporaries of the historical Jesus can become so in the power of the Spirit.[10] And the ascension means that this eucharistic becoming involves us in a future quite different from that of the world.

There are some, of course, who seek no such liberation from the past; today there is a definite entrenchment of traditionalist forces against the threat posed by historicism. It should be admitted, however, that the traditionalist puts himself at a great disadvantage if he too identifies Jesus-history with universal history. The logic of the eucharist, which is not linear and insists on taking us *back* to the future, may offer him at least a modicum of support. But that logic makes little or no sense in the context of a thoroughgoing evolutionism. When will he learn that 'God has no need of a temporal or historical centre'?[11] When will he face the fact that a Christ 'whose features do not adapt themselves to the requirements of a world that is evolutive in structure will tend more and more to be eliminated out of hand'?[12] How he should answer these taunts from the progressivist camp is not at all clear. It may be that the traditionalist is

---

[9] The language may be irreverent but the thought is Augustine's.

[10] For Kerr, the Spirit does not lead us into the presence of the absent Christ, but brings us round instead to an appreciation of 'the presence of the absence.' 'The perils of "spiritualizing" are obvious and should be heeded,' he notes (3), 'but in our day what H. Richard Niebuhr once called the "unitarianism of the Spirit" may be less dangerous and more promising than other theological options before us.'

[11] J. Bowden 1988:173, following Tom Driver.

[12] Teilhard 1971:212 (quoted J. Houston 1980:33).

simply condemned to being propelled backwards into a future pioneered, religiously speaking, by those who (like Kerr) are quite content with an absent Jesus and a present Christ.

We note in passing that all of this is being fought out, not only on the field of liturgics or of moral theology, but in today's heated debate over ecumenism. Is ecumenism to be a quest for some specifically churchly unity, or for some greater global unity that is still coming, to which that of the church is purely instrumental? This question (the Barmen question again!) cannot be settled without deciding once more whether Jesus himself is to be regarded in a utilitarian way. Meanwhile, the deadlock continues. Those who look to the past cling tightly to the security of their own tradition, or imagine themselves to be rediscovering some yet more primitive purity. Those who look to the future urge the church to take the next step towards its own redundancy, to press on to some yet grander catholicity by embracing the world's emerging identity as its own.[13] And that redundancy is just what is happening in those sectors of the church which have already decided in favour of the immanent or cosmic Christ, that is, in favour of ascension of the mind. There, where Jesus of Nazareth is thought to have been too long on the mountain for his story to be taken seriously any more, ecclesial self-assertion is rapidly rebounding as ecclesial self-negation, through a riotous investiture of religious significance in the stories (personal or collective) of the surrounding societies.

It may well be objected that we are making too much of a radical fringe, thus caricaturing the option before us. This grasping after the divine in our time, after the elusive immanent Christ – which really means an endless chasing after the future – should it not be regarded as an unhealthy compulsion? No doubt it should, but what blasphemy against Kant! Besides, what else is left to those who have acceded to the demand to let the man of Nazareth pass quietly into obscurity?

> The main purpose of the church is not to remember Jesus. Its main purpose, surely, is to participate now, in present-future time, in the redemption of the world.

In not a few synods this statement would draw a round of applause, would it not? Often it would not even be recognized for what it is (another golden trinket for the fire) since it has such a comforting traditional ring to it. After all, it is just one more example of the western propensity to let the church stand in for Jesus. In other words, it is still a perverted form of mariology.[14]

The same must be said, unfortunately, of the views of certain would-be critics of the conservative and progressivist forces at work in the church

---

[13] David Jenkins' foreword to Bowden's book is entitled, 'Toward the Next Stage of Christian Catholicity.'

[14] T. Driver 1981:11 (for a more sympathetic perspective, cf. D. Hall 1996:441).

today. We are thinking especially of Graham Ward, whose treatment of the ascension in *Radical Orthodoxy* might have served to expose the compulsion, but instead unwittingly reproduces it.[15] According to Ward the ascension, as scripture narrates it, is the culmination of a series of 'displacements' of the body of Jesus, belonging to an economy of deferred identity. It consummates a process of destabilization or withdrawal which begins already with the virgin birth, a verticalizing process which renders God himself open or permeable to the world, and the world permeable to God. The messianic body of the God-man just keeps on growing in ever new combinations and permutations, embracing (through symbolic mediation) ever new dimensions of human experience.[16] Ward's thesis, of course, stripped of its obfuscations and its postmodern flare, reduces to a familiar refrain: the ascension as the sublation of the all-too-definite humanity of that 'gendered Jew,' as he likes to call him, for the sake of an advancing divinization in which absence becomes the dialectical ground for presence, and ecclesiology smothers eschatology.[17]

Let us go a step further, then, in search of the radical fringe, which like that of the cosmos itself seems to recede faster than we can approach it. There is a place here, at the end of our study of the Origenist option, for the *reductio ad absurdum*. We may find it in Thomas Altizer's discussion of the risen, contemporary Christ in his book *The Descent into Hell*. For the pessimistic postmodernist, of whose nihilism Ward would not approve, the risen one comes into being (ascends in that Hegelian and Straussian sense) as the embodiment in the human race 'of the eternal death of Jesus.' That is, he becomes present and actual for us only insofar as we ourselves are prised open to eternal death.[18] He is there when and as every trace of

---

[15] See J. Milbank *et.al.*, 1999:163ff. (released as proofs of the present work were in preparation, and noted with the kind assistance of Ralph Norman).

[16] The absenting of Jesus, says Ward (176), 'is not a decisive break.' 'The withdrawal of the body of Jesus must be understood in terms of the Logos creating a space within himself, a womb, within which (*en Christoi*) the Church will expand and creation be recreated. In this way, the body of the Church and the body of the world are enfolded through resurrection within the Godhead. The body of Jesus Christ is not lost, nor does it reside now in heaven as a discrete object of veneration (as Calvin thought and certain Gnostics before him). The body of Jesus Christ, the body of God, is permeable, transcorporeal, transpositional. Within it all other bodies are situated and given their significance.' To which it may be remarked in passing that among these 'Gnostics' we will presumably have to number Irenaeus – who in the sexual cast and hermeneutical ingenuity of Ward's 'nascent theology of the ascension' would certainly find a familiar diet.

[17] Ward (181 n. 47) quotes Michel de Certeau (in Ward 1997:146f.) as follows: 'The Jesus event is extended (verified) in the manner of a disappearance in the *difference* which that event renders possible. Our relation to the origin is [a] function of its increasing absence. The beginning is more and more hidden by the multiple creations which reveal its significance.' *Précisément*.

[18] 'The resurrected Christ who is the embodiment of the eternal death of Jesus is the Christ who has descended into Hell. Hell is the point or arena where Christ is present in the world, and Christ is actual for us only insofar as we are open to eternal death.' (1979:142)

transcendence, including and especially the unique human person, is 'annulled and dissolved,' reconstituted as identical with the whole.

> Has not history itself become the arena and the expression of the negation and dissolution of primordial and transcendent Spirit? . . . Is Christ [not] present for us and in us at those points at which we pass through a dissolution of transcendence? . . . Only this passage of life unto death realizes the presence of the Kingdom of God, so that wherever death is not fully actual and real, there the Kingdom has not yet fully appeared . . . The death of the transcendence of God embodies the death of all autonomous selfhood, an end of all humanity which is created in the image of the absolutely sovereign and transcendent God.[19]

Here is the end, in both senses of the word, of the theology that grasps.[20] The advent of a universal or catholic consciousness, the epiphany of a Christ 'who is totally here and now,' warns Altizer, will necessitate 'the loss of all we have known as identity and selfhood.' Once we can accept this, he concludes, 'the way "up" will be the way "down": an ascension to Heaven will be *identical* with a descent into Hell.'[21]

We will make this provocative claim for the provocative Altizer, that he represents at least one legitimate outcome of the doctrine of Mind ascending. For that doctrine does justify an eschatological faith which aspires to mount 'an absolute assault upon the givenness of the world which it confronts.'[22] That doctrine does sanction an approach to presence which inverts the relation of contemporaneity, the hope of the *sursum corda*, and the salvific import of the eucharist. That doctrine does invite the conflation of ascending and descending, if not this vertiginous anti-gospel that calls for nothing less than the abolition of God and man together.

* * *

It was the author of Hebrews who aptly compared the eucharistic situation of the church to that of Israel at the foot of Sinai. Her saviour is ascended into the presence of the Holy One, lost to view in that impenetrable cloud overhanging the mountain. Down below rumours of glory emanate from

---

[19] Quoted from 144, 148, 154.

[20] This is the place to note that Catherine Pickstock, co-editor of *Radical Orthodoxy* with Ward and Milbank, offers in her fine monograph, *After Writing*, a very astute critique of that grasping which Altizer's thought exemplifies. Unfortunately this book too came to hand after *our* writing, and we are unable to benefit here from her analysis. The eucharistic and theological grounding of Pickstock's thought we suppose to be quite different from Ward's, even if we may still need to enquire as to whether the problem of the absence is being underestimated.

[21] See 213f. Descent and ascent, as mere thesis and antithesis, must have their synthesis. So must telling our own stories, and having no story at all.

[22] Ibid. 148.

the elders, but he himself is nowhere to be seen, except by the eye of faith. His ascension has created a time of testing for his people, a time for discipline, for perseverance, for patient waiting; or, it may be, for something else:

> When the people saw that Moses was so long in coming down from the mountain, they gathered around Aaron and said, 'Come, make us gods who will go before us. As for this fellow Moses who brought us up out of Egypt, we don't know what has happened to him.'[23]

A time of testing – and the doctrine of the ascension itself seems to belong to this testing, since it necessarily raises the question as to what has become of Jesus, and with it the possibility of grasping instead of waiting.

We have adjudged the doctrine of ascension of the mind as a type of grasping, as open therefore to the charge of idolatry. But what of the approved option, ascension in the flesh? Our examination of Barth left us with some unfinished business here, to which we must now attend. Right along we have maintained that this doctrine, often said to be the product of an outmoded cosmology, is precisely not that. Rather it entails a subordination of cosmological interests to those of Jesus-history. That was certainly Barth's position, yet we had to ask whether Barth made good his escape from speculative or cosmological theology. We saw that he did not fully overturn the idea of a natural opposition between the divine and the creaturely, and that this failure brought artificial closure to Jesus-history by means of a construction that in its own way also confused descending with ascending. Noting the secondary effects on ecclesiology, we concluded that a theological programme which means to take its direction from Jesus-history must make some alterations or adjustments to his doctrine of ascension in the flesh.

That is a point already made in T. F. Torrance's important book, *Space, Time and Resurrection*, thought it is not only Barth whom Torrance undertakes to correct.

> The way we interpret the ascended and advent *humanity* of Christ and its cosmic and eschatological import for human and physical existence in space and time, will determine more precisely how we regard the resurrection of Jesus Christ in body. A concept of the ascension in which the humanity of Jesus is swallowed up in the Spirit or Light of the eternal God, or a concept of the eschatological future which has little more material content to it than that somehow the future is more real than the past or the present, and in which the humanity of the advent Christ is replaced by 'hope', would appear to reflect in the last analysis a rather docetic understanding of the resurrection, and that in its turn would surely reflect a similar docetic understanding of the incarnation. Hence the 'human realism' with which we interpret the ascension and the final

---

[23] Exod. 32:1, NIV; cf. Heb. 12:18ff., which must of course be read with chap. 3 in mind. (See further my 'Eucharist, Eschatology and Ethics,' forthcoming.)

advent of 'this same Jesus' is likely to prove a real test for the 'human realism' in our understanding of both the historical and the risen Jesus Christ.[24]

Torrance does not criticize Barth's treatment of the hypostatic union, and seems even to presuppose it at times, which may help to account for certain inconsistencies in his argument. But he does begin disentangling ontology and soteriology just the same. Death is not regarded as something natural to man. Neither is the Son's grounding of the relationship between God and man in his own person run together with his soteriological recapitulation of that relationship.[25] For that reason Torrance's construction is more clearly asymmetrical than Barth's. In the retroactive transformation by which the earthly life of Jesus is taken up into his new existence there is not only a revelation of that life, but a new movement or development of it. And because it is a movement in his own flesh there are now *two* times rather than one: our own, in which Jesus was crucified, and that of Jesus himself, who has gone to the Father.[26]

Such a construction requires an open, eschatologically determined cosmology like that of Irenaeus. 'The healing and restoring of our being carries with it the healing, restoring, reorganizing and transforming of the space and time in which we now live our lives in relation to one another and to God.'[27] And here an Irenaean-like answer to the Where? question also begins to emerge, even if we have one or two reservations about Torrance's own way of approaching the matter. Jesus is neither alone with the Father (though in one sense he is always that) nor walking still along our road, so to speak. He goes to the Father in such a way as to prepare a place for us, 'refounding history from this new beginning,' in Balthasar's expression.[28] His ascension is a vital part of his priestly

---

[24] 1976:25f. To this work we gladly acknowledge a significant debt of inspiration and guidance.

[25] According to Torrance (ibid. 73; cf. 54), 'the resurrection reveals that what divides man from God is not the discrepancy between the finite and the infinite, since God is not limited by man's incapacities and weaknesses, although that discrepancy does become a real disjunction for us when it is infected by sin and guilt and enmity.' Descending and ascending are therefore discussed, not only in terms of the ontology of the incarnation, but also in terms of 'the gap between the time of the new man and the time of the old man.' The distinction is imperfectly drawn, however, and is sometimes heavily compromised (see 123ff., 132).

[26] See 96ff. The resurrection is 'the same event' (the earthly life of Jesus) taking place in a new way, yet somehow there is a 'beyond' to the resurrection which through the ascension is translated into a new life and ministry as our heavenly high priest. Here again the construction is vague, but it is clear that Torrance desires neither to separate the heavenly session from the earthly work, nor to *reduce* it to the same.

[27] Ibid. 91.

[28] Balthasar 1967:287; cf. Torrance 86ff. We want, however, to distance ourselves from Torrance's suggestion at the end of the book that resurrection be understood in the light of the natural stratification of reality. 'The universe that is steadily being disclosed to our various sciences,' he observes elsewhere (1985:ix), 'is found to be characterised throughout time and space by an ascending gradient of meaning in richer and higher forms of order. Instead of levels of existence and reality being explained reductionistically from below in materialistic

work, and his priestly work leaves nothing untouched, because all that he commits to the Father is in turn handed over to the Spirit. In this way it is determined from 'above,' that is, from the transformed place and time where Christ can say to the faithful, ' Fear not! I am the first and the last, and the living one.'[29]

The concept is admittedly a difficult one. We have tried (and for this we must beg our fellow travelers' indulgence) to pursue its complex logic a little further in Appendix B. What needs to be noticed here is that the Where? question is not only reversed, making Jesus-history primary, but it is given an answer that demands and allows only baptism and the eucharist as its proper articulation. Jesus ascends to the Father's right hand in the sense that the whole of creation is reorganized around him. That reorganization is *not* something that works itself out within the terms of our own spatio-temporal processes, for ours is the very space and time that requires reorganization. Yet it *is* a spatio-temporal process, since it is we ourselves who are made the objects of it and, with Jesus, its participants and beneficiaries.[30] This is precisely what the sacramental foundations of the church attest. This indeed is what God begins to effect through them, and hence through the whole liturgical and evangelical life of the church, not excluding even its cultural and scientific contributions. Since Jesus is with the Father, none can say where he is according to the canons and criteria of man. But for the same reason – that he is in fact with the Father – it has become possible for human beings to give their answer by being relocated, sacramentally, at the point of turning from the putative kingdoms of man to the messianic kingdom of God.[31]

Given his own adjustments in this direction, we are not surprised to find in Torrance that the eucharistic qualification of ecclesial life returns to prominence, along with the high-priestly ministry of Christ.[32] In an earlier book, *Royal Priesthood*, he was already trying to work out an

---

and mechanistic terms, the lower levels are found to be explained in terms of higher, invisible, intangible levels of reality.' That may be so, but surely to think along such lines is not yet to think eschatologically. Eschatology points us to a higher level of existence only by pointing us first of all to the miraculous *reconstruction* of our existence. This vital distinction is overlooked by D. Hardy (1996:145ff.) also, when he speaks of 'the continued "searching" of the Spirit to further develop the congruence of the world and humanity with God's abundance, and thereby to fulfil God's bond in Christ with the unfolding of the cosmos.' Hardy knows that we must not ignore eschatology. But are creation and eschatology really 'different aspects of the same dynamic,' as he contends? (Cf. T. Kelly 1993:189ff., who asks similar questions in rebuffing J. Honner's misguided attempt [1991:15ff.] to think together 'incarnation, eucharist, resurrection, and physics' into a new ontology inspired by quantum mechanics.)

29 Rev. 1:17; cf. 4:1ff.
30 Cf. Eph. 1:17ff.
31 Cf. Marion 161ff.
32 See 1976:98ff., 112ff. Torrance leans on Irenaeus, Calvin, and W. Milligan.

ecumenical ecclesiology that took into account the implications of ascension in the flesh.

> In the doctrine of the Church as the Body of Christ everything turns upon the fact of the resurrection of Jesus Christ in Body and His ascension in the fulness of His Humanity . . . To demythologise the ascension (which means, of course, that it must first of all be mythologised) is to dehumanise Christ, and to dehumanise Christ is to make the Gospel of no relevance to humanity, but to turn it into an inhospitable and inhuman abstraction . . . Mysticism and rationalism, sacramentalism and institutionalism, always go readily together whether in their 'Catholic' or in their 'Protestant' forms – and in both man is starved for the sheer Humanity of the Son of God.[33]

But as soon we look to the humanity of Christ, he says, we are asked to deal with the 'eschatological reserve' that belongs to our union with him. We are forced, in other words, to reckon honestly with the absence of Jesus in every assertion of his presence. The church lives in the world as the community in which this absence is, or should be, acutely felt and acknowledged. Straddling the two times, it must accept the pain of the tension between them, affirming both its existence in history and its existence contrary to history.[34] When it does so, the grasping approach to presence tends to disappear. A powerful interest in the parousia begins to take its place.[35]

Torrance thus helps us to get the story of Jesus moving again, and as soon as that happens Barth's revolution is complete. The whole dangerous game from Origen to Altizer is nullified. When absence is taken seriously and the missing third member – the parousia – is added to the descent and ascent scheme, the symmetry is broken, the suffocating circle is opened up. What emerges as of first importance is not a pattern but a particular, namely, 'this same Jesus,' who will come in like manner as he departed.[36] Naturally there is not, and cannot be, a triumph of the particular in any abstract sense, to counter the imperialist threat of ἀνάβασις νοός.[37] But there is certainly the triumph of a particular man, and with him of a whole world of particulars as recreated by God. It is to that vision – the

---

[33] See 1993:43ff. (first edition 1955).

[34] 'The Church thus lives, as it were, in two times . . . Because of its participation in the time of the new creation, the Church can continue to live on earth and in history only through being crucified with Christ to the time-form of this world' (1976:99; see also 1993:51).

[35] Cf. 1965:151f. (following John Knox), 1976:99ff., 1993:58ff.

[36] It is 'by the man Jesus that God will finally judge the earth, and by the man Jesus that resurrection and the new creation will finally come upon the old creation.' Thus will 'the vast cosmic significance of the incarnation of the Word . . . be made clear and manifest to all' (1976:103).

[37] Just weeks before his death, speaking on Swiss radio, Barth set his life's labour once more under the familiar signature, warning against any such abstraction: 'The last word which I have to say as a theologian and also as a politician is not a term like "grace", but a name, "Jesus Christ"' (Busch 496).

vision of a new creation in which God is God and humanity authentically human, and the world a fruitful place – that the doctrine of ascension in the flesh leads.

There is one thing that requires to be added, however, of a critical nature. In the background faint echoes of Augustine's retraction theory still linger in Torrance. Which is to say, the question of Jesus' universal lordship, precisely as a particular man, is often begged or even undermined by pointing directly to his divinity.[38] Dietrich Bonhoeffer – whose stirring 1933 christology lectures also reject any compromise of Christ's ascended humanity, insisting that what is overcome by him is our fallen condition and not our finite nature as such – makes a similar mistake. The incarnate one is able to make himself the centre of our existence, corporately and individually, simply because he *is* the incarnate one.[39] What we miss in both these theologians is Irenaeus' thoroughly pneumatological way of thinking about Jesus, about the church, and about the 'reorganization of the mystery of the sons of God;' in short, his combination of the creaturely and the epicletic. We note with approval that, in Torrance's exposition of the eucharist, Calvin's co-ordination of Jesus and the Spirit reasserts itself as the basis for a comprehensive eschatological worldview.[40] But Colin Gunton is right to suggest that in the doctrine of the resurrection he gives inadequate attention to the Spirit's role, and that is true as well in his treatment of the ascension.[41] To look beyond Jesus' humanity to the operation of his divinity in order to explain his 'towering authority' over the world is a move that runs counter to everything we have been saying. We must look instead to the Spirit, whose task it is in the ascension to present Jesus to the Father as beloved son and heir, and to present him to us also, in his heavenly session, as brother and Lord.

Where the Spirit is in view together with Jesus' humanity, we are more firmly on the trinitarian ground Barth, Torrance and Bonhoeffer all desire. We are also on the way to a pluralism that refuses to front for the insidious christomonism of the Origenist tradition.[42] Ephesians 4 (a passage much abused in that tradition) is instructive here. It is not Christ who is

---

[38] Cf. 1976:124, 132, 154f. The influence of the later Alexandrians is powerful here, as elsewhere in Torrance.

[39] What Bonhoeffer (1978:43ff.) does is in most respects quite profound, however. He turns us from false questions as to *how* a man can be God, or *how* he can be present with us, to *who* questions – questions about his and our identity in mutual relation. In particular, and this is very Irenaean, he asks us not to avoid an hamartiological problem by substituting an ontological one: 'The doctrine of the incarnation and the doctrine of the humiliation must be strictly distinguished from each other . . . The incarnation is related to the first [and the new] creation; the humiliation is related to the fallen creation.' (106f.)

[40] Cf. 1976:147ff., Walker 71f.

[41] 1992:62f. The Nestorians were correct (if for the wrong reason) to insist on the Spirit's role in the ascension.

[42] Cf. Teilhard's (1964:46) telling remark: 'Pluralism, far from being the ultimate end of evolution, is merely a first outspreading whose gradual shrinkage displays the true curve of Nature's proceedings.'

identified as ὁ ἐπὶ πάντων καὶ διὰ πάντων καὶ ἐν πᾶσιν; that of course is the 'one God and Father of all.' Christ, in consummation of the promise of Eden and of Sinai, is rather ὁ ἀναβὰς ὑπεράνω πάντων τῶν οὐρανῶν ἵνα πληρώσῃ τὰ πάντα.[43] And it is only by means of the Spirit, who distributes 'to each one of us'[44] the gifts which flow from Christ – including the resurrection of the dead and the life of the world to come – that this human work of filling and fulfilling, satisfying and perfecting, is achieved.

Ecce Homo!

'The question at the back of this episode,' writes Leslie Houlden, referring to the story of the ascension, 'is that of the permanent centrality of Jesus.' We agree. We also happen to think that the church, or that portion of it which represents the remnants of Christendom, is coming to a crossroads which defies all indecision on the matter. A choice about the centrality of Jesus will have to be made, and made with the doctrine of the ascension in mind. But according to Professor Houlden the Where? question is a non-question, and here we must differ.[45] The Where? question cannot be avoided either. Carelessly asked, as at Sinai, it already betrays a fatal lack of interest in its subject. Diligently asked, it helps to elicit an answer about who that subject is, whether we should still be expecting him, and what we should be doing in the meantime. It helps to clarify the choice between ascension in the flesh and ascension of the mind, and with it the nature of the eucharistic situation.

The answer we have been advocating is a disturbing one. It is not disturbing because, in maintaining that Jesus has gone in the flesh to the Father, it refuses to admit that 'we do not know what has happened to him.' On the contrary, it is disturbing because it states quite categorically that we do not know; that we cannot place him, spatially or temporally or materially or spiritually, with respect to ourselves; that he is not above us or ahead of us or alongside us or within us, even if each of these metaphors has something helpful to say about his actual relation to us. It is disturbing because it challenges the assumption that to talk about a human being who cannot be so placed is meaningless, and because it implies that every attempt to define him as something *other* than a human being is really an act of violence designed to force him to yield his meaning on our terms. It is disturbing because it challenges our entire frame of reference, physical and metaphysical, by allowing one particular man to

---

[43] i.e., 'far above all rule and authority, power and dominion, and every title that can be given, not only in the present age but also in the one to come,' so that he might become 'head over everything for the church' (Eph. 1.21f., NIV; cf. 4.4–13). Ought we to see in 2:4–7 a reference to Exodus 24? The entire context is surely Sinaitic in the first instance.

[44] Eph. 4:7; cf. Acts 2:3.

[45] Allowances being made, of course, for the context of his statement (1991:177ff.; cf. 1992). C. Cocksworth (202f.) also regards the question as a 'cul-de-sac.'

stand over against us as a question mark against our very existence. The ascension, as J. G. Davies perceptively remarks, is God's own *Ecce homo!*[46]

We want in conclusion to develop this allusion with the help of the Apocalypse, a rather obvious source for the doctrine of the ascension to which we have not yet made recourse. But first let us recognize an objection, namely, that it is really we who seek to preserve a prior frame of reference. Why do we keep repeating the words 'this same Jesus'? And why must Jesus' identity remain bodily identity? Or, if bodily, why in Irenaeus' sense rather than Origen's? Are we not in danger of a merely sentimental attachment to Jesus, of the clinging that he himself forbade? Of course, this objection has been with us all along, and we have been answering it all along. We will not respond by turning back to scripture and creed, or by pressing on to discuss complex questions in theological anthropology about the meaning of identity or of personhood – vital subjects which belong to a fuller treatment of ecclesiology as such, precisely in connection with the doctrine of the ascension.[47] We will only remind the reader that to press this objection is to reject either the Christian belief in the redemption of the whole person, or in flesh and blood as constituent elements of the person.[48] Doubts about the substantiality of the human subject on *any* level are the unsurprising consequence.

That said, we must pause a moment over another and more pertinent form of the objection. Does the position we are taking on the ascension not invite the suspicion (even among those who are no friends of Strauss) that we are operating christologically with a naïve individualism? And is that individualism not in fact counter-ecclesial? When we say 'Christ,' explains John Zizioulas, 'we mean a person and not an individual; we mean a relational reality existing "for me" or "for us."'

> Here the Holy Spirit is not one who *aids* us in bridging the distance between Christ and ourselves, but he is the person of the Trinity who actually realizes in history that which we call Christ, this absolutely relational entity, our Saviour . . . All separation between christology and ecclesiology vanishes in the Spirit.[49]

Now if the church is indeed, as Ephesians asserts, τὸ σῶμα αὐτοῦ, τὸ πλήρωμα τοῦ τὰ πάντα ἐν πᾶσιν πληρουμένου, will we not want eventually to say

---

[46] 1969:16.

[47] Cf. C. Morse 1994:169. Such a treatment we hope to offer in a subsequent work.

[48] *Constituent* elements – we are not wanting to assert that the physical body is the most significant aspect of human personhood, identity or presence, whether in the eucharistic situation or even at the parousia. But we do want to side with Irenaeus: 'As therefore, when that which is perfect is come, we shall not see another Father, but him whom we now desire to see . . ., neither shall we look for another Christ and Son of God, but him who [was born] of the Virgin Mary, who also suffered, in whom we trust, and whom we love' (*AH* 4.9.2; cf. 5.14.4). See also C. S. Lewis 1978:143ff.

[49] 1985:110f.; cf. 137f., however, for an eschatological qualification.

something very like this? And if so, would we not be better off to eschew protracted talk of ascension in the flesh, for fear of throwing up a narrow and competing meaning of σῶμα – of getting stuck on what Zizioulas calls the biological hypostasis rather than the ecclesial?[50] Would we not be wiser, at all events, to let the Where? question alone, or at least to be content, as Zizioulas appears to be, with an answer like Bonhoeffer's? The *pro nobis* structure of Christ's being, says Bonhoeffer, means that he remains, albeit in a hidden liturgical way, at 'the centre of human existence, of history and of nature.'[51] This would appear to fit nicely with the view of the Apocalypse. Certainly it would deliver us from any temptation to think of him, in Luther's sardonic phrase, as 'a stork in a nest in the treetop'![52]

Let us not be hasty, however. That Jesus' personal identity cannot be defined in terms of mere individuality, since it is perichoretically constituted by his unity with the Father and the Spirit, is not in doubt here. That it is also constituted by his union with the church is not in doubt either, as our discussion of Irenaeus will have made clear. All that has been ruled out is any construal of his union with the church as a denial of his absence, hence of the eschatological qualification of ecclesial being.[53] That, and any denial of his material particularity, as if the latter were itself a barrier to ecclesial being. Under fallen conditions the body, like the soul, impedes as well as serves communion, whether with God or with fellow creatures; this is plain enough. But under the conditions of the new creation the case is otherwise, and those are the conditions that

[50] 'The body tends towards the person but leads finally to the individual' (ibid. 51). This individualization must be overcome through the birth of the ecclesial hypostasis in baptism, i.e., in union with Christ, who has his identity from the Spirit in and as the communion of a pneumatic 'body' (113 n. 116).

[51] For Bonhoeffer the Where? question belongs within the Who? question: 'Christ is Christ, not just for himself, but in relation to me' (1978:47; see 58ff.). He is therefore genuinely present, temporally and spatially, in a unity of act and being, as word and sacrament and ecclesial community. This new form of the humiliation of the God-man is his *only* form between the resurrection and the parousia. But see n. 53 below.

[52] See J. McLelland (Empie and McCord) 42f. R. Jenson (1/201ff.) steers well clear of the said temptation, while also trying to avoid a disembodied Christ: 'It is safe to say that most modern believers, whatever doctrine they may formally espouse, actually envision the risen Christ as *not* embodied, as a pure "spirit," or perhaps as embodied in a very thinned-out fashion, as – not to be too fine about it – a spook. A body requires its place, and we find it hard to think of any place for this one.' Jenson, like Brunner, proposes the church itself as the body, hence as the proper answer to the Where? question. But in reply see Farrow (*et. al.*) 1999:92f.

[53] Christ and his church are present only eschatologically, only as the Spirit makes a way across the boundary line that has been drawn through all things, even time itself, by Jesus-history. Bonhoeffer (1978:60) recognizes this in pointing out that if Jesus is the mediator between God and man, he is the mediator also between us and ourselves, that is, between 'the old and the new existence.' That is why his presence is a hidden presence, and his ecclesial body an entity in the world but not of it – why Christianity must be 'religionless' or, as we would say, ambiguous.

appertain in the case of Jesus, or rather, are made to appertain for and through him. We see no reason, then, to sustain this form of the objection either; nor do we think that the theologians mentioned above would wish us to. Zizioulas, like Bonhoeffer, is explicit: 'the biological and the eschatological hypostases are not mutually exclusive.'[54] As for Luther's jibe, does it not lose its force when (following Zizioulas) we understand the sacraments as nothing less than eschatological events? That is, as events in which the Spirit begins here and now his inscrutable work of expropriating human beings, and the time and space of human beings, for the new creation which Christ has gone to prepare? But lest we stray further into matters that must be reserved for another day, we turn now to our concluding reflection, the homiletic character of which we will make no effort to disguise.

* * *

In the eucharistic vision which opens the Apocalypse, John encounters at close quarters Daniel's famous son of man, dazzling in the Melchizedekian splendour of his heavenly session.

> On the Lord's Day I was in the Spirit, and I heard behind me a loud voice like a trumpet . . . I turned around to see the voice that was speaking to me. And when I turned I saw seven golden lampstands, and among the lampstands was someone 'like a son of man,' dressed in a robe reaching down to his feet and with a golden sash around his chest. His head and hair were white like wool, as white as snow, and his eyes were like blazing fire. His feet were like bronze glowing in a furnace, and his voice was like the sound of rushing waters. In his right hand he held seven stars, and out of his mouth came a sharp double-edged sword. His face was like the sun shining in all its brilliance. When I saw him, I fell at his feet as though dead.[55]

Ecce homo! Thus accosted, John instantly recognizes in himself one who belongs to a race that is 'turned backwards.' In the presence of the exalted one, the living one, he experiences himself as but a shade, a dead man. At

---

[54] 1985:52 n. 46. Zizioulas is following Maximus, to be sure, and our differing treatments of Maximus do suggest areas in which agreement is not complete. We think Zizioulas himself over-inclined to see eschatology as an answer to an ontological rather than an hamartiological problem – i.e., to suffering 'from createdness' – and we do not wish to contrast the biological with the ecclesial in the same way that he does. But the corporate Christ of which Zizioulas speaks does not invite a denial or sublation of particularity, even of bodily particularity. Our bodily nature must be adapted to a truly catholic and communal form of life (in which each person belongs to the whole and the whole to each person) but it will not be abandoned. Nor should we suppose that because each member of the church is in some sense 'Christ' that there is no more need to confess one man, Jesus, as *the* Christ. (Cf. also Pannenberg 3/628ff.)

[55] 1.10ff., NIV.

the head of his work he sets a word of warning for the church and for the world, conjoining Daniel's ascension motif with a premonition of the parousia:

> Behold! He is coming with the clouds
> and every eye will see him,
> even those who pierced him;
> and because of him all the tribes of the earth will wail.[56]

Is this not a sobering word for those who suppose that humankind is advancing in the right direction, who may even think with Strauss that christology should not stop short with Jesus? Does it not have something disquieting to say to all who would resolve by degrees the problem of the presence and the absence, ignoring ancient prophecies about 'minglings without cohesion' and the resolute look in the eye of the coming one?[57] Yet it is a word implicit in every eucharist, given with the food which sustains those who, even on far-flung islands, wait patiently in their precarious position at the foot of the mountain.

In the epicletic interim between the ascension and the parousia, it is the privilege and burden of the eucharistic community to hear the *Ecce homo!* and to echo it around the world, whatever the cost. It may be that it has already been pronounced clearly enough by God himself, if with an irony greater than any Roman procurator's. Pilate, who thrust Jesus forwards at the Stone Pavement, could only put him as a question to a few people, but God has put him as a question to everyone simply by withdrawing him into the sanctuary of his own house. Does Jesus' incomprehensible absence not confront us with the anomalous character of our alienated place and time?[58] But who understands the divine irony? Who is really aware of this absence? As an absence without parallel it is little noticed, much less identified for what it is, even where talk of absence (in the abstract) may be all the rage. Indeed, it would not be noticed or identified at all but for the work of the Spirit, who here and there tantalizes us with a real presence so that we may discover what real absence is, thus learning to love and long for Jesus' appearing.[59]

---

[56] κόψονται ἐπ' αὐτόν (1.7).

[57] Michelangelo captured that look on the wall of the Sistine Chapel, which portrays Jesus descending like Moses into the camp of the revelers, his intercessions on the mountain at an end. Not surprisingly, some find this too an embarrassing work which requires extensive demythologizing (see H. Küng 1992:168f.; cf. Rev. 19:11ff.).

[58] Augustine is right to maintain that the withdrawal of Jesus is theologically significant; only we do not face the issue it raises by inquiring about Jesus' *divinity* but about Jesus himself.

[59] The *kontakion* for the feast of the ascension tries in vain to assure us that we have 'in no wise' been parted from our Lord, even if it be understood as looking ahead to Pentecost. For Pentecost does not *resolve* the problem of the presence and the absence. It *creates* it, by adding a presence which discloses the absence.

The *Ecce homo!* must be repeated eucharistically, then, if it is to be heard where it needs to be heard. But what if the church which hears it begins to forget the absence? What if it thinks that what it has to offer the world is pure presence?[60] Worse than the world's ignorance of Jesus' absence, worse far than its fumbling after the right name for something it nonetheless intuits, is the church's failure to proclaim the absence clearly, to witness in its every act of worship that it really is 'looking for his coming again with power and great glory.' Is the ascension already the Father's *Ecce homo*? Yet only proleptically, only with the intention of bringing Jesus out again and setting him before us once more as the man he is. Not the ascension by itself, but the ascension and the parousia together, constitute the *Ecce homo!* which in the eucharist is heard and repeated. Christ has died, Christ is risen, Christ will come again; for God 'has fixed a day on which he will have the world judged in righteousness by a man whom he has appointed.'[61] Nothing is more important for the world to know than that, since it too, in a quite different sense, is in a precarious position! But if even the church will not acknowledge the absence of Jesus how can the world hope to learn of it? How can it hope to have its attention drawn now, before the parousia and the day of wrath, to him whose intercession with the Father does not preclude but requires that he come also as judge?[62]

The church that forgets the absence inevitably begins to misunderstand and misconstrue the presence. It is the sick church of Laodicea, which knows neither how far nor how near its Lord really is. It is the church that no longer wills to live in eucharistic precariousness, that no longer sees the link between the eucharist and martyrdom. Martyrdom, as the Apocalypse teaches, is the truest manifestation of Jesus' heavenly session, which – as the effecting in all things of the recapitulation he has accomplished – is a mystery that cannot otherwise declare itself except in the resurrection. Martyrdom reproduces the *Ecce homo!* without compromise, pronouncing its 'amen' in human flesh and blood, for the sake of the world. As such it rightly interprets the eucharistic offering, and the Christian calling to inhabit the present in a transformative way.[63] The

---

[60] G. O'Collins (1995:309ff.) is quite mistaken to choose 'presence as a notion capable of synthesizing a fully deployed Christology,' however many 'attractive features' such a christology might display.

[61] Acts 17.30f., NRSV.

[62] Cf. again Exod. 32:9ff.

[63] This transformative way, just because it engages human existence without reservation, can and does lead to other manifestations of the heavenly session of Jesus, in individual lives and in society at large. It may therefore lead to situations in which martyrdom is *not* an immediate experience of the church. Yet martyrdom remains that for which the church is, or should be, ready in the conduct of its redemptive mission (see Caird 1966 *passim*, Marion 195ff., S. Hauerwas 1991:35ff., O'Donovan 1996:212ff., M. Banner 1998:22ff.). The martyr's action is truly an action in waiting, and the company of martyrs recapitulates the action of the crowd at Sinai and of the mob before Pilate, by owning Jesus as their king

church that is no longer the martyr church, or must look for its martyrs among those whose death, however noble, is for lesser names than the name of Jesus, is in imminent danger of ceasing to be the church. And where the doctrine of the ascension is used to marginalize rather than to exalt Jesus, this must quickly become the case. A doctrine of his departure that is not also a doctrine of his impending return is a doctrine capable of converting absence into presence *without* martyrdom. As such it is a doctrine which makes the church sick, just where the world most needs it to be healthy.

In the Spirit, however, as the rest of John's opening vision testifies, life and vitality are granted not only to the sick but even to the dead. In the Spirit even Laodiceans may find themselves feeling the touch of the Master's hand and standing on their feet again. Through an open door in heaven they may glimpse and experience something of what John saw and experienced: the praise of God and of the Lamb, flowing like glorious new wine from a creation in transformation.[64] Caught up in this chorus of praise, they too may learn to embrace their vocation as the wine press of the Spirit, situated redemptively at the tear- and blood-bespattered junction between two histories and two worlds.[65]

Here also is a sobering thought, perhaps the most sobering of all. It is kept at bay by those who accuse the Spirit of having a thinning effect on Jesus, that is, of making him present on terms the world can recognize and accept. To withdraw this accusation is of course to admit that the ascension means two histories, and two histories two competing projects in the making of man – one the work of God's own hands, the other *homo faber ipsius*.[66] Today such an admission may seem especially difficult, and the ecclesiology it supports awkward and contrary. But the alternative is to identify the ascended one as someone other than Jesus, and in due course to cease being troubled by eucharistic visions at all. That is a path on which we may expect only this: to arrive at Damascus without incident.

---

at the cost of their *own* death. Hence the promise that is made to them: 'To him who overcomes, I will give the right to sit with me on my throne, just as I overcame and sat down with my Father on his throne' (Rev. 3:22, NIV; cf. 1 Thess. 1:9f.).

[64] See 4.1ff.

[65] The wine press of the Spirit is an Irenaean concept; the Apocalypse speaks rather about the wine press of God's wrath. But to be the former, the church must be prepared to anticipate redemptively the latter. (Cf. Milligan 199, who might have answered Strauss rather differently in his 1891 Baird Lectures had he made more of this point.)

[66] Cf. J. McIntyre 1957:82, D. Farrow 1989:23ff.

Appendix A

Biblical Resources

1. New Testament Ascension References

The following list of texts[1] is not intended to be exhaustive, but simply to indicate at a glance the high profile of our subject in the apostolic documents. Thematically related passages (touching, e.g., on Christ's universal authority, heavenly priesthood, or parousia) in the New Testament, and those in both Testaments (see especially the Psalms) which in one fashion or another develop the ascension motif, are too many and too difficult to sample effectively in this way. We have therefore confined this list mainly to passages which point to the ascension more or less directly, though not all of these are included either.

Matthew
26:64 you will see the Son of Man sitting at the right hand of the Mighty One and coming on the clouds of heaven

Mark
14:62 [ibid.]
16:19 he was taken up into heaven and he sat at the right hand of God

Luke
9:31 they spoke about his departure
9:51 as the time approached for him to be taken up to heaven
24:51 he left them and was taken up into heaven

John
1:18 who is at the Father's side
3:13 no one has ever gone into heaven except the one who came from heaven

---

[1] Quotations are from the New International Version.

6:62	What if you see the Son of Man ascend to where he was before!
14:2	I am going [to my Father's house] to prepare a place for you
20:17	I am returning [ἀναβαίνω] to my Father

Acts

1:9	he was taken up before their very eyes
2:34	David did not ascend to heaven
3:21	he must remain in heaven until the time comes
5:31f.	God exalted him to his own right hand . . . we are witnesses
7:56	I see heaven open and the Son of Man standing at the right hand of God.

Romans

8:34	Christ who died – more than that, who was raised to life – is at the right hand of God
10:6	'Who will ascend into heaven?' (that is, to bring Christ down)[2]

2 Corinthians

12:2	I know a man in Christ who was caught up to the third heaven – whether it was in the body or out of the body I do not know

Ephesians

1:20	when he raised him from the dead and seated him at his right hand
4:7–13	who ascended higher than all the heavens

Philippians

2:9	therefore God exalted him to the highest place
3:14	the upward call of God in Christ Jesus

Colossians

3:1	set your hearts on things above, where Christ is seated

1 Timothy

3:16	was taken up in glory

---

[2] Note the parallelism in this passage: 'Who will ascend into heaven?' is matched to the confession 'Jesus is Lord.' 'Who will descend into the deep?' is matched to 'believe in your heart that God raised him from the dead.' The resurrection is God's deliverance of Jesus; the ascension is Jesus' enthronement.

Hebrews
    1:3   he sat down at the right hand of the Majesty in heaven (*passim*)
    4:14   a great high priest who has gone through the heavens
    6:19f. the inner sanctuary behind the curtain where Jesus, who went before us, has entered on our behalf
    7:26   exalted above the heavens
    8:4   if he were on earth, he would not be a priest
    9:11   he went through the greater and more perfect tabernacle that is not man-made, that is to say, not a part of this creation
    9:24   he entered heaven itself

1 Peter
    3:21f. by the resurrection of Jesus Christ, who has gone into heaven

Revelation
    11:12 they went up to heaven in a cloud
    12:5   and her child was snatched up to God and to his throne

2. The Descent–Ascent Motif in Scripture

The following diagram, if carefully pondered in the light of our comments in chapter two, says more in some twenty words than might be said in several thousands. It requires to be read vertically (Eden–Calvary, etc.) as well as horizontally. The asterisks mark those members which in some way subvert the series, and the two arrows indicate that after the ascent of Christ the upper and lower lines may each be read consecutively.

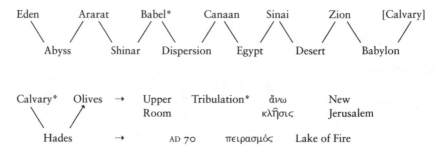

Having pondered it we might want to draw it differently, of course, or indeed in a number of different ways, for diagrams of this kind are necessarily both cryptic and somewhat arbitrary. In any case, the richness of the motif, and of the narrative from which it is abstracted – including the life of Jesus, which recapitulates the whole in some detail – invites other attempts.

3. The Rhetorical Structure of Hebrews

The following analysis makes no attempt to display the more complicated substructures in the content of this epistolary sermon, but only to demonstrate that its rhetorical shape consciously mirrors Hebrews' central focus on the significance of the ascension of Jesus. The sermon is clearly moulded by a series of carefully balanced exhortations (following on an opening eulogy) to which is matched a series of messianic titles reflecting the ascension motifs of cult and monarchy. In between these exhortations fall the famous warning passages, one for each section, as well as the expositions of Pentecost lections, key psalms, and other related passages. The structure, without being at all rigid, is remarkably consistent. Combined with the overall theme of pilgrimage – 'bringing many sons to glory,' 2:10 – it produces a powerful effect indeed:

Chaps 1–12
The Homily

1:1–4	3:1	4:14–16	8:1–6	10:19–25	12:1–3	12:28–29
ὅθεν...	οὖν...	κεφάλαιον	οὖν...	τοιγαροῦν...		διό...
		'the main point'				

'we have
a high priest who
sat down at the right hand'

'draw near'   'draw near'

'sharers of a heavenly calling,   'let us run . . . fixing
concentrate on Jesus'   our eyes on Jesus'[3]

'he sat down at the right hand'   'let us be grateful'

Son	High Priest Apostle	High Priest Son	High Priest Λειτουργὸς	High Priest Son (29)	'author and mediator perfecter' (24)

Chap. 13
epistolary exhortations
benediction: 'that Great Shepherd'

In its large central section Hebrews invites us to superimpose on this rhetorical structure a simple diagram of the earthly tabernacle, to serve

---

[3] 3:1 κατανοήσατε τὸν ἀπόστολον καὶ ἀρχιερέα τῆς ὁμολογίας ἡμῶν, Ἰησοῦν
12:2 ἀφορῶντες εἰς τὸν τῆς πίστεως ἀρχηγὸν καὶ τελειωτὴν Ἰησοῦν

as the symbol of Jesus' reception in the uncreated Holy of Holies. This entry (i.e., his ascension to the Father) in turn spells out an altogether new existence for man, and with him, for the whole creation:

οἰκουμένη μέλλων
(existence *coram Deo*)

↑

– – – – Χριστός – – – –

οἰκουμένη
(fallen existence)

Κόσμος

Some fail to take adequate notice of this dynamic, liturgical way of viewing things, in which old/new, inner/outer, higher/lower, visible/invisible, shakeable/unshakeable, etc., are apt (if inadequate) expressions of a non-dualist cosmology: a cosmology of transposition, we might say, a transposition accomplished in and through the ascension of Jesus, who thus becomes the priest-king of creation. He 'passes through' and is 'exalted above the heavens' not only by becoming pre-eminent in honour, but by re-ordering the fundamental structures of created life around himself, making it presentable to God in and with himself. Neither the writer of Hebrews nor the writer of the Apocalypse, who takes up a similar viewpoint though working in a different genre, could hope to be much more specific than this. Then again, neither can we.

Appendix B

Exaltation and Pre-existence

In *Born Before All Time?* Karl-Josef Kuschel has rightly argued that many biblical statements about pre-existence have an eschatological context and require to be considered in that light.[1] That is something not often noticed. Pre-existence is usually discussed in the rather different terms which arise directly from the confession that Jesus-history is also divine history, the history of Immanuel, 'God with us.' Such is the pre-existence the Nicene Creed has in view when it tells us that the Son is 'eternally begotten' of the Father or (using spatial rather than temporal imagery) that he 'came down from heaven.'[2] Unlike Kuschel we take no issue with any of this. If Jesus really is God giving himself to us, then we must be prepared to speak of his pre-existence *as* God; that is, we must be ready to engage with all seriousness in trinitarian discourse.[3] Yet Kuschel's primary point stands. The eschatological setting of so much of the biblical interest in Jesus' pre-existence suggests that another sort of discussion is also in order alongside the traditional one.

Before opening up that discussion, however, it will be helpful to clear away two related errors. First, pre-existence as God (let us call it P[1]) cannot properly be construed in terms of creaturely time, any more than the movement into our flesh can be construed in terms of creaturely space.

---

[1] Hence our title, which in its mixture of spatial and temporal language is something of an oxymoron. Our agreement with Kuschel is already a qualified one, however, since he would say 'all' where we have said 'many.'

[2] The term προϋπάρχειν was coined earlier by Justin (*Dial.* 48.1; cf. Kuschel 393) to refer to the fact that the Christ was not merely a man among men but *God* among men.

[3] Kuschel wants to speak about the origin of Jesus in God's own 'prior time,' and therefore of his mission as one that 'affects the being of God from eternity' (492ff.). But he does not want to speak in terms of an immanent Trinity, only of a dynamic 'unity of creation, revelation and redemption' revealed through Jesus (390). The 'event of Jesus' is the Word of God, the full revelation of God, and as such 'a factor in determining God's nature.' Hence Scripture can speak of him as the eternal Son, but the creed strays into mythology with its 'God from God,' etc. (Unfortunately, Kuschel fails to reckon with Athanasius' analysis of Θεολόγειν and μυθολόγειν.)

'He came down' is not a literal expression implying somewhere that is up; likewise, 'he pre-existed' does not look back to the period from creation to incarnation, nor yet to some primordial time before creation or indeed bracketing it. Both expressions (which ought not to be restricted to the past tense, since no tense nor any combination of tenses can do them justice) are simply ways of saying that the fact that the Father has a Son, and the Son a Father, is not a fact contingent upon the creation.[4] Otherwise put, both are ways of acknowledging the divine otherness and freedom of the one who gives himself, and is given to us, as a man.

Second, it follows from this that we certainly must not make any exclusive correlation between P[1] and that movement within Jesus-history which culminates with the cross and the descent into hell, as if that were the only course the incarnate one could take.[5] P[1] simply affirms that he *is* the incarnate one, whether descending or ascending. Thus in Philippians 2 (a passage which in our judgment does make reference to P[1], albeit in the naïve language of the past tense) we are invited to draw a line between the incarnation as such and the story which it comprises. God becomes man, the creator a creature:

ἐν μορφῇ θεοῦ ὑπάρχων
οὐχ ἁρπαγμὸν ἡγήσατο τὸ εἶναι ἴσα θεῷ
ἀλλὰ ἑαυτὸν ἐκένωσεν
μορφὴν δούλου λαβών.[6]

But it is as a man, in the freedom of his creaturehood, that he descends and ascends:

ἐν ὁμοιώματι ἀνθρώπων γενόμενος
καὶ σχήματι εὑρεθεὶς ὡς ἄνθρωπος,
ἐταπείνωσεν ἑαυτόν
γενόμενος ὑπήκοος μέχρι θανάτου —
θανάτου δὲ σταυροῦ!

---

[4] Because of the incarnation it *is* a fact of creation, or we would not know it to be a fact at all. But it is a fact which does not derive from or depend upon creation, or even upon the will to create; just the reverse.

[5] In order, i.e., to *be* incarnate. That such was his only true course as the Father's obedient Son, in his act of reconciling fallen man, we readily admit (cf. Barth, CD 4/1:194). But we do not want to limit the person and work of Christ to his act of reconciliation.

[6] It has been proposed, of course, that the reference in the first stanza of this hymn is not to God the Son *per se*, but to a 'heavenly man' of some sort. But such a man has foreign, docetic features which the apostle would not have recognized. The only heavenly man in which the hymn is interested is the one who comes into view in the last stanza, namely, the exalted Jesus. We have already argued this at length (1986:53ff.) against Oscar Cullmann, though we have since found N. T. Wright's construction of the matter (1983:359ff.) more persuasive than our own. Wright recognizes an Adamic framework yet argues convincingly that the first stanza has 'nothing to do with a pre-existent *man*' (383), but is indeed incarnational.

διὸ καὶ ὁ θεὸς αὐτὸν ὑπερύψωσεν
καὶ ἐχαρίσατο αὐτῷ τὸ ὄνομα τὸ ὑπὲρ πᾶν ὄνομα
ἵνα ἐν τῷ ὀνόματι Ἰησοῦ πᾶν γόνυ κάμψῃ ...
καὶ πᾶσα γλῶσσα ἐξομολογήσηται ὅτι κύριος Ἰησοῦς Χριστὸς ...

Confusion on this point has the very serious side-effect of conflating P¹ with that other form of pre-existence (let us call it P²) about which we must now speak: the pre-existence of a *man*, a pre-existence which is disclosed to us and interpreted for us chiefly through the ascension.

We shall find evidence of P² in two other passages, namely, the prologue to John and the *carmen Christi* in Colossians 1. Along the way we will take further note of Kuschel, expanding on our differences. We will also try to draw some conclusions as to the proper meaning of P² in the light of our own eschatological approach. This will permit us to make a number of remarks that will help to indicate how our position differs from that of Karl Barth, who is perhaps the chief exponent of P².

Colossians 1

Tom Wright, who takes the view that 'the contrast of Adam and Christ is somewhere near the heart of Paul's thought,' offers a balanced approach to Colossians 1:15–20 within the wider context of Pauline christology. Facing the scandal of the cross from the higher ground of Jesus' astonishing vindication, Paul saw that Jesus had not only assumed Adam's place as lord of the world – a role to which Israel as a nation aspired – but also Israel's place as the world's redeemer, a calling she had effectively refused. He therefore sought to present Jesus as the true image of God, says Wright, '*both* in his obedience unto death *and* in his new state of post-resurrection existence as "life-giving spirit"' (i.e., in the old creation as in the new).[7] If the people of the Torah were meant to stand in for Adam, displaying the wisdom and righteousness of God to a fallen world, the crucified one had now stood in for them. He it was, therefore, who had turned out to be the centre and climax of creation, and as such its 'pre-existent' blueprint.

Wright thus upholds a conviction we have tried in our own way to articulate elsewhere, namely, that in this passage εἰκών can and should 'be given its full force of "the *human* image of God."' Karl Barth, for one, agrees. It is certainly 'the Son *in concreto* and not *in abstracto*, Jesus Christ,' of whom we are reading here.[8] The text runs as follows:

---

[7] *Pace* J. Dunn (1980) *et.al.*, Wright is careful to observe that Paul's insights turn on the axis of crucifixion–exaltation and do not flow from the latter only (1983:384ff.; cf. *The Climax of the Covenant*, chap. 6).

[8] CD 2/2:98f. (cf. Farrow 1986:93f., 126ff., 176ff.).

ὅς ἐστιν εἰκὼν τοῦ θεοῦ τοῦ ἀοράτου
πρωτότοκος πάσης κτίσεως
ὅτι ἐν αὐτῷ ἐκτίσθη τὰ πάντα ἐν τοῖς οὐρανοῖς καὶ ἐπὶ τῆς γῆς
τὰ ὁρατὰ καὶ τὰ ἀόρατα
εἴτε θρόνοι εἴτε κυριότητες εἴτε ἀρχαὶ εἴτε ἐξουσίαι
τὰ πάντα δι᾽ αὐτοῦ καὶ εἰς αὐτὸν ἔκτισται·
καὶ αὐτός ἐστιν πρὸ πάντων
καὶ τὰ πάντα ἐν αὐτῷ συνέστηκεν
καὶ αὐτός ἐστιν ἡ κεφαλὴ τοῦ σώματος τῆς ἐκκλησίας

ὅς ἐστιν ἀρχή
πρωτότοκος ἐκ τῶν νεκρῶν
ἵνα γένηται ἐν πᾶσιν αὐτὸς πρωτεύων
ὅτι ἐν αὐτῷ εὐδόκησεν πᾶν τὸ πλήρωμα κατοικῆσαι
καὶ δι᾽ αὐτοῦ ἀποκαταλλάξαι τὰ πάντα εἰς αὐτόν
εἰρηνοποιήσας διὰ τοῦ αἵματος τοῦ σταυροῦ αὐτοῦ
εἴτε τὰ ἐπὶ τῆς γῆς εἴτε τὰ ἐν τοῖς οὐρανοῖς.

Colossians, then, seems to provide a bold statement of P²: Jesus of Nazareth, the image of the invisible God and the ἀρχή of his kingdom, is twice πρωτότοκος. He is the firstborn in the old creation and in the new, 'existing before all and going before all,' as Irenaeus has it.[9] We would not have known that about him, of course, but for his preceding us into the new. On that basis, however, we can and must speak of him not merely as a blueprint for creation but as its very foundation – in him, through him, and for him all things cohere and receive their being. But what exactly is meant by such a statement, which appears to stretch Adam christology to the breaking point? That Jesus goes before all into the new creation is a straightforward gospel claim. That he does so because he has gone before all in the old is plain enough. But was it not by way of the cross as a reconciling act that he went before us? How do we get from soteriology to ktisiology, from eschatology to protology? What is behind such a move and how should we interpret it? At least three ways present themselves.

Tom Wright is wary here. He wants to make the first πρωτότοκος honorific, and regard its ὅτι clause as a piece of incarnational theology. He observes that 'the one the Colossians know as *their* Lord is Lord of the whole world as well as the church, and he is this not merely by right of redemption (1:20) or conquest (2:15) but, more fundamentally, by right of creation (1:16f.).' But with this 'more fundamentally' Wright is talking about Christ in his 'divine splendour prior to becoming human,' that is, about P¹ not P². What Christ does in freeing us from our sin reveals who he is – God in person, the creator come as redeemer. The move to protology is made by recognizing his *divine* dignity.[10] P², supported by

9 *AH* 2.22.4.
10 Wright, it should be said, acknowledges P¹ as a natural corollary of the biblical witness to Jesus, who not only accepts the call to live redemptively in the world but in dying for it is

allusions to the Torah, does not disappear entirely on Wright's construction, but is reduced to the notion that the world was made by God with Jesus in mind (i.e., for his own appearance as the living charter for a new humanity). Adam christology thus retains its integrity after all, since the main burden of protology comes to rest on the pre-incarnate Son.

It might be said that this view inclines towards the first of the two errors about P^1 to which we pointed above.[11] But our main difficulty with it is that we do not see anything that justifies the proposed change in referent. Where in *this* passage are we invited to look away from the humanity of the Son even for a moment? Is it not exactly the one who suffered the cross and who lives as head of the church who is said to be before all things, such that 'all things hold together in him'? Does not the parallelism, firstborn of creation and firstborn from the dead, suggest that the title is not merely honorific? Do not the twin ὅτι clauses point to the one Jesus Christ, who is the bond between the old creation and the new? Indeed, is it not precisely by way of this strangely *eschatological* doctrine of pre-existence that the hymn attempts to give real meaning to Jesus' universal lordship?[12]

If we accept that there is but one referent in the hymn, we might choose with Kuschel to read it instead as a mythopoeic piece. It is Jesus who is said to be before all things, that is, to provide the ground of creation as well as its goal. But this pre-existence (P^2) is a poetic category not a 'speculative' one.[13] The hymn, then, is not saying a great deal more about Jesus himself than the previous option suggests. Indeed it is saying far less, for there is no uncreated divine Son who comes into view, no incarnational theology in that sense. Rather it is a man who is bravely proclaimed as the mediator of all God's works from beginning to end.[14] It is not as though that man literally pre-exists, however. In the last analysis the point of the hymn is strictly a theological one. Its author wants to assure us, in spite of every hostile force at work in our world, that God is

---

found to have done what only God *can* do, namely, deliver the people from their sins. He is therefore recognized as coming from God and indeed as being God, so that it is not surprising to find the hymn referring also to his divine dignity (cf. 1:19, 2:9).

[11] Does God think, plan and act temporally apart from the incarnation? With the authors of scripture we may speak *as if* he does, but only apophatically as it were.

[12] The Council of Sardica (AD 343; cf. Athanasius, *Ari.* 2.64) insists that 'firstborn' refers to the incarnate one, but also applies it only to the resurrection or new creation. To differ on this point is not to take issue with Wright's thesis that Adam christology, wisdom christology, and incarnational theology belong together. We differ only on the shift in referent between πρωτότοκος πάσης κτίσεως and the first ὅτι clause, a shift reversed presumably between ἐν αὐτῷ συνέστηκεν and αὐτός ἐστιν ἡ κεφαλή.

[13] We have used the term 'mythopoeic' advisedly, even if for Kuschel 'poetic' means precisely *not* 'mythological,' i.e., not speculating about divisions in God; in our judgment these latter terms are being misused.

[14] In Colossians we are not dealing with Paul but with a later figure who *for the first time* makes creation 'a distinct theme of christology' (p. 332; see 327ff.). Kuschel also argues, of course, that Paul himself had no incarnational theology in the classical sense.

always consistent with himself; that he is the great reconciler, whose good purposes will not fail. And to claim confidently that God is and always will be the God of reconciliation revealed in Jesus Christ, it is necessary to insist that he always *was* such. Nothing more or less than that is being said by projecting the human Jesus backwards onto the foundations of the world.

On Kuschel's view the doctrine of pre-existence becomes a function of Christian hope. Here the move to protology is an existential one, so to speak, in which it is wagered that the *love* of God (definitively revealed in Jesus) will in the end show itself fundamental to everything. The great attractiveness of this reading is that it does away with the problem of pre-existence altogether. For P^2, thus interpreted, is not really P^2 at all but a more digestible form of P^1, stripped of its trinitarian complications. It serves but one purpose, *viz.*, to reassert a christological understanding of the character of God in the face of crises which appear to threaten that understanding. Unfortunately, we can only regard Kuschel's proposal with deep suspicion. Exegetically it smacks of a vicious circularity; theologically it appears to have its real starting point in 'the end of metaphysics' rather than in Jesus-history.[15] Above all, it depends upon an unresolved dichotomy between act and being, a dichotomy rejected at Nicaea for very good reasons. Only God can reveal God, only God can redeem us. If we lose sight of that fact, opting with Kuschel for a heavily functionalist christology, we end up reducing the person of Jesus to his work and our *carmen Christi* to a *carmen spei*.

There is a third possibility, which is to read with Karl Barth in a more literal way: Jesus himself really is God's original word-act in creation and redemption. This reading does not begin with (though it is well able to address) human hopes and fears. It begins rather with the testimony about Jesus, who in the plain prose of 3:1–4 is said to be 'seated at the right hand of God,' from whence he will appear in glory. The line of thought is a realist one, in other words, controlled by Jesus-history not by some real or imagined crisis of confidence in Colossae. And it moves from eschatology to protology *not* by referring away from Jesus to God (as even Kuschel appears to do) but by allowing the outcome of his human life to inform us about his full human import. He who sits at God's right hand somehow shares with God in all that God does; he is with God in the beginning as he will be with him at the end.[16]

[15] p. 503 (the phrase is Bernhard Welte's). Like Wright, Kuschel rejects a metaphysical approach for what he calls a 'confessional' one. Unlike Wright he wants to ground statements about pre-existence existentially in 'the experience of a real historical threat' (221) or more generally in 'human spiritual experiences' of the exalted, pneumatic Christ (494). This leads apparently to 'a genuinely biblical ontology,' which has the merit of remaining remarkably vague.

[16] Kuschel, of course, can make similar-sounding claims: 'So from the perspective of the end of time, all time can be understood in trust, faith and hope as being shaped "in Christ" . . . If the exalted Christ is with God, God is "essentially" never other than the Father of Jesus Christ . . .' (363).

The epistle to the Hebrews offers an instructive parallel in support of such a reading. In Hebrews the knowledge that Jesus sat down at the right hand of God leads to the further confession that what happens with him happens ἐφάπαξ, once for all. This ἐφάπαξ is not a poetic cipher for a strictly theological truth.[17] Rather it is cashed out in terms of the twin doctrines of pre-existence and parousia, which preserves its human and temporal content. It is Jesus who is expected to return; likewise it is Jesus who actually pre-exists, 'sustaining all things by his powerful word.'[18] The same pairing of doctrines occurs in Colossians. In 1:16–17 the ἐφάπαξ logic is articulated in terms of pre-existence through the combination of the πρό and the three spatial prepositions ἐν, διά, εἰς. In 3:4 it is thought out in terms of the parousia: 'When Christ, who is your life, is revealed, then you also will be revealed with him in glory.'

Now plainly to take this line requires some new thinking about the relations that govern creaturely existence! But is that not just what is going on here? Colossians appears to be exploring a christologically, and hence an ecclesiologically, controlled interpretation of the cosmos.[19] All existence is said to involve, in one form or another, participation with Jesus – a notion that finds its pithiest expression in 1:17, where τὰ πάντα ἐν αὐτῷ συνέστηκεν provides an analogue to the clause that follows it, καὶ αὐτός ἐστιν ἡ κεφαλὴ τοῦ σώματος τῆς ἐκκλησίας. In a realist framework, of course, we cannot avoid asking how this can be so, or at least what meaning we might give to such strange claims as must result from so robust a concept of P². In what way is Jesus of Nazareth constitutional for all creation?

Barth's own attempt to clarify things is something we have touched on in Chapter 5. The incarnate Son, if indeed he participates in the inner life of the Trinity, certainly takes 'the same full share' in God's being and work in creation.[20] Put the other way round, everything God does *ad extra* he does as the God and Father of our Lord Jesus Christ, who (in his own person) is 'at the Father's side.' Barth's insistence that God's being is in his act, and his act in his being, excludes any concept of the incarnation as merely episodic. As God's self-disposition in time, the man Jesus lives a history which belongs to God and is backed by God's own indissoluble temporality. For all its creaturely particularity it cannot be confined by,

---

[17] i.e., a timeless qualification of every time – something perhaps like Schleiermacher's 'original perfection' (*CF* §60).

[18] Cf. Heb. 1:1ff., 9:23ff. It is the logic of Kuschel's position that the parousia must be left out of account, which it is.

[19] We ought not to overlook the fact that the church (as the community of the Spirit) is the only tangible consequence of the ascension. If the order *christology, ecclesiology, cosmology* is maintained in our theo-logic, the possibility of a healthy and appropriate doctrine of the church as 'κόσμος of the cosmos' emerges.

[20] *CD* 4/2:94. P¹, in other words, implies P², the precedence of Jesus in everything creaturely – ontologically and therefore epistemologically, not (*pace* Kuschel?) epistemologically only.

but rules over, its own spatio-temporal boundaries. It becomes constitutional for every creaturely history, and for history as a whole, since (by divine election) it is constitutional for the creator himself.[21]

In staking these claims Barth wants to steer clear of deification, that is, the confusion of P[1] and P[2]. The creator may be a man, he says, but it is not a man who creates. Rather a man is implicated, included, co-opted in the divine work of creation and wields – by grace, in a creaturely way – divine authority over it. But Barth, as we observe in Chapter 5, makes the second of the two errors mentioned above. Since he associates divinity (P[1]) too closely with descent, and humanity with ascent, he falls after all into what is quite arguably a form of deification. Jesus' resurrection begins to look rather like a shift from inauthentic human temporality to authentic divine temporality. This in turn distorts Barth's view of P[2], transposing it into a rigid doctrine of election with universalist tendencies; the twin elements of the ἐφάπαξ (pre-existence and parousia) begin to run together. How P[2] ought to be seen we must shortly attempt to say, but it is time to carry this whole discussion over into John, perhaps the richest of all biblical resources in the matters that concern us.

John 1

It is generally agreed that John 1 owes a great deal to Sirach 24. In both texts it is said that God's pre-existent wisdom or word, through which he creates the world, finds a place to reside *in* the world, declaring God to it.[22] For Sirach that place is the temple in Jerusalem, where wisdom is embodied as Shekinah and Torah. For John, on the other hand, the residence of the divine word is a human being: ὁ λόγος σὰρξ ἐγένετο καὶ ἐσκήνωσεν ἐν ἡμῖν, καὶ ἐθεασάμεθα τὴν δόξαν αὐτοῦ, δόξαν ὡς μονογενοῦς παρὰ πατρός . . .[23] There are of course many interpretive problems connected to John 1, but the famous prologue commands our undivided attention when it dares to identify the 'only-begotten,' ὁ ὢν εἰς τὸν κόλπον τοῦ πατρός, first and very deliberately with God, and

---

[21] Cf. CD 2/2:257ff. Kuschel (96ff.) offers a lengthy account of this 'speculative intensification of the christology of pre-existence,' and eventually adapts aspects of it to his own construct, as we will notice in due course.

[22] Both writers are looking back to Gen. 1f. and Exod. 33ff., along with Prov. 8.

[23] Wright (1992:410ff.) points up the contrast this way: The wisdom tradition, he says, like the Hebrew scriptures generally, wants to tell Israel's story as 'the true and redeeming story' of the whole creation. John however, like the New Testament generally, tells the story of *Jesus* as the true and redeeming story of Israel. Jesus not only reveals God's glory in the world, which Israel has failed to do, but drives away the darkness that has beset his own people. Here Wright recalls 1 Enoch 42, which in its 'terrifying parody of Sirach's beautiful poem' suggests that wisdom was unable to remain with Israel and instead returned to heaven, leaving its unoccupied place to iniquity; the gospel of the incarnate and crucified one is able to answer to this pessimism in a way the wisdom tradition could not.

then also quite specifically with Jesus of Nazareth.²⁴ This twofold identification certainly involves an assertion about Jesus' pre-existence: Ὁ ὀπίσω μου ἐρχόμενος ἔμπροσθέν μου γέγονεν, ὅτι πρῶτός μου ἦν. But what sort of assertion?

Wright's view is consistent with his reading of Colossians. While it is quite true that the centre of the cosmos is being shifted by John from Jerusalem to Jesus, the pre-existence question concerns P¹ not P². Barth's view is also consistent. He affirms both P¹ and P², pressing the ident-ification between Jesus and the Logos back into the very first verse of the prologue.²⁵ Kuschel is no exception. He again denies P¹ in the orthodox sense, while arguing for a version of P² that is meant to take its place. 'There can be no question here of the pre-existence of the man Jesus, as Barth saw it,'²⁶ nor of any departure from standard Jewish monotheism:

> The Johannine writings are not interested in protology in isolation and for its own sake, whether in speculation about divine beings before all time, or in the assumption that the man Jesus is pre-existent in the temporal sense. Rather, they state in trust that the existence of Jesus Christ 'in the world' owes itself to the initiative of God.²⁷

Drawing out Kushel's more modest claim (*viz.*, that pre-existence has more to do with God than with Jesus) will allow us to elaborate our differences not only with him but with Barth as well, and to present more clearly our own alternative view of P² in the context of John's Gospel.

As Kuschel sees it, 'the basic theological and hermeneutical problem' of the high Johannine christology is to narrate what cannot be narrated. John must 'tell the story of someone in time who is not subject to time,' if in Jesus we are confronted with the full revelation of God. The problem (is it not in fact the two-natures problem, shifted to the narrative itself?) is solved by 'an ingenious abolition of the limitations of time,' already implicit in the primal experience of Easter: Since Jesus is with God, he too is now Spirit. 'The pneumatic, present Christ is no longer limited by time . . . but free from time; he is no longer determined by a before, now and afterwards, but by a contemporaneity which is above time.' John's next move is to fuse the eternal presence of this heavenly or spiritual Christ with 'the earthly time of Jesus the Galilean,' a fusion which – if it is to be

---

²⁴ Cf. John 1:18, Prov. 8:30f.; John 17:4f., Prov. 8:22f. (In spite of John's essentially Jewish character, fruitful comparisons can also be made here with pagan thought; cf. S. Jaki 1990:72ff.)

²⁵ See *CD* 2/2:95ff. for Barth's controversial reading, which certainly complicates the parallel with Sirach but does not destroy it. Nor (if we read vv. 1–5 as a summary of 6–18, much as Gen. 1:1 is a summary of its chapter) does it engage us in any literary convolution. But we need not agree fully with Barth's handling of the prologue in order to argue that P², along with P¹, is a Johannine concept. See below.

²⁶ 'For exegetical reasons,' he says (382), but does not supply any.

²⁷ p. 389; cf. J. A. T. Robinson 1985:389.

cast in narrative form as a Gospel – necessarily involves the step from post-existence to pre-existence. That step cannot be taken without resorting 'to some degree to mythological notions,' but John's achievement is 'that he mythologized less than he could have done.' Jesus is not understood as a God alongside God or as a man literally prior to other men. He is understood rather as one given and confirmed by God as his own definitive self-revelation to man.[28]

We are tempted to say (quite conscious of the irony) that all of this comes out as pure gnosticism, albeit in the guise of a thoughtful compromise between Barth and Rudolf Bultmann, on whom Kuschel also has an eye.[29] For if the revelation in question is objectively anchored in time – in a human being who *is* the Word of God, insists Kuschel – nevertheless it is so only as an event in which Jesus-history becomes spiritually transparent for Christians.[30] It is not really Jesus himself, then, but the 'pneumatic' Christ who belongs at the Father's side, and who as such can be said to pre-exist:

> In John, the statements about pre-existence are a function of his Spirit christology. The Christ exalted by God, the Christ who like God is present at all times as Spirit, was also 'in the beginning' as Word; he was in the time of Jesus; and he will also be in the future.[31]

In short, there are two Christs here not one, as there are in every gnostic system. Pre-existence and post-existence belong to the λόγος ἄσαρκος or spiritual Christ, who provides an abiding depth-dimension to the earthly Jesus. As for the move from post- to pre-, that is as easy to allow as it is difficult to narrate, just because this 'Spirit christology' is a christology of contemporaneity, or rather of time-denying *simultaneity*.[32]

Were Barth himself to respond to Kuschel he would doubtless protest that no such compromise with Bultmann is possible.[33] Yet we must bring the charge that Barth helps to lay the foundation for Kuschel's gnostic rendering of John, since it is from Barth that Kuschel derives the notion of simultaneity – a notion closely bound up with the former's own understanding of P². Before proceeding we need to show how that is so,

---

[28] pp. 384ff.

[29] We are ignoring Kuschel's attempted trialogue between Barth, Bultmann and Harnack, for we must not allow ourselves to be dragged into the enticing theo-politics of *Born Before All Time?*– an ambitiously ecumenical work powered by its own underlying myth: 'despite all the disputes about truth, the primal power of reconciliation *before* all creation can resolve all differences *in* creation' (339).

[30] pp. 494f.

[31] p. 389; *n.b.* that the Word who is 'in the beginning' is the λόγος ἄσαρκος (381).

[32] Cf. 496f.

[33] Who *is* this spiritual Christ, Barth might well ask, if not in fact the deposit of our faith in Jesus, hypostatized and indeed divinized? Kuschel tries hard to avoid this conclusion but it is not clear that he can. Any attempt to hold together the subjective and objective poles of the doctrine of revelation without recourse to a full trinitarianism must land itself in this dilemma.

permitting ourselves therefore a further brief digression into Barth's problematic doctrine of time.

We begin with the question of God's time. Barth is quite right to read off from the fact of the incarnation God's freedom for man and for temporal existence; hence to insist that God's eternity must not be defined in opposition to time, any more than as infinitely extended time (time-lessness and sempiternity are both rejected). But he is wrong to attempt to articulate that eternity as real or authentic time, that is, as pure duration, a perichoretic 'simultaneity of beginning, middle and end.' To do so is only to repeat the common error of venturing a model of eternity (of the Trinity!) by way of a negative judgment on time.[34] If that negative judgment were not obvious enough from the claim that 'eternity is just the duration which is *lacking* to time,'[35] it would become so from the fact that the incarnation is brought in precisely as the salvation of time. By taking time and making it a form of his eternity, God lends to it the duration it lacks. And what is this durable time? It is finite creaturely time – the time appointed to each of us between birth and death – but time that does not pass away. It is time fixed in God as in a secure bracket, its beginning, middle and end gathered up by the Trinity into a proper perichoresis. It is plainly time for God, in other words, but we are justified in asking how far it is time for man; for it is time in which the creature's possibilities are already 'exploited and exhausted.'[36]

This circular reasoning from time to eternity and back again we must regard as an unfortunate remnant of natural theology in Barth. We cannot square it either with scripture or with Barth's own best insights, but only repeat that it is closely bound up with his actualism. Since the incarnation does not merely accomplish atonement but *is* atonement, Barth's crucial distinction between created time and fallen time tends to melt away; but that is the very distinction which should have prevented him from seeing the problem of time in terms of its not being eternity, and so from misconstruing eternity as the saviour of time.[37] The distortion this introduces into his doctrine of God is a matter beyond our present scope; it will do simply to record our suspicion of all attempts to expound the Trinity in terms of beginning, middle and end – or origin, movement and goal, or past, present and future, or any other set of spatio-temporal

---

[34] *Pace* Kuschel 496; see CD 2/1:608ff.

[35] Emphasis ours. Barth looks over his shoulder nervously here, wary that his thesis not be reversed. Eternity is the very ground of time; time is certainly not the motion or vitality lacking in eternity. (God's *nunc stans*, he says, includes a *nunc fluens*.) But the damage is already done. Creator and creature are mutually defining.

[36] CD 3/3:84ff.

[37] Barth's acceptance of death as a feature of our created humanity is a sign of his failure to follow through with this distinction, and with his own attack on 'Chronos' (i.e., on a natural theology of time). This departure from the biblical perspective has huge ramifications for his view of the resurrection.

abstractions.[38] What concerns us directly is the way his views on time feed back into his christology and into his doctrine of pre-existence.

Barth's notion of simultaneity or pure duration allows him to speak of Jesus-history as a history that simply *is* – here as there, now as then, 'the same yesterday, today and forever.' That is how he understands pre-existence, which is rather hard to distinguish from post-existence.[39] In Barth's favour it must be said that he makes no move at all in Kuschel's direction, that is, away from the earthly Jesus. Just the reverse. He sees all this as a great improvement over the formless (pneumatic?) Christ of the ubiquitarians. As we argue in Chapter 5, however, that is something of an illusion. Is it not just as easy to see it as a translation of the ubiquity doctrine into temporal terms? Can a history that is said to be both here and there, then and now, still be held to be concretely human and particular (the *concretissimum*!) in any meaningful sense? Can we really expect the one who is and has this history to return, as Barth encourages us to do? Or has a too-radical actualism led to the substitution of a history for a person, such that we must accuse Barth too of reducing the person to his work and eschatology to epistemology?[40] If so, a line may be drawn, albeit reluctantly, from Barth to Kuschel, tracing out a growing erosion of Jesus' temporality in connection with P[2].

What then? Are P[2] and simultaneity so tightly interwoven that we must abandon the former with the latter? We do not think so. Indeed, John will not permit us to do so. That P[2] is intended by the prologue along with P[1] is clear from the way the Baptist's testimony – 'after me comes a man who has surpassed me because he was before me' – is confirmed by Jesus in chapter 8. 'Before Abraham was, I am' may be nothing less than a claim to divinity, but it is also a claim about Jesus' humanity: 'Abraham your father exulted that he should see *my* day; and he did see and was glad.'[41] It may even be (and here we can say that we find his exposition much more compelling than Kuschel's) that Barth is right to find P[2] already in verse 1 of the prologue. There is no need to rehearse his well-known

---

[38] God's eternity certainly entails, as the incarnation declares, a 'readiness' for time. But the positive value of that fact is in its negation of every hypothesis about the divine eternity constructed as a denial of time – including Barth's, though it does not recognize itself as such. Whenever we go beyond that negation, moving from the assertion that a man's time is also 'God's time for us' to the assertion that the Trinity is somehow 'temporal,' we are actually on the road back to monism.

[39] Cf. 3/2:483f., 4/1:313, 4/3:223ff., 298ff., etc.

[40] Our criticism of Barth's actualism really ought to take us back to the idea of God as *actus purus*, a notion he takes up almost as if with this one stone he could fell all objections to the incarnation and render an adequate account of the divine freedom for man; but we cannot do that here. We can only suggest that the theology of eternity with which he supports his christology makes it even more difficult for him to recover for the Reformed tradition what Schleiermacher set aside, namely, the ongoing priesthood of Christ.

[41] 8:56; cf. 1:15, 30. P[1] is implicit, of course, in the use of the divine name ('the name you gave me,' 17:11).

treatment of the passage, which turns on the conviction that John is not appending the name Jesus to the title Logos, but the title Logos to the name Jesus. Suffice it to say that any alternative which cannot match the coherence which that conviction supplies is working with a weaker hand.[42] But how can we understand and articulate P[2] in a way that neither sets up a second Christ alongside Jesus nor compromises his human temporality with any hidden, unintended deification? The answer lies in a point that Kuschel conveniently overlooks and Barth, to some extent, miscontrues.

Let us come to that point by agreeing first of all that, logically speaking, the prologue is meant to be read from back to front; it does not interpret Jesus' end from the standpoint of his beginning, but his beginning from the standpoint of his end. That Jesus comes from God follows from the fact that he goes to God, that he is with God in the beginning from the fact that he is with him in the end. And it is from the standpoint of this end (his being at the Father's side) that we are entitled to extrapolate, not only his own beginning, but the beginning of all things in and with him – that is, his pre-existence (P[2]). But just because eschatology precedes and interprets protology, it is vital that we get our eschatology right. Irenaeus, on whose feast day we happen to be writing, knew what the front-line defense against gnosticism should be, namely, the notion of descent and ascent in the flesh. But this line of thought, vital as it is to the Gospel of John, is imperiled by Barth's actualism, and completely overturned by Kuschel's spirit-christology.[43] It is precisely here that their respective views of P[2] go wrong and need to be corrected.

Descending and ascending, coming and going, being sent and returning – these are the themes which help to frame the Gospel of John in its attempt to identify Jesus as the messiah and Son of God in whom we are to believe.[44] It will not do to take all of this language poetically, or even as a restrained mythologizing of Jesus-history in order to make the point that here, in this man, we encounter an expression of the love of God that has eternal validity. We *may* do this, of course, following Kuschel's lead, but only if we are prepared *inter alia* to overlook the fact that John's Jesus is one who regards his future presence at the Father's side as a humanly active one. 'I go to prepare a place for you' represents the Godward side of his activity: 'Go and say to my brothers, "I am ascending to my Father and your Father, my God and your God."' The humanward

---

[42] The parallel with Sirach certainly must not be allowed to dominate the prologue, since the shift from Shekinah/Torah to Jesus of Nazareth as the earthly locus of the Logos necessarily entails a radical alteration of the Logos concept itself – an alteration which must affect *both* our view of God *and* our view of creation.

[43] Kuschel ignores the fact that the Spirit is very definitely *'another* counselor' (14:16), and John's emphasis on the eschatological *absence* of Jesus. Cf. 6:61f., 20:24ff., 21:22.

[44] Cf. Nicholson 21ff.

side is indicated in the promise: 'I will not leave you orphans; I am coming to you.'[45]

Now when we understand Jesus' post-existence as a humanly active one, not in any mythological sense albeit in a most inscrutable one, we are free to understand his pre-existence as a human reality also. Indeed we ought to do so. In chapter 17 Jesus prays, 'glorify me in your own presence, Father, with the glory which I had with you before the world existed.' Or again, 'I desire that where I myself am those also may be with me, that they may behold my glory, which you have given me because you loved me before the founding of the world.' In other words, Jesus' departure or exodus (i.e., his death, resurrection and ascension) is consistently presented by John as a *restoration* to glory, just as Moses' arrival at Sinai with the people of Israel was for him a return as well as an advance.[46] It would be nonsensical, not to say Apollinarian – and John's Gospel is neither – to have the human Jesus asking to be restored to his divine glory (P^1).[47] The glory in view is rather the glory of a man uniquely loved by the Father πρὸ τοῦ τὸν κόσμον εἶναι, a man uniquely related to the Father in a way that other men are not nor ever can be. It is the glory of the God-man, the only-begotten, 'full of grace and truth,' the glory of him whose face enlightens the world and everyone in it. This too may be taken as an actual condition of Jesus' existence, though it is once again quite inscrutable – as inscrutable as the virgin birth, which John may very well be expounding here in his usual dialogical way.[48]

But what will we mean by P^2 if we approach it thus? If not what Kuschel means, not what Barth means either, though Barth (like Irenaeus) explicitly joins the virgin birth to the ascension as the historical envelope in which the mystery of the God-man is wrapped. For Barth this pair of mysteries appears to be reducible to the single mystery of Easter, from which we learn that Jesus-history really is God with us, and that it is therefore 'immune from dissolution and above the need of coming into being.'[49] No doubt there is something to this from the standpoint of John's Gospel.

---

[45] Today there is much agreement that the prologue is all of a piece with the Gospel. Of its many echoes in later chapters, the resonance of 1:18 in 14:1ff., 17:1ff., 20:16f., etc. is among the most important.

[46] We agree with Nicholson (21ff.) that this whole complex of ideas, as a question about origin and destiny, serves to structure John's interpretation of Jesus. We might convey our own rather different reading, however, by making an epexegetical distinction between coming and going, as that which defines Jesus' humanity in relation to God, and descending and ascending, as that which further defines him over against 'this world' (cf. 3:1–21). And of course we are allowing that the definition of his humanity *vis-à-vis* God does not exclude, but includes, belief in his divinity.

[47] Brown (2/740ff.) reflects the ambiguity of the passage but also exacerbates it. John's Gospel is not kenotic, he tells us, yet it is the manifestation of Jesus' divine glory that is being sought here.

[48] Dialogue with God, appropriately enough in the present case, not with his disciples or his opponents.

[49] *CD* 1/2:115; cf. 3/2:453.

In our midst has stood one not generally recognized for who he is. Like Melchizedek he appears on the Johannine stage as one who is without beginning and without end, or rather who has God for his beginning and end; like Moses he is sent from God and returns to God. Unlike either, however, he stakes the claim for himself, 'I and the Father are one.' He not only declares the divine name but possesses the divine name. Therefore what can be said of Melchizedek and Moses only poetically can be said of him in actuality. Nevertheless, we do not propose to understand either his beginning (P^2) or his end (the ascension) quite as Barth does, for we have detected a worrying Eutychian tendency in Barth that is not evident in John.

To Kuschel we say: If we wish to reject mythology at the protological end we must first reject it at the eschatological end; that is, we must exchange ascension of the mind for ascension in the flesh. Then we will not imagine that John is seeking to abolish the limitations of time or to narrate the unnarratable, but only to draw the proper conclusions *from* his narration, that is, from the outcome of Jesus-history.[50] But to Barth we also say: It will not do to treat the divine-human time of Jesus as time that simply is ('eternal time' in that sense). Ascension in the flesh does not bring closure to the time of Jesus as such but only to his sojourn ἐν τῷ κόσμῳ, where κόσμος means (as often in John) the world in its alienation from God.[51] With the ascension Jesus-history does not come to an end but to a new beginning: 'I am going off to prepare a place for you; and when I do go and prepare a place for you, I am coming back to take you along with me, so that where I am, you also may be.'[52] But if that is the case we are not talking about simultaneity or pure duration, and it is not to that concept that P^2 should be linked. We must find some other way to understand it.

Our proposal is to identify P^2 as a real temporal priority, but one which is defined in terms of the *freedom* with which this man, Jesus Christ, disposes himself *vis-à-vis* creation and the rest of humanity.[53] This way of getting at P^2 takes much from Barth, but allows us two distinct advantages. First, it allows us to emphasize with Paul, John and Irenaeus that it belongs to the human Jesus to choose the *incognito* of the cross; to let his glory be hidden beneath the murk of a world distorted by the devil and by men

---

[50] Can John be teaching a 'drop in' theory of the incarnation with his many references (1:14, 7:33, etc.) to Jesus' brief sojourn with us? On the contrary, he is indicating the descent and ascent of the Man of Nazareth: 'You are from below; I am from above. You are of this world; I am not of this world.' Hence, 'you have no idea where I come from or where I am going' (8:14ff., NIV). As a reference to the incarnation *per se* all this would be pure tautology; as a rebuke to the κόσμος (i.e, to a distorted world *in* its distortion) it makes great rhetorical sense. Jesus is not rebuking men for being men, but for being sinners! P^2 and P^1 thus support rather than compete with each other.

[51] Cf. *CD* 3/2:453f., where Barth appears to be in two minds about this.

[52] 14:2f. (trans. R. E. Brown); cf. 7:33f., etc., and the act of *new* creation in 20:19ff.

[53] Cf 2:1ff. and 13:3ff., which may be taken as paradigms of this freedom.

who prefer darkness to light, even while disclosing it to those given him ἐκ τοῦ κόσμου.[54] Barth obscures that by equating incarnation and atonement, by failing to distinguish between the fact of Jesus-history and its actual shape or content. For Barth there can be no incarnation without the cross, and by implication no creation without the fall. Jesus comes and stands where he must come and stand. But, as we saw in Chapter 3, for Irenaeus it is a genuine question as to why Jesus stands where he stands, and this question witnesses to a more profound doctrine (at least at this point) of the freedom of the human creature as such. The freedom of Jesus is a freedom grounded in God, for it is God's freedom *as* man, but it is more obviously than in Barth also and as such a freedom *for* man. Irenaeus is working with what may be described as an open ontology, in which the interaction between Jesus and ourselves has a real and decisive bearing on the way things are.

To be sure, Barth takes a page from Irenaeus when he makes the move to which we are objecting. We must query the way Irenaeus himself links Christ and creation when, in a much debated passage, he says that the latter is called into existence that the saviour might not exist in vain.[55] The risk of a new determinism – and with it the collapse of relationality – arises unless it is made completely clear that pre-existence and mutuality of influence are not contradictory notions. Surely then creation does *not* come into existence in order to prevent the saviour from saving in vain; the saviour saves because creation proves to have need of his salvation. Given the inherent danger in christology of generating a false universalism (i.e., a christomonism) this disagreement is hardly insignificant.[56] But the main direction of Irenaean thought is a safer one, and points us to the other advantage, namely, the emphasis we are now able to place on the Spirit. Pre-existence (P^2) and post-existence do allow us to speak of an ἐφάπαξ, but the ἐφάπαξ must be understood in terms of the activity of the Spirit. If to be is in fact to bear the fruit of communion, as we tried to show in Chapter 3, then it is in just this way – as the head of the Spirit and therefore as the champion of free and genuine human being – that the Son 'goes before' the creation and provides for it a footing with God.[57]

---

[54] Worldly men, like Pharaoh's host, see only the dark side of the Cloud of the Presence (Exod. 14:19f.).

[55] *AH* 3.22.3 (cf. Wingren 92f.).

[56] Forster (138) points out that Irenaeus reconceives history around Jesus – rather than projecting him backwards or upwards into some timeless eternity – in order to avoid the *unreality* of history in gnosticism. Yet he suggests that the doctrine of recapitulation threatens to swallow history up after all. If it *does* so threaten, it is precisely at this point.

[57] Yet as it happens this going-before does indeed have a soteriological dimension; ascending involves descending. Note here that eschatology and protology do communicate. Receiving 'power from the Father over our life,' Jesus brings it down to us who are afar off (cf. *Demo.* 52, 97; *AH* 5.1.1, 20.2, etc.). Understood from this standpoint the pre-existence of Jesus is not 'so bizarre a doctrine' as A. T. Hanson (1982:92) imagines it to be.

P^2 as we are trying to understand it – and we recognize that here any addressing of the How? question must be very modest indeed – requires, and in Irenaeus receives, a strong pneumatology just where Barth puts his concept of 'eternal time.' It is in the relation with Jesus that is made possible for every human being by the Holy Spirit that space and time themselves can be regarded, together with the persons to whom they belong, as open forms or structures of our existence.[58] That is one thing the ascension testifies to. Indeed, it is only in and with the ascension as a brand new beginning that our world is actually so ordered to Jesus that P^2 can ultimately be said to hold true. The pre-existence of Jesus in and for our world is *fully* a feature of our world only retroactively, by recapitulation.[59] While Barth might be happy with much of what we have just said, his own very limited use of the notion of recapitulation betrays the problem to which we have pointed:

That the creature may continue to be in virtue of the divine preservation means finally that – itself actual and active within its limits – it may continue before him eternally. We have already seen what is meant by the phrase 'within its limits.' It does not only mean a limitation to its own particular place. It means also a limitation of its possibilities and capacities, of its develpment and operation. Above all, it means a limitation of its existence in itself and as such . . . [T]he time will come when the created world as a whole will only have been. In the final act of salvation history, i.e., in the revelation of Jesus Christ as the Foundation and Deliverer and Head of the whole of creation, the history of creation will also reach its goal and end. It will not need to progress any further, it will have fulfilled its purpose. Everything that happened in the course of that history will then take place together as a recapitulation of all individual events. It will be made definitive as the temporal end of the creature beyond which it cannot exist any more. Its life will then be over, its movement and development completed, its notes sounded, its colours revealed, its thinking thought, its words said, its deeds done, its contacts and relationships with other creatures and their mutal interaction closed, the possibilities granted to it exploited and exhausted. And in all this it will somehow have a part in that which Jesus Christ has been and done as Foundation and Deliverer and Head. It will not need any continuance of temporal existence. And since the creature itself will not be there, time which is the form of its existence will not be there. Yet this does not mean that its preservation by God is terminated. It is a preservation within appointed limits . . .[60]

[58] What we are talking about here is a perichoresis of persons, not of tenses (cf. John 17). The latter notion we may safely reject without falling into a naïve doctrine of sempiternity. Why should the eschaton not include movement and progress, which belong to the human finitude that God blesses and, in the Son, underwrites?

[59] The ordering of all things to Jesus means that he really is the beginning and the end, but since this ordering, as it actually happens, requires and involves judgment and redemption – i.e *re*ordering – it is visible to us only as the mystery of the church, which is the witness to Jesus' ascension. (Cf. Zizioulas 1985:182f. n. 39.)

[60] CD 3/3:87f.

Is this not effectively a closed rather than an open concept? With it we might further compare and contrast that of John, which arguably is the Gospel of recapitulation. To do so would take us back, however, to a discussion of the connection between the ascension and the eucharist, opened up in Chapter 6. But that we cannot do here.

A Bibliography of Works Cited*

Alsup, John E. *The Post-Resurrection Appearance Stories of the Gospel Tradition*. Calver Verlag, Stuttgart, 1975.

Altizer, Thomas J. J. *The Descent Into Hell: A Study of the Radical Reversal of the Christian Consciousness*. Seabury, New York, 1979.

Anglican Church of Canada. *The Book of Alternative Services*. Anglican Book Centre, Toronto, 1985.

Aquinas, Thomas. *Summa Theologiae*, vol. 55, trans. C. Thomas Moore; vol. 56, trans. David Bourke. Blackfriars, London, 1976.

Athanasius. *St Athanasius: Select Works and Letters: Nicene and Post-Nicene Fathers of the Christian Church*, second series, vol. 4. Eds. P. Schaff, H. Wace and A. Robertson. Eerdmans, Grand Rapids, 1980.

Augustine. *Expositions on the Book of Psalms: Library of Fathers*. 6 vols. Trans. H. M. Wilkins. John Henry Parker, Oxford, 1847–1857.
The City of God: The Fathers of the Church: Writings of Saint Augustine, vols 6–8. Trans. G. Walsh, D. Zema, *et.al.* Catholic University of America, Washington, 1950–54.
Sermons on the Liturgical Seasons: The Fathers of the Church, vol. 38. Trans. M. S. Muldowney. Catholic University of America, Washington, 1959.
The Confessions of St Augustine. Trans. John K. Ryan. Image, Garden City, 1960.
The Retractions: The Fathers of the Church, vol. 60. Trans. Mary I. Bogan. Catholic University of America, Washington, 1968.
The Trinity. Trans. Edmund Hill; ed. John E. Rotelle. New York City Press, 1991.

Aulén, Gustaf. *Christus Victor: An Historical Study of the Three Main Types of the Atonement*. Trans. A. G. Hebert. Macmillan, New York, 1969.

---

* Excluding incidental references to some ancient works.

Balthasar, Hans Urs von. *Kosmische Liturgie. Das Weltbild Maximus' des Bekenners*. 2nd ed. Herder, Freiburg, 1961.
A Theology of History. Sheed & Ward, London, 1963.
A Theological Anthropology. Sheed & Ward, New York, 1967.
'In Retrospect.' *Communio* 2.3, Fall 1975, pp. 197–220.
Heart of the World. Trans. Erasmo S. Leiva. Ignatius, San Francisco, 1979.
The Glory of the Lord: A Theological Aesthetics. 7 vols. Eds. J. Fessio and J. Riches. Ignatius, San Francisco, 1982–89.
Mysterium Paschale. T&T Clark, Edinburgh, 1990.
'Eternal Life and the Human Condition.' *Communio* 18, Spring 1991, pp. 4–23.

Baker, A. E., ed. *William Temple and His Message: Selections from his Writings*. Penguin, Harmondsworth, 1946.

Banner, Michael. 'Christian Anthropology at the Beginning and End of Life.' *Scottish Journal of Theology* 51.5, 1998, pp. 22–60.

Barrett, C. K. *The Gospel According to St John*. 2nd ed. SPCK, London, 1978.
Church, Ministry, and Sacraments in the New Testament. Eerdmans, Grand Rapids, 1985.

Barth, Karl. *Dogmatics in Outline*. Trans. G. T. Thomson. SCM, London, 1949.
Church Dogmatics, vols. 1–4. Eds. G. W. Bromiley and T. F. Torrance. Trans. G. W. Bromiley *et.al*. T&T Clark, Edinburgh, 1956–75.
Anselm: Fides Quaerens Intellectum: Anselm's Proof of the Existence of God in the Context of His Theological Scheme. Trans. Ian W. Robertson. SCM, London, 1960.
The Humanity of God. Trans. Thomas Wieser and John Newton Thomas. John Knox, Atlanta, 1960b.
Theology and Church: Shorter Writings 1920–28. Trans. L. P. Smith. SCM, London, 1962.
The Epistle to the Romans. 6th ed. Trans. Edwin C. Hoskins. Oxford University Press, 1968.
'My Relation to Soren Kierkegaard.' Acceptance Speech on receiving the Sonning Prize, May 1963. Trans. Louis Pojman. *TSF Bulletin*, May–June 1968, pp. 3–4 (abridged).
Action in Waiting. Including 'Joy in the Lord' by Christoph Blumhardt. Plough, Rifton, 1979.
Letters 1961–1968. Trans. and ed. G. W. Bromiley. Ed. Jürgen Fangmeier and Hinrich Stoevesandt. Eerdmans, Grand Rapids, 1981.
The Theology of Schleiermacher. Trans. Geoffrey W. Bromiley. Ed. Dietrich Ritschl. Eerdmans, Grand Rapids, 1982.
The Göttingen Dogmatics: Instruction in the Christian Religion, vol. 1. Trans. Geoffrey W. Bromiley. Ed. Hannelotte Reiffen. Eerdmans, Grand Rapids, 1991.

Bartsch, H. W., ed. *Kergma and Myth: A Theological Debate*, vol. 1. Trans. R. H. Fuller. SPCK, London, 1953.

Bateson, Gregory. *Mind and Nature: A Necessary Unity*. Bantam, Toronto, 1980.

Bauerschmidt, F. C. 'Julian of Norwich – Incorporated.' *Modern Theology* 13.1, 1997, pp. 75–100.

Benoit, Pierre. *Jesus and the Gospel*, vol. 1. Trans. Benet Weatherhead. Herder and Herder, New York, 1973.

Berner, Ulrich. *Origenes: Erträge der Forschung*, Band 147. Wissenschaftliche Buchgesellschaft, Darmstadt, 1981.

de Bie, Linden J. 'Real Presence or Real Absence? The Spoils of War in Nineteenth-Century American Eucharistic Controversy.' *Pro Ecclesia* 4.4, 1995, pp. 431–41.

Blair, H. A. *The Kaleidoscope of Truth: Types and Archetypes in Clement of Alexandria*. Churchman, Worthing, 1986.

Blake, William. *The Complete Poetry and Prose of William Blake*. Rev. ed. Ed. David. V. Erdman. Anchor, New York, 1988.

Blocher, Henri. *In the Beginning: The Opening Chapters of Genesis*. InterVarsity, Leicester, 1984.

Bloom, Allan. *The Closing of the American Mind*. Simon & Schuster, New York, 1987.

Bockmuehl, Markus. '"The Form of God" (Phil. 2.6): Variations on a Theme of Jewish Mysticism.'*Journal of Theological Studies*, NS, 48.1, April 1997, pp. 1–23.

Boelhower, Gary John. 'The Process Christology of John Cobb, Jr: Christ as Creative Transformation and Jesus as a Unique Structure of Human Existence in a Pluralistic Age.' PhD, Marquette University, 1988 (UMI).

Bonhoeffer, Dietrich. *Christ the Center*. Trans. Edwin H. Robinson. Harper & Row, San Francisco, 1978.

Bousset, Wilhelm. *Kyrios Christos*. Trans. John E. Steely. Abingdon, Nashville, 1970.

Bouwsma, William J. *John Calvin: A Sixteenth-Century Portrait*. Oxford University Press, 1988.

Bowden, John. *Jesus: The Unanswered Questions*. SCM, London, 1988.

Braaten, Carl E. *No Other Gospel: Christianity Among the World's Religions*. Fortress, Minneapolis, 1992.

Braaten, Carl and Robert Jenson, eds. *Christian Dogmatics*, vol. 1. Fortress, Philadelphia, 1984.

British Council of Churches. *British and Irish Churches Respond to BEM. Analysis and Implications of The British and Irish Churches' Responses to the Lima Report on Baptism, Eucharist and Ministry.* Inter-Church House, London, 1988.

van den Brom, Luco J. 'Can Anything Good Come from Nazareth?' *Society for the Study of Theology*, Oxford, April 1994.

Bromiley, Geoffrey W. *Historical Theology: An Introduction.* Eerdmans, Grand Rapids, 1978.

Brown, Colin. *Philosophy and the Christian Faith: A Historical Sketch from the Middle Ages to the Present Day.* InterVarsity, London, 1973.

Brown, Peter. *Augustine of Hippo. A Biography.* Faber and Faber, London, 1967.

Brown, Robert F. 'On the Necessary Imperfection of Creation: Irenaeus' *Adversus Haereses* iv, 38.' *Scottish Journal of Theology* 28, 1975, 17–25.

Bruce, F. F. *The Epistle to the Hebrews.* The New International Commentary on the New Testament. Eerdmans, Grand Rapids, 1964.

Brunner, Emil. *The Mediator: A Study of the Central Doctrine of the Christian Faith.* Trans. Olive Wyon. Lutterworth, London, 1934. *The Christian Doctrine of Creation and Redemption: Dogmatics*, vol. 2. Trans. Olive Wyon. Westminister, Philadelphia, 1952.

Buccellati, Giorgio. 'Ascension , Parousia, and the Sacred Heart: Structural Correlations.' *Communio* 25.1, Spring, 1998, pp. 69–103.

Buckley, James M. 'A Field of Living Fire: Karl Barth on the Spirit and the Church.' *Modern Theology* 10.1, January 1994, pp. 81–101.

Buckley, Michael J. *At the Origins of Modern Atheism.* Yale, Newhaven & London, 1987.

Bultmann, Rudolf. *Theology of the New Testament*, vol. 1. Trans. K. Grobel. SCM, London, 1952.

Busch, Eberhard. *Karl Barth: His Life from Letters and Autobiographical Texts.* Trans. J. Bowden. Fortress, Philadelphia, 1976.

Cabasilas, Nicholas. *A Commentary on the Divine Liturgy.* Trans. J. M. Hussey and P. A. McNulty. SPCK, London, 1977.

Caird, G. B. *A Commentary on the Revelation of St John the Divine.* Black's New Testament Commentary. Hendrickson, Peabody, 1966.

The Language and Imagery of the Bible. Westminster, Philadelphia, 1980.

Calvin, John. *Commentary Upon the Acts of the Apostles,* vol. 1. Trans. and ed. Henry Beveridge. T&T Clark, Edinburgh, 1879.
The First Epistle of Paul the Apostle to the Corinthians. Trans. J. W. Frazer. *Calvin's Commentaries.* Eds. D. W. and T. F. Torrance. Oliver and Boyd, Edinburgh, 1960.
Institutes of the Christian Religion. Library of Christian Classics, vols xx, xxi. Ed. John T. McNeill. Trans. Ford Lewis Battles. Westminster, Philadelphia, 1960.
Tracts and Treatises on the Doctrine and Worship of the Church, vols. 1 and 2. Trans. Henry Beveridge. Eerdmans, Grand Rapids, 1958.

Cannon, William Ragsdale. *History of Christianity in the Middle Ages: From the Fall of Rome to the Fall of Constantinople.* Baker, Grand Rapids, 1960.

Chadwick, Henry. *The Early Church.* Penguin, Harmondsworth, 1967.

Church, Philip A. F. 'The Cult and the Monarchy: A Study in the Development of Two Old Testament Themes in the Epistle to the Hebrews.' MCS Regent College, Vancouver, 1982.

Clark, H. W. *The Cross and the Eternal Order: A Study of Atonement in its Cosmic Significance.* Lutterworth, London, 1943.

Clark, Mary T. *Augustine of Hippo: Selected Writings.* SPCK, London, 1984.

Clements, Keith W. *Friedrich Schleiermacher: Pioneer of Modern Theology: Selected Writings.* Collins, London, 1987.

Cocksworth, Christopher J. *Evangelical Eucharistic Thought in the Church of England.* Cambridge University Press, 1993.

Congar, Yves M. J. *I Believe in the Holy Spirit,* vols. 2 and 3. Trans. David Smith. Geoffrey Chapman, London, 1983.

Cousins, Ewert H., ed. *Hope and the Future of Man.* Fortress, Philadelphia, 1972.

Crockett, William R. *Eucharist: Symbol of Transformation.* Pueblo, New York, 1989.

Cross, F. L. and E. A. Livingstone, eds. *The Oxford Dictionary of the Christian Church.* 2nd ed. Oxford University Press, 1983.

Crouzel, Henri. *Origen.* Trans. A. S. Worrall. T&T Clark, Edinburgh, 1989.

Cullmann, Oscar. *The Christology of the New Testament*. Rev. ed. Trans. Shirley C. Guthrie and Charles A. M. Hall. Westminster, Philadelphia, 1963.
Christ and Time: The Primitive Christian Conception of Time and History. Rev. ed. Trans. Floyd V. Filson. Westminster, Philadelphia, 1964.

Dalferth, Ingolf U. *Theology and Philosophy*. Basil Blackwell, London, 1988.

Danielou, Jean. 'The Meaning and Significance of Teilhard de Chardin.' *Communio* 15, Fall 1988, pp. 350–60.

Dante, Alighieri, *The Portable Dante*. Ed. P. Milano. Trans. L. Binyon, Viking, New York, 1947.

Davies, J. G. *The Spirit, the Church and the Sacraments*. The Faith Press, London, 1954.
He Ascended Into Heaven. Lutterworth, London, 1958.
'Ascension of Christ.' *A Dictionary of Theology*. Ed. Alan Richardson. SCM, London, 1969.

Davies, Robertson. *Fifth Business*. Penguin, New York, 1977.

Davies, W. D. and D. Daube, eds. *The Background of the New Testament and Its Eschatology*. University of Cambridge, 1954.

Deuser, H. *et.al.*, eds. *Gottes Zukunft – Zukunft der Welt: Feschrift für Jürgen Moltmann*. Christian Kaiser, Munich, 1986.

Dewald, Ernest T. 'The Iconography of the Ascension.' *American Journal of Archaeology*, second series. *Journal of the Archaeological Institute of America* 19.3, 1915, pp. 277–319.

Dionysius. *Pseudo-Dionysius: The Complete Works*. Trans. C. Luibheid. Paulist Press, New York, 1987.

Dix, Gregory. *The Shape of the Liturgy*. Dacre, Westminster, 1945.

Dostoevsky, Fyodor. *The Brothers Karamazov*. Trans. Andrew H. MacAndrew. Bantam, Toronto, 1981.

Dowley, Tim, ed. *Eerdman's Handbook to the History of Christianity*. Grand Rapids, 1977.

Driver, Tom F. *Christ in a Changing World: Towards an Ethical Christology*. SCM, London, 1981.

Dru, Alexander. *The Journals of Søren Kierkegaard*. Oxford University Press, London, 1938.

Drummond, Henry. *The Ascent of Man*. Hodder & Stoughton, London, 1894.

Dulles, Avery. *The Catholicity of the Church and the Structures of Catholicism.* Clarendon, Oxford, 1985.
Models of the Church. Expanded ed. Image, New York, 1987.

Dumbrell, William J. *Covenant and Creation: A Theology of Old Testament Covenants.* Thomas Nelson, Nashville, 1984.
The End of the Beginning: Revelation 21–22 and the Old Testament. Baker, Grand Rapids, 1985.

Dunn, James D. G. *Jesus and the Spirit: A Study of the Religious and Charismatic Experience of Jesus and the First Christians as Reflected in the New Testament.* SCM, London, 1975.
Christology in the Making: A New Testament Inquiry Into the Origins of the Doctrine of the Incarnation. Westminster, Philadelphia, 1980.

Edwards, Denis. 'The Relationship Between the Risen Christ and the Material Universe.' *Pacifica* 4.1, February 1991, pp. 1–15.

Edwards, M. J. 'Origen no Gnostic, or on the Corporeality of Man.' *Journal of Theological Studies* (NS) 43, 1992, pp. 23–37.
'Origen's Two Resurrections.' *Journal of Theological Studies* (NS) 46. 2, October 1995, pp. 502–18.

Ellingworth, Paul. 'Jesus and the Universe in Hebrews.' *Evangelical Quarterly* 58.4, October 1986, pp. 337–50.

Ellis, E. Earle. *The Gospel of Luke* The New Century Bible Commentary. Ed. Matthew Black. Eerdmans, Grand Rapids, 1991.

Ellul, Jacques. *The Subversion of Christianity.* Trans. Geoffrey W. Bromiley. Eerdmans, Grand Rapids, 1986.
What I Believe. Trans. G. W. Bromiley. Eerdmans, Grand Rapids, 1989.

Empie, Paul C. and J. I. McCord, eds. *Marburg Revisited: A Re-examination of Lutheran and Reformed Traditions* Augsburg, Minneapolis, 1966.

Eusebius of Caesarea. *Oration in Praise of Constantine: Nicene and Post-Nicene Fathers,* Second Series, vol. 1. Eds. P. Schaff and H. Wace. Trans. A. C. McGiffert and E. C. Richardson. Hendrickson, Peabody, 1995.

Evans, C. F. *Resurrection and the New Testament.* SCM, London, 1970.

Evdokimov, Paul. *Le Christ dans le pensée Russe.* Cerf, Paris, 1970.

Farrow, Douglas. 'Form and Function: A Response to the Functional Christology of Oscar Cullmann.' ThM, Regent College, Vancouver, 1986.

The Word of Truth and Disputes About Words. Eisenbrauns, Winona Lake, 1987.
'Showdown: The Message of Second Thessalonians 1:1–12 and the Riddle of the "Restrainer."' *Crux* 25.1, March 1989, pp. 23–26.
'St Irenaeus of Lyons: The Church and the World.' *Pro Ecclesia* 4.3, Summer 1995, pp. 333–55.
'The Doctrine of the Ascension in Irenaeus and Origen.' *ARC* 26, 1998, pp. 31–50.
'In the End is the Beginning: A Review of Jürgen Moltmann's Systematic Contributions.' *Modern Theology* 14.3, July 1998b, pp. 425–47.

Farrow, Douglas, David Demson and J. Augustine Di Noia. 'Robert Jenson's *Systematic Theology*: Three Responses.' *International Journal of Systematic Theology* 1.1, March 1999, pp. 89–104.

Fee, Gordon D. *God's Empowering Presence: The Holy Spirit in the Letters of Paul.* Hendrickson, Peabody, 1994.

Fitzmyer, Joseph A. 'Ascension and Pentecost.' *Theological Studies* 45, Spring 1984, pp. 409–40.

Flannery, Austin P., ed. *Documents of Vatican II.* Eerdmans, Grand Rapids, 1975.

Ford, David F. *Barth and God's Story: Studies in the Intercultural History of Christianity*, Bd. 27. Verlag Peter Lang, Bern, 1981.

Ford, David. F., ed. *The Modern Theologians: An Introduction to Christian Theology in the Twentieth Century.* 2nd ed. Blackwells, Cambridge, 1997.

Forster, Peter. 'God and the World in Saint Irenaeus: Theological Perspectives.' PhD, Edinburgh, 1985.

Forsyth, P. T. *The Person and Place of Jesus Christ.* Independent, London, 1948.

Fox, Matthew. *The Coming of the Cosmic Christ.* Harper & Row, San Francisco, 1988.

Franklin, Eric. 'The Ascension and the Eschatology of Luke-Acts.' *Scottish Journal of Theology* 23.2, May 1970, pp. 191–200.
Christ the Lord: A Study in the Purpose and Theology of Luke-Acts. Westminster, Philadelphia, 1975.

Frei, Hans W. *The Eclipse of Biblical Narrative: A Study in Eighteenth and Nineteenth Century Hermeneutics.* Yale, New Haven, 1974.
The Identity of Jesus Christ: The Hermeneutical Bases of Dogmatic Theology. Fortress, Philadelphia, 1975.

Frye, Northrup. *The Great Code: The Bible and Literature*. Academic Press, Toronto, 1982.

Gage, Warren Austin. *The Gospel of Genesis: Studies in Protology and Eschatology*. Carpenter/Eisenbrauns, Winona Lake, 1984.

Galloway, Allan. *The Cosmic Christ*. Nisbet, London, 1951.

Garascia, Mary Martha. 'The Search for an Ascending Christology: An Examination of the Christology of John B. Cobb, Jr. and its Implications for Revisionary Christology.' PhD, The Iliff School of Theology and the University of Denver, 1988 (UMI).

Gerrish, B. A. *Grace and Gratitude: The Eucharistic Theology of John Calvin*. Fortress,Minneapolis, 1993.

Gilkey, Langdon B. 'Cosmology, Ontology, and the Travail of Biblical Language.' *Journal of Religion* 1961, pp. 194–205.

Gilson, Etienne. *The Unity of Philosophical Experience*. Charles Scribner's Sons, New York, 1937.

Gore, Charles, ed. *Lux Mundi: A Series of Studies in the Religion of the Incarnation*. 11th ed. John Murray, London, 1891.

Grabar, André. *Christian Iconography: A Study of its Origins*. Bollingen Series 35.10. Princeton University Press, 1968.

Gregory Nazianzen. *Select Orations of Saint Gregory Nazianzen. Nicene and Post-Nicene Fathers of the Christian Church*, second series, vol. 7. Eds. P. Schaff and H. Wace. Trans. C. G. Browne, J. E. Swallow, and E. H. Gifford. Eerdmans, Grand Rapids, 1983.

Greer, Thomas H. *A Brief History of the Western World*. 4th ed. Harcourt Brace Jovanovitch, San Diego, 1982.

Guilding, Aileen. *The Fourth Gospel and Jewish Worship*. Oxford University Press, 1960.

Gunton, Colin E. *Becoming and Being: The Doctrine of God in Charles Hartshorne and Karl Barth*. Oxford University Press, 1978.
Yesterday and Today: A Study of Continuities in Christology. Eerdmans, Grand Rapids, 1983.
'Barth, the Trinity, and Human Freedom.' *Theology Today* 43. 3, October 1986, pp. 316–30.
The Actuality of Atonement: A Study of Metaphor, Rationality and the Christian Tradition. T&T Clark, Edinburgh, 1988.
The Promise of Trinitarian Theology. T&T Clark, Edinburgh, 1991.
Christ and Creation. Paternoster/Eerdmans, Grand Rapids, 1992.

The One, the Three and the Many: God, Creation and the Culture of Modernity. Cambridge University Press, 1993.
'Unity and Diversity: God, World and Society.' *Society for the Study of Theology*, Cardiff, 1993.
Theology through the Theologians. T&T Clark, Edinburgh, 1996.

Gunton, Colin E. and Daniel W. Hardy, eds. *On Being the Church*. T&T Clark, Edinburgh, 1989.

Guzie, Tad. *Jesus and the Eucharist*. Gracewing, Leominster, 1995.

Hall, Douglas J. *Professing the Faith: Christian Theology in a North American Context*. Fortress, Minneapolis, 1993.

Hall, Thor. *The Evolution of Christology*. Abingdon, Nashville, 1982.

Hanson, A. T. *The Image of the Invisible God*. SCM, London, 1982.

Hardy, Daniel W. *God's Ways with the World: Thinking and Practising Christian Faith*. T&T Clark, Edinburgh, 1996.

Harnack, Adolf. *History of Dogma*. 3rd German ed., vols. 1 and 2 (1896), trans. Neil Buchanan; vol. 3 (1897), trans. James Millar. Williams & Norgate, London.
The Acts of The Apostles. Trans. J. R. Wilkinson. Williams & Norgate, London, 1909.
What is Christianity? Trans. T. B. Saunders. Fortress, Philadelphia, 1986.

Harris, Murray J. *Raised Immortal*. Marshall, Morgan & Scott, London, 1983.

Hart, Trevor and Daniel Thimell, eds. *Christ in our Place*. Paternoster, London, 1989.

Hartwell, Herbert. *The Theology of Karl Barth: An Introduction*. Gerald Duckworth, London, 1964.

Hauerwas, Stanley. *After Christendom?: How the Church is to Behave if Freedom, Justice and a Christian Nation are Bad Ideas*. Abingdon, Nashville, 1991.

Hayes, Zachary. *The Hidden Center: Spirituality and Speculative Christology in St Bonaventure*. Paulist Press, New York, 1981.

Healy, Nicholas M. 'The Logic of Karl Barth's Ecclesiology: An Analysis, Assessment and Proposed Modifications.' *Modern Theology* 10.3, 1994, pp. 253–70.

Hefner, Philip. 'Theological Methodology and St Irenaeus.' *Journal of Religion* 44, 1964, pp. 294–309.

Hegel, G. W. F. *The Phenomenology of Mind.* Trans. J. B. Baillie. George Allen & Unwin, London, 1949.
The Philosophy of History. Trans. J. Sibree. Dover, New York, 1956.
Lectures on the Philosophy of Religion. The Lectures of 1927. Ed. Peter Hodgson. Trans. P. Hodgson, R. Brown and J. Stewart. University of California, Berkeley, 1988.

Heine, Susan. *Christianity and the Goddesses: Systematic Criticism of a Feminist Theology.* Trans. John Bowden. SCM, London, 1988.

Hengel, Martin. *The Son of God: The Origin of Christology and the History of Jewish-Hellenistic Religion.* Trans. John Bowden. Fortress, Philadelphia, 1976.
Acts and the History of Earliest Christianity. Trans. John Bowden. SCM, London, 1979.

Heppe, Heinrich. *Reformed Dogmatics: Set Out and Illustrated from the Sources.* Rev. and ed. E. Bizer. Trans. G. Thomson. Baker, Grand Rapids, 1978.

Heron, Alasdair I. C. *A Century of Protestant Theology.* Westminster, Philadelphia, 1980.
The Holy Spirit: The Holy Spirit in the Bible, the History of Christian Thought, and Recent Theology. Westminster, Philadelphia, 1983.
Table and Tradition. Toward an Ecumenical Understanding of the Eucharist. Handsel, Edinburgh, 1983b.

Hick, John. *Death and Eternal Life.* Collins, London, 1976.
Evil and the God of Love. Macmillan, London, 1985.
God and the Universe of Faiths. Oneworld, Oxford, 1993.

Hick, John and Paul F. Knitter, eds. *The Myth of Christian Uniqueness.* SCM, London, 1987.

Himmelfarb, Martha. *Ascent to Heaven in Jewish and Christian Apocalypses.* Oxford University Press, 1993.

Hobbes, Thomas. *Leviathan.* Ed. C. B. MacPherson. Penguin, London, 1968.

Hong, Howard V. and Edna H. Hong. *Søren Kierkegaard's Journals and Papers,* vols. 1–7. Assisted by G. Malantschuk. Indiana University Press, Bloomington, 1967–78.

Honner, John. 'A New Ontology: Incarnation, Eucharist, Resurrection, and Physics.' *Pacifica* 4.1, February 1991, pp. 15–50.

Hoogland, Marvin P. *Calvin's Perspective on the Exaltation of Christ.* Free University of Amsterdam. J. H. Kok, N. V. Kampen, 1966.

Horne, Brian. 'Beyond Tragedy.' Preaching the Ascension, I. *Theology* 94, May–June 1991, pp. 168–73.

Houlden, J. L. 'Beyond Belief.' Preaching the Ascension, II. *Theology* 94, May–June 1991, pp. 173–80.
Jesus: A Question of Identity. SPCK, London, 1992.

Houston, James. *I Believe in the Creator*. Eerdmans, Grand Rapids, 1980.

Hughes, P. E. *The True Image*. InterVarsity, Leicester, 1989.

Hunsinger, George. *How to Read Karl Barth: The Shape of His Theology*. Oxford University Press, 1991.

Hurst, L. D. *The Epistle to the Hebrews: Its Background of Thought*. Society for New Testament Studies Monograph Series 65. Cambridge University Press, 1990.

Inge, W. R. *Personal Religion and the Life of Devotion*. Longmans, Green & Co., London, 1924.

Irenaeus. *The Demonstration of the Apostolic Preaching*. Translations of Christian Literature, Series IV. Gen. eds, W. J. Sparrow Simpson and W. K. Lowther Clarke. Trans. J. Armitage Robinson. SPCK, London, 1920.
Against Heresies. Ed. and trans. Alexander Roberts and James Donaldson. American ed. A. Cleveland Coxe. *The Ante-Nicene Fathers*, vol. 1. Eerdmans, Grand Rapids, 1987. Greek and Latin quotations from *Sancti Irenaeus: Libros quinque adversus haereses*, ed. W. Wigan Harvey, Cambridge, 1857.

Jaki, Stanley L. *The Saviour of Science*. Scottish Academic Press, Edinburgh, 1990.

Jamros, Daniel P. 'Hegel on the Incarnation: Unique or Universal?' *Theological Studies* 56, 1995, pp. 276–300.

Janson, H. W. *History of Art*. 3rd ed. Rev. Anthony F. Janson. Harry N. Abrams, Prentice-Hall, New York & Englewood Cliffs, 1986.

Jantzen, Grace. 'Ascension and the Road to Hell.' *Theology* May–June 1991, pp. 163–65.

Jenson, Robert W. *The Triune Identity: God According to the Gospel*. Fortress, Philadelphia, 1982.
The Unbaptized God: The Basic Flaw in Ecumenical Theology. Fortress, Minneapolis, 1992.
The Triune God. Systematic Theology, vol. 1. Oxford University Press, New York, 1997.

John of Damascus. *The Orthodox Faith*. Trans. F. H. Chase. The Catholic University of America Press, Washington, 1958.

John Paul II. *Veritatis Splendor*. To all the Bishops of the Catholic Church Regarding Certain Fundamental Questions of the Church's Moral Teaching. Vatican translation. St Paul's Books and Media, Boston, 1993.

Johnstone, William, ed. *The Cloud of Unknowing* and *The Book of Privy Counseling*. Image, Garden City, 1973.

Jones, D. Gareth. *Teilhard de Chardin: An Analysis and Assessment*. Eerdmans, Grand Rapids, 1969.

Joyce, James. *A Portrait of the Artist as a Young Man*. Penguin, London, 1992.

Julian of Norwich. *A Lesson of Love: The Revelations of Julian of Norwich*. Ed. and trans. Fr John-Julian. Darton, Longman & Todd, London, 1988.

Jüngel, Eberhard. *Karl Barth: A Theological Legacy*. Trans. Garrett E. Paul. Westminster, Philadelphia, 1986.

Justin Martyr. *First Apology*. Ed. and trans. Alexander Roberts and James Donaldson. American ed., A. Cleveland Coxe. *The Ante-Nicene Fathers*, vol 1. Eerdmans, Grand Rapids, 1987.

Kaiser, Christopher B. *Creation and the History of Science: The History of Christian Theology*, vol. 3. Series ed. Paul Avis. Marshall Pickering, London, 1991.

Kant, Immanuel. *The Philosophy of Kant: Immanuel Kant's Moral and Political Writings*. Ed. Carl J. Friedrich. Random, New York, 1949. *Religion Within the Limits of Reason Alone*. Trans. T. M. Greene and H. H. Hudson. Harper Torchbooks, New York, 1960.

Kasper, Walter. *Theology and Church*. Trans. Margaret Kohl. SCM, London, 1989.

Kelly, J. N. D. *Early Christian Doctrines*. 5th ed. A & C Black, London, 1977.

Kelly, Tony. 'A New Ontology? A Response to a Recent Suggestion.' *Pacifica* 6.2, June 1993, pp. 189–209.

Kerr, Hugh T. 'The Presence of the Absence.' *Theology Today*, 43.1, April 1986, pp. 1–4.

Kierkegaard, Søren. *Philosophical Fragments or a Fragment of Philosophy*, by Johannes Climacus. Trans. D. F. Swenson. Princeton University Press, 1936.

Attack upon 'Christendom.' Trans. Walter Lowrie. Beacon, Boston, 1956.
Concluding Unscientific Postscript. Trans. D. F. Swenson and W. Lowrie. Princeton University Press, 1968.
The Sickness Unto Death: A Christian Psychological Exposition for Edification and Awakening, by Anti-Climacus. Trans. A. Hannay. Penguin, London, 1989.
Practice in Christianity. Ed. and trans. H. V. Hong and E. H. Hong. Princeton University Press, 1991.

Kikawada, Isaac M. and Arthur Quinn. *Before Abraham Was: The Unity of Genesis 1–11.* Abingdon, Nashville, 1985.

Kim, Dai Sil. 'Irenaeus of Lyons and Teilhard de Chardin: A Comparative Study of "Recapitulation" and "Omega."' *Journal of Ecumenical Studies* 13.1, 1976, pp. 69–93.

Kline, Meredith G. *Images of the Spirit.* Baker, Grand Rapids, 1980.

Koch, G. *Die Auferstehung Jesu Christi.* Tübingen, 1965.

Koch, Klaus. *The Rediscovery of Apocalyptic.* Trans. Margaret Kohl. SCM, London, 1972.

Komonchak, J. and M. Collins, D. Lane, eds. *The New Dictionary of Theology.* Gill & Macmillan, Dublin, 1987.

König, Adrio. *The Eclipse of Christ in Eschatology: Toward a Christ-centred Approach.* Eerdmans, Grand Rapids, 1989.

Küng, Hans. *Theology for the Third Millennium: An Ecumenical View.* Trans. Peter Heinegg. Doubleday, New York, 1988.
Credo: The Apostles' Creed Explained for Today. Doubleday, New York, 1992.

Künneth, Walter. *The Theology of the Resurrection.* Trans. James W. Leitch. SCM, London, 1965.

Kuschel, Karl-Josef, *Born Before All Time?: The Dispute Over Christ's Origin.* Trans. John Bowden. SCM, London, 1992.

LaCugna, Catherine M., ed. *Freeing Theology: The Essentials of Theology in Feminist Perspective.* HarperCollins, San Francisco, 1993.

Larranaga, Victorien. *L'Ascension de Notre-Seigneur dans le Nouveau Testament.* Institut Biblique Pontifical, Rome, 1938.

Lasch, Christopher. *The True and Only Heaven: Progress and its Critics.* Norton, New York, 1991.

Lawson, John. *The Biblical Theology of Saint Irenaeus*. Epworth, London, 1948.

Lessing, G. E. *Lessing's Theological Writings*. Ed. and trans. H. Chadwick. A & C Black, London, 1956.

Levi, Peter, ed. *The Penguin Book of English Christian Verse*. Penguin, Harmondsworth, 1984.

Lewis, C. S. *The Great Divorce*. G. Bles, London, 1946.

Miracles: How God Intervenes in Nature and Human Affairs. Collier, New York, 1978.

Libreria Editrice Vaticana. *Catechism of the Catholic Church*. Paulist Press, Mahwah NJ, 1994.

Limouris, Gennadios, ed. *Church Kingdom World: The Church as Mystery and Prophetic Sign*. Faith and Order Paper No. 130. World Council of Churches, Geneva, 1986.

Lincoln, Andrew T. *Paradise Now and Not Yet*. Cambridge University Press, 1981.

Lindars, Barnabus. *The Theology of the Letter to the Hebrews*. Cambridge University Press, 1991.

Logan, Alastair H. B. *Gnostic Truth and Christian Heresy: A Study in the History of Gnosticism*. T&T Clark, Edinburgh, 1996.

Lohfink, Gerhard. *Die Himmelfahrt Jesu*. Kosel, Munich, 1971.

Lossky, Vladimir. 'Concerning the Third Mark of the Church: Catholicity.' *One Church* 19, 1965, pp. 181–87.
In The Image and Likeness of God. Eds. J. Erickson and T. Bird. Mowbrays, London, 1974.
Orthodox Theology: An Introduction. Trans. Ian and Ihita Kesarcodi-Watson. St Vladimir's, Crestwood, 1978.
The Vision of God. Trans. Asheleigh Moorhouse. St Vladimir's, Crestwood, 1983.

Louth, Andrew. *Denys the Areopagite*. Geoffrey Chapman, London, 1989.
Maximus the Confessor. Routledge, London, 1996.

de Lubac, Henri. *The Religion of Teilhard de Chardin*. Trans. R. Hague. Desclee, New York, 1967.
'Teilhard de Chardin in the Context of Renewal.' *Communio* 15, Fall 1988, pp. 361–75.

Lyons, J. A. *The Cosmic Christ in Origen and Teilhard de Chardin*. Oxford University Press, 1982.

MacKintosh, Hugh R. *Types of Modern Theology: Schleiermacher to Barth*. Nisbet, London, 1937.

Macquarrie, John. *Jesus Christ in Modern Thought*. SCM, London, 1990.

Maddox, Robert. *The Purpose of Luke-Acts*. T&T Clark, Edinburgh, 1982.

Maile, John F. 'The Ascension in Luke-Acts.' *Tyndale Bulletin* 37, 1986, pp. 29–59.

Malantschuk, Gregor. *Kierkegaard's Thought*. Ed. and trans. by H. V. Hong and F. H. Hong. Princeton University Press, 1974.

Maloney, George A. *The Cosmic Christ: From Paul to Teilhard*. Sheed & Ward, New York, 1968.

Marion, Jean-Luc. *God Without Being*. Hors-Texte. Trans. T. A. Carlson. Univerity of Chicago, 1991.

Markus, R. A. *Saeculum: History and Society in the Theology of St Augustine*. Cambridge University Press, 1970.

Marrevee, W. H. *The Ascension of Christ in the Works of St Augustine*. University of Ottawa Press, 1967.

Martensen, Hans. *Christian Dogmatics*. Trans. W. Urwick. T&T Clark, Edinburgh, 1890.

Maximus Confessor. *Selected Writings*. Trans. George C. Berthold. SPCK, London, 1985.

May, Gerhard. *Creatio ex Nihilo: The Doctrine of 'Creation out of nothing' in Early Christian Thought*. Trans. A. S. Worrall. T&T Clark, Edinburgh, 1994.

McBrien, Richard P. *Catholicism*. Harper & Row, San Francisco, 1981.

McCool, Gerald A., ed. *A Rahner Reader*. Darton, Longman & Todd, London, 1975.

McCormack, Bruce L. *Karl Barth's Critically Realistic Dialectical Theology: Its Genesis and Development 1909–1936*. Clarendon Press, Oxford, 1995.

McDannell, Colleen and Bernhard Lang. *Heaven: A History*. Yale University Press, Newhaven & London, 1990.

McDonnell, Kilian. *John Calvin, the Church, and the Eucharist*. Princeton University Press, 1967.

McGinn, Bernard. 'Resurrection and Ascension in the Christology of the Early Cistercians.' *Cîteaux* 30, 1979, pp. 5–22.
 The Calabrian Abbot: Joachim of Fiore in the History of Western Thought. Macmillan, New York, 1985.

The Foundations of Mysticism. Crossroad, New York, 1995.
The Growth of Mysticism. Crossroad, New York, 1996.

McIntyre, John. *The Christian Doctrine of History*. Eerdmans, Grand Rapids, 1957.

McKim, Donald, ed. *How Karl Barth Changed My Mind*. Eerdmans, Grand Rapids, 1986.

McPartlan, Paul. *The Eucharist Makes the Church: Henri de Lubac and John Zizioulas in Dialogue*. T&T Clark, Edinburgh, 1993.

Sacrament of Salvation: An Introduction to Eucharistic Ecclesiology. T&T Clark, Edinburgh, 1995.

Meyendorff, John. *Christ in Eastern Christian Thought*. St Vladimir's, Crestwood, 1975.

Milbank, J., C. Pickstock and G. Ward, eds. *Radical Orthodoxy: A New Theology*. Routledge, London, 1999.

Milligan, William. *The Ascension and Heavenly Priesthood of Our Lord*. MacMillan, London & New York, 1892.

Milner, Benjamin Charles Jr. *Calvin's Doctrine of the Church*. E. J. Brill, Leiden, 1970.

Minns, Denis. *Irenaeus*. Geoffrey Chapman, London, 1994.

Molnar, Paul D. *Karl Barth and The Theology of the Lord's Supper. A Systematic Investigation*. Peter Lang, New York, 1996.

Moltmann, Jürgen. *Theology of Hope: On the Ground and the Implications of a Christian Eschatology*. Trans. J. W. Leitch. SCM, London, 1967.
The Crucified God: The Cross of Christ as the Foundation and Criticism of Christian Theology. Trans. R. Wilson and J. Bowden. SCM, London, 1974.
The Church in the Power of the Spirit: A Contribution to Messianic Ecclesiology. Trans. Margaret Kohl. SCM, London, 1977.
The Future of Creation: An Ecological Doctrine of Creation. Trans. M. Kohl. Fortress, Philadelphia, 1979.
God in Creation: A New Theology of Creation and the Spirit. Trans. M. Kohl. SCM, London, 1985.
Theology Today: Two Contributions Towards Making Theology Present. Trans. John Bowden. SCM, London, 1988.
The Way of Jesus Christ: Christology in Messianic Dimensions. Trans. M. Kohl. SCM, London, 1990.
The Spirit of Life: A Universal Affirmation. Trans. M. Kohl. Fortress, Minneapolis, 1992.

The Coming of God: Christian Eschatology. Trans. M. Kohl. Fortress, Minneapolis, 1996.

Morse, Christopher. *Not Every Spirit: A Dogmatics of Christian Disbelief*. Trinity, Harrisburg, 1994.

Moule, C. F. D. 'The Ascension – Acts i.9.' *The Expository Times* 68, 1957, pp. 205ff.

Muir, Edwin. *Collected Poems*. Faber & Faber, London, 1963.
An Autobiography. Hogarth, London, 1987.

Myers, J. M. and O. Reimherr, H. N. Bream, eds. *Search the Scriptures*. Gettysburg Theology Studies 3. E. J. Brill, Leiden, 1969.

Nebelsick, Harold P. *Circles of God: Theology and Science at the Frontiers of Knowledge*, No. 2. Scottish Academic Press, Edinburgh, 1985.

Neill, Stephen and N. T. Wright. *The Interpretation of the New Testament, 1861–1986*. 2nd. ed. Oxford University Press, 1988.

Nelson, James B. *Body Theology*. Westminster/John Knox, Louisville, 1992.

Nicholson, Godfrey C. *Death as Departure: The Johannine Descent–Ascent Schema*. SBL Dissertation Series 63. Scholars Press, Chico, 1983.

Niebuhr, Reinhold. *The Nature and Destiny of Man*, vol 2. *Human Destiny*. Charles Scribner's Sons, New York, 1964.

Nietzsche, Friedrich. *Twilight of the Idols and The Anti-Christ*. Trans. R. J. Hollingdale. Penguin, London, 1968.

Nolland, John. *Word Biblical Commentary*, vol. 35c: Luke 18:35 – 24:53. Ed. Ralph P. Martin. Waco, 1993.

Norris, Richard A. *God and the World in Early Christian Theology*. A & C Black, London, 1966.

O'Collins, Gerald. *Christology: A Biblical, Historical, and Systematic Study of Jesus*. Oxford University Press, 1995.

O'Donovan, Oliver. *On the Thirty-Nine Articles: A Conversation with Tudor Christianity*. Paternoster, Exeter, 1986.
Resurrection and Moral Order: An Outline for Evangelical Ethics. Eerdmans, Grand Rapids, 1986b.
The Desire of the Nations: Rediscovering the Roots of Political Theology. Cambridge University Press, 1996.

O'Grady, Colm. *The Church in Catholic Theology: Dialogue with Karl Barth*. Corpus, Washington, 1969.

Origen. *Contra Celsum*. Trans. H. Chadwick. Cambridge University Press, 1953.
Prayer/Exhortation to Martyrdom. Trans. J. J. O'Meara. *Ancient Christian Writers* 19. Green, London, 1954.

On First Principles. Trans. G. W. Butterworth. Peter Smith, Gloucester, 1973.

O'Toole, R. F. 'Luke's Understanding of Jesus' Resurrection-Ascension-Exaltation.' *Biblical Theology Bulletin* 9.3, 1979, pp. 106–14.

Ouspensky, Leonid and Vladimir Lossky. *The Meaning of Icons*. Trans. G. E. Palmer and E. Kadloubovsky. St Vladimir's, Crestwood, 1983.

Owen, John. *The Works of John Owen*, vols. 1 and 8. Ed. W. H. Goold. The Banner of Truth Trust, Edinburgh, 1967.

Pannenberg, Wolfhart. *Jesus – God and Man*. 2nd ed. Trans. Lewis L. Wilkins and Duane A. Priebe. Westminster, Philadelphia, 1968.
The Apostles' Creed in the Light of Today's Questions. Trans. Margaret Kohl. SCM, London, 1972.
Systematic Theology. 3 vols. Trans. G. Bromiley. Eerdmans, Grand Rapids, 1991–98.

Parsons, Mikeal C. 'The Departure of Jesus in Luke-Acts.' *Journal for the Study of the New Testament* Supplement Series 21, Sheffield, 1987.

Passmore, John. *The Perfectibility of Man*. Charles Scribner's Sons, New York, 1970.

Paul, Jean. *Siebenkäs*. Hrsg. von Klaus Pauler. Edition text + kritik. München, 1991.

Peck, M. Scott. *People of the Lie*. Simon & Schuster, New York., 1983.

Pelikan, Jaroslav. *The Christian Tradition: A History of the Development of Doctrine*, vols 1–5. University of Chicago Press, Chicago and London, 1971–89.
Jesus through the Centuries: His Place in the History of Culture. Yale University Press, New Haven, 1985.

Percy, Walker. *The Thanatos Syndrome*. Collins, London, 1987.

Perrin, Norman. *The Resurrection Narratives*. SCM, London, 1977.

Peters, Ted, ed. *Cosmos as Creation: Theology and Science in Consonance*. Abingdon, Nashville, 1989.

Petry, Ray C., ed. *A History of Christianity: Readings in the History of the Church*, vol. 1. Baker, Grand Rapids, 1981.

Pickstock, Catherine. *After Writing: On the Liturgical Consummation of Philosophy*. Blackwells, Oxford, 1998.

Plato. *The Works of Plato*. Trans. Jowett; ed. Irwin Edman. The Modern Library, New York, 1956.

Plekon, Michael. 'Kierkegaard, the Church and Theology of Golden-Age Denmark.' *Journal of Ecclesiastical History*, 34.2, April 1983, pp. 245–66.
'Kierkegaard and the Eucharist.' *Studia Liturgica* 22.2, 1992, pp. 214–36.

Polanyi, Michael. *Personal Knowledge: Towards a Post-Critical Philosophy*. University of Chicago, 1962.

Popper, Karl. *The Open Society and its Enemies*, vol. 2. *The High Tide of Prophecy: Hegel, Marx, and the Aftermath*. Routledge & Kegan Paul, London, 1962.

Prigogine, Ilya and Isabelle Stengers. *Order out of Chaos: Man's New Dialogue with Nature*. Fontana, London, 1984.

Przywara, Erich. *An Augustine Synthesis*. Sheed & Ward, London, 1936.

Rae, Murray. *Kierkegaard's Vision of the Incarnation: By Faith Transformed*. Oxford University Press, 1997.

Rahner, Karl. *On the Theology of Death*. Herder & Herder, New York, 1961.
Theological Investigations. 23 vols. Darton Longman & Todd, London, 1961–92.
Foundations of the Christian Faith. Trans. William V. Dych. Darton Longman & Todd, London, 1978.

Rahner, Karl, ed. *A Concise Sacramentum Mundi*. Burns & Oates, London, 1975.
Sacramentum Mundi, vol. 5. Theological Publications in India, Bangalore, 1978.

Ratzinger, Joseph. 'Ascension of Christ.' *Encyclopedia of Theology*. Ed. Karl Rahner. Burns & Oates, London, 1975.
Introduction to Christianity. Trans. J. R. Foster. Seabury, New York, 1979.
Eschatology: Death and Eternal Life. Trans. Michael Waldstein. Ed. Aidan Nichols. The Catholic University of America Press, Washington, 1988.

Redeker, Martin. *Schleiermacher: Life and Thought.* Trans. John Wallhausser. Fortress, Philadelphia, 1973.

Reimarus. *Fragments.* Ed. C. H. Talbert. Trans. R. S. Fraser. SCM, London, 1971.

Rist, John M. *Augustine: Ancient Thought Baptized.* Cambridge University Press, 1994.

Ritschl, Dietrich. *Memory and Hope: An Inquiry Concerning the Presence of Christ.* Macmillan, New York, 1967.
The Logic of Theology: A Brief Account of the Relationships Between Basic Concepts in Theology. Trans. John Bowden. SCM, London, 1986.

Robinson, J. A. T. *The Priority of John.* SCM, London, 1985.

Robinson, J. M. 'Ascension.' *The Interpreter's Dictionary of the Bible.* Abingdon, New York, 1962.

Roebuck, Stuart, ed. *Christ and the Cosmos.* Report on the Research Consultation Held at the Luton Industrial College on April 3–5, 1987. Westminster College, Oxford, 1988.

Rowdon, Harold H., ed. *Christ the Lord: Studies in Christology Presented to Donald Guthrie.* InterVarsity, Leicester, 1982.

Sanders, E. P. *Paul and Palestinian Judaism: A Comparison of Patterns of Religion.* SCM, London, 1977.

Satinover, Jeffrey. *Homosexuality and the Politics of Truth.* Baker, Grand Rapids, 1996.

Schleiermacher, Friedrich. *On Religion: Speeches to its Cultured Despisers.* Trans. John Oman. Harper & Row, New York, 1958.
The Christian Faith. Various trans., eds. H. R. MacKintosh and J. S. Stewart. T&T Clark, Edinburgh, 1989.

Schrade, H. 'Zur Ikonographie der Himmelfahrt Christi,' *Vorträge der Bibliothek Warburg, Vörtrage* 1928–29. *Uber die Vorstellungen von der Himmelsreise der Seele,* 1930.

Schwöbel, Christoph and Colin Gunton, eds. *Persons, Divine and Human.* T&T Clark, Edinburgh, 1991.

Scott, Nathan A. Jr. *The Broken Centre: Studies in the Theological Horizon of Modern Literature.* Yale, New Haven, 1966.

Segundo, Juan Luis. *The Historical Jesus of the Synoptics,* JNYT, vol. 2, 1985.
The Humanist Christology of Paul, JNYT, vol. 3, 1986.

An Evolutionary Approach to Jesus of Nazareth: Jesus of Nazareth Yesterday and Today, vol. 5. Trans. John Drury. Orbis, Maryknoll, 1988.

Shapland, C. R. B. *The Letters of Saint Athanasius Concerning the Holy Spirit*. Epworth, London, 1951.

Sittler, Joseph A. 'Called to Unity.' *Ecumenical Review*. 14.2, January 1962, pp. 177–87.

Sölle, Dorothee. *Beyond Mere Obedience*. Pilgrim, New York, 1982.

Staniloae, Dimitru. *Theology and the Church*. Trans. Robert Barringer. St Vladimir's, Crestwood, 1980.

Steiner, George. *Real Presences*. University of Chicago Press, 1989.

Stempvoort, P. A. van. 'The Interpretation of the Ascension in Luke and Acts,' *New Testament Studies* 5, 1958, pp. 30–42.

Strauss, David F. *The Life of Jesus for the People*. 2nd ed. 2 vols. Williams & Norgate, London, 1879.
The Life of Jesus, Critically Examined. Trans. George Eliot. 2nd ed. SCM, London, 1973.

Suchocki, Marjorie Hewitt. *God Christ Church: A Practical Guide to Process Theology*. Crossroad, New York, 1982.

Surin, Kenneth. *Theology and the Problem of Evil*. Basil Blackwell, Oxford, 1986.

Sykes, S. W., ed. *Karl Barth: Studies of his Theological Method*. Clarendon, Oxford, 1979.
Karl Barth: Centenary Essays. Cambridge University Press, 1989.

Tannehill, Robert C. *The Narrative Unity of Luke-Acts: A Literary Interpretation*. 2 vols. Fortress, Minneapolis, 1990.

Teilhard de Chardin, Pierre. *Le Milieu Divin*. Ed. Bernard Wall. Collins/Fontana, London, 1960.
The Future of Man. Trans. Norman Denny. Collins, London, 1964.
Hymn of the Universe. Trans. Gerald Vann. Collins, London, 1965.
The Phenomenon of Man. Trans. B. Wall. Collins/Fontana, London, 1970.
Christianity and Evolution. Trans. R. Hague. Collins, London, 1971.

Temple, William. *Readings in St John's Gospel*. MacMillan, London, 1947.
Nature, Man and God. MacMillan, London, 1960.
Christus Veritas. MacMillan, London, 1962.

Thompson, Bard. *Liturgies of the Western Church*. Fortress, Philadelphia, 1961.

Thunberg, Lars. *Microcosm and Mediator: The Theological Anthropology of St Maximus the Confessor*. C.W. K. Gleerup, Lund and Einar Munksgaard, Copenhagen, 1965.
Man and the Cosmos: The Vision of St Maximus the Confessor. St Vladimir's, Crestwood, 1985.

Tillich, Paul. *Systematic Theology*, vol. 2. *Existence and the Christ*. SCM, London, 1957.

Tolkien, J. R. R. *The Silmarillion*. Ed. Christopher Tolkien. Unwin, London, 1979.
The Letters of J. R. R. Tolkien. Eds. Humphrey Carpenter and Christopher Tolkien. Houghton Mifflin, Boston, 1981.

Toon, Peter. 'A Message of Hope for the Rump Parliament.' *Evangelical Quarterly* 43.2, April–June 1971, pp. 82–96.
The Ascension of our Lord. Nelson, Nashville, 1984.

Torrance, Alan J. *Persons in Communion: Trinitarian Description and Human Participation*. T&T Clark, Edinburgh, 1996.

Torrance, James B. *Worship, Community, and Triune God of Grace*. Paternoster, Carlisle, 1996.

Torrance, James and Roland Walls. *John Duns Scotus*. Nutshell Series No. 1. Handsel, Edinburgh, 1992.

Torrance, T. F. *Theology in Reconstruction*. SCM, London, 1965.
Space, Time and Incarnation. Oxford University Press, 1969.
Theology in Reconciliation: Essays Towards Evangelical and Catholic Unity in East and West. Geoffrey Chapman, London, 1975.
Space, Time and Resurrection. Grand Rapids, Eerdmans, 1976.
Reality and Evangelical Theology. Westminster, Philadelphia, 1982.
Reality and Scientific Theology: Theology and Science at the Frontiers of Knowledge, vol. 1. Scottish Academic Press, Edinburgh, 1985.
The Trinitarian Faith. T&T Clark, Edinburgh, 1988.
Royal Priesthood. 2nd ed. T&T Clark, Edinburgh, 1993.

Tracy, David and Nicholas Lash, eds. *Cosmology and Theology. Concilium*. T&T Clark, Edinburgh, 1983.

Trigg, Joseph Wilson. *Origen*. SCM, London, 1983.
'The Angel of Great Counsel.' *Journal of Theological Studies*, NS, vol. 42, pt 1, April 1991, pp. 35–51.

Troeltsch, Ernst. *Writings on Theology and Religion*. Trans. and ed. R. Morgan and M. Pye. Westminster/John Knox, Louisville, 1990.

Underhill, Evelyn. *Mysticism: A Study in the Nature and Development of Man's Spiritual Consciousness*. 12th ed. Methuen, London, 1930.

Wainwright, Geoffrey. *Eucharist and Eschatology.* 2nd ed. Epworth, London, 1978.
    Keeping the Faith: Essays to Mark the Centenary of Lux Mundi. Ed. G. Wainwright. Fortress, Philadelphia, 1988.

Wakefield, Gordon S., ed. *A Dictionary of Christian Spirituality.* SCM, London, 1983.

Walker, William G. 'The Doctrine of the Ascension of Christ in Reformed Theology.' PhD, Vanderbilt University, 1968 (UMI).

Wallace, Ronald S. *Calvin's Doctrine of Word and Sacrament.* Oliver & Boyd, Edinburgh, 1953.

Ward, G., ed. *The Postmodern God.* Blackwell, Oxford, 1997

Watson, Francis. 'Ambiguity in the Markan Narrative.' *King's Theological Review* 10.1, Spring 1987, pp. 11–16.
    Text and Truth: Redefining Biblical Theology. T&T Clark, Edinburgh, 1997.

Webster, John. *Barth's Ethics of Reconciliation.* Cambridge University Press, 1995.
    'Jesus in the Theology of Eberhard Jüngel.' *Calvin Theological Journal* 32.1, 1997, pp. 43–71.

Wiener, Philip P., ed. *Dictionary of the History of Ideas*, vol. 4. Charles Scribner, New York, 1973.

Wesche, Kenneth P. 'The Soul and Personality: Tracing the Roots of the Christological Problem.' *Pro Ecclesia* 5.1, 1996, pp. 23–42.

Whitehead, A. N. *Science and the Modern World.* Cambridge University Press, 1933.

Williams, Rowan. 'Ascension of Christ.' *A New Dictionary of Christian Theology.* Eds. Alan Richardson and John Bowden. SCM, London, 1983.

Wingren, Gustaf. *Man and the Incarnation: A Study in the Biblical Theology of Irenaeus.* Trans. Ross MacKenzie. Oliver & Boyd, Edinburgh, 1959.

Wood, Ralph. *The Comedy of Redemption: Christian Faith and the Comic in Four American Novelists.* University of Notre Dame Press, South Bend, 1988.

World Council of Churches. *Baptism, Eucharist and Ministry.* Faith and Order Paper No. 111. Geneva, 1982.
    Confessing One Faith: Towards an Ecumenical Explication of the Apostolic Faith as Expressed in the Nicene-Constantinopolitan Creed (381). Faith and Order Paper No. 140 (Study Document). Geneva, 1987.

Wright, N. Thomas. 'Adam in Pauline Christology.' *SBL Seminar Papers*. Ed. K. H. Richards, Scholar's Press, Chico, 1983, pp. 359–89.
The Climax of the Covenant. Fortress, Minneapolis, 1991.
The New Testament and the People of God: Christian Origins and the Question of God, vol. 1. Fortress, Minneapolis, 1992.
Jesus and the Victory of God: Christian Origins and the Question of God, vol. 2. Fortress, Minneapolis, 1996.

Wybrew, Hugh. *The Orthodox Liturgy: The Development of the Eucharistic Liturgy in the Byzantine Rite*. SPCK, London, 1989.

Yeago, David S. 'Jesus of Nazareth and Cosmic Redemption: The Relevance of St Maximus the Confessor.' *Modern Theology* 12.2, April 1996, pp. 163–93.

Yourgrau, Wolfgang and Allen D. Breck, eds. *Cosmology, History, and Theology*. Plenum Press, New York and London, 1977.

Zizioulas, John D. 'Human Capacity and Human Incapacity: A Theological Exploration of Personhood.' *Scottish Journal of Theology* 28, 1975, pp. 401–47.
Being as Communion: Studies in Personhood and the Church. St Vladimir's, Crestwood, 1985.
'Preserving God's Creation.' Three Lectures on Theology and Ecology. *King's Theological Review* vols. 12.1, 12.2, 13.1, 1989–90.

Zwiep, A. W. *The Ascension of the Messiah in Lukan Christology*. E. J. Brill, Leiden, 1997.

Index of Names

Index of Subjects

Index of Biblical References

Old Testament

New Testament

See also Appendix A.